THE CAPTURED

ALSO BY

SCOTT ZESCH

Alamo Heights

ST. MARTIN'S PRESS
NEW YORK

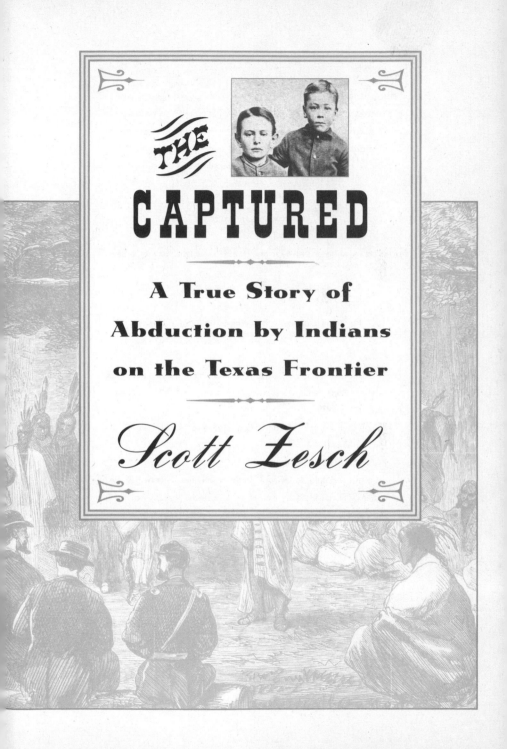

THE
CAPTURED

A True Story of
Abduction by Indians
on the Texas Frontier

Scott Zesch

www.stmartins.com

BOOK DESIGN BY DEBORAH KERNER/DANCING BEARS DESIGN

Maps on pages x, xi by David Cain

Library of Congress Cataloging-in-Publication Data

Zesch, Scott.
    The captured : a true story of abduction by Indians on the Texas
frontier / Scott Zesch.— 1st ed.
    p. cm.
Includes bibliographical references (p. 333) and index (p. 349).
ISBN 0-312-31787-5
EAN 978-0312-31787-4
    1. Korn, Adolph, d. 1895. 2. Indian captivities—Texas. 3. Apache
Indians—Social life and customs. 4. Comanche Indians—Social life
and customs. 5. Whites—Texas—Relations with Indians. 6. Whites—
Texas—Cultural assimilation. I. Title.

E87.K76Z47 2004
976.4004'9725—dc22   2004046765

First Edition: November 2004

10 9 8 7 6 5 4 3 2 1

FOR ZACH AND BEN:
This is your heritage.

Contents

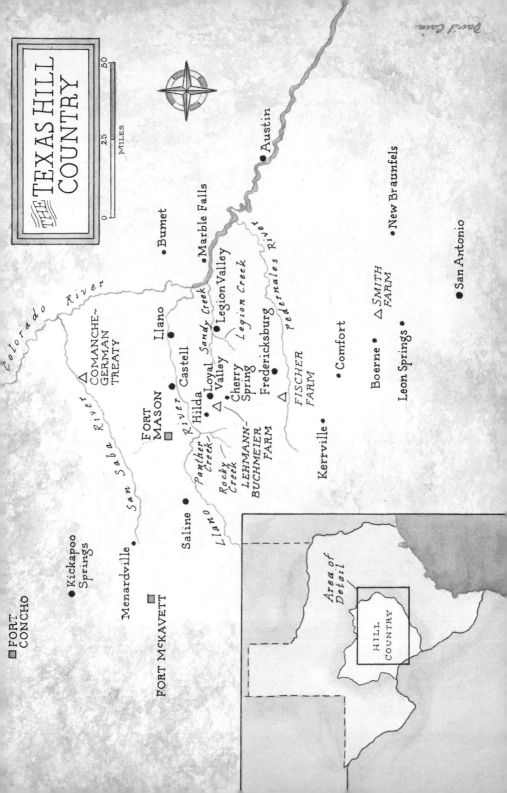

Let us now sing the praises of our
ancestors in their generations.
There were those who made a name for
themselves by their valor;
Those who gave counsel because they
were intelligent;
Those who led the people by their knowledge
of the people's lore—
All these were honored in their generations,
and were the pride of their times.
Of others there is no memory;
They have perished as though they had
never existed;
They have become as though they had
never been born.
But their name lives on generation
after generation.

—EXCERPTED FROM
ECCLESIASTICUS 44

Prologue

The Trail

I f I'd been looking for it, I never would have found it. I came across it by accident on a hot, still afternoon in June. I was wandering alone through a neglected corner of the Gooch Cemetery in Mason, Texas, mulling over the names of forgotten pioneers who dreamed big and died young. With a sideways glance, I saw it, barely sticking out above the dry weeds in the miserly shade of a mesquite tree—just a tiny concrete stub with a funeral home plaque, a temporary marker that had served its purpose too long. It read:

ADOLPH KORN

-1895

Even though the letters were weatherworn, the name leaped out at me. He was my own kin, and this cemetery was located on the outskirts of my hometown, my family's settling place for six generations. But I never knew he was buried there. And Mason is one of those small towns on the fabled Texas frontier where people take pride in knowing these things about their ancestors.

I stopped and stared at the plaque. The date of birth was missing; the year of death was earlier than I would have expected. Then I thought: *It's shameful. My family has let this pathetic chunk of concrete stand as his only monument. As if we're embarrassed to claim him.*

I vaguely remembered my grandparents' stories about Adolph Korn. He was a stepbrother to Granny Hey, my grandmother's grandmother. I'd heard the family yarn about how he was kidnapped by Indians when he was a child. After he returned to his people, he refused to sleep indoors. For a while, he even lived in a cave like a wild man. He ate raw meat. Now and then he took his rifle and disappeared into the hills for several days, never explaining his absences when he returned.

Other than those bits and pieces, no one seemed to know much about him, not even the most basic facts. For instance: *How old was he when he was captured?*

"About ten," my grandfather thought.

"Twelve," said Granny Hey.

Eight, according to a fellow captive's narrative.

How long did he stay with the Indians?

"Three or four years," recalled my grandfather.

Twelve, in Granny Hey's memory.

The Korn family history book said six.

Which tribe was he with?

No one knew.

His story had so many gaps and inconsistencies that I doubted whether much of it was true. Still, it wasn't implausible. Indians and their captives were facts of bygone life in the Hill Country of central Texas, the rural region north of San Antonio and west of Austin. I'd spent my first eighteen years in Mason County, an area with a rich Native American past. Until my ancestors edged them out, the Comanches, Apaches, and Kiowas had hunted deer in those brushy hills and buffalo on the grassy flats below. On that same ground, Native Americans and immigrant Americans had fought some of their last, desperate battles over who would control this country. It was clear who'd won. I didn't even know where the Comanches, Apaches, and Kiowas had gone after they were driven away.

I'd grown up on the cattle ranch my family had claimed as our home since Indian times. It consisted of two square miles of steep, rocky hills lying between the Llano and James Rivers, eight miles south of Mason. As a child, I rode my horse past the blackened mounds of long-ago Indian camps, climbed into caves decorated with faded Indian pictographs, and occasionally found discarded arrowheads and flint knives the rain had washed up.

I was surrounded by reminders of the Indian wars as well. My sixth-grade Sunday school teacher was a daughter of an Indian captive. During my high school days, my friends and I sat by the road and drank Lone Star in front of the historical marker at a rounded hill known as Todd Mountain, where a group of Indians had attacked a family and captured a white girl in 1865. On the hill where Granny Hey had lived were the foundations of Fort Mason. From that post, Robert E. Lee and the soldiers of the Second Cavalry had protected my ancestors from Indians until the Civil War called the army away.

I was also aware, even as an adolescent, that Mason and its closest neighbors—Llano, Fredericksburg, Junction, Menard, Brady, and San Saba—had once been much more lively and significant places than the complacent "last picture show" towns they'd become by the 1970s. A century earlier, this had been the heart of the Texas frontier mythologized by countless western movies and novels, the domain of independent cowboys and their archenemies, the Indians. Still, I never gave much thought to the people who came before me, not even to my family's own Indian warrior.

By the time I was grown, the story of my uncle Adolph's life with the Indians seemed beyond reach. He'd died at the turn of the twentieth century, and the only relatives I'd ever known who could actually remember him were Granny Hey's last surviving children. Aunt Kate, Aunt Fay, Aunt Net, and Aunt Mag had spent their childhoods in the 1880s and 1890s with Adolph Korn. As girls, they shied away from their odd uncle who walked with a limp and had a habit of picking them up by their pigtails. They didn't understand why he still acted like an Indian many years after he came home.

I wish I'd asked them about him, or at least listened to their tales more carefully. However, by 1970 they'd all died and taken their stories with them. Virtually no eyewitnesses were left. Eighteen years later, I no longer had my grandmother to tell me what she'd heard. As each generation passed, our elusive uncle Adolph receded further into the realm of legend, soon to be lost to history.

I call him Uncle Adolph by way of reclamation. In our family, we always referred to him as Adolph Korn, for he was never really one of us. But seeing his grave got me stirred up. For the first time, this obscure ancestor seemed real. I wondered if there was a trail leading to his story.

As soon as I got home that day, I called Julius DeVos, a local historian who catalogued Mason's cemeteries, to make sure this was *our* Adolph Korn. "Yes, that's your relative," he assured me.

Then I asked him a question that I should have been able to answer myself: "Why wasn't he buried with the rest of the family?"

"Well, Adolph was always a little strange," explained Julius.

That did it. I decided it was time to find out who this shadowy figure really was—or at least get enough information to give him a decent headstone.

His story was unusual but not unique. Dozens of children on the Texas frontier were captured by Southern Plains Indians in the 1800s and adopted into the tribes. Many came to prefer the Native American way of life, resisting attempts to rescue them. Long after they were forced to return to their former families, they held fast to what they'd learned while they were away. Some anthropologists call these assimilated children white Indians.

Not all of the captives were white, though. The Plains Indian raiders abducted European-Americans, Mexicans, Mexican-Americans, African-Americans, and Native Americans from other tribes. They didn't discriminate as to whom they killed or kidnapped—or whom they eventually adopted as their own.

The white Indians who rode with the native warriors willingly took part in their horse-stealing raids, which sometimes led to the gruesome deaths of my fellow Texans. Having a captive in the family brought this history uncomfortably close to home. My relative was a German-Texan boy, much like myself, who grew up in a gentle, religious household, instilled with a set of values that most Americans consider absolute and universally desirable. Don't eat with your hands. Don't take what's not yours. Don't kill other people. After spending only three years among the Indians, my uncle Adolph had thrown aside all his old ways of thinking. Did he come to see his own people's morals as hypocritical and untrustworthy? Or were his dormant personality traits finally coming out, once he was liberated from the people who pressured him to act like a "good boy"? One other question troubled me: under the same circumstances, would I have become like him?

The documented facts of my uncle Adolph's life were fragmentary and inconclusive. Like many white Indians, he kept his secrets, leaving few tracks. However, I learned from my research that practically all of the captured children went through similar experiences. To better understand my ancestor's captivity, I expanded my search to include other children who lived with the Comanches or Apaches at about the same time, especially those who chose to talk about their experiences.

One of them, Herman Lehmann, eventually got away from his Apache captors, only to join a group of Comanches rather than return to his own kin. Another, Rudolph Fischer, chose to spend his entire adult life with the Comanches. Uncle Adolph's campmate, Temple Friend, was brought back to his white family in robust health but soon withered away. Dot and Banc Babb, Clinton and Jeff Smith, and Minnie Caudle defended the native people throughout their lives. While these captives' stories were alike in many respects, each contributed something unique to my understanding.

Most of Uncle Adolph's fellow captives lived until the 1930s or 1940s, which meant I would be able to find people who knew them personally. I placed ads in Texas newspapers, posted messages on genealogy Web sites, crashed family reunions, and even left a note in a bottle at one captive's grave. Soon the responses came pouring in. Like me, the descendants of other captives grew up hearing stories, and they were eager to pass them on. They also wanted to know how many of the family legends were true. One woman sent me successive e-mails with funny, poignant anecdotes about her grandfather's rough readjustment to the white world. She concluded: "I don't see how all these little things can be of any interest to someone writing a book." However, I was spellbound. The details were fascinating; significant patterns of behavior started to emerge.

I also needed to get to know the native people Uncle Adolph lived among. Why did their culture and their hard way of living have such a strong hold on him? When I began my search, I was sorely uninformed about the Native American tribes who inhabited this continent before my ancestors arrived, and popular culture had only reinforced familiar stereotypes. I'd seen movies such as *The Searchers,* with its ruthless Comanches who attacked Texas settlers without provocation. I'd also seen later films such as *Little Big Man* and *Dances with Wolves,* in which vindictive U.S. soldiers splattered even more blood in the Indian camps. I suspected that the truth fell someplace outside these extremes, but I didn't know where.

Through the Internet, I contacted some Comanches in Oklahoma. I didn't know how I'd be received, for the Comanches hated the Texans in the old days and blamed them for all of their troubles. However, they encouraged me to come visit them. When I got to Lawton, I was invited to their meetings, their church services, and their homes. Over tables spread with platters of roasted meat and homemade bread, they shared with me their stories, songs, and aspirations. We had more in common than I'd realized. Their ancestors adopted many non-Indian children, and a number of those children grew up and married into the tribe. Like me, most contemporary Comanches have captives in their family trees.

The captives' trail took me from central Texas to the vast prairies of Oklahoma and Kansas and the open plains of the Texas Panhandle. I refused to let Uncle Adolph and the other white Indians rest in peace. Their story still speaks to us, and they have much explaining to do. These children witnessed a brutal chapter in the history of America from a unique perspective. For a short time, they became "the other."

Their trail begins in the Texas Hill Country, where European immigrants lived miserably and in terror of Indians.

Part One

A Fate Worse Than Death

Chapter One

New Year's Day

They had no reason to feel afraid when they first saw the three figures on horseback, riding steadily across a distant ridge. Even when the horsemen started heading their way, there was no cause to panic. It was noon, broad daylight. The riders were probably just some neighbors returning home from church. Maybe they were travelers on their way to Fredericksburg. They might be U.S. soldiers or Texas Rangers on patrol. There were many good reasons to believe they weren't Indians. Still, as the riders drew closer, the two miles of riverbank that separated the shepherds from the village seemed like a great expanse.

It hadn't seemed nearly as far that morning, when they'd let the sheep drift upstream. Along the south edge of the Llano River, the herd was greedily ripping up the dry grass. The sheepdog trotted back and forth, keeping the flock from straying. The herders were ten-year-old twin brothers, Adolph and Charlie Korn, with identical broad faces, light flaxen hair, and high foreheads. Adolph had a scar in the middle of his chin. The boys spoke only German.

The hillsides in that region were thick with live oaks, agaritas, and persimmons. The twins kept losing sight of the three horsemen, weaving in and out of the brush. As always, the boys were defenseless. Still, they didn't try to hide; it wasn't their habit to be cautious. Everyone knew that Indians raided on summer evenings when the air was warm and the moon was full, not on a crisp New Year's Day just before a new moon.

The sheep scattered and bleated as the horses galloped into their midst. Adolph was sitting on a log, calmly eating his lunch, when he got his first good look at the three Apache men rushing toward him. Charlie, a short distance away, dove into the bushes and kept quiet. He watched, petrified, as his twin tried to dash for safety. One of the Apaches grabbed Adolph, hit him over the head with a pistol, and hoisted him onto his horse.

Then the Apaches disappeared into the brush like phantoms, as silently as they had come. It was over and done with so quickly that it didn't seem real. The sheep went back to grazing, as if nothing had happened. As if Charlie Korn still had a twin brother.

Those three Apaches dealt my ancestors the hardest blow of their lives on that first day of 1870. My uncle Adolph's capture was the worst and last in a series of disasters his family withstood during their ten-year bout with the Texas frontier. They'd come to this hard, wild country by choice, and their decision turned out to be a poor one.[1]

Grandpa Korn should have stayed in San Antonio, where his family was safe and modestly prosperous. My great-great-great-grandfather was a gentle soul, an immigrant candy maker who loved to host dances and German songfests and play Santa Claus at Christmas. A small, wiry man with large eyes and heavy eyebrows, he walked around the plazas of San Antonio with sweets in his pocket, ready to offer them to his pupils from the Methodist Sunday school. Never very strong, Grandpa Korn had weighed just over three pounds at birth and grew to a height of only five feet three inches. He wasn't cut out for life on the frontier.

Still, he felt the lure of the unspoiled wilderness a hundred miles northwest of San Antonio. His friends told him about the bountiful rivers and springs, the ample grazing land for cattle, the gently sloping hills covered with sturdy oaks and flowering yuccas. Hardly anyone lived there: just a handful of fellow German immigrants and a few soldiers and some drifters from the southeastern states. Grandpa decided to give the ranching business a try.

For all its delicate beauty, the Texas Hill Country is an unexpectedly harsh land. Rainfall is erratic, and the area is prone to drought. Cattle that are round-bellied and healthy during the spring, when the countryside is flowering with bluebonnets, winecups, and red Indian blankets, may be wasting away by the end of summer. Mesquites, junipers, and prickly pear spread uncontrollably, draining the shallow aquifer and choking out the native grasses. Bold outcroppings of limestone and granite give the landscape its rugged appeal; but that same rock also underlies the fragile topsoil, waiting to crack the blade of a plow. Grandpa Korn didn't know about that. He was thinking of the money he would make from raising and selling beef cattle. The U.S. Army needed to supply its frontier forts, and the urban markets in Texas and beyond were expanding.

Most of his experience had been in trade, not agriculture. Grandpa Korn—his full name was Louis Jacob Korn—had lived in America twenty-four years before he came to the Hill Country. He'd left his home in Meissenheim, Germany, at the age of nineteen and arrived in New York in 1836. Like many immigrants, he moved around a lot, looking for better opportunities. In 1839 he relocated to New Orleans, then left Louisiana for Texas in 1845. For a few years, he tried farming near New Braunfels, a German-American enclave northeast of San Antonio. He also went into business as a confectioner, and that seemed to suit him. By 1848, at age thirty-one, he was doing well enough to marry Friedrika Grote, a neighbor. Over the next nine years, they had five children.

In the mid-1850s, Grandpa moved his family to San Antonio, where the market for his candies and pastries was larger. It was a good time to be living there. During that decade, San Antonio temporarily eclipsed Galveston to become the largest, most vibrant city in Texas. Businesses flourished, soldiers and traders came and went, and smart new buildings sprang up every month. Grandpa Korn opened his confectionery shop on Market Street, just east of Plaza de las Islas (Main Plaza). His specialty was elaborately decorated wedding cakes, which he displayed in the front window. Louis and Friedrika Korn's children played hide-and-seek in the ruins of the Alamo.

In 1858 Friedrika died unexpectedly of a fever, leaving Grandpa with five children under the age of ten. He needed help, and he found a new partner who was just as needy. Less than a year after my great-great-great-grandmother's death, Grandpa Korn married Johanna Bartruff, a recently widowed immigrant from Germany. She was twenty-one, exactly half his age. Grandpa also adopted her three-month-old twins, Charlie and Adolph.

Louis and Johanna Korn's amalgamated family numbered nine by the time they set out for the Hill Country in the latter part of 1860, and their spirits were high. They awoke each morning to see a light frost on the tall, brown grass and a misty blue haze over the hills ahead. They had every reason to believe that after a few years of hard work and sacrifice, they'd be cattle barons. The nation had just elected a controversial new president, Abraham Lincoln, and South Carolina was threatening to break away from the United States, but that wasn't likely to have much impact on people out in the hinterland.

The Korns established their new home on the eastern edge of Mason County, near the German-American settlement of Castell. They weren't one of the first families there; Castell and its founders had already survived thirteen winters by 1860. The Korns arrived to find a close-knit, orderly community of 137 people whose homes were nestled among the sprawling oaks and native pecan trees. The Llano River was wide and shallow, its clear water pouring over low ledges and swirling around gray and pink rock islands. Ten-acre farm plots with log cabins—what passed for civilization in that remote outpost—already lined the grassy lowland along the north bank of the river. The Korns became members of Castell's Methodist church, the only other token of civilized life in the area.

Although the children of Castell grew up in an idyllic natural setting, everyday life was far from utopian. The older Korn children, accustomed to the relative comfort and urbanity of San Antonio, must have been appalled by their new living conditions. "People living now as we had to live then would be looked on as mighty sorry white trash," declared my granny Hey. She was ten years old when the Korn family arrived in Castell.

Popular culture, especially western movies, has tended to elevate the living standards of settlers on the Texas frontier during the 1860s. In John Ford's *The Searchers,* for instance, the pioneer family lives in a rustic but comfortable house of several rooms. Its wood-plank floors are covered by woven rugs. The glass windows are curtained. The family eats substantial meals off elegant Blue Willow china neatly laid out on a long, polished table, with plenty of spare dishes on the shelves. Their clothes are tidy and look barely worn. A rocker and a padded armchair wait invitingly beside the fire. On the mantel of the broad fireplace sits a kerosene lamp and a handsome clock.

A typical house in Castell during the 1860s would have looked nothing like that. The immigrants' dwellings were crude log cabins of one or two rooms. The walls never quite fended off the strong gales of a winter norther; however, they did manage to trap the one-hundred-plus-degree heat of August. The floors were hard-packed dirt. No matter how many times a housewife swept them, they still wouldn't seem clean. The thatched roofs leaked. The windows had no screens or glass, only shutters. During the daytime, a person could either leave them open and risk an invasion of grasshoppers, wasps, and mosquitoes, or close them and sweat in a dark room. Cooking was done over an open fire, either in the fireplace, if the family was fortunate enough to have one and the weather wasn't sweltering, or else outside the cabin. At night the only source of light was a twisted rag dipped in tallow and set on a tin plate. It was barely enough to read by; but that didn't matter, because there was hardly anything to read, except the family Bible and maybe an almanac. Most of the children were illiterate, anyway.

The settlers around Castell supplemented their simple diets with whatever they could take off the land: deer, turkey, rabbits, wild plums and grapes, persimmons, even prickly pear apples and weeds. Occasionally, the native plants they ate turned out to be poisonous, making them seriously ill. They didn't do much canning or preserving to store food for the winter, because they didn't have jars. They rarely got wheat flour for bread, and they were desperate for corn. Any time U.S. soldiers camped nearby, the locals scoured the ground afterward for corn their horses might have left uneaten. They also tried to keep a little whiskey on hand to trade the soldiers for grain. "It was a 'lucky' that could afford corn bread, black molasses, bacon and beans six days in the week and biscuits for dinner on Sunday," said Granny Hey. The children dreaded the arrival of visitors during the Sunday meal, because they had to wait and eat at the second table.

Money was scarce. Sometimes the men of Castell left home to take odd jobs such as splitting rails, leaving their wives and children to fend for themselves. As Granny Hey recalled, "Many of the Germans who later became wealthy would work twelve hours a day for fifty cents, and save thirty-five cents of it." Even when the settlers had money, there wasn't much food for sale.

The Korn children didn't attend school—there wasn't any. Sometimes a teacher would attempt to hold classes for a few days or weeks at one of the settlers' houses. Usually, however, the children were needed at home. Like the adults, the youngsters spent almost every day carrying out tedious and repetitive chores. Johanna Korn often told her stepdaughters, "I hope you poor children won't have to work and live as hard as we women have to work and live." She seemed to overlook the fact that they already did. Granny Hey and her sisters hauled water, gathered firewood, milked cows, ground corn (or acorns when there was no corn), herded livestock, made soap, sewed, and washed clothes. The laundry list wasn't extensive; each family member had only about two suits of clothing, made of coarse cotton fabric or deerskin. The kids had no shoes. Their feet and arms itched from frequent brushes with stinging nettle, cat's-claw, and thistles. As they went about their work, they had to watch out for diamondback rattlesnakes along the sandstone ledges and cottonmouth moccasins in the river bottom.

It soon became obvious to Grandpa Korn that Castell wasn't quite the paradise he had envisioned. Yet perhaps, at the end of the day, in the tranquil moments just before dark, Grandpa paused from his hard labor to watch a fiery sunset over the Llano River, observe a skittish whitetail deer at its evening watering, or listen to a bobwhite quail signaling its mate, and thought to himself: *Maybe this wasn't a mistake. Stop thinking about San Antonio, New Orleans, New York. This is home now.* Somehow, he was going to make it tolerable.

Then everything fell apart. Grandpa Korn had invested $1,200 in cattle—his life savings, plus all of the proceeds from the sale of his confectionery in San Antonio. According to Granny Hey, he "never got one dollar back." It's hard to account for the Korns' complete failure in the cattle business, though the outbreak of the Civil War only a few months after they arrived in Castell must have been a factor. Cattlemen in Confederate Texas had lost their single biggest consumer, the federal army. None of the ranchers in the Hill Country could get reliable information about where and when to sell their livestock; mail arrived once a week at most. Another factor may have accelerated the family's downward slide: the Korns were city folk with little experience raising livestock. The grazing land was unfenced; some of their wild cows strayed and never returned, or were stolen by rustlers or Indians.

Living conditions plummeted during the Civil War, even though Mason County was far from the battlefronts. Even basic foodstuffs were hard to come by. "We had to eat careless weeds and lambsquarter," Granny Hey remembered. "Supper for us children was usually a bowl of mush without milk or cream." The Korns were desperate. They had to try another line of work, and quickly, even at the cost of their self-respect. In a land where a man's status was measured by the head of cattle he owned, Grandpa Korn was soon reduced to raising sheep. What's worse, the smelly, thickheaded animals didn't even belong to him. Louis Korn merely tended the sheep for their owner in exchange for part of the profits.

In search of new grazing land for the sheep, the Korn family left their home in Castell late in 1862 for the hardscrabble country of the

Saline Valley, west of Mason. They brought with them the few milk cows they'd managed to keep for household use. Sometimes the family camped out with the sheep. Whenever they stopped in one place for a few months, they put up a makeshift shanty.

As Granny would say: *like mighty sorry white trash.*

The countryside in the Saline Valley was much rougher and less hospitable than Castell. The hills dropped off suddenly in craggy precipices rather than gentle slopes. Tough, scraggly junipers and daggerlike sotol plants dotted the ridges. The soil was stony, the cliffs a pale yellow caliche. Whereas the families of Castell lived close together, the settlers of Saline were widely dispersed. Some of their cabins were six or seven miles apart—ideal targets for Indian raiders. Indian attacks had increased in the region, for Fort Mason and the other federal army posts on the frontier were left in disarray once the nation split apart.

Unlike Castell, Saline had only a handful of German-American residents. The Korns settled three miles east of the farm of Grandpa's friend, Adolph A. Reichenau, a German immigrant who had moved to Saline from Castell a short time earlier to run cattle. Reichenau, with his heavy dark beard and blue eyes, was a rough-hewn, hardy adventurer who'd served as a soldier and Texas Ranger. As soon as the Korns saw the Reichenaus' compound, they knew what they could expect in the Saline Valley. The two-room log cabin was enclosed by a heavy picket fence made of sharpened cedar poles, with small holes cut so they could shoot at attackers. It wasn't a home; it was a fortress.

The Reichenaus weren't overreacting, for the threat of Indian raids was very real. On April 2, 1862, only a few months before the Reichenaus and the Korns arrived, the Saline community had been shocked by a triple murder. When a settler named Felix Hale went to his elderly neighbors' place to return a wash kettle, he found their cabin on fire and feathers from a mattress strewn about the yard. Near the house, he discovered the charred body of Henry Parks, age seventy-seven. His wife, Nancy, seventy-two, had been killed near the cow pen. Along the creek lay the body of their twelve-year-old grandson, Billy. All three had been scalped.

Hale rode off to spread the news, and a Texas Ranger captain named John Williams quickly raised a scouting party to look for the Indians who had killed the Parks family. Some of the neighbors offered to ride with him. However, when Captain Williams asked one smart aleck in the Saline community to join him on the Indian hunt, the man refused, saying he hadn't lost any Indians.

That sort of response wasn't uncommon. If western movies have underplayed the harsh living conditions on the Texas frontier, they've also exaggerated the bravery and self-reliance of the farmers who lived there. On the whole, the Texas settlers were ordinary folks, no more or less courageous than their kin in Tennessee or Wisconsin or Pennsylvania. Many of these people had moved to Texas because they hadn't succeeded back home. Often, they remained there in the face of adversity not because they were stouthearted but because they were trapped. Poverty kept them from relocating and starting over, especially during the miserable years of the Civil War and Reconstruction. One Mason County pioneer wrote in 1868: "I would get away from here if I could but I am too poor. . . . I have been living on the frontier since 1853 and I now curse the day when I commenced it."[2]

When Indians came around their homesteads, the settlers were usually outnumbered, and they seldom stood and fought to defend their homes if they had a chance to hide or escape. Clinton Smith, a young white captive who went on raids through Texas with the Comanches, recalled: "[W]e fearlessly went to the ranches and stole horses out of pens in the daytime. The white people would dash into their houses whenever we appeared, and we would go boldly into the pens and get the horses."[3]

A few months after the Parks murders, the Reichenaus were startled one afternoon when a sorrel pony belonging to an eight-year-old neighbor boy, Billy Schumann, came galloping into their compound, riderless. The Schumanns, who had sold their farm near Fredericksburg the year before to move to Saline,[4] were building a cabin nearby. Two of Adolph Reichenau's sons took off with some other men to see what was wrong. Ten-year-old Gus Reichenau rode Billy's pony toward the Schumann farm. As they drew near, the pony became agitated and wouldn't go any closer. Before long they found the naked body of Billy's father, Gus Schumann, near Little Saline Creek, with fourteen arrows in his back. About three hundred yards away lay Billy, also naked, shot with twelve arrows.

The tiny community had witnessed five murders in a single year: 1862, the year the Korns and the Reichenaus migrated to the area. Although neither family lost any of its own members to Native American raiders in the Saline Valley, they had their share of close calls over the next few years. That's how my ancestors, who had no personal reason to hate the native people, became Indian fighters. To the Korns and their neighbors, Indian raiders were just hazards of frontier life, like rattlesnakes or rabies or rustlers. Settlers such as Grandpa Korn didn't see themselves as intruders on Native American hunting grounds. They weren't aware that their mere presence there helped precipitate the last and bloodiest phase of warfare between Native Americans and all other Americans.

Each time the Korns drove the sheep herd into virgin grazing territory, they moved farther from their neighbors and deeper into Indian country. One bright midnight, my granny Hey and her stepmother, Johanna Korn, got out of bed to let some calves out of the pens. As Granny was lowering the bar, she noticed a crouching figure. "I thought at first it was a cow and said, 'Huah.' The Indian jumped up and nearly scared me to death. I shouted to my stepmother to run. We caught up our dresses and ran to the house as fast as we could." Granny slammed the door so quickly that she caught part of her skirt in the doorjamb. "The Indian was right behind me," she claimed, "and stuck his head through an open panel in the door and took a wild glance about the room."

Meanwhile, other Indians came riding out of the brush and

started circling the house. "Get the gun, Daddy, get the gun!" Granny screamed. Before Grandpa could fire a shot, the raiders left. According to Granny Hey, they were afraid of the dogs. One of the Indians lost his saddle when he took off. The next morning, Uncle Adolph found it and claimed it for his own. "Before my stepmother would allow my brother to use it," said Granny, "she put it in a pot of boiling water to kill the bugs." The Indians also dropped some beads, which Granny Hey and her sisters were delighted to claim.

White settler histories are full of tales like Granny's. It's too bad that we have so few raiding stories from the natives' point of view. The Texas pioneers, who were busy defending themselves and scratching out a meager living, didn't have the luxury of mulling over the more interesting questions. For instance, why did the Indians bother to stake out the Korn house if the family had so little worth taking? Were they hoping to capture the children? Did the Indian who stuck his scowling face through the door envy or scorn the way these impoverished settlers lived in their cramped hovel? And why did the Indians circle the cabin and put on such a show if they weren't planning to attack? Were they scared off, or did they just lose interest?

One Comanche captive, Clinton Smith, described an almost identical incident from the other side of the cabin door. He reported that the Comanches sometimes chased settlers into their shacks just for fun. When the white family in his story sprinted to their cabin, as Granny Hey and Johanna Korn had done, "[w]e all gave the war-whoop, just to see how fast those people would run. . . . We had a big laugh. The house was an old log affair, with only one hole in it, and a big old slathery boy was running so fast he missed the hole and went half way around the house before he could stop and turn back and hit the hole."[5]

Anything for an occasional laugh. Life was hard and potentially short for both the Native Americans and the immigrants. As a former Comanche raider named Mamsookawat explained in his later years, perhaps only half jokingly: "We shot the white men, because it was better to shoot them than to let them starve."[6]

Three years after the murders of 1862, the people of the Saline Valley were still living in a state of anxiety, expecting at any moment to hear that another neighbor had been killed and mutilated. Adolph Reichenau's family awoke on the morning of January 8, 1865, to discover that they'd been raided during the night. Someone had made off with the laundry they'd hung out to dry the previous evening. A storm had blanketed the area with about fourteen inches of snow, so the Reichenaus were able to follow the thieves' tracks to a pasture near their cabin. Sure enough, they found signs of an Indian camp. Then they saw something so chilling that they forgot about their stolen laundry. Some small footprints circled a tree over and over again. It appeared as if someone, probably a child, had been tethered to the trunk.

Later that morning, a tired, grim party of men from neighboring Mason County arrived in Saline. They were tracking some Indians who had captured a thirteen-year-old girl, Alice Todd, the day before, about four miles south of Fort Mason. The Indians had killed the Todd family's servant girl and mortally wounded Alice's mother. Her father had abandoned his family during the attack, claiming he couldn't control his horse. The Reichenaus, the Korns, and the other neighbors realized what had happened during the night, while they slept soundly—Alice Todd, bound to a horse and shivering from cold and trauma, passed by their cabins, unable to cry out for help. At the same time, they felt a guilty sense of relief that it wasn't one of their children.

A few of the men of Saline joined in the search for Alice Todd. Nothing caused the Texas settlers to hate Indian raiders more than the abduction of women and, especially, children. To their way of thinking, captivity truly was a fate worse than death. Death at the hands of Comanches or Apaches elevated ordinary dirt farmers to the status of martyrs in the quest for western expansion. Captivity, on the other hand, was unspeakably degrading. Life among the natives turned virtuous women into sexual slaves and civilized children into savages.

Alice Todd was at that in-between age where she could be subjected to both types of ruination.

The rescue party pursued the raiders north into Menard County, then northwest beyond Fort Concho, a total distance of over a hundred miles. Snow was still falling, and the searchers lost the Indians' trail several times and had to circle around for miles to find it again. The men and the horses were exhausted and badly chilled. At the foot of the Staked Plains, the tracks indicated that the Indians had divided into three groups. It was hopeless. Alice Todd was lost, another casualty of the frontier.[7]

After the Civil War officially ended on April 9, 1865, the frontier settlers hoped that peace and order would soon be restored. However, Indian raids in Texas only got worse. That summer the people of the Saline Valley heard nothing but bad news from the surrounding settlements. On July 26, 1865, Indians attacked and killed a man named Henry Kensing in southern Mason County. They raped and mortally wounded his pregnant wife, Johanna. Only three days later, the Comanches captured a thirteen-year-old boy, Rudolph Fischer, close to his parents' farm outside Fredericksburg. Ten days after that, Eli McDonald and his sister-in-law, Gill Taylor, were killed by Kiowas in adjacent Gillespie County. McDonald's wife, Caroline, and their two children, two nieces, and a nephew were all taken captive.

At about the same time as the attack on the McDonalds' farm, Saline got hit. This time the victim was thirty-four-year-old Fred Conaway. He was last seen at the Reichenau place on his way to get a yoke of oxen. He'd been gone several days when Adolph Reichenau rode by his house and asked Conaway's wife, Martha, where he was.

"God, I don't know," she blurted out. Martha Conaway, five months pregnant, was frazzled by then. She'd been keeping her four young children close to her in case there were Indians around. When night fell, she hadn't built a fire or lit a lamp.

Adolph Reichenau and a few other men rode in search of Fred Conaway. They were about to give up when they noticed some buzzards circling. Along the edge of the Llano River, they found his partially decomposed body. He'd been suffering from two gunshot wounds and apparently was trying to quench his thirst at the time he died. One hand was dangling in the water. It was the hottest month of the summer, and the smell of decay was so strong they didn't try to haul his body back home. Instead, they buried him beneath a nearby tree. Later, they found signs that he'd furiously battled some Indians from inside a cave and had apparently killed or wounded at least one of them.

After Conaway's death, the people of Saline began to question whether it was really worth trying to stay there. One of them, Rance Moore, lost 2,100 head of cattle and fifty-two saddle horses to a large party of Indian raiders in the daytime hours of August 8, 1866.[8] He decided to move to the town of Mason for safety. He'd helped bury his neighbor, Fred Conaway, and had lived in fear of Indians much too long. Even in town, however, his family didn't feel secure. On the night of February 5, 1867, Moore awoke in terror when he heard a noise in the horse stable. He spotted a single, shadowy figure prowling about the corral. Like most Indian fighters, Rance Moore shot first and investigated afterward. The boy he'd killed was his own son, Daniel, five days shy of his fifteenth birthday.

At the time the Saline settlers learned about the Moore family's tragedy, it had been a year and a half since they'd lost anyone in their community to Indians. They started to lower their guard. On the morning of October 12, 1867, fifty-five-year-old Frank Johnson, a patriarchal figure with a long, white beard, went to look for his horses. He didn't take his gun—and he didn't come home. His wife, Betsy, wasn't too worried. Once before Frank had set out for a neighbor's house to get some cornmeal for breakfast and was gone for three months. However, the men of the community decided not to wait that long to look for him. They found his body several miles from his home, scalped and shot with arrows.[9]

One by one, the families of the Saline Valley gave up and left. Adolph Reichenau lost nine horses to Indian raiders in June 1868, seventeen more in December of that year, and another twenty-five in March 1869.[10] He moved his family east to a place on the Llano River called Hedwig's Hill. Betsy Johnson and her family returned to their former home, the Legion Valley community in southern Llano County, shortly after Frank was murdered in the fall of 1867. The Korn family went back to Castell in 1869. The Johnsons and the Korns hoped they could still find some semblance of serenity on the frontier if they stayed in settlements where the houses weren't so far apart. Both families would be proven wrong.

For Grandpa Korn, the 1860s should have been the era in which he established his place in life. As the decade drew to a close, however, he had nothing to show for his ten years in the Hill Country. He had stoically withstood Indian raids, but he hadn't managed to profit from occupying the natives' home. He had foundered in the cattle business, his American dream scrapped for salvage. Worst of all, he had failed his children. Louis Korn's mother had been able to speak seven languages, and Louis himself could read and write both German and English. Most of his own offspring spoke only German and were illiterate. Grandpa even had to send them to work for other families for wages. During the last weeks of 1869, as his children halfheartedly observed the German St. Nicholas traditions and scavenged wild plums and berries for an improvised Christmas pudding, Grandpa Korn tried to convince himself that the next decade would be better.

But New Year's Day 1870 was just another working day in Castell. The ten-year-old twins, Charlie and Adolph, rose early and left the cabin to go to their usual job: herding sheep for their neighbor, August Leifeste. They wouldn't be home till dusk, so their mother sent lunch with them—perhaps some dried meat, if they had any, and a hunk of the previous night's cornbread. Johanna Korn watched her boys leave the cabin. When she casually told Adolph good-bye, she couldn't have imagined it would be for three years. Or that when he returned, her son would be a stranger who despised everything she stood for.

* * *

August Leifeste was afraid something bad had happened when his sheepdog came home alone. He started to go check on his shepherds, the Korn boys. Before he got far, he could hear Charlie's frenzied shouts upriver, followed by Louis and Johanna Korn's cries of panic. Within minutes Leifeste, Grandpa Korn, and some other men from Castell were searching frantically for Adolph, calling his name and whistling. In that boundless brushland, it was useless. The European settlers were no match for the Apaches when it came to navigating the wilderness.

Adolph Korn heard the men calling, not far behind. However, he was afraid his captor would hit him again or even slit his throat if he cried out. His head was still throbbing where the Apache had smacked it with a pistol. Gradually, the voices of his father and his neighbors faded in the distance. All he could hear was the pounding of horses' hooves.

The three Apaches who captured him probably came from the Fort Sill region of Indian Territory, although they may have been from New Mexico or even Arizona.[11] Regardless, they were a long way from home, and they weren't out for pleasure. Adolph traveled north with them for about twelve days. Each day his hope of rescue grew fainter.

After a raid, the Southern Plains Indians rode hard, stopping only a few moments for rest or water, sometimes not eating for several days. If they killed a calf or a deer along the trail, they often didn't bother to cook the meat before they ate it. It took too long to build a fire, and the smoke would give away their location. Typically, they tied the captives to a horse to prevent their escape. Sometimes, the Apaches stripped off a captive's "white" clothes and made him ride naked until they could get to an Indian camp, where the women would dress him in buckskin and moccasins.

Finally, they reached a Quahada village in Indian Territory. The Quahadas were the most bellicose division of the Comanches, the ones who refused to report to their Indian agent and made no treaties with the federal government. Their camps had the appearance and at-mosphere of a traveling circus: the tepees, constructed of tanned buf-falo hides and long poles, were easily assembled and disassembled, and the mood was festive when a successful raiding party showed up.

As a captive, Adolph was the property of the man who abducted him and was subject to his whims. His Apache owner decided to trade him to some Quahadas at the camp for a sorrel horse, a pistol and am-munition, a blanket, and some other trinkets. During the early weeks of his captivity, Adolph served as their menial. One of his chores was taking care of a Comanche child, who was sick at the time. When the child died, some of the tribesmen wanted to kill Adolph, but an old woman intervened and saved his life. He was severely whipped in-stead.[12]

That wasn't his worst trial. As the Comanches were preparing to move on to new hunting territory, Adolph was thrown from a horse, badly injuring his leg. The Comanche men debated what to do with him. Adolph didn't understand their language, but no translation was necessary. Crippled, he had little value as chattel and no future as a warrior. He wouldn't be able to keep up with them, and they often had to stay on the move in case U.S. soldiers or Texas Rangers were after them. They could abandon him to fend for himself. However, they were a long way from any settlement, and with his lame leg he would almost certainly starve to death before he found help. The sim-plest and most humane solution would be to drive a lance through his chest.[13]

Then a Comanche woman, most likely the same one who had saved him before, came forward to beg for his life. Maybe she took pity on him. Perhaps she'd lost a son of her own. Or maybe she just felt that he still had potential as a warrior if his leg healed properly, and she knew the tribe needed more fighting men to resist the Texas invaders. There's no record of what she said, but she must have put up a spirited argument, for the boy was spared.

This Comanche woman helped Adolph travel two miles to the next camp by holding up his injured leg while he crawled. No doubt his hands were cut and bloody and swollen from thorns by the time they reached camp, but at least he was alive. The child prisoner had survived his closest call. While his leg was healing, the old woman nursed him and protected him, sometimes even hiding him in a snow-bank from those tribesmen who still thought he should be killed. Adolph would always feel indebted to her. Alone in a world of unfa-miliar sights and sounds, he had a new mother to guide him.

Grandpa Korn refused to believe that the Indians would have killed Adolph after going to so much trouble to get away with him. He traveled to San Antonio to report the kidnapping at the military head-quarters. As a result, officers in charge of scouting parties were or-dered to search for the boy. Grandpa Korn also wrote to the Texas governor, and his cry for help went up and down the chain of com-mand. The Texas secretary of state notified the commissioner of In-dian Affairs in Washington, who contacted the Indian Office's superintendent in Lawrence, Kansas, who directed the Indian agent at Fort Sill to ask the tribal chiefs if they knew what had become of Adolph Korn.

Despite this show of authority, the army, the governor, and the commissioner of Indian Affairs were powerless to do anything more than publicize the boy's disappearance. The Indian Office's superin-tendent in Lawrence issued a circular, making a plea on the Korns' be-half: "His parents are poor, but hope to hear something of their child from some out-post of civilization where Indians trade; therefore all Texas and frontier papers will confer a favor on the afflicted, by giving this notice publication."[14] "All Texas and frontier papers": Adolph could be anywhere. The Korns didn't even know which tribe was holding him. The commissioner in Washington directed the agents under his authority to inquire among the Kiowas and Comanches, the tribes that most frequently raided in Texas. He was essentially saying, "The boy is in Texas, Indian Territory, Kansas, or New Mexico, un-less he's elsewhere." No news came back.

For ten years, Grandpa Korn had felt the shame of not being able to provide for his children. Now he'd failed in an even more important duty of a man on the frontier: to protect his family. He'd let his twin boys wander perilously far from the village, just so they could earn the money he didn't have, and now one of them hadn't come home, and the other was traumatized. For all he knew, the Indians had bashed out Adolph's brains with a rock, just as they'd done a couple of years before to two infant granddaughters of Betsy Johnson, the Korns' former neighbor from Saline. Or maybe they were torturing Adolph, putting him through a slow and agonizing death. Grandpa knew he had let it happen.

It was his wife who decided they'd stayed on the frontier long enough. The move to the Hill Country had been Grandpa's idea to start with. Johanna Korn had trusted her husband and kept watch over his dreams, waiting patiently for things to get better. But after her boy disappeared, she declared that she would no longer live in that wild country and put her other children at risk. The Korns packed up their meager belongings and returned to San Antonio. A decade after Grandpa Korn had set out to make good in Castell, he was back where he started.

But Louis and Johanna Korn's Hill Country ordeal was not yet over, for the boy they'd left behind there, if he had survived, was still wandering somewhere on the prairie, a prisoner in the hands of savages. The Korns had become part of a small circle of heartsick parents across Texas who faced each day by reassuring themselves that some captured children eventually came home. However, each night they tossed fitfully, racked by the knowledge that others, like Alice Todd, did not. There was nothing the Korns could do to improve the odds of Adolph's recovery. Only one decision remained within their hands: how long to wait before giving up hope.

Chapter Two

Germans in
Comanche Land

At the time my uncle Adolph roamed the plains with the Comanches, they had no central government. The scattered tribal groups made their collective decisions in local village councils. Nowadays the Comanche Nation is headquartered in a sprawling, modern complex on a low hill nine miles north of Lawton, Oklahoma. It's the center of tribal government, business, and social services, but I went there to contemplate a treasured part of my own heritage. Hanging behind the receptionist's desk is a handsome mural on a tanned buffalo hide. It reaffirms a treaty the Comanches made with my German-Texan forefathers in 1847:

> We are the Promise of our Ancestors
> We agree to uphold
> the Treaty of Peace
> made between
> the People of Fredericksburg
> and
> the Comanche Nation
> We are not afraid of war; we choose peace
> We shall walk the path of
> peace and protect each other
> We shall give support to those
> among us in need

We shall not recognize any line
of distinction between us because
we are one people and choose
to live together as such
We reaffirm these ideals so
our children will be our promise

1997

———— ·•· ————

The signers of the mural are descendants of people from two strikingly different cultures who attempted to tolerate one another and coexist peacefully in Texas during the mid-1800s. I decided to take a closer look at the unusual relationship between the Comanches and the German immigrants, because it might have some bearing on why my German ancestor became such a thorough Comanche convert. Anthropologist A. Irving Hallowell pointed out that Indianization depended on a number of variables, one of which was the captive's "previous attitude toward the people of the second culture."[1] Three of the captives I tracked—Adolph Korn, Rudolph Fischer, and Herman Lehmann—spent their childhood within thirty-five miles of one another, growing up among German-Texans whose first contacts with Native Americans had been mostly positive.

The bond of friendship between the Comanches and the German settlers of central Texas has been enshrined in both people's mythologies, and over the decades the story has been glorified and distorted by selective memory. Still, the Comanche-German treaty is remarkable, possibly even unique in American history. In the bloody annals of Indian-white relations in the nineteenth century, it's hard to find other instances when white settlers and Plains Indians successfully negotiated a private agreement. Although their utopia didn't last, the Comanches and the Germans seemed to have had an understanding for a short time. The story of those few golden years provides a heartbreaking glimpse into an America that might have been.

* * *

Could the final, bloodiest years of the Indian wars on the Texas frontier have been avoided? What if someone had just drawn a boundary line through Texas—Indian hunters on one side, non-Indian farmers on the other? It sounds simplistic, but that's what both the Comanches and Sam Houston wanted. Shortly after Texas became an independent republic in 1836, Mopechucope (Old Owl) and several other Penateka Comanche chiefs starting talking with Houston, the Texas president, about dividing the territory: Indians in the north and west, settlers in the south and east. Since the Penatekas were the southernmost division of the Comanches, they were the ones most directly threatened by white expansion.

Mopechucope, a small, wrinkled man who wore a dirty cotton jacket that belied his stature, was the Penatekas' principal advocate for a line of demarcation across Texas. In March 1844, he dictated a letter to Sam Houston, describing a line that he wanted to "run between our countries," from the Brazos River to the Colorado River below the mouth of the San Saba, then straight to the Rio Grande.[2] Houston, who was popular among the Comanches, agreed that a boundary line would be a good idea, but he felt it would never work, for two reasons. The Comanche elders who made the treaties were notoriously ineffective when it came to restraining the high-spirited young men of their tribe, who raided where they pleased. And Houston was just as powerless to control the white settlers. He admitted, "If I could build a wall from the Red River to the Rio Grande, so high that no Indian could scale it, the white people would go crazy trying to devise means to get beyond it."

Nonetheless, the line through Texas remained the focal point of the Comanches' talks with the whites for several years. In the summer of 1846, a multitribal delegation of Native American chiefs traveled to Washington to meet with President James K. Polk and discuss the boundary question. After passing through one town after another and realizing that the white people were "more numerous than the stars," the chiefs were prepared to accept a compromise. However, they were stymied by an odd problem created by an agreement they hadn't made. On December 29, 1845, the U.S. government had approved the annexation of Texas as a state; the independent Republic of Texas was formally dissolved on February 19, 1846. Prior to joining the union, Texas had opened all of its so-called "vacant" land—that is, Indian hunting grounds—to non-Indian settlers. One of the stipulations of the annexation agreement was that the state would retain title to that territory. That meant the federal government didn't own the land that the Indians occupied in Texas and therefore had no legal authority to establish a line of separation. Meanwhile, the Texas state government was selling the Native Americans' homeland to immigrants and developers.

The governor pro tempore of Texas, Albert C. Horton, realized that the racial problems in the state were potentially explosive. The Indian, Anglo, and Mexican inhabitants of Texas had enjoyed sporadically peaceful relations during the 1840s, but any balance they'd achieved had been both hard-won and fragile. On June 1, 1846, Horton issued a proclamation imploring Texans to "abstain from trespassing" on debatable lands, that is, "all the territory above and bordering on our present Settlements." Horton thought it was "of vital importance to the peace of our frontier" that "no collision should take place between our citizens" and the Native American tribes in Texas.[3]

Horton's proclamation came on the heels of an alarming development. Only three weeks earlier, a small group of German immigrants had started a new settlement called Fredericksburg on the southern fringe of Comanche hunting grounds.[4] Most of the founders of the village were impoverished but industrious artisans and farmers who had left Germany for a number of reasons, including overpopulation, crop failures, and the desire to avoid conscription. They'd been lured to the wilderness of Texas by the enthusiastic promises of the Verein zum Schutze deutscher Einwanderer in Texas (Society for the Protection of German Immigrants in Texas), an organization of idealistic noblemen that brought more than seven thousand immigrants to start a colony in Texas between 1844 and 1846.

The Germans hadn't been in Fredericksburg long before a few Comanches ventured into their midst, observing the settlers with wary curiosity. The native people camped in the village and gaped at its inhabitants: strange, frightened, unhealthy men and women in comical attire, clearing timber in the heat of the day. To the Comanches, who were able to satisfy their own needs from the land without taming it, the Germans seemed pitiful and pigheaded, waging war on nature rather than simply enjoying its bounty. Their scraggly beards repelled the Comanches, whose own men fussed over their appearance and were careful to pluck all their facial hair. The Comanches also thought the white people had strong body odor.

Before long the Comanches discovered that they could trade with the Germans. They brought fresh deer and buffalo meat into the village, which the Germans purchased "for the most trifling considerations." They also sold the Germans horses, mules, deer hides, honey, and other goods. The trade that developed was enormously beneficial to the immigrants, who otherwise might have starved during that first miserable year.

By founding Fredericksburg, the Germans had taken one tentative step over the line (which was still not officially defined) into Comanche territory. That was nothing compared to what they planned to do. The Society for the Protection of German Immigrants in Texas had purchased rights to settle German colonists throughout the Fisher-Miller Land Grant, a tract of over six thousand square miles of semiarid country in west central Texas. The grant was bounded by the Colorado River on the north and the Llano River on the south, extending westward from the junction of those two streams almost to the Pecos River. That land comprised the principal hunting grounds of the Penateka Comanches. Fredericksburg, located south of the grant, was merely a way station for German immigrants who intended to penetrate the vast expanse of Comanche land and make their homes there.

Once they arrived in the Texas Hill Country, the Germans realized that they couldn't go ahead with their plans for a colony unless they reached some sort of agreement with the dreaded Comanches. Timing was critical; the contract required the Germans to survey the grant by the first of September 1847. One immigrant, Alwin Sörgel, summed up the fears of many of his fellow colonists when he wrote: "What tribe the size of the Comanches has ever relinquished its hunting grounds without a fight so the white men can plow it or an increasing number of palefaces can kill off or drive away the wild life, their chief source of sustenance? . . . How are the Germans, unfamiliar with warfare, to resist them?"

Since the Comanches could easily overrun and annihilate the small German settlements, diplomacy was the immigrants' only option. On January 22, 1847, an expedition of about forty men left Fredericksburg to explore the wilderness north of the Llano River and try to meet with some Comanche leaders.[5] For an interpreter, the Germans hired Lorenzo de Rozas, a Mexican who had been kidnapped by the Comanches as a child and was familiar with their ways. He was probably the first Indian captive the Germans ever met.

Meanwhile, the Comanches kept a suspicious eye on the white men once they crossed the Llano River and entered the grant. On February 5, 1847, about seven or eight Comanches carrying a white flag approached the Germans' camp. Their leader was Ketumsee, a minor Penateka chieftain who would later become a principal band chief. Wasting no time with pleasantries, he demanded to know what the Germans were doing there. He announced that he believed the white men had come to wage war. He pointed out that he had notified his distant kinsmen of this intrusion, and that the Germans were surrounded by throngs of armed Comanches.

Comanche-German relations might have ended in a bloodbath right there. Fortunately for everyone involved, the German expedition was headed by a thirty-four-year-old aristocrat named John O. Meusebach, who was well aware of the Comanches' skill in battle and also took a genuine interest in their culture. Remaining calm, he announced that the Germans had come in peace and brought presents, and that if the Comanches came to visit Fredericksburg, they would

be shown the same hospitality the Germans expected from the Comanches.

Ketumsee was satisfied with Meusebach's response. He invited the
Germans to visit his camp on the San Saba River and promised to
summon other Comanche chiefs in the area to a large peace council.
Two days later, the Germans reached Ketumsee's village, far from any
American settlement. Over the next few days, the Germans were immersed in Comanche society, which they found both captivating and
appalling. One of them complained that the Comanches were "very
untidy," picking lice off one another and then eating them. The immigrants became seriously concerned about their food supply, for
"when we prepared our meals, they crowded in with such a ravenous
hunger that we could scarcely satisfy our own hunger." However, they
were favorably impressed by the Comanches' ceremonial attire, which
they described as "indeed beautiful and in good taste." They also admired the comfort and functionality of their hosts' buffalo-hide tepees, which they thought offered more protection against wintry gales
than their own log cabins.

While they were in Ketumsee's camp, the Germans met two Indian captives. That experience left them shaken. The first was Warren
Lyons, a young white man from Fayette County, Texas, who had
spent nearly a decade with the Comanches.[6] He could still speak some
English. The Germans tried to persuade him to go back with them.
However, according to Ferdinand von Roemer, a young German scientist who had joined the expedition to study the geology of the region, Lyons "did not entertain our proposition and assured us several
times that he liked his present condition very much and that he had
no desire to return to the pale faces." With Warren Lyons was a Mexican boy of about eight, who was suffering pitifully from cold and
hunger. He was obviously Lyons's slave. Roemer asked Lyons how the
boy had come to be with the tribe.

Lyons replied quietly, "I caught him on the Rio Grande."

Roemer was stunned: "This was said in a tone of voice as if he
were speaking of some animal."

Even the most benevolent whites believed that the ultimate goal of contact between European-Americans and Native Americans was to elevate the latter. Yet here was a white boy, raised in a civilized home, who clearly preferred the natives' way of life. Even worse, Lyons had adopted Indian customs to the point of taking a captive of his own. For the German idealists who hoped to live as one with the Comanches in the wilderness, Warren Lyons, the strapping white Indian, provided a sobering warning of what that might mean. If the two peoples ever truly blended, the resulting culture might be more aboriginal than Teutonic.

The peace council took place on March 1 and 2, 1847, in another Comanche village located in a serene valley on the lower San Saba River. From a distance, the arriving Germans thought they were approaching an army camp. Between twelve hundred and fifteen hundred Comanches had gathered for the event. They'd set up a long string of tepees along the water in the shade of live oaks and pecan trees. Comanche men, women, and children ran to gawk at the Germans as they entered the village.

When it came time for the solemn council, the Comanches arranged buffalo hides in a circle around a smoldering fire that would be used to light the peace pipe. John Meusebach represented the Germans. About twenty Penateka chiefs and headmen participated in the council, although Mopechucope, Santa Anna, and Pochanaquarhip (Buffalo Hump) were the primary spokesmen.

Even though interpreters were present, the Comanches and the Germans didn't communicate very well at the council. The problem wasn't just the language barrier. As their remarks demonstrated, Indians and whites simply couldn't understand one another's ways of thinking. To start with, the two sides had very different ideas about who were the parties to their agreement. The Germans believed they were making a treaty with the "Comanche Nation." There was no such thing. A Comanche chief only had the authority to speak for his group. The Germans didn't understand that they were negotiating with the Penatekas, their nearest Comanche neighbors, and no one else.

Meusebach got the council started on the right foot by telling the Comanches that the Germans were "united with the Americans; they are our brothers and all of us live under the same great father, the President." Since he was still new to Texas, Meusebach may not have fully realized how fortuitous it was that he'd chosen the word "Americans" rather than "Texans." The Comanches hated the Texans, whom they thought were treacherous murderers and land-grabbers, but they were willing to negotiate with the Americans. They didn't fully grasp that the Texans had recently become Americans themselves.

The terms of the Comanche-German agreement were simple, covering only a few basic points:

1. The Germans were free to visit any part of the land grant between the Llano and San Saba Rivers.
2. The Comanches were free to visit the German communities.
3. The Comanches would not disturb the fledgling German settlement on the Llano River.
4. Each side would help the other fend off marauding tribes and bring criminals to justice.
5. The Comanches would allow the Germans to survey the uninhabited parts of the grant.
6. The Germans would give the Comanches $3,000 worth of presents.
7. Both sides would work to maintain peaceful relations.[7]

The Comanches still had strong misgivings about settlers building homes inside the grant, their hunting ground. Meusebach assured them that he was not trying to force them from their land; the Germans and Comanches would live side by side. However, these promises of peaceful coexistence didn't alleviate the Comanches' true fear: farmers, by their mere presence, tended to drive out the wild game. Even though the Comanches might benefit marginally from trade with the settlers, they would gain no real advantage from sharing their territory with the Germans if that meant losing the buffalo and the deer.

Meusebach more effectively allayed their fears by telling them that the amount of land the Germans needed was small, and that they would confine their settlements to the area along the Llano River, the southern edge of Penateka hunting grounds. Still, Mopechucope replied: "There is one thing which does not please my heart, if you set your wigwams along the water you call Llano." He said he would need to consult with all his men before he could give a firm reply.

Mopechucope went on to say, "I know that the people who call themselves Texans wish to draw a line of distinction between us and the pale faces." Apparently, he was referring to his earlier discussions with Sam Houston about a boundary line across Texas, a line the Comanches still wanted for their own protection. Mopechucope would need to confer with other Comanche chiefs to see if they thought the proposed German settlements would interfere with the establishment of an acceptable dividing line.

The Germans, misunderstanding Mopechucope's remark, thought he was referring to a line of racial segregation rather than territorial demarcation. Meusebach replied: "I do not scorn the red brothers because they have a darker color, and do not regard the whites as noble because they are lighter in color. If our great father and president wishes to draw a line of distinction, let him do so. We shall not see the distinction because we are brothers and wish to live together as brothers." The Germans went to great lengths to assure the chiefs that they regarded the native people as equals, not realizing that the Comanches' real concern was land, not bigotry.

Meusebach made a bolder suggestion, one that may have shocked some of his white colleagues: "After our people and yours have lived together for a time, it may happen that some will want to intermarry." The chiefs didn't respond to this proposal. They may have found it embarrassing, even offensive. Comanches normally didn't condescend to marry people from outside the tribe, nor did they welcome adult white males into their families. Meusebach then qualified his proposal: "Soon our young warriors will speak your language and, if they are so inclined and can reach an agreement to marry, I know of no objections." He made it clear that he was referring to his "warriors," German men, taking Comanche brides and bringing them to the German settlements—not to German women going to live with native men in Comanche camps. The Germans had seen Warren Lyons and his Mexican captive; they knew what could happen to white people who lived too long among the Comanches.

The strong personal bonds formed at the council of March 1847 would be more effective in keeping the peace than the actual terms of the agreement. The men primarily responsible for the treaty all hoped their very different peoples could coexist without either having to forgo its way of life, but that wasn't really possible. Among the Germans, the only observer who took a clear-eyed, unsentimental look at the Comanches' prospects for the future was the young scientist, Ferdinand von Roemer. After returning to Germany, he wrote in 1849:

> It is apparent that Indians of Texas, as well as the Red Race in North America, will be driven from their homes and eventually be exterminated. The most beautiful lands have already been taken from them, and restlessly moving forward, the white, greedy conqueror is stretching forth his hand to take their new hunting ground also. . . . The Comanches very likely will hold out longest in their stony plateau. The prevailing unfertility of the soil and the inaccessibility of their homes will serve to protect them more against extermination than their number and warlike disposition.[8]

The treaty got off to a rocky start once the Germans began surveying the land grant. Around July 13, 1847, the leader of the surveying party went to check on four of his men who were working along the Llano River. All he found at their camp were their hats and the tracks of several horses. Afraid that the Indians had captured them, he immediately gave the alarm. Before the Germans could determine what had happened to the four missing surveyors, the Comanche chief Santa Anna, whose people had frequently paid friendly visits to the surveyors' camps, inexplicably told them that they must leave. He said that his men wouldn't allow any further surveys. Shortly afterward, he left the region "very suddenly and under suspicious circumstances with all the women and children of his tribe," heading north at a rapid pace.

The Germans were worried that their peace treaty had failed. Meusebach reportedly raised a militia of about sixty men to go into the grant and protect the surveyors if necessary. Two companies of Texas Rangers were stationed near Fredericksburg, prepared for an all-out war.

In August Santa Anna returned to Fredericksburg expressing "every disposition to be friendly with the white people." He wanted to explain his sudden departure the month before. At the time he'd delivered his threat to the surveyors, he wasn't aware that four members of their party were missing. Later, when he heard about their disappearance and learned that the Texas Rangers were heading for Fredericksburg, he realized that his people were prime suspects. He decided to move his women and children to a safe place until he could clear the air.

Santa Anna also brought tragic news. He reported that he had visited a camp of Waco Indians, who were holding a ceremonial dance around the scalps of the four surveyors. The Wacoes later denied this, protesting that none of their people had been in the region at the time. Instead, they blamed the Comanches. A cynical Houston journalist harrumphed that both tribes "are so treacherous that it is difficult to decide whether they depend upon their innocence or upon their adroitness in lying to exculpate themselves in this instance."[9]

Aside from this one tragedy in the summer of 1847, the arrangement between the Comanches and the Germans worked admirably, if not perfectly. The Comanches brought buffalo hides and tanned deerskins to Fredericksburg to trade for manufactured goods. Santa Anna and his brother, Sanaco, who later became a major war chief, were frequent visitors in the German village during 1847. The Comanche women constructed drums from leftover German cheese containers. Comanche children played with those of the immigrants and helped them gather acorns for their coffee.

Although the Germans spoke glowingly of the Comanches as a people, most of them didn't really enjoy dealing with the tribesmen one on one. Peace treaty or not, a Comanche warrior was still plenty frightening up close. The Germans were also irritated when the Comanches would show up at mealtime and expect unlimited hospitality, or when their women and children would pilfer small articles that the settlers could scarcely afford to replace. Clara Feller, who was living in Fredericksburg at the time, related a typical story: "The rascals had a habit of taking whatever they could easily get away with and not even returning thanks for it. One day while I was at home alone, in walked a big buck Indian. I had just made a successful bake of bread and was exceedingly proud of it. . . . The big scamp sized up everything, spied my bread, picked it up and walked off with it. My fear turned to helpless rage, to all of which the Indian paid no more attention than if I had been a bird chirping in a bush."[10]

Nor did the Comanches feel completely at ease in town. If the German men in Meusebach's expedition had felt nervous camping among hundreds of armed warriors, a night in Fredericksburg was just as unsettling for some Comanches. When Mopechucope came to visit, he was invited to stay in a settler's log cabin, but he vacated his room before daybreak, inexplicably shaken, and never returned to Fredericksburg.

Other cross-cultural exchanges were more enjoyable for both sides, especially in the smaller German settlements on the Llano River outside of Fredericksburg. In November 1847, Santa Anna, with about one hundred of his men and their families, paid a visit to the German settlers at Bettina, an experimental communistic colony started by enthusiastic students from Darmstadt. Louis Reinhardt, one of the founders, recalled: "For everything we gave them we were paid back three-fold. . . . Whenever we came into their camp, they would spread out their deer skins, bring out morrals full of the biggest pecans I ever saw, and tell us to help ourselves." In nearby Castell, where the Korn family would eventually settle, friendly native women cared for the German-American children while their parents worked in the fields. William Schmidt, who spent his childhood near Castell, said that the Comanches "never stole a horse or anything else from us." One day a Native American man picked up William's older sister, Sophie, rode off with her on his horse, then brought her back a little later, laughing.

Those early days saw the fulfillment of the vision of cooperation and mutual support spelled out by Meusebach, Santa Anna, and Mopechucope. No one realized they would end soon, especially not the immigrants. One of them even boasted, "The Americans know well that the Indians have an ineradicable hatred against them—a natural result of the many injustices they have suffered; whereas the Indians treat the Germans very kindly." Another wrote, rather smugly, that the Indians "see in the conduct and actions of the Germans a distinct difference from that of the old-time Texans. . . . Because of the kindness shown them, the Indians do not transfer to the German newcomers their old hostility against the Texans."

Sadly, it didn't take long for the peaceful relations between the Comanches and the Germans to deteriorate. There's no single reason why. A series of unrelated events, beginning only a year after the peace treaty, all played a role.

In 1848 the U.S. Army established Fort Martin Scott on the outskirts of Fredericksburg to keep the peace on the frontier. The Comanches knew that the soldiers weren't there for their benefit, and they felt less welcome in town. Texas Rangers were also stationed near Castell to protect the German settlers from Indian raids.

Early in 1849, the body of a German laborer was found about twenty miles from Fredericksburg. He'd been lanced, stripped, and scalped—a warning that not all was well between the Germans and the native people.[11] No one knows why he was killed. However, Marie Leifeste Donop, the daughter of one of Castell's original settlers, related, "Some of the white people became angry with the Indians and began beating them in trades and mistreating them. That's what my father said started the trouble with the Indians." Later in 1849, both Santa Anna and Mopechucope died during a cholera epidemic. The Germans lost their two best Comanche friends.

In 1850 the Comanches made one of their last recorded visits to Fredericksburg, and it wasn't peaceful. Two Comanches got in an argument with an Indian of the Tonkawa tribe and stabbed him to death. Later that year, the federal government negotiated a new treaty that prohibited the Comanches from traveling south of the Llano River without express, written permission from an Indian agent or military officer.[12] It placed no similar restriction on whites venturing north.

By 1851 renegade Indians had started moving into the region, including Comanches from northern divisions that had not signed the treaty with the Germans. A chief of the Lipan Apaches who visited Fredericksburg reported that the Comanches were still disposed to be peaceable and friendly toward the whites, except for some "bad men among them who cannot be restrained."

Meanwhile, the pattern of white settlement was changing. The Germans had originally established compact, European-style villages surrounded by small farm plots. They eventually discovered that the stony, arid land of the Texas Hill Country wouldn't allow them to farm as they had in Germany. They started occupying larger and more widely dispersed tracts. More significant, they began competing with the native people for wild game, which the Comanches had thought they would never do.

Indian raiders began stealing the Germans' horses and household goods. In 1852 some citizens of Fredericksburg put together a petition complaining about the conduct of certain Comanches and Lipan Apaches encamped in the area, "praying that measures may be taken to stop their outrages" and that these Indians "be removed from the Llano." On investigation it was found that the Germans' account of the depredations was "greatly exaggerated." The thefts were committed by a few drunken Indians, "who were made so by unprincipled white men who reside in Fredericksburg and vicinity and sell liquor to the Indians."[13]

Around 1854 the townspeople took matters into their own hands. Early one morning, an ailing Comanche boy, about thirteen years old, approached the home of a German settler near Fredericksburg, begging for food and medicine. No one knows what made the settler so angry or suspicious, but he immediately tried to grab the Comanche. The boy dodged him, jumping behind the man's wife for protection. He even dropped his bow and arrow to show that he meant no harm. Still, the German caught him and bound his hands and feet. The boy implored the man's wife to help him, but she refused. The man put him on a wagon and hauled him into Fredericksburg. A crowd gathered, drawn by the ruckus, and the Germans held a long discussion over what to do with the prisoner. Some thought he was a spy. Eventually, they took him to the outskirts of the village, where they forced him to gather firewood. Then the lynch mob tied the young Comanche to the trunk of a pecan tree, raised their shotguns, and blasted him more than thirty times. Finally, they used the wood he'd gathered to cremate his body.[14]

Although there were still some friendly contacts between Native Americans and German settlers well into the 1860s, violent encounters became the norm after 1850. At least nineteen German-Americans were murdered by Indians around Fredericksburg and the surrounding German communities between 1850 and 1870, some reportedly by Comanches. No one kept a record of how many native people, Comanche or otherwise, were killed by German-Americans during that same period. However, by the time the Civil War broke out, the Germans of the Texas Hill Country were battling Native American raiders as fiercely and frequently as any other settlers living in central Texas.

One significant difference remained, however. What set the German immigrants apart was not how they responded to the Indian threat in practice but how they spoke about the native people in the abstract. The typical feelings of other frontier settlers toward Indians were summed up in the no-nonsense words of one Mason County pioneer from Virginia: "They ought to be all killed off. There is no better way to get rid of them."[15] Many of the Germans, in contrast, continued to defend the Indians and see their side of the conflict even during the years they were fighting them, blaming the troubles on the "Americans" or "old-time Texans." That way of thinking—tolerant of the natives, arrogant toward non-German whites, and blind to their own culpability—permeated the insular German settlements during Uncle Adolph's boyhood.

The German-Texans of the Hill Country, still congratulating themselves over the bond they'd formed with the native people in the 1840s, clung to their idealized notions of a Comanche-German Camelot long after the brief era of peaceful relations had passed. In 1855, while the farms around Fredericksburg were being hit by Indian warriors, a resident named Theodore Specht wrote that he "found among these so-called 'wild people' good and bad persons, but never such poor specimens as are to be found among civilized nations." The German community made excuses for the Indians even when they raided, attributing fault to everyone but their own people and the natives themselves. Specht blamed federal Indian policy and government agents. In 1877 an unnamed newspaper correspondent from Fredericksburg argued that Indian raids were understandable because the establishment of military posts on the frontier "provoked the red men to anger," and the soldiers' persecution of the natives "incurred their hatred for every pale face."[16] A pioneer named Therese Marschall von Biberstein Runge, who grew up during the Indian scares of the 1860s, nonetheless maintained that the Native Americans "were people of great honor defending their homes." Adolph Korn and the other German captives most likely heard their families and neighbors express these sorts of sentiments in their formative years.

The reality of their daily lives was another matter. Theodore Specht acknowledged in 1855: "Where in 1846 we dared to go hunting and fishing, in common with the Indians or alone, without any risk, now we must expect to be mercilessly shot down and scalped by the same Indians who were formerly our friends." As raids intensified and horror stories accumulated during the 1860s, the German immigrants lived in a climate of fear. They stayed close to home and barred their cabin doors at night. Some never walked across an open field without first ducking behind a tree to see if there were Indians around. Occasionally, they got careless. Sometimes they just didn't see the raiders in time.

After it happened, Gottlieb Fischer must have tried to convince himself there was nothing he could have done to prevent it. He'd heard that twenty-five or thirty Indians had been seen camped near Fredericksburg that week. They were probably Comanches.[17] Some people said they'd even come within a couple of miles of town. And by 1865, Indians in the vicinity almost always meant trouble. Still, the settlers had to go on with their daily lives.

The Fischers' farm, six miles southwest of Fredericksburg on the north bank of the Pedernales River, was isolated and vulnerable to attack. Gottlieb and his wife, Sophie, had purchased the land in 1851,[18] when the Indians were still friendly. Back then the place had seemed more like the New World paradise that the German noblemen who headed the colony had promised: one hundred ten acres of rolling meadows in a shady dale, the river bottom lined with tall trees. Fourteen years later, at age fifty-one, he was still struggling to make a living from it.

The abduction occurred on a main road in broad daylight, around noon on a sunny, calm Saturday, July 29, 1865. Fischer had sent his oldest son, Rudolph, to look for some stray cattle. Times were hard; the war had ended only three months earlier, and the family couldn't afford to lose any livestock.

Rudolph should have been more careful. He wasn't a helpless, ignorant child. He was a young man, thirteen and a half years old,[19] a fine-looking boy with curly black hair, dark eyes, and a fair complexion. Certainly, he knew to watch out for raiders. The boy had heard stories about Indian abductions. At least he was old enough to know not to struggle too much or the Indians would kill him. He might have even gone with them without putting up a fight.

A scouting party had tried to follow the Indians that took Rudolph. They'd come near them twice, but finally they'd lost the trail. It might have been better if they'd found him dead. When Mrs. Runge's son, Herman, had been killed by Indians ten years earlier, she'd been greatly comforted by one witness's report that he'd probably died before he was scalped. Then again, what if the search party had found Rudolph's body in the same position as Billy Schumann's, Gus Schumann's son in the Saline Valley: drawn up in a cramped heap, probably in the last throes of a death struggle as he was being scalped?

The Fischers knew there was some hope Rudolph might make it back to them alive. Gottlieb tried to get information from Indian traders, but they weren't any help. At Christmastime, desperately missing his son, the broken man wrote to Pres. Andrew Johnson, giving him a full account of Rudolph's disappearance: "When he was carried off he was barefooted, wore a straw hat, hickory striped shirt and buckskin pants. On the lower part of his belly he has got a mark, the exact likeness of a Catfish." As months went by with no news, hope started to fail him. By the spring of 1866, Gottlieb Fischer was willing to believe that his son had been killed. It was easier to mourn Rudolph than to wait for him.

He didn't know that Rudolph now answered to the name Asewaynah (Gray Blanket),[20] or that when he saw his boy again, the boy would be a man. Not a man as he pictured him, but a painted, solemn Comanche warrior. Asewaynah had spent his first thirteen years among settlers who taught him that the Indians were noble people fighting for their homeland, and he had taken those lessons to heart. One day he would help the native people make their final stand against the white invaders on the plains of Texas.

Chapter Three

The Bosom
of the Comanches

Rudolph Fischer and Adolph Korn, like many white Indians, left no explanation of how they made the transition from docile farm boys to Comanche warriors. "He didn't care to discuss his life," says Rudolph's granddaughter, Josephine Wapp. "We thought we shouldn't ask him questions if that was how he felt." Nor did Adolph Korn reveal much about his time away. Perhaps he didn't talk about it because he thought the family wasn't interested. Maybe he felt it was none of our business. For whatever reasons, he kept his secrets, and no one knows exactly what happened to him during his first months with the Comanches. The only way for me to understand his captivity was to study other child captives of post–Civil War Texas who went through similar experiences and chose to tell their stories— Dot and Banc Babb, Herman Lehmann, and Clinton and Jeff Smith.

The first of these to be captured were the Babbs. The two siblings from north Texas lived with the Comanches in 1866–1867, only three years before Uncle Adolph was kidnapped. They left a wealth of information about their early months as captives. Dot Babb published a memoir, *In the Bosom of the Comanches,* in 1912. Banc also wrote a short account of her time with the tribe.

One of Dot's granddaughters, Miri Hargus, traveled to Oklahoma in 1989 and tried to find out more about him from the Comanches. When she returned home to Seattle, she visited her grandchildren's elementary schools and shared his story with their classes. Sadly, Mrs. Hargus died just as I was starting my own search, so we never got to compare notes. Her daughter Leslie told me, "She was always proud of her grandfather and his efforts to present the Comanches as something besides savages." That's what drew me to the Babbs' story as well. In both of their narratives, Dot and Banc Babb spoke glowingly, sometimes idealistically, of their captors.[1] Their admiration for their adoptive people might not be so surprising if their captivity hadn't begun in a frenzy of bloodshed and terror.

The raiders were in a foul mood long before they reached the Babb place. It should have been a quick, easy trip. They'd started out as thirty-two young men from the Nokoni division of the Comanches, looking for adventure and a chance to test their mettle. Their leader, Persummy, was a brother to the Nokonis' principal chief, Terheryaquahip (Horseback). They'd dipped down into north Texas from Indian Territory, raided four farms in Jack and Wise Counties, and taken several horses. However, something had gone terribly wrong; six of their men had lost their lives along the way. The white enemies had even scalped one warrior, so that his life was forever annihilated, his spirit unable to enter the next world.

Persummy's group rode hard across rolling prairies and low hills thick with oaks and native grasses—what used to be good buffalo-hunting country, before the white settlers moved in. Around mid-afternoon on September 14, 1866, they came upon a log cabin on the scrubby flatlands near Dry Creek, about twelve miles west of Decatur. Two white children, a boy and a girl, were resting and playing in the yard near a brush arbor. The Comanches didn't see any men around. A white woman yelled from the doorway, and the two children looked up. Then they ran to the cabin and slammed the door. Persummy's group headed in their direction. The Nokoni raiders were about to have their satisfaction.

The people trapped inside the cabin waited anxiously for the Comanches to make their next move. Isabel Babb, the mother, tried to stay calm. She spoke as little as possible, because she didn't want the children to hear the fear in her voice. There wasn't much she could do to get ready for an onslaught. The door didn't even have a lock or a bar. Isabel had always known there were Indians around; but, like everyone else, she never really believed they would bother her family. Nor had she learned to be afraid of the native people. Before moving to Texas, she'd lived peacefully beside the Winnebago Indians in Wisconsin Territory.

Her husband, John, and their oldest boy, Court, had gone to Fort Smith, Arkansas, to trade some cattle for horses. They weren't expected back for another three weeks. Her son Dot was fourteen and could fire a rifle. But her daughter Banc was only ten, too little to defend herself, and Isabel couldn't protect her and the infant, Margie, too. A young Civil War widow named Sarah Jane Luster was also in the cabin. She'd been staying with Isabel and keeping her company while John and Court were away.

They all heard the war whoops. A moment later, a Comanche man threw open the door and stepped in. Isabel, knowing she couldn't fend off the intruders, tried to shake the man's hand and even offered him a chair. Ignoring her, he walked back to the bed and started stripping off the linens. Other raiders poured into the house and began taking clothes and bedding. They jerked off the mattresses, tore up the fabric cases, and shook feathers into the air. They also broke up the furniture. Some helped themselves to the milk.

Dot ran back to the corner to get a rifle off the rack, but the Comanches easily overpowered him. They took the gun away and whipped him over the head with their quirts. Isabel cried out, "Don't fight back, Dot! They'll kill you." She was clutching the baby in one arm, and her other arm was wrapped around Banc, sheltering the girl in her skirt. Two of the Indians grabbed Banc by the arms and started to lead her away. Isabel put the baby on the bed. She followed Banc and clung to her hand, trying to stop the Comanches from taking her. Suddenly, one of the men reached for a large knife and plunged it into Isabel's body four times. She fell onto the bed beside the baby.

The raiders forced Sarah Luster down from the loft where she'd been hiding and took her and Banc outside. Two men came back in the house; they were surprised to find Isabel still alive. A Comanche named Omercawbey (Walking Face) drew a bow and shot her in the left side with an arrow. Then the raiders scalped her alive. Dot managed to pull the barbed arrow out of his mother's flesh and tried to comfort her. Omercawbey then pointed an arrow at him. The last thing Isabel said to her son was: "Go with him and be a good boy." A warrior grabbed Dot by the arm and led him to the door.

Outside the cabin, Sarah and Banc were already placed on horses, each behind a Comanche man. Banc called out, "Dot, don't let them hurt me." The ten-year-old girl had already given her captor a hard time, clinging to one of the posts of the brush arbor so tightly that the skin was ripped from her hands when he pried her loose. She also slipped off the horse before the man got her secured. However, Banc had made up her mind not to cry. Later, her captor, whose name was Kerno, told her that if she'd cried, he would have killed her.

Dot couldn't do anything to help his sister. He was also put on a horse behind a warrior. "The Comanche pulled my arms around in front of him and held me by pressing his own arms tight against his side," he recalled. "I thought I could get away, but I soon found out I was being held. I tried to bite the Indian then, but there was no place I could get my teeth into."

As they left the Babb place, the Comanches took six of the family's mares, adding them to the herd. They also killed Dot's colt. Then they moved fast up Dry Creek in the direction of Indian Territory, disappearing into the woods.

A few hours later, Sheriff Bob Cates and a volunteer posse of about twenty-three men from Decatur arrived at the Babb farm. They'd been following the Comanches' trail of destruction all afternoon. On a hill about two hundred yards from the Babb house, they'd found some of John Babb's carpentry tools. The cabin was eerily quiet when they rode up. They called out, but no one answered. They got off their horses. Feathers from the bed were scattered about the yard. One man pulled an arrow out of a dead sheep.

When they entered the cabin, all talking stopped, except for a few muffled exclamations. Isabel Babb, bleeding profusely but by then mercifully unconscious, was breathing her last. And the infant, Margie, unharmed but grotesquely smeared with Isabel's blood, was trying to nurse at her dying mother's breast.

By then it was dusk. The new moon hadn't reached its first quarter, and the men knew there wouldn't be enough light to pursue the Indians after dark. Early the next morning, Sheriff Cates and the posse started following the raiders' tracks northwest. Along the way, they found pieces of calico and strips of clothing hanging from the brush. They speculated that Sarah Luster was ripping her clothes, trying to leave a trail for them. After about forty miles, the Indians' tracks split off in several directions, and the searchers had no idea which path to follow. They'd also run out of food. Exhausted and defeated, they turned back.

The Comanches and their captives were heading northwest at a rapid pace, barreling across open prairies where there were no settlements. They rode full speed through the night, stopping only two or three times for their sweaty horses to rest. Unlike their white pursuers, the Comanche fighting men had trained themselves to go long distances without food or water. Sometimes they purposely chose escape routes with no water so the whites wouldn't try to follow them.

They wouldn't let the three prisoners off their horses during the flight. The girl captive, Banc Babb, lost control of her bodily functions. The Comanches must have been amused, for they gave her a nickname that meant "Smell Bad When You Walk." Unfortunately for Banc, the name stuck.

By the next morning, they'd reached the northern plains of Texas, country not yet inhabited by white settlers. About six miles northwest of present-day Henrietta, Texas, they arrived at the Little Wichita River, which was on a rise. The Comanches, not knowing whether they were still being pursued, decided to risk crossing it. They got off their horses and led the captives over the roaring floodwaters atop a large accumulation of driftwood. The Comanches forced the horses to swim the swift stream. Then they took off west.

If the three captives had been too terrified at first to notice how uncomfortable they were, they could think of nothing else after a night on horseback. Their legs were sore, their backs ached, they hadn't slept, and Banc was sitting in her own excrement. The mid-September sun was blistering and burned their faces. They hadn't had anything to eat since they'd left home.

At around eleven o'clock, when the raiders reached Holliday Creek, they found the remains of a big steer that the wolves had attacked, crippled, and partially devoured. They stopped there. When Dot's captor jumped down from the horse they were sharing, the boy tumbled awkwardly to the ground. "I tried to get up and go over to Banc," he recalled, "but I was too numb. I couldn't walk. When I fell back, the Indians laughed at me. Then I made a face at them. They slapped their bare legs and laughed louder than ever." Banc didn't notice these pratfalls. She was fixated on the dead steer. The men built a fire and started cooking the meat. As Banc later related, "I was so hungry that I begged for some of the raw meat, and they gave me a small piece, which I ate greedily and begged for more. . . . I reached for a piece myself, when an Indian hacked my finger with his knife. I reached with my other hand and he hacked it, so I decided to quit reaching."

They got back on their horses and kept pushing on at a steady clip, leaving plumes of dust behind them in the clear autumn air. Banc was able to sleep a little as she rode behind Kerno. At sunset they reached the Red River just below the mouth of the Pease River. By then the raiders felt safe enough to stop and rest. They camped on the south bank of the stream for several days, waiting for the floodwaters to subside. Meanwhile, most of the Comanches went off to hunt buffalo. The three prisoners had to stay behind in camp with their guard. In the daylight, they were allowed to move freely and talk with one another. At night the two Babb children and Sarah Luster slept together, with their captors surrounding them.

On the morning of the fifth day, they crossed the Red River just below the mouth of the North Fork, which put them on the grassy prairies of Indian Territory. Banc thought the men looked very relieved: "I presume it was because they considered that they were out of Texas and at home again." They kept moving northwest, passing through large sand dunes and crossing the North Fork of the Red River between Stinking and Otter Creeks. The buffalo were ample, so they had plenty of meat. They crossed the North Fork again the following morning and stayed overnight on the Washita River. The next day, they reached the Canadian River northwest of present-day Elk City, Oklahoma, and set up camp.

Sarah Luster had given up hope that a search party would find them. She was twenty-six and beautiful and, as Dot explained delicately, "the helpless victim of an unspeakable violation, humiliation, and involuntary debasement." All this time, Sarah had been making plans to escape. On the seventh night, while their captors slept, she and Dot talked quietly. Sarah told Dot that he should tie a certain good stallion near the camp the next day. She felt sure a particular mare would stay with the stallion. They'd take off the following night while their guards were asleep. They planned to ride through the water of the Canadian River, which was only two or three feet deep, so the Comanches couldn't track them. Dot didn't want to leave without his sister, however. "Banc is a little girl, Dot," Sarah told him. "She is in no danger now with the Indians, and I know we cannot get her away without noise. We will escape and send the soldiers for Banc." Dot was still troubled, but Sarah convinced him that her plan was their best hope.

The following day, Dot did as Sarah had instructed him. Around one o'clock in the morning, Sarah woke Dot. They crawled slowly away from their captors, moving for a short interval and then lying still, until they reached the place where the stallion was waiting. Sarah found a bridle for the horse. They led him to a log where she could climb on. The mare came up to them in high spirits. Sarah whispered for Dot to get another bridle and get on the mare. Before he could bridle the mare, several Comanches awoke. The men started shouting and running toward them. Dot told Sarah to go on without him. She took off into the night, unnoticed by their captors.

Dot dropped the bridle he was holding and started walking toward camp, as if nothing had happened. An hour later, the warriors discovered that Sarah was missing. About eight or ten men went after her. They returned at daybreak, empty-handed and furious. They held Dot responsible. Early that morning, the men scratched a mark in the ground and made Dot stand there. They unbuttoned his shirt and ordered him to hold it open. Then they punched him in the chest with an old pistol, ripping his skin and causing him to fall back each time. Dot knew better than to cry or beg for mercy. Next, the Comanches made Dot stand against a big cottonwood tree. The men formed a line about twenty or thirty yards in front of him. Some drew their bows; others aimed pistols at him. Banc started sobbing, then fell on the ground and threw a blanket over her head.

Dot just wanted to get it over with. He made signs for the Comanches to shoot. Instead, they lowered their weapons and walked up to him. A few men tied Dot to the tree with a rawhide rope. They piled dry grass, leaves, and brush at his feet. They placed flint and steel nearby, ready to start a fire. Banc was so completely seized with terror that she did a strange thing: she began laughing hysterically. Even Dot smiled uncontrollably from fright. Then, in the maddeningly democratic fashion of the Comanches, the men held a council. Dot, "more than ever tired of these preliminaries," again made signs for them to hurry up and be done with it. He recalled, "I couldn't stand to hear Banc screaming, so I motioned for them to go on and set the fire." Instead, the men came forward and said to Dot, in broken English: "Heap wano you." They untied him. Dot had passed the test. As he explained in later years, "I never was scared. I never get scared until after everything is over."

At that point, the Comanches divided into several parties and left in various directions. Dot and Banc went with different groups. The Babb children wouldn't see each other again while they were with the Comanches. And they'd seen Sarah Luster for the last time. After a grueling ride and a second captivity by Kiowas, she escaped once more and found her way to freedom near Fort Zarah, Kansas.

The Southern Plains Indians had two reasons for capturing women and children during raids rather than killing them or leaving them behind. The first was commercial. Captives could be held for ransom or traded to other tribes. The second was adoption. Captives could be used to replace family members who had died, or just to build up the tribe generally. The Indians were hampered by low birth rates and had lost many of their own people to warfare, smallpox, and cholera. If the captives proved their worth and were adopted, they were granted full tribal rights and treated as natural-born Native Americans.

The practice of taking captives long predated the arrival of Europeans in America and continued right up until the reservation period. Captives taken during a successful raid were considered spoils of war, like horses or guns or clothing. Indians couldn't understand why non-Indians got so upset about it. Most of the captives were children between the ages of seven and fourteen. Younger children were too much trouble to care for during the getaway and were likely to cry; older ones were hard to retrain and usually tried to escape. Occasionally, the Indians took adult women, such as Sarah Luster, to hold for ransom or use as concubines. Hardly any grown men, or even boys over the age of fourteen, were captured. They were usually killed if they put up a fight or got in the way.

Whatever the reasons for taking captives, the practice was common. "We are all descendants of captives," said Ronald Red Elk at a Comanche gathering I attended in Lawton. I heard this refrain several times in Oklahoma. "Whenever they went on a raid, they were interested in capturing young boys," Comanche elder Vernon Cable told me. "Someone to ride the horse, to be a warrior, to help them in their battles. It didn't matter if they were black or Mexican or white. When the captives got to be about twelve or thirteen years of age, they were Comanches."

And so Dot and Banc Babb, and later my uncle Adolph Korn, became members of the tribe. They had two choices: adapt and enjoy their new life, or resist and live in miserable bondage.

By her second week of captivity, Banc Babb was completely alone in a world she couldn't comprehend. She no longer had Dot and Sarah for company. After Banc and her brother went their separate ways, her captor, Kerno, and his Comanche group continued up the Canadian River, riding hard for several more days.

During the trip, Banc spent one night in the camp of a Comanche group whose chief had a white captive living in his home. She said the captive was a teenage boy; most likely, he was Rudolph Fischer, who was fourteen years old by that time and had been with the Comanches a little more than a year. Although Rudolph had grown up in the German-American enclave of Fredericksburg, he could speak a little English. Banc and the boy talked about where they were from and how they were captured. According to Banc, "The Indians seemed to have a good time listening to us talk our funny language." The next morning, she left with her captors, and she wouldn't see another white face for seven months.

Three days later, as the sun was setting, Banc reached the village of the Comanche group with whom she would live. The first glimpse of a large Comanche camp was an unforgettable sight. The clusters of buffalo-hide tepees were strung along a stream for several miles, making the village look more populous than it really was. Family members set up tents near one another. Hundreds of horses grazed nearby. Her captors rode up to one tepee after another, greeting their friends. Eventually, they started to dismount and relax.

After a triumphant raid, the returning warriors were met with shouts of joy and songs of victory. Children rushed to find out what their fathers, brothers, and uncles had brought home from the trip. The people in the village also wanted to see the new captive. Soon

Banc was surrounded by men, women, children, and dogs, all curious to get a look at her. They pulled the white girl one way and then the other. Before she was even off her horse, she had managed to kick several people in the face. The Comanches were going to learn to keep their hands off Banc Babb.

Once she was on the ground, the Comanche children flocked around her. The small boys were naked; the older ones were clad in breechcloths, leggings, and moccasins. The girls wore buckskin dresses. The children were especially interested in stroking Banc's long, blond hair, for she was the first white child most of them had ever seen.

Kerno, the man with whom Banc had shared a horse for more than a week, led the girl to the lodge of his sister, Tekwashana, a young widow with no children of her own. He presented the girl to her to raise as her daughter. As it turned out, this woman's husband had been killed by white men a short time earlier. Banc didn't describe Tekwashana's appearance, but she probably wore moccasins and a buckskin dress decorated with multicolored beads, fringes, and small pieces of iron and tin. Comanche women paid little attention to their hair, usually hacking it off crudely. However, they carefully painted their faces with red and yellow lines. That night the Comanches held a big feast to celebrate the return of the warriors. They enjoyed flat bread, coffee, and sugar—luxuries Banc would seldom have during her time with the tribe.

Over the next few weeks, Banc adjusted quickly to the Comanche way of life. Her family consisted of about thirty-five people, who occupied seven or eight lodges. She slept in Tekwashana's tepee on a bed of dry grass, blankets, and thick buffalo robes. The Comanches kept a fire burning inside their tepees for warmth; a flap at the peak let the smoke out. On cold nights, Tekwashana would stand Banc in front of the fire, turning her around until she was warm. Then she'd wrap her in a buffalo robe, furry side in, and tuck her into the bed next to the tepee wall.

From the moment she got up each morning, Banc was ready to

eat, and she seemed to have no trouble getting used to the Comanches' diet of mostly meat. She also liked the informality of their
meals. Her family had no fixed hours for dining, but ate whenever
they were hungry. She remembered, "We never sat down to eat, just
stood around the kettle of meat, and with the stick we would spear a
piece of meat from the kettle, hold it to our mouth and bite off as
much as we could conveniently chew."

Banc came to treasure her Comanche ornaments. Tekwashana
outfitted her with brass bracelets, silver earrings with long chains, and
an elaborate headdress made of shiny pieces of metal attached to long
strips of cloth. Before long Banc learned to ride horseback, and she
enjoyed racing her horse as fast as it would run so she could glance
back at her blond hair and headdress trailing in the breeze. Her hair
didn't stay blond, though. Eventually, the Comanche women mixed
buffalo tallow and charcoal together and rubbed it in her hair to make
it dark. Banc thought they did this so she would fit in with the other
children. It's also possible that they didn't want her to stand out if any
traders, Indian agents, or army officers visited their camp.

Although Banc had to gather wood, fetch water, and help move
camp, she was young enough to escape the hardest work that befell
Comanche women. Most days she did whatever she pleased. As she recalled, "Every day seemed to be a holiday; children came to play with
me and tried to make me welcome into their kind of life." She also
chose to take part "in many a chase after the buffalo, deer and antelope," which she thought was more fun than staying in camp.

It's not clear when Banc started speaking Comanche. In one account, she said, "I wasn't with them long until I could talk their
lingo." In another, she recalled that she was "some time learning to
speak their language." She wasn't shy, however. Whenever anything
happened in the village that she didn't understand, she plied Tekwashana with questions until she was satisfied. Tekwashana seldom
scolded or even corrected her. Banc said, "She was always very
thoughtful of me and seemed to care as much for me as if I was her
very own child."

* * *

After the Babb children were separated, Dot traveled with his captors for ten days until they reached a Comanche village on the Arkansas River. Persummy, who had led the raid through Wise County, claimed Dot as his own but placed him in the home of his sister and her husband, Watchoedadda (Lost Sitting Down). Dot was given an equally unflattering name: Nadernumipe (Tired and Give Out).

Dot's experience in his Comanche village was markedly different from Banc's. The role of every young Comanche man, including potential adoptees, was to become a good horseman, hunter, and warrior. While Banc was enjoying an unstructured life, Dot went into training. His teacher was his Comanche father, Persummy.

One day Persummy, painted and bedecked in horns and feathers, told Dot to follow him into the sand hills for a demonstration. He then handed Dot his six-shooter, instructing the boy to fire at his torso each time he charged and at his back each time he retreated. If Persummy was testing Dot, he did so at great personal risk. He made four charges and retreats. Dot fired six shots, and each time Persummy deflected the bullets with his buffalo-hide shield. Afterward, rather than gloating over his own skill and bravery, Persummy complimented Dot on his accuracy and said he would make a trustworthy warrior.

Even while he was in training, Dot wasn't punished by the Comanches for his mistakes, and only once was he in danger among them. One day when he went for water with some Comanche girls, the mother of a slain fighting man, crazed with grief, came running at him with a large butcher knife, shrieking and moaning. Most likely her son had been killed by whites and she was out to take revenge. Dot managed to outrun her. Eventually, she stopped and slashed herself to death.

Like his sister, Dot didn't have much trouble adapting to Comanche living conditions, including the food. He described his favorite Indian meal: "Whenever a buck killed a buffalo calf, the squaw rushed up and split the calf open. She scooped every bit of the milk out of its stomach just as quickly as she could and gave it to the children. It was the sweetest stuff I ever tasted, and was thick like our gelatin." He also claimed that Comanche beds, consisting of dried buffalo hides suspended between four poles and covered with buffalo robes, were comfortable enough. "I've slept in lots worse beds in white folk's houses many times," he once remarked.

Persummy drilled his new son in the specifics of battle; but other than that, Dot learned his new people's customs through observation and experience rather than actual instruction. Even though he was training to become a warrior, he didn't know how assertive he should be, or what station a boy his age was supposed to assume in village life. Early on, the Comanche women appropriated him as their servant. They made him help move the tepees, carry wood and water, and cook the meat. Dot, accustomed to obeying his mother, did what they told him. Eventually, the other young men his age hinted that the women were taking advantage of him; as a warrior, he didn't have to do those household chores. Dot explained how he liberated himself: "One day an old squaw told me to put some wood on the fire. I didn't do it. She hit me a devil of a lick across the back."

That was the only blow he received while he was with the Comanches. It was worth the pain, however, for he had won his independence. From that day on, he enjoyed the life of a Comanche man: breaking wild horses, hunting deer and buffalo, practicing with his bow and arrow, lounging around camp—and leaving the manual labor to the women.

The final stage of a Comanche warrior's training was experience in an actual battle. Persummy took Dot on his first raid with a group of fifteen men. They'd been gone from camp six days when they surprised seven Caddoes chasing buffalo along the Washita River. At that time, the Comanches and Caddoes were at war. In the short fight that followed, the Comanches killed six of the Caddoes, but had to chase the seventh several miles. Finally, Persummy shot him twice, knocking him off his horse. When the Comanches approached him, the

Caddo was sitting up, badly wounded but still conscious. Persummy handed Dot his pistol. Then he commanded the boy to shoot the Caddo in the head. Dot described his response in three simple words: "This I did."

As far as anyone knows, this was the first time Dot had killed a person. The incident raises a host of questions. Did he do it because he thought he had no choice, or did he shoot the man willingly? Was he certain the Caddo was going to die anyway and wanted to put an end to his suffering? Did he feel guilty afterward? Or did he think the murder was justified, since his fellow Texans never thought twice about killing Indians? Was he trying to win his adoptive father's approval? Did he already consider himself a Comanche and think of the Caddo as an enemy of his people? No one knows the answers, for Dot refused to satisfy his readers' curiosity about the killing. His autobiography is noticeably terse and vague when it comes to recounting his experiences as a warrior. Like most returned captives, Dot didn't reveal too many details about what he did on the warpath.

Dot's next adventures as a raiding warrior pulled him even further away from the values of his upbringing. It was one thing to kill an enemy in battle; it was quite another to attack non-Indian civilians in their homes. Yet Dot accompanied the Comanches on two raids into Mexico, where they killed seven adults and captured three Mexican children. Moreover, Dot's repeated use of the word "we" in describing these raids suggests that he was a full participant: "we captured," "we killed."

Dot wanted to go with the Comanches on their raids into Texas, but they wouldn't let him. They were afraid he would try to escape. At first he would have; he was elated "at the thought of getting back and finding an opportunity to detach myself from my savage captors." Later, however, he made up his mind that if they would let him go to Texas, he wouldn't try to run away. Still, the Comanches never put him to the test of possibly killing one of his own people.

After only a few months among the Comanches, fourteen-year-old Nadernumipe Dot Babb, Tired and Give Out, had become a budding

Comanche warrior. When asked in 1926 why he thought the Comanches wanted to keep him, he replied simply: "Wanted to make an Indian out of me. Wanted to build up their tribe."

In October 1866, John Babb and his oldest son, Court, returned from Arkansas to a home that no longer was. The previous month, his neighbors had buried Isabel, his wife of twenty-one years, in a quiet, shady spot about a quarter of a mile from the ruins of their cabin. At least his infant, Margie, was unharmed. However, he had no way of knowing where Dot and Banc were, or if they'd even survived.

He began his search for his children as soon as he learned what had happened. For families of Indian captives, the most important contact in the government was the federal Indian agent for the tribe thought to be holding the children. In the Babbs' case, that was the Kiowa-Comanche agent, Col. Jesse H. Leavenworth, a native of Vermont who had spent much of his life on the western frontier. Like a number of ex-army Indian agents, Leavenworth had fought Indians during his military days but preferred making peace with them.

The years 1865 and 1866 had been a period of both triumphs and failures for Colonel Leavenworth. He'd witnessed the recovery of a number of captives from the Kiowas and Comanches, including Sarah Luster.[2] However, the work of locating captives and arm-twisting the Indians into turning them over was slow, unpredictable, and frustrating. To make matters worse, Leavenworth wasn't popular among the Indians, partly because he demanded that they give up their captives without payment. They were becoming less inclined to surrender their captives to him.

Although Dot Babb was reported dead at various times, Leavenworth had reason to be hopeful. He knew that the Nokoni chief Quenahewi (Drinking Eagle) disapproved of the September raid into Wise County by the young men of his division. He was also able to confirm that the Babb children were still alive at the time their captors reached Quenahewi's camp. Leavenworth was confident that Quenahewi would promptly surrender the two children to him, but by December 1866, three months after their capture, he hadn't been able to learn any more about them.[3]

Quenahewi wasn't the only person who was trying to obtain the Babbs' release. Dot was sighted in a Comanche camp by Brit Johnson, an African-American sharpshooter "of splendid physique" who was moving among the Indians, trying to recover captives. His wife, two of his children, and four other people had been captured in Young County, Texas, during a raid in 1864, and afterward he made several trips to the Indian villages. Johnson was generally well received by the Comanches, for he had known some of them in his younger days and had learned a little of their language. A frontier hero in his day, Brit Johnson was credited with recovering several captives, and "[f]or these acts of chivalry he never asked any remuneration."[4] (His legendary journeys served as inspiration for *The Searchers*.[5]) While Johnson was camped across the Cimarron River from the Comanches, he and Dot spoke with each other. Johnson assured Dot he would try to ransom him. However, he didn't have any money at the time, and he'd traded all his horses except four, which he needed to bring other captives back to Texas.

Meanwhile, in February and March 1867, Capt. E. L. Smith, the commanding officer of Fort Arbuckle, Indian Territory, got actively involved in the search. He asked Horace P. Jones, the government interpreter, to try to recover the Babbs. Jones said he lived too far from the Comanche villages to deal with the captors effectively. He recommended that Smith engage Jesse Chisholm, "a person of intelligence and tact" who had extensive prior experience with the Comanches and was thought "worthy to be trusted with the business." Chisholm, who was half-Scottish and half-Cherokee, was a veteran Indian trader, guide, and interpreter, by then in his early sixties. (He is remembered today as the namesake of the Chisholm Trail, the main cattle-driving route between Texas and Kansas.)

Chisholm had been able to secure the release of several Indian captives in the past. He was also believed to know the whereabouts of Dot Babb. In April 1867, Captain Smith authorized Chisholm to negotiate for the captives' ransoming. At the same time, Smith laid before him the government's dilemma, a matter of increasing concern among policy makers in Washington:

> Although my sympathies have been warmly enlisted in behalf of these captives and their friends, it has not been thought sound policy by the Government, to encourage this inhuman business, by holding out inducements to continue it by the eager offer of large ransoms, or indeed by any act that might appear to commit it to the practice of ransoming at all. Neither on the other hand is the Government insensible to the cruelty of remaining idle or indifferent in a matter of so much interest to the relatives of these captives and to the captives themselves, but it is anxious to exert its full power in their behalf, in such a manner however as may tend to restrain this barbarous speculation.[6]

Captain Smith further instructed Chisholm that any ransoms paid (which were "really the rewards of treachery and lawlessness") should be made as small as possible. In the end, however, Chisholm was no more successful than Quenahewi or Brit Johnson in getting the Babbs away from their captors.

By early 1867, John Babb couldn't wait on the government any longer. Placing his son Court and the infant, Margie, in the care of their neighbors, he left Wise County on January 25, 1867, and traveled to Fort Arbuckle to see if he could do anything to expedite the search.[7] There, he got to know Horace P. Jones, the interpreter. Jones, whose own great-grandfather had been an Indian captive, was a congenial, outdoorsy man who had lived most of his thirty-eight years in close contact with Indians. He'd even been adopted by the Penateka Comanches, the division that had made the peace treaty with the German immigrants two decades earlier. They placed great trust in him and thought he was a man of his word.

Jones promised John Babb that he'd make further inquiries about his children. He engaged a man named Jacob J. Sturm to search for them. Sturm, a self-styled doctor from Tennessee, had worked and lived among the Caddo and Waco Indians and married a Caddo woman. Meanwhile, John Babb sent word to his father in Wisconsin to try to raise as much as $800 to use if necessary in recovering Dot and Banc. He decided to wait in Indian Territory until he found out whether they were still alive.

One day in April 1867, Banc Babb returned from gathering firewood to find Tekwashana crying in their tepee. She explained that a man had come to their village to take Banc back to her father. The rescuer was Dr. Sturm, who had located Banc while her people were camped near the site of Verden, Oklahoma. Banc told her Comanche mother that she wanted to leave with him. Tekwashana hung her head and refused to talk. Banc hurried to find the tepee where Sturm was meeting with her captors. The Comanches demanded ransom for Banc's release, and Sturm paid $333 for her.

When Banc got back to her tepee that night, Tekwashana had fastened the flap and wouldn't let her inside. Her Comanche mother told her, "If you want to leave me, it is because you do not love me." By that time, Tekwashana's brother, Kerno, had been killed during another raid into Texas. Banc was all she had. Tekwashana also thought of herself as Banc's only protector against their white and Indian enemies.

Banc couldn't get her Comanche mother to let her come in. As much as she longed to see her white father, she also wanted to be near Tekwashana that night. She walked around to the side of the tepee where the bed was located. After a while, she fell asleep on the ground there.

During the night, Banc woke when she felt Tekwashana shaking her shoulder. She carried the girl inside the tent, where she had prepared some dried meat and two bottles of water. When Banc asked what was happening, Tekwashana explained they would run away and hide until Dr. Sturm left. Then they'd come back home. Banc didn't protest this plot to escape. They left the village under the cover of darkness. Banc was still sleepy, so her mother carried her on her back. When Tekwashana got tired, they stopped to rest. The two of them traveled this way until noon the next day, when they hid in a large depression in the ground and took a nap.

They woke suddenly when they heard someone calling. Dr. Sturm had tracked them. Angry with Tekwashana, he took Banc away from her and put the girl on his horse. He told Tekwashana she would have to walk. Then they headed back to camp, Tekwashana trailing behind, brokenhearted. That was the last time Banc saw her Comanche mother.

The next morning, Dr. Sturm started for Fort Arbuckle with Banc. When they got there, he delivered the girl to the commanding officer, Capt. E. L. Smith, who made out a voucher for the amount Sturm had paid in ransom. John Babb was overjoyed to see one of his lost children. Banc was also "tickled to death" to be back with him. However, as she remembered, "I had been with the Indians so long, I had forgotten how to speak English. Although I could understand what was said to me, when I tried to talk to my father, it would be in Comanche."

John Babb told his daughter that her brother had been located near the New Mexico border. Dot had been discovered in a Nokoni Comanche camp by a trader named Mike McCleskey,[8] a hardy fellow who "could drink whiskey like throwing slop down a slophole." The trader had spoken to the young white Indian, asking where he was from. Dot gave McCleskey his father's name and address.

John and Banc Babb stayed in Indian Territory with the family of Joseph Chandler near Pauls Valley, waiting for further word about Dot. Chandler's wife, a Mexican woman named Tomassa, understood the culture shock Banc was experiencing. She had also been a Comanche captive; after her recovery, she had voluntarily returned to the tribe.

Around the middle of May 1867, the Nokoni chief Horseback visited Fort Arbuckle and told the new commanding officer, First Lt. Mark Walker, that he had Dot Babb "in his possession" and was willing to surrender him. However, he was "anxious to be remunerated for this trouble," as he claimed it had "cost him considerable to get the child from its captors." (Dot's captor, Persummy, was Horseback's brother. While it's possible that the chief had purchased the boy from Persummy, Horseback's claim that he'd already paid for Dot's release was probably bogus, as Dot made no mention of being sold.)

Lieutenant Walker wasn't sure how to handle this situation. He knew that the higher-ups in both the army and the civilian Office of Indian Affairs had started to grumble about the practice of paying ransom for captives. Walker didn't promise Horseback any money or presents, but instead reminded him vaguely of his treaty obligations to return captured children. Meanwhile, Walker wrote to his superiors for further instructions.

Now that Dot was finally located, his father was terribly eager to have him brought in at any cost. He was worried that if ransom were refused, Horseback, who seemed determined to make a profit off the boy one way or another, might sell him to a different band or tribe, and Dot would be lost once more. Horace Jones, the interpreter, arranged for a friendly Penateka Comanche chief known as Esihabit (Milky Way) to go to Horseback's camp and try to negotiate Dot's release.

Esihabit arrived in Horseback's village with two of his wives and spoke at length with the Nokonis. They weren't willing to give up Dot, no matter what Horseback had told Lieutenant Walker, and they made "a display of much obstinacy." According to Dot, they finally agreed to let him decide for himself whether to remain with the Comanches or go back home. (In reality, they were probably just soliciting Dot's opinion; his owner would have made the final decision.) Horseback and several of the Nokonis felt certain that Dot had become Indianized and would want to stay with them. Dot surprised them. He made an "instant and unalterable" decision to accompany Esihabit to Fort Arbuckle and go back to Texas with his father. Dot reported that Esihabit had to pay ransom to Horseback, consisting of horses, saddles, bridles, blankets, and other gifts.

Although Dot had stated his preference without hesitation, his parting with his Comanche companions turned out to be much more difficult than he'd expected, for "many mutual attachments had been formed." As he described his departure: "Not a few cried and wept bitterly, and notably one squaw and her son who had claimed me as son and brother and as such were my guardians and protectors, and to whose immediate family and household I had been attached. . . . Their kindnesses to me had been lavish and unvarying, and my friendship and attachment in return were deep and sincere, and I could scarcely restrain my emotions when time came for the final good-bye."

Meanwhile, John Babb had become impatient. In June 1867, he left Banc in the care of Joseph and Tomassa Chandler, while he and Horace Jones went to search for Dot themselves. They met Esihabit's party on the Washita River, near the site of present-day Anadarko, Oklahoma. Dot described this meeting with his father as a scene of "convulsive joy or hysteria." John Babb broke down, overcome with emotion. Esihabit later told Indian agent Jesse Leavenworth that he could not bear to see the white man weep for his child. When the party reached Fort Arbuckle, Lieutenant Walker gave Esihabit $210 in cash, plus articles of clothing worth $23.75, to cover his costs in procuring Dot.

In the summer of 1867, Dot and Banc finally made it home to Texas, where they went through a rough period of acculturation. A neighbor, H. H. Halsell, remembered that they "had adopted Indian ways and habits."[9] Banc said, "It was rather a hard job for me to get my tongue twisted back so I could talk English again to my folks and friends." Dot agreed: "When I got back from the Indians, I talked like an Indian. I quit talking for a long time because I couldn't talk like white people."

Not long after Dot's recovery, Lieutenant Walker received a belated communication on how to handle Horseback's ransom demand. His instructions came from no less an authority than Lt. Gen. William T. Sherman, the scourge of both the Southern rebels and the

Native Americans, and the man who was soon to become the commanding general of the U.S. Army. Sherman railed against the practice of paying for stolen children, proclaiming that it was "better the Indian race be obliterated. . . . There must be no ransom paid." He directed Walker to tell the Comanches that Dot Babb "must be surrendered or else war to the death will be ordered." Apparently, Walker had already settled with Esihabit before he received this scathing order. The controversy over paying ransom for captives would flare up repeatedly for several more years.

Banc and Dot Babb became only partially Indianized after spending seven and nine months, respectively, with their captors. Despite the strong bonds they formed with individual Comanches, they never lost their desire to go back to their own people and resume their former way of life. Of all the captives I followed, they were the only ones who said they willingly left their captors. After they were ransomed, the Babb siblings were able to reenter the white world successfully. As Dot's obituary accurately summed up, "He brought back from his life with the Indians the natives' love of nature, their skill and daring, but at the same time he didn't lose his background as a white man."

Still, it is remarkable that the Babbs became as assimilated as they did. More than anything else, their story provides a benchmark for how rapidly the child captives could acquire the ways of their captors. "People may think that is strange," Banc said in one interview, "but really a nine-year-old [sic] child reacts very quickly to surroundings." After less than a year among the Comanches, Dot and Banc had practically lost their ability to speak English. Even though the Babbs had been victims of a Comanche raid, Banc soon came to enjoy the raiders' festivities in her village, and wrote, "It was always fun to go to a war dance." Dot's quick transformation was even more unexpected, because he was already a teenager when it happened, less impressionable and more independent than his sister. No doubt he passed up opportunities to escape when the Comanches took him into Mexico.

After an apprenticeship of merely nine months, the fourteen-year-old white boy had developed a taste for raids and battles.

Most of what my family knows about our own Comanche warrior comes from the narrative of one of his fellow captives, Clinton Smith. By the time Clinton met Uncle Adolph in captivity, my ancestor had been with the Comanches about fourteen months and was already one of them.[10] His experience provides another benchmark. Although the child captives assimilated at different rates and to varying degrees, nearly all of them came to prefer the native people's society once they'd stayed with them more than a year. Historian James Axtell found that the children abducted by Indians in colonial America "took little time," in some cases no more than six to nine months, to "fall in with" the natives and forget their past lives.[11] If Dot and Banc Babb had spent just a few more months with their Comanche families, chances are they would have made a different choice.

Chapter Four

Legion Valley

few months after the Comanches surrendered the Babb children, several influential leaders of the tribe signed a watershed
treaty that would mark the beginning of the end of their
nomadic way of life. In October 1867, representatives of the Comanches, Cheyennes, Arapahoes, Kiowas, and Kiowa-Apaches gathered on Medicine Lodge River in southern Kansas to meet with a
government peace commission. It was the last great Indian council of
this type, and the peace treaty that was signed on October 21 would
be the last ever made with the Southern Plains Indians. Not every division of these tribes deigned to participate in the treaty talks. Among
the absentees were the warlike Quahada Comanches, who eventually
counted among their numbers my uncle Adolph Korn, Rudolph Fischer, and several other captives.

The gathering at Medicine Lodge was huge and spectacular. The
treaty meetings, which began on October 19, were held in a grove
along the river. Although the event was billed as a council, there was
no real negotiating. The peace commission had already decided the
terms of the agreement. The Indians were to go live on their reservations and stop roaming. They had to give up their extensive hunting
territory. They could still hunt south of the Arkansas River as long as
the buffalo held out—which wasn't expected to be long. However,
they couldn't settle permanently off the reservation. They had to stop
raiding white settlements and taking captives. In short, the commis-

sion was asking the Indians to stop being Indians. They were to become like white people and settle in one place, so that the real white people who wanted to move onto their hunting grounds could do so without fear of being attacked.

In exchange for the concessions forced on these tribes, the government promised to provide them with houses, farms, agricultural implements, schools, churches, teachers, carpenters, doctors, and all sorts of things they didn't want. The peace commissioners tried to convince the Indians that this radical change was necessary for their well-being. Senator John B. Henderson bluntly put the native people's dilemma before them: "The whites are settling up all the good lands. . . . When they come, they drive out the buffalo. If you oppose them, war must come. They are many, and you are few. You may kill some of them; but others will come and take their places." The Treaty of Medicine Lodge allowed the Indians little time for transition; the wandering hunters were required to become sedentary farmers at once. As a safety net, the government agreed to provide them annuities for thirty years. The commissioners made it clear that if the Indians refused to comply with these terms, they would face the wrath of the U.S. Army.

The treaty didn't stop Indian raids into Texas. The Quahada Comanches, in particular, were contemptuous of treaties and derided their fellow Native Americans who made peace agreements with the whites. Besides, no matter what the Indians had agreed to in Kansas, they'd always thought of Texas as a free-for-all. Although some Texans thought Native Americans had "a revenge to satisfy on every man, woman and child of the white race,"[1] most raids weren't really about vengeance or necessity or driving settlers off the land. The Southern Plains Indians raided because raiding was what they did. Raids were as much a part of their culture as hunting buffalo, constructing tepees, or wearing moccasins and buckskin.

The main purpose of a typical raid was horse gathering. The Comanches depended heavily on horses, not only for transport but also for currency. Raids were also rites of passage, the primary means by which young men proved their prowess. The only way a boy could gain status was to demonstrate that he was braver, stronger, or cleverer than his peers. Until he had returned from a raid with some horses, a captive, or a scalp that he'd taken himself, no one would respect him or ask for his advice.

Non-Indians had their own terms for what these raiders did. *Stealing. Kidnapping. Murder.* To the Plains Indians, however, taking an enemy's property, children, or hide was not only daring but also honorable. They wouldn't think of chastising a young warrior who took part in a raid any more than non-Indians would condemn a war hero for conduct that, in everyday society, would be criminal.

Murder wasn't the objective of most raids. Still, Mexican-Americans, European-Americans, and African-Americans who were unlucky enough to encounter a raiding party along the road or in a field might be killed for sport or practice, or perhaps as a precaution. Occasionally at the end of a raid, when the excitement was at its height, the young Indian men would launch a full-scale assault on some unfortunate settler's cabin.

According to Texas folklore, Indians raided during the season between the arrival of the spring grass and the fall buffalo hunts, and during a full moon, when they had ample light for a quick night getaway. (Hence, the expression "Comanche moon.") That seems logical, but it's not true.[2] In reality the settlers were vulnerable to Indian attacks any month of the year and any time of the month. They had no way of predicting when or where the next strike would take place. Although the number of non-Indian civilians murdered by Native Americans was small compared with deaths from diseases and accidents, the grisly reports of Indian depredations generated enough hysteria to cause a significant number of Texas settlers to abandon the frontier.

So many, in fact, that Gen. William T. Sherman eventually made a fact-finding tour of the remote settlements in Texas. Although Sherman had little sympathy for Plains Indian raiders, he reserved his harshest invective for the citizens he was duty-bound to protect. He blamed white settlers such as my ancestors for creating conditions that encouraged Native Americans to raid. While visiting Fredericksburg, Fort Mason, Menardville, and Fort McKavett, he observed that the people "expose women and children singly on the road and in cabins far off from others, as though they were safe in Illinois. . . . If the Comanches don't steal horses in Texas, it is because they cannot be tempted."[3]

But tempted they were. My grandpa Korn and his neighbors in the Saline Valley suffered their heaviest losses from Indian raids in the years after the Treaty of Medicine Lodge. On October 12, 1867, at the exact time the Indians were gathering at the council in Kansas, Frank Johnson was killed by raiders near his home. In 1868 and 1869, Grandpa's friend Adolph Reichenau lost a total of fifty-one horses in three separate raids on his farm.

The frontier families deserted the hardest-hit areas such as the Saline Valley for places they thought would be safer. The Korns returned to their former home on the Llano River in Castell. The Reichenauses moved to Hedwig's Hill in Mason County. Betsy Johnson, Frank's widow, went back to Legion Valley in nearby Llano County, where several of her relatives lived.

These settlers didn't necessarily find security in more populated communities. By the summer of 1868, Indians were stealing horses in plain daylight near Castell.[4] Over the next few years, Grandpa Korn and his friends would watch helplessly from a distance as painted men on horseback made off with their most valuable property. In Legion Valley, twenty miles to the southeast, Grandpa's former neighbor, Betsy Johnson, would see much more horrible sights.[5]

Legion Valley wasn't a town or even a village. Smaller than Castell, it was just a rural settlement of about one hundred people, most of them related by blood or marriage. Their log cabins were scattered throughout a scenic vale that was bounded on the east and south by rugged hills thick with junipers, oaks, and blackjack trees. Just below

Cedar Mountain to the east, Legion Creek flowed into Sandy Creek, a tributary of the Colorado River. The nearest town, Llano, was fifteen miles to the north.

By 1868 the community still didn't have a school or church or store. Its only real center was Betsy Johnson, Frank's widow. The matriarch of the large Johnson clan was only in her midforties. Seven of her twelve children were under age twenty; her youngest was just three. Betsy was the community's nurse and adviser, the one to whom everyone turned for help when a baby was coming or a wife was ill. After Betsy's husband was killed by Indians in October 1867, she and her younger children went to stay with the family of one of her married daughters, Samantha Bradford, in the Bradfords' cabin on Legion Creek.

During the first week of February 1868, a heavy rain fell in Legion Valley, followed by a cold front that turned the moisture to snow. The sky was cloudy and bleak. It was a miserable time to be outdoors, but most of the men of the community had picked that week to take to the road. Betsy's son Asa Johnson (they called him "Boy") had started to Austin with a drove of hogs. Boy's older brother Thomas (known as "Babe") was also away from home on business. Their young wives, Samantha and Rebecca, were staying with their mother-in-law at the Bradfords' house.

On Tuesday, February 4, while the frozen ground was still spotted with patches of snow and ice, a neighbor named John Friend came over to the Bradford place. John was married to Betsy Johnson's great-niece, Matilda; they lived a mile and a half to the west, across Legion Creek. He was planning to go to the mill at Fredericksburg the next day to get some lumber for the floor of his new cabin. The trip was twenty-five miles each way, so he'd have to stay there overnight. His nineteen-year-old wife was eight months pregnant with her first child, and he was worried about leaving her alone. John asked Betsy's daughters-in-law, Samantha and Rebecca, if they'd go stay at his house with Matilda the following evening. They said they would. By the next day—Wednesday, February 5—the air was still cold, but the snow and sleet had stopped. At nine o'clock that morning, John Friend left for Fredericksburg in a wagon drawn by a team of two horses.

Meanwhile, at the Bradfords' cabin, the community's tireless matriarch, Betsy Johnson, was called into service once more. Betsy's eighteen-year-old niece, Amanda Townsend, appeared at the door with a message. Her mother, Nancy, was expecting a baby and was having a rough time with the pregnancy. Amanda asked if Aunt Betsy could go stay with her. Betsy Johnson was being pulled in many directions at once. She was also looking after another niece, eight-year-old Malinda Ann Caudle, whom everyone called "Minnie." The girl had been experiencing fever and chills. Betsy decided Minnie would be all right without her for one evening; Amanda could look after the girl. Betsy dressed for the cold and left the Bradford place to go sit through the night with her sister-in-law, Nancy Townsend.

Later that afternoon, Samantha and Rebecca Johnson got ready to go over to the Friends' cabin to stay the night with Matilda, just as they'd promised John the day before. They wrapped their shawls tightly around their heads and necks. Rebecca decided to take her three-year-old daughter, Nancy Elizabeth, with them. Her two older children, Will and James, would stay with the Bradfords that night. Rebecca's sister-in-law, Samantha Johnson, also took her baby girl, Fielty, eighteen months old. She was expecting her second child.

The young Johnson wives didn't think of their mission to Matilda Friend as a chore. Instead, it would be a break from the monotony of their hard, solitary lives. Social events were rare in Legion Valley, and an evening at Matilda's would be something akin to a slumber party or girls' night out. That's probably why their unmarried cousin, Amanda Townsend, decided to go with them. Eight-year-old Minnie Caudle wheedled an invitation as well. A half sister to Samantha Johnson, she was a bright girl with blue eyes and light-colored hair. She convinced the adults that despite her fever, she wasn't too sick to

walk the mile and a half to the Friends' cabin. The six of them—
three young women, two infants, and one girl—set out for the Friend
place anticipating a quiet evening together, away from their husbands
and the responsibilities of home.

The frosty, overcast weather somehow made for a comforting sunset.
A thick bank of gray clouds diffused the sun's last, piercing rays in
breathtaking shades of orange and purple. The heaviness of the damp
air gave the women a feeling of tranquility. Their work was done. The
horses were hobbled, the evening meal under way. By the time darkness set in, they'd be huddled around the fire with the children,
warming their hands and resting, gazing at the big, black kettle as
their supper simmered to a finish.

Outside the cabin, Minnie Caudle was playing with Temple
Friend, John's seven-year-old son from his first marriage. He was a
rather frail, fair-complexioned child with dark eyes, light auburn hair,
and "quite an intellectual countenance." The women heard Temple
and Minnie running and laughing, throwing snowballs at each other.
Their noises were reassuring; as long as the women could hear them,
the children must be all right. They'd been cooped up indoors during
the snowfall that week, so they were allowed to play as long as they
wanted.

Suddenly the children's yells sounded different, more like
screams. They were shouting "Someone's stealing Button!" as they
sprinted toward the house. Matilda rushed outside. Samantha, Rebecca, and Amanda were close behind her. They saw a man near one
of the ponies that was hobbled about two hundred yards from the
cabin. Matilda climbed up on the log fence to get a better view. The
lone figure she saw was unmistakably an Indian. The women watched
as he removed the hobbles. Then he leaped on the pony, bareback,
and took off to the southwest.

The four women waited anxiously to see whether the Indian was
gone for good. A few moments later, about fifteen figures on horseback approached at a gallop, charging the house. The women ran back

inside the cabin and barred the door. Then they watched from a window as the raiders drew near and stopped.[6] Among them were a couple of women. Some of the Indians dismounted and walked confidently toward the house.

Matilda Friend handed her husband's double-barreled shotgun to one of the other women. When the Indians broke open the door, she screamed, "Shoot!" Her friend was too petrified to react. Matilda grabbed the shotgun out of her arms. She used it to try to frighten the Indians away from the door, but the man at the front of the group lunged into the house and wrested the gun away from her.

Matilda was the only one in the cabin who put up any fight. She picked up a chair and knocked the gun out of the man's hands. He drew his bow and shot her in the arm. With her good arm, she grabbed a smoothing iron and hurled it at him. It struck him on the side of the head. He collapsed. She reached for the iron again. The man quickly recovered, and he shot her with another arrow, this time in her left side. The arrow went all the way through her body, coming out below her right breast. She fell onto the bed, pretending she was dead. Meanwhile, other Indians poured into the cabin and led the women and children outside. After seeing what had happened to Matilda, they decided not to struggle.

Once the prisoners were all outside, the Indians came back inside the cabin. They started stripping the house of everything they could carry away: bedding, clothes, a Spencer rifle, the shotgun, a six-shooter, a sidesaddle, and some money from a box on a shelf. They dragged Matilda off the bed and dumped her facedown on the dirt floor. Then they carried the featherbeds and straw ticks out into the yard, tore them open, emptied the feathers, and took the cloth.

Matilda's attacker reentered the house. He drew a knife, slashed the back of her left hand to the bone three times, and stabbed her left breast twice. Then he started scalping her. First, he cut a strip almost two inches wide and three inches long from the back of her head, just below the crown. Not satisfied, he took a larger section from the front part and right side of her head. Finally, he cut off the rest of her hair and inflicted several severe blows to what was left of her scalp. Matilda Friend, still fully conscious, somehow managed to keep from crying out.

When her attacker left the cabin, she tried to get up from the floor so she could see what was happening to the others. She wasn't able to stand. Instead, she crawled to a small opening in the side of the house. Wiping the blood out of her eyes, Matilda watched as the Indians placed the three women and four children on horses. It was almost dark by the time they headed out. Then she saw her attacker coming back toward the house. Matilda hurried to the spot where he'd left her on the floor and tried to place herself in the same position as when she was scalped. The man approached her, still not satisfied she was dead. He grabbed the arrow sticking out from her side and jerked it back and forth, then up and down. She didn't flinch. The man went back out to join his companions.

Once Matilda was sure the Indians were really gone, she pulled herself up off the floor. She found a piece of cloth and wrapped it around her head to stop the bleeding. Then she stepped outside to make her way toward the home of her cousin, Samantha Bradford. Before she left, she took time to pick up the things the Indians had scattered around the yard and put them inside the cabin, bending over carefully so she didn't agitate the arrow shot through her chest.

The sky was cloudy, but Matilda knew her way in the dark. After everything she'd been through that evening, the freezing temperature wasn't likely to bother her. However, she was weak from trauma and loss of blood. The searing pain of the multiple knife wounds and the arrows lodged in her arm and breast, as well as the baby protruding from her belly, caused her to walk slowly. Along the way, she stopped to scoop up some snow. She used part of it to quench her thirst and put the rest on her head to bathe her face and stem the flow of blood.

It was eight o'clock by the time Matilda saw the faint light coming from the Bradford cabin in the grove of live oaks. She tried to call out, but she didn't have the voice. The dogs growled and barked as she approached. Her cousin's husband, Jack Bradford, opened the door and emerged hesitantly. He saw a strange apparition staggering in the shadows, its head wrapped in a bloody cloth and arrows protruding from both sides. Jack ran back inside and slammed the door. Matilda summoned enough strength to holler and tell him who she was. Jack came back out. This time he rushed to her side and supported her.

It wasn't until she got inside that the Bradfords saw how horribly she was wounded. The sight of Matilda Friend—two arrows sticking out of her, blood oozing from her scalp and down her face—caused them to panic. They were sure the Indians were still in the area and would come for them next. The Bradfords decided that they weren't going to ride for a doctor, sit with Matilda and comfort her, or even take time to remove her blood-soaked clothes or dress her wounds. What they did was place her in front of the fireplace and quickly retie her bleeding head. They put a bucket of water by her side and threw a quilt on the floor. At Matilda's insistence, Jack finally agreed to extract the arrows, cutting them below the feathers and pulling them through. Before they abandoned her, the Bradfords told Matilda not to lie on their bed; they didn't want their linens bloodied. Then Jack and Samantha woke the children and fled with them, leaving their cousin alone to die. For the rest of that freezing night, the Bradford family hid in a cedar thicket.

The temperature had dropped sharply after sundown, but eight-year-old Minnie Caudle was too much in shock to notice the numbness in her hands and face. The Indians who had taken her moved fast and spoke little. Minnie was tied behind one of the women in the raiding party, a fat Comanche who was to become her adoptive mother. The woman drew a blanket around her so that she didn't suffer terribly from exposure.

The Indians and their seven captives hadn't gone far when Samantha Johnson's infant daughter, Fielty, started to cry. Everyone tensed.

The noise would give away their location if a search party was following them. The man who was carrying Fielty choked her, trying to make her stop. Samantha was riding behind him on the same horse. In a panic, she tried to take her baby away from him. He got so angry at both of them that he grabbed the infant by the ankles and dashed out her brains against a tree. Minnie Caudle saw it happen. The murdered infant was her niece, her half sister's child.

That first night, they camped on a small mountain not far from the Friend house. The Indians took shelter from the icy blasts of wind in a cedar brake and kept a fire blazing. That was risky, for the light could lead a rescue party straight to their camp; but the night was too miserable not to have any heat. Minnie's new mother slept with her to keep her warm. She also sheltered the girl from some of the terrifying sights and sounds that followed. It would be an endless night of suffering for the two Johnson women and Amanda Townsend, who were raped and tormented as they sobbed and prayed aloud.

The two older children, Minnie and Temple, realized that they mustn't cry, not even when they saw worse sights the second day. Shortly after they left camp the next morning, the Indians decided that they didn't want to risk traveling with a wailing infant. One of them grabbed Rebecca Johnson's three-year-old daughter, Nancy Elizabeth, and slit her throat. They held up her body by the feet as blood flowed out, letting her head dangle right in front of Rebecca. The child's mother screamed and fainted. The Indians laughed at the spectacle. Then they took off again.

Around noon they stopped. The raiders held a conference. The five remaining captives couldn't understand what they were saying, but they knew the Indians were debating something. Finally, the men grabbed the two Johnson women. Before Minnie could see any more, her Comanche mother threw a blanket over her head.

The day after the raid, the small town of Llano was in an uproar over the shocking news. About a dozen men, outraged by the atrocity, had already formed a posse to pursue the Indians. When they reached the cabin of Jack Bradford in Legion Valley around ten o'clock that night, the tiny, close-knit community was already in mourning. Earlier that evening, Spence Townsend, the father of one of the captives and a brother of Betsy Johnson, had found the frozen, battered body of Samantha Johnson's baby girl on the side of Cedar Mountain, close to the Bradford house. Eighteen-month-old Fielty Johnson, the first infant to die, was lying in a heap at the foot of a blackjack tree. Bits of fabric, hair, and clothes clung to the bark. It was too late and too cold for the search party to start following the Indians' trail. They spent the night outdoors at the Bradford house warming themselves by a fire.

Around midnight John Friend drew near to Legion Valley in his wagon loaded with lumber. A messenger had gone to meet him along the road. The man lent John his horse and offered to drive the slow wagon for him. John took off, spurring the horse to a gallop. First he stopped briefly to inspect the damage at his house. Then he rushed to the Bradfords' cabin to see his wounded wife. Matilda was conscious and remarkably calm, nursed by Betsy Johnson and Hardin Oatman, the physician from Llano. Miraculously, she hadn't lost her baby. John tried to convince her everything would be all right. But his boy, Temple, was still unaccounted for, and he wasn't sure if Matilda was going to make it through another night. John was also racked by guilt. If he hadn't asked Rebecca and Samantha Johnson to spend the night with his wife, they and their children would be safe at home. His only consolation was that his ten-year-old daughter, Florence, had been away at boarding school when the raid happened.

Before sunrise the next morning—Friday, February 7—the searchers started following the steep, rocky trail through the brush along the hillside. The journey began horribly. The men heard John Oatman, the physician's son, cry out for them to stop. About fifty yards from where the murdered infant had been found the previous evening, he discovered the body of three-year-old Nancy Elizabeth Johnson, lying facedown on a flat limestone rock. He recalled: "As I approached it, I thought that it had been stripped to go to bed when it was taken and that it had on a white night cap with a lock of yellow hair sticking out on the back of its head. But when I got to it, I found that it had been scalped, taking all the hair off its head except a small space next to its neck on back of its head, and that what I thought was a night cap was the flesh of its naked scalped head."

Near that place, the men found beds of cedar boughs and grass. They doubted whether anyone had slept there. Instead, they speculated that the beds were where "the Indians had mistreated the women in a nameless way." One of the men became so distraught that he started experiencing heart problems. The others convinced him to turn back.

John Oatman and another man carried the frozen body of the second infant back to the Bradford cabin. John Friend and the doctor, Hardin Oatman, were waiting there for news. Meanwhile, John had found a way to occupy his time. He was using the lumber he'd brought from Fredericksburg to build coffins. He and Dr. Oatman buried the two children.

About three or four miles up Cedar Mountain, the posse found the prints of bare feet. Since the Indians usually wore moccasins, the men guessed that these were the tracks of the white women. For the first time, their spirits rallied. If the three adult prisoners had survived that far, maybe they were still alive.

Around ten o'clock that morning, they reached a place called Gamble's Gap, after trailing the raiding party another four miles. The Indians had stopped near there and left two of their captives behind. Samantha Johnson, perhaps because she was pregnant, hadn't even tried to flee. It looked as if she had just sat down on the limestone rock, naked and humiliated, and given up. The spear had entered her body just under her right shoulder blade and had come out on her left side above her hip. Her throat was also slashed, and she'd been scalped. Apparently, she was going into premature labor at the time she died. Samantha's sister-in-law, Rebecca Johnson, also stripped of her clothing, had managed to run about fifty yards before she fell. A spear went through the center of her body. She'd been both scalped and disemboweled. The men had to identify her mainly by process of elimination, because some wild hogs had eaten out her intestines and torn most of the flesh from her face and thighs. The search party stopped long enough to borrow a wagon from a nearby settler and haul the bodies down the hillside to his house.

The trail then took the men up four more rough miles through thick persimmon and cat's-claw to a craggy spot aptly called Hell's Half Acre. There they were startled to see a red flag flying. They couldn't believe that they'd actually managed to sneak up on the Indians, whom they thought were long gone. That meant they'd have to fight them to rescue the remaining three captives. These men were farmers, not soldiers, and they were about to go to battle with some of the best-trained warriors in the land. It took all the courage they could muster to charge up the hill into the thicket, their pistols drawn and their rifles ready for action.

But no one was there. They dismounted and looked around. They found the remnants of an Indian camp: a dying fire, more tracks, and some scraps of cooked meat. Spence Townsend picked up one of the small pieces of flesh the Indians had discarded. It had a long lock of yellow hair attached. The men heard him scream, "This is my poor child's hair!"

Then they noticed a foot trail leading away from the camp into the brush. There they found the last of the adult prisoners, Amanda Townsend. According to the news accounts, her remains were "an indescribable mass of flesh." Her head was crushed to pieces. Around her body, the men found rocks covered with blood, hair, and brains. She'd been scalped, and her throat was cut. Amanda's father was there to see it all. One final outrage perhaps caused him more grief than all the others: his daughter had been "tied in a position that the fiends could satisfy their brutal lusts."

By then the posse had given up all hope. The only task that remained for them was to find the mutilated bodies of the two older children, Temple and Minnie, and they were in no hurry to do that. They continued the search for five days, but the Indians eluded them.

Near Devil's River, their horses finally gave out from exhaustion. Some of the men had to lead their mounts by the reins. They stopped to let them drink at one of the waterholes where the raiding party had been.

One of the men took a close look at the ground. He shouted in excitement. The others crowded around. They saw some footprints too small for the adult Indians to have made. Either Temple Friend or Minnie Caudle might still be alive. Perhaps both of them had survived.

After that first night when they camped on the hillside, the Indian raiders rode three days and three nights without stopping to rest or eat a proper meal. Minnie Caudle, whose legs were sore and raw from riding bareback behind her Comanche mother, was still suffering from chills and fever. At one point, the Indians stopped by a cornfield and collected some husks. They boiled them and made signs that she should drink the water. After that her fever broke, and she felt much better.

Minnie's great-grandson, Damon Benson, remembers her talking about the flight northwest from central Texas. "She said they'd ride a horse till it fell from exhaustion. Then they'd jump off of it, split it open and grab a gut, about three or four feet long, and just pop it over their heads like you would a rope and eat it raw. They'd grab another horse and take off, riding full tilt all the way."

This was the first time the two white children had been outside the Hill Country. After long days of hard riding across the plains, the raiding party reached Palo Duro Canyon in the Texas Panhandle, a favorite gathering place for the Comanches and Kiowas. This vast, deep canyon, sixty miles long and six miles wide, took Minnie and Temple by surprise, opening up suddenly before them after they'd crossed a seemingly endless expanse of level land. The raiding party descended eight hundred feet over rocky trails to the bottom of the canyon, which was watered by the Prairie Dog Town Fork of the Red River. They set up camp in the peaceful valley and rested there awhile, safe from soldiers and Texas Rangers. Other Indians were probably staying there as well.

By then the moon was full. The landscape, dotted with small hardwood shrubs and defined by buttes and pinnacles, looked like a wonderland in the moonlight. The colors of the steep canyon walls were stunning, especially at dawn, when the sun's first rays gradually illuminated the stratified layers of burnt red, gold, and dusty green.

One day the Indians sent Minnie and Temple to the river to fill a wooden bucket with water. The stream was shallow, and they took turns using a tin cup to dip the water into the bucket. Temple was playing along the edge of the stream. Minnie got tired of doing all the work and handed Temple the cup. They got into an argument. Temple swung the empty tin cup and hit Minnie in the stomach.

When they got back to the camp with the bucket of water, the Indians ushered them to the teepee of the group's headman. He was sitting inside, slowly drawing the blade of his knife back and forth across a sharpening stone. Suddenly, he grabbed Temple by the hair on the back of his head and laid the boy across his knees. He pressed the blade of the knife against his neck. Through signs and gestures, he made them understand that he was going to cut off Temple's head for hitting Minnie. The terrified children started wailing and pleading for mercy. Eventually, the man made Temple understand that if he'd never strike Minnie again, he would let him live.

That was the only time the children were afraid of the Indians in camp. Later, Minnie and Temple came to realize that the man was just fooling with them. Considering what they'd witnessed during their flight from Legion Valley, no one could blame them for taking him seriously.

At some point, Minnie Caudle and Temple Friend were separated and went with different Comanche groups. The story of Temple's time with the tribe has been lost. All that's known is that he eventually ended up with the same group of Quahada Comanches that was holding my ancestor, Adolph Korn.

Minnie's experience has survived only through one published interview and a few anecdotes she passed along to her descendants. According to family lore, Minnie was treated well by the Comanches, especially the women. They dressed her in buckskin and greased her body with tallow to keep her dry during the rain and snow. At night her new mother told her stories around the fire. Minnie said that this woman "was very kind to me" and "always treated me as her own child." The girl slept on a pallet near the wall of the woman's tepee. The Comanche women "wouldn't let the Indian men bother her in any way," says a grandson, Frank Modgling. "They were good to her. The Indian ladies knew that Grandmother liked her meat cooked, so they cooked it for her. When they passed by salt licks, they would get some salt so they could season her food for her."

"She always spoke well of them," agrees great-grandson Damon Benson. "The woman that took care of her would cook her meat better than she would for the Indians. Grandma said she was not mistreated in any way."

One night Minnie was nearly trampled by accident. Her great-granddaughter, Neoma Benson Cain, remembers her telling the story: "She said that the Indians were real jokesters. They'd stampede their own horses right through the camp, and just laugh! One of the horses stepped on the edge of the tepee, and it grazed her head. From then on, she always put her bed away from the wall."[7]

Like Banc Babb, Minnie spent only half a year with the Comanches. During the summer of 1868, several kidnapped children were recovered in Kansas. The process of redeeming captives was touch-and-go. The Comanches and Kiowas were angry with their agent, Col. Jesse Leavenworth, because he was no longer offering them ransom for captives. Once that summer, the Kiowas reportedly delivered two children to him, then changed their minds and took them back. (Leavenworth denied this story, asserting: "I have never failed to get a captive when they came near me."[8]) Although the Indians peevishly refused to turn over any more captives to Colonel Leavenworth, they were on good terms with J. E. Tappan, the post storekeeper at Fort Larned, Kansas, and were willing to negotiate with him. In July 1868, the Kiowas delivered Eliza and Isaac Briscoe, two siblings captured in Parker County, Texas, to Tappan.

Around the same time, the Comanches announced they would give up their captives, but they made it clear that they expected payment—two ponies at a minimum. The willingness of the Kiowas and Comanches to trade their captives that summer was partly the result of food shortages. Newspaper accounts described members of these tribes as "sullen and impudent because of the scarcity of provisions among them." Buffalo were few in the region, and they had not received the guns and ammunition that the government had promised them for hunting other game.

In late July, Col. Edward W. Wynkoop, the dapper Cheyenne-Arapaho Indian agent of the Upper Arkansas Agency at Fort Larned, was visiting a Comanche camp near the post when he noticed a white girl among them. He was able to talk with her. Fortunately, the girl remembered her name—Malinda Ann Caudle, or Minnie, as she was called. She could still speak English. Wynkoop told the Comanches that they must bring her to Fort Larned and surrender her.

No one knows whether Minnie's Comanche mother fought to keep her (or even who actually owned the girl), but the general feeling was that the white children must be traded for badly needed supplies. The Comanches brought Minnie to Fort Larned on July 25, 1868, and presented her to the post's commanding officer, Capt. Henry Asbury. Apparently, she wasn't afraid of either her captors or the white people, for she answered questions freely. Although Captain Asbury claimed that Minnie spoke English "very well," he appears to have had some problems communicating with her. He understood Minnie to say that her parents had been killed, and that she had two or three brothers who were captives.

Captain Asbury wasn't especially worried that the Comanches would harm the girl or leave the region with her, for he decided not to try to take her by force. Before the Comanches left with Minnie that day, they promised to bring her and the other captives back to Fort

Larned. They asked Asbury how much he would pay for them. He replied vaguely, "Bring them in, and I will talk about trading them." Meanwhile, he wrote to his superior officer for instructions on whether or not to pay ransom.

He hadn't received a response by the time the Comanches returned with Minnie Caudle two days later.[9] However, the federal Indian agent at Fort Larned, Colonel Wynkoop, demanded that they give up the girl without ransom. They were resentful; but they also knew that the Indian agents had the power to withhold their annuities. They agreed to hand her over.

Wynkoop brought Minnie to his house so that his wife, Louise, could take care of her. The Wynkoops were a dashing couple. He was a social, polished gentleman, an amateur actor, and, according to the British journalist Henry Morton Stanley, a "skillful concoctor of drinkable beverages." She was a former actress who had gained many admirers while touring the mining camp circuit in Colorado. The Wynkoops gave Minnie a doll, and the girl, thrust into yet another unfamiliar situation, became obsessively attached to it.[10]

Shortly after Minnie was released, a newspaper reporter arrived when Louise Wynkoop was giving her a bath in a big wooden tub, trying to scrub the tallow off her. The journalist couldn't wait to interview her; he burst into the room. "She ducked under the water and would not talk to him, wouldn't even look at him," says great-grandson Damon Benson. "She was embarrassed."

Colonel Wynkoop interviewed Minnie, whom he described as a "bright intelligent girl." He learned the names of her parents and brothers, as well as the circumstances of her capture. There was only one problem: she was unable to state exactly where in Texas her family lived. Wynkoop had a hard time figuring out to whom she belonged. Apparently, he had never received a copy of the circulars that the Texas governor sent to authorities in Indian Territory and New Mexico concerning Minnie and Temple.[11]

Minnie's case was brought to the attention of the commissioner of

Indian Affairs in Washington, who in turn contacted the Texas governor for help in locating her parents. Governor E. M. Pease notified the commissioner that Minnie's family resided in Llano County. Since the Caudles were poor, he requested that the Indian agency have her sent to the nearest military post, where the officers might arrange a ride for her. After a journey of three or four months that took her to Fort Harker, the town of Leavenworth, and Cherokee Town (near Fort Cobb), Minnie finally made it home to Llano. The celebration over her return was muted, for Temple Friend's fate was still unknown.

Still, the Friend family hadn't given up hope; Temple's recovery seemed imminent. On July 31, 1868, four days after Minnie's release, representatives of the Kiowas and Comanches came to Fort Larned to meet with Thomas Murphy, a superintendent of Indian Affairs. Murphy demanded that the Indians give up all their white captives. They promised they would deliver Temple to their new agent at Fort Cobb when they received their annuities. By October that still hadn't happened.[12] Eventually, the Comanches returned to the plains with Temple.

Meanwhile, the Friend family relocated. Matilda had given birth to a healthy baby girl, Belle Jane, less than a month after the massacre. According to local lore, Matilda's face was still so badly swollen from the scalping and beating that she wasn't able to see her baby for more than seven weeks. A few months after the baby was born, the Friends packed up and left Texas for good. They traveled by covered wagon, driving nine hundred head of steers up the Chisholm Trail, until they reached their new home of El Dorado, Kansas, in September 1868. John and Matilda purchased a one-hundred-sixty-acre farm a mile east of town, and John opened a meat market on Main Street. For four more years, the Friends continued searching for Temple.

The fledgling settlement of Legion Valley foundered after the raid of 1868, its soil stained by blood and the site forever poisoned by the memory of what had happened there. Betsy Johnson and several of her children moved to Hays County, Texas, not far from Austin. The two widowers, Babe and Boy Johnson, left Legion Valley and eventually remarried. The Friends and Johnsons weren't the only ones whose lives were shattered by the events of February 5, 1868. Jack and Samantha Bradford had to leave the area, their reputations destroyed by a single lapse of courage when they abandoned Matilda Friend that night. The families' log cabins became empty, crumbling shells, and the community finally vanished altogether. Even the graves of the five victims have been lost.

When the Apaches kidnapped my uncle Adolph Korn, the only physical injury they inflicted on anyone was a smack on his head with a pistol. Similarly, the Comanches simply nabbed Rudolph Fischer as he walked along a deserted road. A number of other rural youngsters were scooped up and whisked away without bloodshed while they were tending livestock or working in fields. Captivity began in a horribly different way for some children, including Dot Babb and Minnie Caudle. Dot watched the Comanches stab, shoot, and scalp his mother. Minnie was present when her captors brutally terrorized, raped, and butchered her half sister, niece, and three cousins. Even though her Comanche mother shielded her from some of the worst sights, she said: "I remember how they suffered. They cried and prayed all the time and they knew they were going to be murdered."

Historian J. Norman Heard, who studied more than fifty captivity cases from across America, observed: "Frequently, the surviving members of the family were compelled to carry the scalps of their parents and little brothers and sisters, an experience which would seem likely to have instilled in them such a hatred of Indians as to make assimilation impossible."[13] Yet that wasn't the case. Minnie Caudle's great-granddaughter, Neoma Benson Cain, recalls, "She would not hear a word against the Indians." Neoma's brother, Damon Benson, agrees: "She always took up for the Indians. She said they were good people in their way. When they got kicked around, they fought back, because it was their land to start with, their hunting ground, their living."

Dot Babb was even more defensive of the Comanches. He was known to say on many occasions, "Bad Indians were made bad by bad white men." When asked if he hated Indians because they'd murdered his mother, he replied: "You wouldn't want to kill every white person you saw because some white person had killed your mother." While Dot never absolved the "very desperate Indian" who shot his mother, he was nonetheless able to rationalize what had happened: "I don't believe they would have killed Mother, but she held on to my sister's hand."

Dot once told an illuminating story about a conversation he had with another customer in a bank in Clarendon, Texas, in the early 1900s. While they were reminiscing about old times, the other man admitted to Dot that he used to go to the Comanche reservation and steal the Indians' horses. Dot listened to his tale in stony silence. When the man finished, Dot told him: "You were the cause of my mother being killed." Recalling this incident in 1926, he added, "I had my mind made up to kill him if he said anything back. I would rather kill that kind of a man than let him live." Dot, having convinced himself that the Comanches raided his parents' farm in retaliation for horse stealing by Texans, went so far as to blame his mother's death on white thieves rather than the raiders who actually killed her.[14]

The ghastly circumstances under which Dot Babb and Minnie Caudle were abducted did not impede their Indianization and had no bearing on their lifelong attitudes toward Native Americans. The sociological literature on Indian captivities offers no explanation for the apparent lack of correlation between violence during capture and a child's ability to assimilate; nor do the captives' own narratives provide much insight on this point. It is worth noting that the Comanche individuals who adopted Dot and Minnie were not the same persons who had killed their loved ones; in fact, Dot never saw his mother's murderer afterward. All the same, these children, who had had little if any previous close contact with Native Americans, were placed in Comanche households shortly after they saw Comanches take the lives of their family members by the most gruesome means. Nonetheless, Dot and Minnie didn't transfer their abhorrence of their relatives' killers to the tribe as a whole. The strong affection they developed for their Native American families and friends somehow enabled them to look past the horror they'd witnessed in those first days—and even find a way to justify it.

Chapter Five

Warriors
in Training

A s late as 1870, the year of Adolph Korn's disappearance, the abduction of children by Indians in the American West still made
the front pages of newspapers across the nation. For people living on the eastern seaboard, these news items read like correspondents' reports from foreign lands. Several generations had passed since
their own immigrant families had lost sons and daughters to the native
people, and to easterners it seemed inconceivable that Indians still
captured children in the United States.

Citizens on the East Coast sympathized with the western families
only up to a point. Many Americans in the long-settled parts of the
country thought the people out West were overstating their Indian
troubles, even falsifying tales of atrocities. They also felt that the
western settlers, who insisted on advancing the frontier at the expense
of the native people, were largely to blame for the bloodshed.

Regional differences of opinion on Indian relations gave rise to
overheated editorials in America's newspapers. Texas journalists lam-
basted easterners, whom they claimed formed their idealized notions
of Native Americans from reading James Fenimore Cooper: "New En-
gland, New York, Pennsylvania, Ohio, &c., have millions who have
never felt hunger, never known what it was to be for days, weeks and
months in a constant state of watchfulness, necessary to preserve life
and property."[1] However, the eastern press wasn't impressed by the
Texans' clamor for more protection in the hinterlands. The *New York*

Tribune lashed out against "that peculiar and unnatural and unjust warfare, which in disguise of frontier defense the settlers have for years past waged against the Indians."[2] The editors of the *New York Herald* suggested that the accounts coming from the Southern Plains were "grossly exaggerated," proclaiming: "Not half the stories of attacks by Indians on white men, on trains, or the killing and scalping of soldiers are true."[3]

A few observers were able to step back and take a long-range, more dispassionate look at the realities of the longstanding conflict between Native Americans and newer Americans. In May 1870, *The New York Times* ran an editorial titled "Red and White," in which the writer summed up "the essential difficulty in the Indian question" by positing: "The coexistence of the two races in close contact is impracticable." The column went on to describe "an incompatibility of temper" between Indians and whites. It pointed out that the Native American, having utterly rejected the European-American's brand of civilization, "has the enterprise and courage to insist that he will live his own life in his own way; and that is a way which is in fatal conflict with the age and its movements."[4]

The culture of the Southern Plains Indians, who lived by hunting and by raiding their enemies, was inimical to the values of virtually all other Americans of the 1870s, whether they descended from Mexicans, Europeans, Africans, or Asians. For that matter, the free-roaming life of the Comanches, Kiowas, and Apaches was alien to some of the more pastoral native people in other regions of the American continent. In hindsight the plains of America afforded ample land to sustain all the people living there in 1870, but the irreconcilable goals of native hunters and immigrant farmers goaded both sides into a hardheaded struggle for dominance. There would be no real peace until one group or the other was annihilated, or at least broken in spirit. When the Lakota chief Red Cloud finally quit fighting the intruders, he reportedly told a white delegation, "We didn't need all this land, and neither did you."[5]

A week after *The New York Times* ran its editorial, two more

German-American boys from the Texas Hill Country, youngsters like Adolph Korn and Rudolph Fischer, got an unwelcome opportunity to learn firsthand about Native American life. One of them, Herman Lehmann, would eventually be the last white Indian to roam the Southern Plains.[6]

After lunch the four children went to the field to scare the birds away from the wheat. It was a radiant spring day, a Monday, May 16, 1870. The countryside had rallied back to life after a bleak winter. It was still too early in the season for the children to think about the hard labor of summer, hoeing weeds and clearing brush in the heat. That day they were going to spend a lazy afternoon playing and sitting in the sun. Shooing birds was easy work.

They weren't expecting the visitors who silently appeared on horseback shortly after one o'clock. A few were dressed in blue army jackets, pants, and overcoats. Others wore nothing but breechcloths and leggings. Some had painted their faces red, black, and white. Their dark hair was plaited. Around their heads, they'd tied rags and handkerchiefs; one wore a small cap decorated with feathers. These men, eight or ten altogether, were armed with bows and arrows, six-shooters, and lances.

The children looked up. They thought they heard the strangers speaking English, but they couldn't be sure, for these children had never been to school and spoke only German. By the time they realized they were in danger, it was too late to run and hide. Their parents' house was three hundred yards away. The Indians grabbed Willie Lehmann where he was sitting. He was eight years old, with sandy hair and light blue eyes. His stepsister, Auguste, a toddler of seventeen months, tumbled from his lap; the men ignored her. An Indian named Chiwat caught nine-year-old Caroline Lehmann as she fled.

Herman, almost eleven, sprinted across the field. He was a slender boy, small for his age. Like his brother, Willie, he had sandy hair and gray eyes. Another Indian named Carnoviste caught him, slapped and choked him, then tore off his blue pants and hickory shirt. Though

Herman was normally bashful, he fought back violently. He yelled, pulled Carnoviste's long black hair, kicked him in the stomach, and bit him. But the Indians were too strong for them. They dragged the three older children to the edge of the wheat field, where their companions were waiting on horseback. Willie's captor tossed him over the rock fence, and other Indians tied him to a horse. Herman nearly got loose from Carnoviste, so Chiwat, who was only about seventeen, came to his aid.

While Carnoviste and Chiwat were struggling to shove Herman over the fence, Caroline managed to break away. She dashed toward the house, screaming for help. The children's mother, Auguste Buchmeier, heard the screams and rushed to the door of the family's log cabin. At first she thought the men chasing her children were cowboys. However, her oldest daughter, Mina, ran to the house and shouted, "Mama, I think it is Indians." Auguste's husband, Phillip Buchmeier, jumped up from his meal, grabbed his gun, and bolted out of the cabin.[7]

Meanwhile, one of the Indians raised his six-shooter and fired at Caroline as she ran across the field. She dropped down in the wheat, unhurt. The Indians didn't have time to go after her. They took off with Herman and Willie before the boys' stepfather could fire any shots. Phillip Buchmeier then tried to round up a posse to follow the raiders' trail. As bad luck would have it, all the men in his sparsely settled neighborhood were out looking for their cattle that afternoon.

When news of the Lehmann brothers' capture reached the community later that day, only one neighbor could truly understand what they were going through. Ten-year-old Minnie Caudle, who had spent six months in a Comanche village, was living with her family in Loyal Valley, about four miles east of Phillip and Auguste Buchmeier's farm on Squaw Creek. Perhaps only she believed that the Indians were not going to harm the boys. She knew they had other plans.

Herman Lehmann was fair-complexioned and freckled. He was also naked. Before long his tender skin was blistered from riding in the midday sun and bloody from brushing against mesquite needles and cat's-claw bushes. Tied to a horse like a slain deer, he couldn't dodge the thorny branches.

They were heading northwest. The Indians stopped to rest for a while on the banks of the Llano River across from the mouth of Willow Creek, only seven miles from the site of the capture. They weren't too worried about a posse overtaking them. During the raid, they'd had a chance to size up the German farmers in the area, and they'd been easy prey.[8] Before they lay down, they tied Herman and hobbled Willie.

Eventually, they pushed on. All Herman and Willie got to eat that afternoon were some berries. They kept riding after the sun went down. The full moon was on the wane, still bright enough to make the raiders' flight easy. In the middle of the night, they came upon a young calf lying down. Carnoviste slew it, cut open its stomach, and ate the milk it had nursed. He motioned for Herman to do the same.

The boy refused.

Carnoviste grabbed Herman and thrust the boy's head into the calf's paunch. He rubbed the contents all over his face and forced some of the mush into his throat. Then he held the boy's nose.

Herman swallowed. Immediately, he vomited.

Carnoviste then cut out the calf's kidneys and liver. He made Herman eat some of the warm, raw organs.

Herman vomited again.

Carnoviste scooped up Herman's vomit, forced it into his mouth, and made him swallow again. Once more it came up.

Then Carnoviste soaked the matter in warm blood and tried again. The blood seemed to settle Herman's stomach, for he was able to keep it down. Carnoviste washed the boy's face, and they took off into the darkness, both riding on the same horse.

When daylight came, Carnoviste was curious to see if Herman knew how to shoot. He took the cartridges out of his pistol and handed it to Herman. They played with the gun for a while, and Herman began to think Carnoviste was easygoing. That opinion soon changed. When Herman couldn't understand what his captor was saying or wanted him to do, Carnoviste smacked the boy until he comprehended.

Finally, the Indians decided to see how well Herman could ride. During their raid in the Texas Hill Country, they'd stolen between twenty and twenty-five horses. They roped a wild pony and tried to put Herman on it. The boy yelled, terrified. He and the pony fought several rounds with each other, with no clear winner. Eventually, the Indians were satisfied and let him off.

Eight-year-old Willie fared better; he wasn't tested as severely, probably because of his youth. Unlike Herman, he got to keep his clothes. His captor also gave him a furry cap made from the scalp of a calf's head and a small pair of deerskin moccasins. The man offered him some raw meat but didn't force him to eat it. As Willie recalled, "He never did beat me or abuse me, but he often frightened me."

That evening the Indians washed and dressed the sores the boys had developed from hard riding and brushing against thorns. Then they painted Herman and Willie like Indians, using black rocks and saliva to obtain a yellowish red hue. Herman was tied securely with ropes at night to keep him from escaping, but Willie was turned loose. He almost got away that night. He remembered, "I rolled down a hill some distance from camp and could have slipped away, but I was too scared. I was too little to know what to do; so I climbed the hill and went back to sleep. Early the next morning I heard roosters crowing, and I knew then that we were not far from a farm house."

While they were riding the next day, one of Willie's new moccasins fell off. He poked his captor in the side, but couldn't get his attention. When the man finally looked back, Willie pointed solemnly to his naked white foot. He was scared that the Indians would beat him for losing the moccasin. Instead, they just laughed.

Like all parents who lost their children to Indian kidnappers, Auguste Buchmeier must have blamed herself. She should have taken the threats more seriously. Reports of horse thefts and brushes with Indians had been circulating through Mason and Llano Counties that month. Only a week before her boys were taken, some Indians had attacked John Brite of Mason while he was driving his wagon to his father-in-law's ranch with his family. As Auguste would soon learn, the Indians who abducted Herman and Willie had tried to take the son and daughter of her neighbors, Johann and Margretha Anderegg, only three hours before they raided her place. One of the raiders had managed to lift the girl onto his horse, but her father jumped on the Indian and finally wrested her away from him. Auguste and her neighbors probably realized the same thing: if the Indians had succeeded in capturing the Anderegg children, they might not have taken the Lehmann boys.

Auguste had let her children roam the woods freely and hadn't taught them to be afraid of Indians, even though tales of killings and captivities circulated through the area. Rudolph Fischer of Fredericksburg had vanished five years earlier and was presumed dead. Temple Friend, one of the children captured in Legion Valley two winters ago, was still missing. His parents had given up on Texas and resettled in Kansas. Just five months before Auguste's own sons were taken, some Indians had stolen Louis and Johanna Korn's boy near Castell, ten miles to the northeast. The Korns had become so distraught that they'd abandoned the Hill Country and moved back to San Antonio.

Unlike the Friends and the Korns, Auguste Buchmeier wasn't going to pack up and leave. From an early age, life had taught her to endure whatever adversity came her way, including the untimely death of her first husband while she was expecting their sixth child. The day her boys were carried off, she and Phillip, her second husband, wrote a letter to the commanders of Fort Concho and Fort McKavett, imploring them to search for Herman and Willie. Unfortunately, no one knew which Indians had taken them. Auguste and Phillip, along with their neighbors in nearby Loyal Valley, believed that the boys' captors were Comanches. Later, the commissioner of Indian Affairs in Washington would suggest that the Indians who raided the Buchmeier home were either Kickapoos who lived in Mexico or the wild Kiowas or Comanches who ranged around the headwaters of the Rio Grande. In ei-

ther case, the commissioner cautioned, the prospects of finding a captive among them were grim, for "[w]ith these Indians the Government
has but little intercourse, there being no agent in charge of them."

The Buchmeiers, their neighbors, and the commissioner in Washington were all mistaken. Somehow, no one suspected that Herman
and Willie Lehmann were in the hands of Apaches.[9]

On their fourth full day of captivity—May 20, 1870—Herman and
Willie Lehmann were riding with the Apaches along a wagon road
about fourteen miles north of Fort McKavett, near the tiny outpost of
Kickapoo Springs, when their captors halted abruptly and pulled off
the road. The two boys were forced to dismount. One Apache stayed
behind to watch the prisoners, while the others rode off.

About fifteen minutes later, the Lehmann boys heard a rapid exchange of gunfire. As it turned out, the letter their parents sent to the
northern forts had produced results. The Apaches had encountered a
patrol of ten African-American troops of the Ninth Cavalry, led by a
short, scrappy sergeant named Emanuel Stance. The soldiers had left
Fort McKavett that day with orders to scout along Kickapoo Creek
and "endeavor to the utmost to intercept the Indians that stole the
two children of Phillip Buckmeier [sic] of Loyal Valley." When they
saw the Apaches riding across the hills, the cavalrymen charged them.
After a short fight, the Apaches abandoned the horses they had stolen
and fled to the hills. The soldiers killed the leader of the raiding party
and recovered nine horses.[10] (In recognition of his leadership on this
mission, Sergeant Stance became the first black regular to receive a
Congressional Medal of Honor.[11])

Soon the Apaches came rushing back to where Herman and
Willie were waiting. They grabbed the Lehmann boys and took off.
Herman rode on the same horse as the Apache in the lead. Willie
shared a horse with the last man in the group. He thought the man
was trying to crowd him off, perhaps to lighten the load and move
faster. The boy clung desperately to his captor. While they were traveling at full speed, Willie fell off the horse and hit the rocky ground

with a thud. He was still clutching a shred of the Apache's black shirt in each hand. His captor either didn't notice that he was gone or thought it was too risky to go back for him.

When Herman glanced over his shoulder and saw that Willie was missing, he thought the Apaches had killed his brother. The two boys wouldn't see each other again for eight years.

Willie's experience after he fell off the horse explains why Indian captives, especially the very young ones, didn't try harder to escape. Lost in the wilds, with no settlements for miles around and no food or water, the captives were faced with the daunting question: *escape to where?*

Willie wandered helplessly across the deserted grasslands, unable to find the soldiers who had just fought against his captors. He was terrified that he would be attacked by wild animals. The child had good reason to be afraid, for buffalo and wolves still roamed the Staked Plains of Texas in 1870, and occasionally a person heard the chilling scream of a mountain lion. As darkness fell, he crawled into some bushes, where he crouched in fear all night.

Water was hard to come by on the prairies of west Texas. During a nighttime shower, Willie was able to catch a few raindrops by holding his head up with his mouth open. At one point, he drank muddy rainwater that had collected in some animal tracks. The only food he found was a piece of cornbread that a traveler had discarded.

By his third day alone, Willie was so weak, hungry, and thirsty that he could walk only a few steps without resting. Around noon he spotted a white man on horseback and called to him in German as he approached. The man didn't understand him and rode on by without trying to help the bedraggled waif. Later that day, Willie saw a freight wagon approaching. As it drew near, the driver spoke to him in German, and Willie climbed aboard. The wagon belonged to a teamster from Fredericksburg. He brought Willie to Kickapoo Springs and left him in the care of some settlers named John and Martha Flanigan. The freighter eventually returned and delivered Willie to his home in Mason County on the evening of Saturday, May 28, 1870.

It was a bittersweet reunion for the Buchmeier family, for Herman was still missing. When Auguste asked her son where he'd left his brother, Willie replied: "Herman has gone on, Mama. They took him on." Willie Lehmann's testimony gave the civil and military authorities their best leads about the Indians who had raided Loyal Valley and kidnapped Herman. The boys' stepfather, Phillip Buchmeier, assured everyone that his stepson's information was reliable, as Willie was a "very clever little chap" who was "not in the habit of telling an untruth." Willie would later summarize his four-day captivity as follows: "During my stay with the Indians I was never whipped or beaten, and besides scares, hard rides and starvation, I was treated well."

Herman and the Apaches traveled northwest across the Staked Plains without sleep, food, or water. They passed some waterholes along the way, but the Apaches wouldn't let Herman drink—possibly to test his endurance. Eventually, Chiwat loosened his bonds. One evening at dusk, they crossed a small stream. Herman slipped away unnoticed and crawled to the creek. The boy was so dehydrated he wanted to feel the water, not just swallow it. He drank and bathed in the stream as evening fell. Before long the Apaches realized he was missing. He heard Chiwat and another Apache named Pinero searching for him. Herman kept still. Eventually, the Apaches gave up and went on without him.

At last Herman had his chance to escape, but he was lost in the wilderness. He'd never been outside the Hill Country before, and his party had passed no settlements along the way. He knew that he couldn't find his way home alone. He might have to wander in the open country for weeks, and he didn't know what he'd eat or where he'd find water. Like his younger brother, the boy was afraid of wolves and mountain lions. As he weighed the merits of freedom and captivity, freedom seemed less appealing. "If I follow the Indians," he reasoned, "they will see that I don't want to leave them. So I will be treated better."

Herman bounded off in the direction the Apaches had gone.

Soon Chiwat and Pinero saw him and stopped. They waited for Herman to catch up to them. As he got close, Pinero grabbed him by the hair and hoisted him onto his horse. Then they took off.

That night in camp, Chiwat and Pinero decided to punish Herman for trying to escape. They tied a rope around his neck, fastening the other end to a bush. They strapped his arms behind his back and tied his feet together. Then they suspended him facedown by tying his arms and feet to a pole, so that his chest just barely touched the ground. Finally, they placed a heavy rock on his back, pressing his face into the dirt. The Apaches left him hanging in that agonizing position all night.

The raiders and their captive had almost reached New Mexico before they got to the Apache camp. To Herman, the village looked as if it were swarming with about 2,500 Indians. The women and children rushed up to Herman. One fat woman grabbed him, pinched him, slapped him, boxed him, and threw him down. A man took a hot iron rod from the fire and used it to burn holes in Herman's ears, so that he, like the Apache boys, could wear earrings on dress occasions. Then the Apache seared marks on the boy's arms, probably as signs of ownership or identification. Herman kicked and struggled and hollered; finally, he fainted from the pain. When he came to, the Apaches were washing him.

The next day, Carnoviste led Herman to a blanket spread with food. The Apaches had bartered with some Mexicans, and the blanket was covered with cakes, breads, sugar, coffee, cooked meats, and raw meat. Herman, for reasons he never could explain, reached for the raw meat. That greatly pleased the Apaches. They patted him to show their approval.

Herman's captor, Carnoviste, adopted the boy. Carnoviste called his new son Enda (White Boy). His wife, Laughing Eyes, was very good to Herman. At the time he came to live with them, she had no children of her own and lavished affection on him. Even after her first baby, Straight Bow, was born, she continued to treat Herman as her natural son.

Herman did small jobs for his adoptive father, Carnoviste. He would fetch the man's horse, bring his food, light his pipe, wash his feet, paint his body, tighten the points on his arrows, and catch lice for him. When Herman wasn't helping Carnoviste, the Apache women made the white boy work for them. He pounded corn, skinned game, built fires, looked after the babies, carried water, and hauled off the dung from camp.

Eventually, Herman was invited to spend more time with Carnoviste. His new father taught him how to ride wild ponies and jump on a horse as it ran by. He learned to crouch close to his horse's neck so that an enemy's arrow wouldn't hit him in battle. The warriors also trained him to use a shield to ward off arrows. The men stood about fifty yards away and shot headless shafts at him, while he moved the shield "as a snake when it tries to charm its prey." As he remembered, "I *had* to learn to use the shield, and I was knocked down several times before I became an adept." Then he added: "All Indians were thus trained." Already the Apache men were starting to treat Herman like one of their own rather than as their slave.

On July 18, 1870, only two months after Herman's abduction, eight Apache raiders, including a woman and a boy, made a quick sweep through southern Mason County. They rode down the Onion Creek branch of Threadgill Creek and shot a farmer named Fritz Brandenberger through the arm. At about three o'clock that afternoon, they reached the Buchmeier place. Phillip Buchmeier and his oldest stepson, Adolph, were working about a mile and a half from their house, preparing to irrigate some land. Auguste was home with seven of her children. Willie and his twelve-year-old sister, Mina, had just returned from watering the horses at the creek. When Mina heard the dogs barking, she stepped outside the cabin and saw the raiding party drawing near. She cried out to the family.

Auguste herded the children into the house. She bolted and barricaded the door behind her. Then she and Mina waited and watched while the smaller children hid. Their only weapon was a double-barreled shotgun. It was loaded, but neither of them knew how to shoot it or reload it. They decided not to fire the gun unless the Indians actually broke inside the house.

The Apaches rode silently around the cabin at a full gallop, waiting to see if anyone would come out or shoot at them. Finally, some of them dismounted. They caught the horses that were grazing in the pasture and saddled them. Then they drew nearer to the house and rode around it, firing their six-shooters at the roof. No one shot back. They jumped off their horses.

The windows of the cabin were covered with curtains. The raiders hurled rocks through them and stuck a lance in the room to see whether anyone was inside. There was still no movement or sound. The Apaches rummaged through the lean-to attached to the cabin and saw a large box in which the family kept its personal goods. They opened it and found a small, unloaded pistol that the children used as a toy. The men had great fun playing pranks with the pistol, pointing it first at one and then another of their unsuspecting comrades, and roaring with laughter when it snapped and the victim flinched. Then they proceeded to rob the storeroom of anything they could carry off: blankets, linens, clothes, harnesses, and saddles.

Meanwhile, one Apache approached a window of the cabin. When he tried to climb inside, Auguste shot at him. She thought she missed, but at least she scared him away. Another Apache tried to climb through the opposite window. Auguste fired at him with the other barrel of the shotgun, wounding him. After the second shot, all the Apaches ran to their horses. They took off immediately, firing several shots at the cabin as they left.

As soon as the family stepped outside, they saw their dog, Max. He'd been wounded by lances and was weak from loss of blood, but was still standing and had never stopped guarding their house. The family also found that the raiding party had left behind a horse that had been stolen at the time of the first raid. The same Indians were responsible for both attacks; the Buchmeier farm had become a target. Two months later, the family packed up and moved to nearby Loyal Valley.

Auguste Buchmeier had no way of knowing that by defending her other children, she'd unwittingly endangered Herman's life. As it turned out, her shotgun blasts during the second attack had wounded two men. One was an Apache named Genava. The other was Herman's adoptive father, Carnoviste.

Back at the Apache camp, the two injured men grunted and howled as their friends picked turkey shot from their flesh. Genava received the more serious wound. He took a full blast to the lower part of his back, and the Apaches were afraid he would die. (He didn't, to Herman's great relief.) Carnoviste's chest was peppered with shot.

The Apaches beat Herman severely to avenge his mother's well-aimed shots. They also showed him the clothing and the toy pistol they'd taken from the box in the storeroom. In the course of the raid, they told him, they'd killed all of his family. After that Herman gave up any remaining hope of returning home. He thought he had nothing left to go back to. Instead, he made up his mind to become the very thing that had terrified him only a few weeks earlier: an Apache warrior.

In 1963 *Frontier Times* magazine reprinted a condensed version of Herman Lehmann's story. During my childhood, my dad saved a well-worn copy of the magazine. I remember curling up on the couch in the dark, high-ceilinged parlor of the old sandstone house where we lived, looking at the magazine many times. The torture was what impressed me the most. The cover illustration showed Herman stripped of his clothing and buried in the ground up to his chest. His head was lifted, and he was screaming in anguish. His Apache captors hovered menacingly above him with lances and rifles, ready to inflict savage torments on the boy.

The picture left a lasting impression on me. I assumed that was how the Indians treated all their captives. When I reread Herman's memoirs as an adult, I was surprised to find that the magazine illustration I remembered so vividly from my childhood bore no resemblance to any of the incidents Herman actually described.[12]

Were the Southern Plains Indians intentionally cruel to their child captives? There's no simple answer, for the children's experiences varied considerably. To a large extent, it depended on the dispositions of their individual captors. The sex and age of the child were also significant. The two girl captives I followed, Banc Babb and Minnie Caudle, were never physically abused during their captivity. Neither was Willie Lehmann.

Dot Babb addressed the issue of the captives' treatment in his memoir:

> Generally the Indians were very considerate of their captives, and I have known not a few to return to the Indians and others that would have returned if they had been given the opportunity. Such captives had found the Indians hospitable and generous, dividing liberally and freely any and everything they had or could get that would minister to the pleasure and comfort of the captured.[13]

When the Indians did inflict physical pain on their child captives, it was the boys, especially those age ten or older, who bore the brunt of the misery. Still, in the cases I've studied, the situations in which Native Americans purposely hurt their boy captives were limited and typically fell into one of three categories. The first was initiation by hazing; sometimes the native women would beat and torment the boys when they first arrived in camp. The second was punishment, usually when they tried to run away or misunderstood an order. The third—and this was rarely carried out—was vengeance for injuries and killings committed by whites. I found no instances when the Indians tortured the children simply for torture's sake.

The Southern Plains Indians lived under mean circumstances in a merciless environment. They were passionate and affectionate, but they weren't gentle people. They had to be tough to survive, and they raised their children to endure great hardships. For the most part, they didn't treat their boy captives any more harshly than they treated their own sons. When Herman Lehmann described how the Apaches taught him to swim by simply tying a rope around his body and tossing him into a pool of deep water, nearly letting him drown while he floundered, he concluded: "The Indian boys were taught by the same process." Roughhousing and deprivation were just part of their training. And the fighting men, hoping to build up their own ranks, were determined to make Indians out of those white boys who could take it.

There were plenty of boys to choose from in Texas. The abductions happened time and again, with only minor variations. During the last week of February 1871, Indians were sighted in a neighborhood less than twenty miles northwest of San Antonio, Texas's second largest city (after Galveston). The local press exclaimed that "with bands of Indians roving about and around San Antonio, we may presume that again our city has become the frontier." Another San Antonio journalist, understandably edgy, reported that "within a short twelve or fifteen miles from the very office where we are now writing, distracted parents are bowed to the very earth with the weighty sorrow of loss of their young children, carried off by these very devils upon whom so much mistaken charity is being expended."[14]

At around nine o'clock on a Sunday morning, February 26, 1871, a raiding party visited the farm of Henry Marion Smith on Cibolo Creek, about twenty-three miles northwest of San Antonio. Henry, a former Texas Ranger and San Antonio city marshal, was a short distance from the house looking for his horses. Two of his sons, Clinton and Jeff, were across the creek herding sheep. Clinton, ten years old, was a good-looking, slender boy with a spare build, dark eyes, and black lashes. His complexion was fair, and his hair was almost white. His eight-year-old brother, Jeff, was also fair-complexioned, with dark eyes, a rather large head, and hair even lighter than Clinton's. Jeff was so shy that he never talked to strangers unless spoken to, and then only to answer their questions.[15]

The Smith boys' stepmother, Harriet, had just given Clinton some matches to burn off the grass on a hillside east of the house. She was watching him to make sure he did it right. All at once, six or seven men appeared behind him, well-dressed and riding good horses. Their hair was short, and they wore black hats. They looked like cowboys out for a Sunday ride. As Harriet would later admit, "I viewed the whole tragedy without fear or excitement."

She watched the men chase Clinton and try to pull him up onto one of their horses. They were just having fun with him, she thought, but she could tell that Clinton didn't like it. She watched him run down into the creekbed, where he disappeared. Harriet expected to see him jump the fence and come home. He never did.

Up close the men looked like Indians. The Smith brothers' first inclination was to run for the house. However, the raiders cut them off, riding between them and home. The two brothers then headed for each other. Clinton took Jeff's hand and they sprinted. When Jeff got tired and fell behind, Clinton carried him on his back and kept running as best he could.

The Indians, a mixed group of Lipan Apaches and Comanches, soon overtook the Smith boys. A Comanche jerked Jeff off Clinton's back, grabbing the younger boy by the hair. He held on to Jeff's white hair while the boy kept running alongside the horse. Then the man pulled him up.

Clinton realized that it was not only useless but also risky to resist anymore. An Apache patted him on the back, indicating that he should get on the horse behind him. Clinton walked up to the man, who took the boy's hand and stuck out his foot to use as a step. Clinton climbed on, and they galloped off.

By the time Henry Smith returned to the house, Harriet was worried. She told her husband that the boys had gone off with some cowboys and never had come back. Henry ran to the place where Clinton had disappeared. He didn't see any sign of him. He couldn't find Jeff, either. He started running in every direction, shouting frantically. As Harriet later wrote: "Then the awful truth burst upon our minds."

Henry got on his horse and tried to follow the kidnappers. Along the way, he asked a man he met to go to Leon Springs, about seven miles west, to let the neighbors know what had happened. The messenger reached there an hour later. In less than ten minutes, store-owner Max Aue and another man named Cardenas rode off to help Henry in his search. Aue, like Henry Smith, was a former Texas Ranger and was ready for action. The small posse followed the Indians' trail as far as they could. All they found along the way was one of Clinton's shoes.

Indian depredations had become so common in Texas that the San Antonio press was almost blasé in reporting the Smith brothers' capture: "We presume, as usual, these children will be offered for ransom by the savages, who have learned by experience, that a hundred dollars is the accredited value of stolen children."

The Indians in the raiding party were used to taking captives from Texas and Mexico and getting away with it. This time, however, they'd picked the wrong boys. The kidnappers were in for a much tougher getaway than they'd expected. The Smith brothers' first cousin on their late mother's side was John W. Sansom, one of the most fearless, energetic, and respected captains of the Texas Rangers. Absolutely determined to bring his young cousins home, Captain Sansom was prepared to show the raiding party that Texas Rangers, like Southern Plains Indians, could ride all day and night without rest or food.

Sansom was stationed near Kerrville at Camp Verde. He learned about his cousins' abduction Sunday night around eleven o'clock and didn't wait for daylight. Within an hour after he got the news, Sansom was on the Indians' trail with all but two of his men—seventeen rangers, "eager for an affray" and ready to "have a fight if possible." They took ten days' rations, expecting to be on the trail at least that long. The rangers headed toward Austin, thinking they might intercept the raiding party. They rode the rest of that night and all day Monday until seven o'clock in the evening. Finally, they stopped to buy corn for their horses.

Meanwhile, the Indians were riding just as relentlessly, trying to lose the rangers. By Tuesday Clinton and Jeff Smith still hadn't had anything to eat. The day before, the Indians had killed a cow. The boys had refused the bloody milk and raw meat their captors tried to give them. By the third day, they weren't so fussy. When the Indians killed another cow, Clinton and Jeff "were watching like dogs" for their portion. The men tossed the boys some raw liver. Clinton was so hungry that he grabbed the first piece away from his younger brother. The Indians laughed at them.

Later that day, the Smith boys witnessed their first murder. When the raiders came upon a man splitting rails, one of the Indians crept up and shot him with arrows. They made Clinton roll the body over so they could have a look at their victim.[16] Afterward, they rode through a stretch of thorny brush. As Jeff recalled, "It ripped our flesh like keen knife blades and we bled like stuck hogs."

Around daylight on Wednesday, March 1, the Indians heard some dogs barking. The Smith boys rallied, thinking they were about to be rescued. As the Indians pressed on, they kept looking back anxiously. The party split up into two groups. Clinton went with one, Jeff with the other. The Indians also set fire to the dry grass, trying to destroy their tracks.

By then the rangers had followed the Indians' trail about thirty-five or forty miles over very rough terrain. When they found the tracks indicating that the raiders had taken off in different directions, Captain Sansom figured they were trying to join other groups of Indians. From signs along the way, he estimated that his cousins' captors were only twelve hours ahead of him.

Meanwhile, the Indians kept watching for the search party, stopping on a high peak to survey the countryside and have a smoke. They offered Clinton some tobacco, but he was too hungry to accept. He said, "I began to think they had quit eating altogether." From there they headed down into a long, brushy draw. Some of the men dismounted and crept off with their bows. Half an hour later, they returned. One of the Indians gave Clinton two pieces of skin and made signs for him to tie them to a shield. They were human scalps. That evening the scattered Indian groups used smoke signals to locate each other. Clinton's bunch rode to join the men who were holding Jeff. They ate some colt meat for supper.

On Thursday morning, the Indians came upon two cowboys riding up a river. Clinton recalled, "As I saw those young men coming, and knowing what was going to happen, I got nervous and wanted to cry out and warn them, but I knew it would not be safe for myself and my little brother." The Indians opened fire on the cowboys, killing both of their horses. However, the cowboys got the upper hand in the short battle that followed. They killed one Indian and wounded another in the shoulder.[17]

By Friday, March 3, Captain Sansom and the rangers had reached the Llano River. They'd followed the Indians' trail westward in a zigzag pattern for another forty miles. The Indians seemed to have gained a little on them. They stopped to get some corn for their horses. The next day, they found signs that the Indians had headed due north after crossing the river. The rangers traveled about forty miles that day, almost to the head of the Llano River. They set up camp once they found good grass for their horses.

That night the rangers met the enemy. Rain, normally a welcome visitor to the parched hills of central Texas, arrived at the worst possible time. By the next morning, the Indians' tracks had been obliterated. The rangers had no choice but to turn back on Sunday, March 5, a week after the chase started. In his report, Captain Sansom wrote: "I must in justice to my men with me on scout say that I never have seen men more determined. Some were truly sick when they saw that it was impossible to catch the Indians and recover the boys which we were satisfied they had."

Meanwhile, the Smith boys, traversing the open plains of northern Texas, saw their first buffalo. The Indians roped one. When Clinton ran up to it, the buffalo turned and knocked the breath out of him. The Indians had a good laugh. As for Clinton, he "was learning the wild savage life pretty fast, but it was in a rather tough way."

They reached a large camp of Mowway's group of Comanches.

Mowway (Shaking Hand) was the principal chief of the Kotsotekas, who ranged primarily in eastern New Mexico. He'd made a name for himself some years earlier when he single-handedly wrestled a grizzly bear and stabbed it to death, and he wore one of the bear's claws in his hair as a reminder. That evening the women celebrated the men's return by preparing a big feast of raw buffalo, horse, and mule meat. They tossed some chunks to the Smith boys, who ate them greedily. Later, the Comanches held a dance over the scalps the raiding party had brought back. Some of them dressed as animals—deer, bear, buffalo, owls, eagles, and turkeys. Clinton and Jeff, as spoils of war, were displayed in the parade along with the scalps.

The day after the boys' arrival, the Comanches painted Clinton and placed a string of beads around his neck. One of the men led him to an arena, where a number of people were waiting. The man's name was Tosacowadi (Leopard Cat).[18] He was a powerful figure who stood six feet tall and weighed about two hundred pounds.

Clinton was terrified, thinking the Comanches were going to kill him there. Instead, some women arrived with a Comanche boy about Clinton's age. The boy entered the arena. Clinton was relieved, but he still wasn't sure what was going on. He didn't have much time to think. The Comanche boy charged Clinton and knocked him down. Clinton didn't resist. He simply picked himself up. Once he was on his feet, the boy knocked him down again. Then he jumped on Clinton and started beating him. Clinton still didn't know what to do, so he did nothing.

Tosacowadi entered the arena and pulled the Comanche boy off Clinton. That was the end of the fighting for that day. Tosacowadi took Clinton by the hand and led him off. He attempted to explain what he should do, but his words and gestures only baffled Clinton more. Then Tosacowadi tried speaking Spanish, and Clinton understood him. As it turned out, the Indians had placed bets on the fight. Tosacowadi wanted Clinton to whip the Comanche boy so that he could win some horses from the women who were promoting him.

Tosacowadi took good care of Clinton, grooming him for the next match.

It took place two days later. Tosacowadi was dressed in beads and a colorful feathered cap with a streamer that reached the ground. He was carrying a tomahawk in one hand and a pistol in the other. The women let out a great cry as they approached the arena with their fighter. Tosacowadi shoved Clinton forward and gave a war whoop.

Then the two boys went at it. The Comanche boy knocked Clinton down and jumped on him. Clinton wrapped his arms around him and locked his teeth in the boy's flesh. The boy began to howl, but Clinton wouldn't turn loose. The women tried to separate them, but Tosacowadi pointed his pistol at them and made them stand back. Other onlookers yelled and laughed. In their excitement, they took out their guns and fired shots into the air. Two Comanches entered the arena and tried to pry Clinton loose from the other boy. Still he held on. They started choking him, and he was finally so strangled that he had to let go. Tosacowadi had won the horses. He took Clinton by the hand and patted him on the head to show his pleasure.

Tosacowadi was so impressed by Clinton's performance that he bought him from his Apache captor for four horses and some beads, powder, and lead. He took him to live with his family. Tosacowadi had a son named Monewostuki, and he made Clinton understand that he wanted them to be brothers.

Just when the Smith boys started thinking everything might turn out all right, their hopes were shattered once more. Clinton and Jeff were separated. Clinton had found a new home with Tosacowadi and the Comanches, but Jeff's Comanche captor decided to sell him to a Lipan Apache.[19] Clinton couldn't keep from crying when "poor little Jeff was tied up and branded like a cow." The Apaches singed the boy's face with a hot iron to identify him. They also stuck large mesquite thorns through his ears to make holes for brass earrings. Not long afterward, they left with him.

One of the Apache women took charge of Jeff, and he said that she treated him "very tenderly (for an Indian)." She made him a buckskin jacket and foxskin cap with a tail hanging down the back. He also wore a breechcloth, a beaded belt, and buckskin moccasins. The woman painted his face red, with blue stripes up and down his forehead. Jeff recalled, "The Apaches gave me plenty to eat, which was more than the Comanches had done, and I began to feel proud of the trade."

The Apaches named Jeff Catchowitch (Horse Tail). Before long he was living the ordinary life of an Apache boy. The most difficult part of his Indianization was the language instruction: whenever he couldn't understand what the Apaches wanted him to do, they would grab his ear, pull it hard, and then point to whatever they were talking about. The Apaches taught him how to use a bow and arrow and gave him odd jobs to do. Like Herman Lehmann, he had to carry water and wood, herd the horses, scrape animal skins, cut switches for arrows, and carry the meat after a hunt. When he wasn't working, Jeff mingled freely with the Apache children, and they were good to him. Since he was only eight, the Apaches didn't take him on raids but left him behind with the women and other children.

Perhaps because he was so young, Jeff was able to adapt to Apache life rather quickly and without much resistance. "At first I felt very lonely," he later recalled. "But after I learned to talk like them and understand everything, I was satisfied living with them."

Meanwhile, Clinton, who had been given the name Backecacho (End of a Rope),[20] also performed menial chores for the Comanches. He helped the women cook meat for the men and dressed their wounds after battle. He also had to herd horses and carry wood and water. In time, however, it became clear to Clinton that the Comanches hadn't purchased him just so he could be their menial. He was being trained to serve the tribe in much more important ways. Clinton recalled occasions when he and the other boys his age were taken to the open flatlands and drilled in battle maneuvers for several hours. They were taught to conceal their bodies behind their horses' necks and shoot while the horses were running at full speed. They were also instructed in how to charge, retreat, circle the enemy, and rescue their fallen comrades. The Comanches had big plans for Back-ecacho Clinton Smith.

By the spring of 1871, when Clinton and Jeff Smith were captured, Rudolph Fischer of Fredericksburg and Temple Friend of Legion Valley were already full-fledged Comanches. Adolph Korn, Herman Lehmann, and the Smith brothers had all passed the initial trial by fire. These timid farm boys were well on their way to becoming juvenile Indian warriors. No one has ever come up with a completely satisfying explanation for how that happened. Anthropologist A. Irving Hallowell pointed out in 1963 that Indianization "has remained a neglected topic of scholarly research,"[21] and this is still the case; most recent scholarship in this area has focused on the captivity narrative as a literary genre rather than the psychology of the captives' transformation.

One avenue for approaching this phenomenon is the "Stockholm syndrome," a term coined in the 1970s to explain why hostages sometimes come to identify with their captors. According to this theory, the victims' behavior is an irrational but natural way of coping with trauma and staying alive. At first the captives are relieved that their abductors, who could have killed them, have chosen to let them live. They also feel betrayed because their own people have failed to rescue them. Over time the captives adopt their captors' values, perhaps to avoid punishment. Eventually, they start to fear the people trying to rescue them; they see their abductors' dilemma as their own. Even after they are released, the victims may continue to sympathize with their captors for several months.[22]

Although the Stockholm syndrome has been documented repeatedly among adult hostages, it doesn't fully explain the metamorphosis these child captives went through. Some of them, especially the younger ones like Minnie Caudle and Banc Babb, do not seem to have had much fear or even awareness that the Indians might harm them, even after they saw other white people attacked. As Jeff Smith recalled, "I suppose I was too small to worry much about my situation." Typically, the child captives did not start to act and think like their captors until they'd spent a few months with the tribe; their acceptance of the native people's values cannot be characterized as an immediate reaction of relief over not being killed. More significant, the captives' affection for their Native American families and their affinity for Indian culture lasted throughout their lives. The medical historian and anthropologist Erwin H. Ackerknecht observed that American Indian captives who returned to white society retained the "outward impassibility of the Indian," often "could no longer sleep in a 'white' house or bed," "showed the same physical stamina as did the Indians," were "unanimous in their praise of the Indian character and of Indian morals," and lived "between the two cultures in a state of great unhappiness."[23]

The extent of the captives' assimilation differed, and not all captured children became converts to native ways. Some anthropologists have suggested that the two most critical factors in the making of a white Indian were abduction at an early age and a long residence with the tribe. The cases of Ole Nystel and Frank Buckelew, two Texas captives who never became assimilated, support this hypothesis in the converse. Nystel spent merely three months with the Comanches in 1867 when he was already fourteen; Buckelew, captured at age thirteen, lived with the Lipan Apaches for eleven months in 1866–1867. Both of these boys successfully resisted Indianization and never lost their desire to escape.

However, the exceptions seem to swallow the rule. Rudolph Fischer and Dot Babb were both as old as Frank Buckelew when they were captured, and they became Indianized. Even younger children such as Adolph Korn, Herman Lehmann, and Clinton Smith, all abducted at age ten, were old enough to have been conscious of their cultural identities and to make choices. Furthermore, Dot Babb spent only nine months with the Comanches—two months less than Buckelew, who rejected the Indians' way of life. Minnie Caudle and Banc Babb spent merely six and seven months, respectively, with the Comanches, yet both acquired their captors' ways and became lifelong defenders of their adoptive people.

Generalizations based on objective factors such as age when captured and duration of captivity are not particularly helpful. The captives' individual personalities seem to have played a more significant role in accounting for the differing degrees of assimilation. The challenges and rewards of adapting to Indian folkways held the greatest appeal for children who were somewhat assertive, liked taking risks, and did not feel bound by cultural or moral absolutes but were open to new ways of thinking.

As an example of this last characteristic, the captives' diverse views on the nature of God and religion are instructive. Frank Buckelew, who did not become Indianized, was drawn to traditional, evangelical Christianity and eventually became a Methodist preacher. He described a Lipan religious ceremony he witnessed as a "strange performance" by "uncivilized beings." Similarly, Ole Nystel, while acknowledging that the Comanches believed in a supreme being, noted how "wrong" they were in "their mode of worship" and described their prayers as "unavailing and misdirected." Banc Babb, on the other hand, was completely nonjudgmental when she pointed out that the Comanches "had their regular time for worshipping their heavenly Father, or as they would say our sure enough Father." In even sharper contrast, Herman Lehmann, who subscribed to mainstream Christianity later in life, nonetheless compared the natives' spirituality favorably to his people's when he remarked, "I have seen just as much earnestness and less hypocrisy among the Indians in their worship as I ever have seen since I came among the whites." He suggested that if the white man would "study our religion and our philosophy, he would find that we are not what he would call pagans, or miscreants, or savages, but we know about as much of the unknowable as he does and have seen perhaps even deeper." Dot Babb also showed his distrust of religious orthodoxy when he said, "I believe there is a hereafter, but I don't know what it is. I've heard some say they know, but I don't believe anyone can actually know."[24]

Other subjective factors that may have influenced these children's transformations included the extent to which an individual captive enjoyed adventure and a carefree, unstructured existence. These qualities of Plains Indian society seem to have been especially appealing to my uncle Adolph, who courted danger while he was with the Comanches and never put down roots afterward. Ironically, captivity opened up a new world of freedom for some overworked farm children, who had previously spent their days herding livestock or hauling rocks or hoeing fields. My granny Hey, Adolph Korn's stepsister, described the children's life in the Korn household: "From a little girl I had to work hard. Not much time left for recreation." While the captives were with the Indians, they were allowed to ride horses, hunt, travel, loaf, and play games. No wonder one German-Texan from the Hill Country recalled that during his boyhood, "I wasn't afraid of the Indians. I guess I figured if they captured me, I'd get to ride and shoot all I wanted to."[25]

However, the thrills, leisure, and mobility of the Plains Indians' unfettered life cannot entirely account for the depth of the captives' attachment to the native people. J. Norman Heard, a historian of frontier America, observed: "It would appear that Indian family life offered much to the fulfillment of the individual which was lacking in the more advanced civilization."[26] Frontier parents in central Texas, preoccupied with the necessities of life and their own daily toil, typically had little spare time to instruct their young. Although Granny Hey maintained that parents in those days shared a close bond with their children and loved them dearly, few mothers and fathers gave their sons and daughters any formal education or even taught them practical skills such as swimming, hunting, shooting, and horseback riding. My grandpa Korn was fully literate, but he never taught his children to read and write. Herman Lehmann's mother could write German very well. However, she "was trying to make a living for her children," says Gerda Lehmann Kothmann, Herman's niece. "She didn't have time to teach them."

The Comanches and Apaches not only received the child captives warmly and without prejudice; they also spent much time training them, making them feel significant in tribal society. Dot Babb, Herman Lehmann, and Clinton Smith took lessons from their adoptive fathers in riding, fighting, and shooting. Banc Babb's Comanche mother taught her to swim, took her to religious ceremonies, and instructed her in tribal lore. Perhaps the captives, in turn, felt a need to prove that they were worthy of their Indian parents' investment in them. Historian James Axtell reached that conclusion when he studied captives from colonial America: "Although fear undoubtedly accounted for some of the converts' initial behavior, desire to win the approval of their new relatives also played a part."[27] Not long after their initiation into tribal life, Adolph Korn, Rudolph Fischer, Temple Friend, Herman Lehmann, and the Smith brothers would have many occasions to demonstrate to their new families what they were made of.

Part Two

In the Wilds

Chapter Six

As Mean an Indian
as There Was

At daybreak the buffalo hunters were startled by the sounds of war whoops and horses' hooves pounding the prairie. They hadn't even rubbed the sleep out of their eyes when they saw the horsemen charging. Too late the hunters realized their mistake. The campfire that had kept them warm and content the night before had also given away their location. Unable to get to their horses before the onslaught began, they threw off their blankets and reached for their guns. The hunters crouched and fired desperately; but they were greatly outnumbered by the two dozen Comanches. By the time the sun had cleared the horizon and the gunfire had ended, only one hunter was still alive. He threw down his rifle and raised his hands. Then he watched the Comanches plunder his camp, stripping the bloody corpses of his companions, their eyes frozen in disbelief that death could have taken them so unexpectedly.

The Comanches grabbed the lone survivor and shoved him toward one of their horses. The buffalo hunter didn't resist. His captors made signs for him to get on the horse. He did as he was told. It wasn't necessarily a good thing that the Comanches were sparing his life; he knew they might be planning to subject him to vengeful torture at their camp.

He would be sharing the horse with one of the youngest warriors, a slender, diffident boy about eleven or twelve years old. It took the buffalo hunter a moment to comprehend that the painted savage in buckskin and beaded moccasins was a white boy. His long, matted hair was crawling with lice and bleached ash blond from riding in the sun. His skin, which must have once been quite fair, was now bronzed and rough like rawhide leggings. The Comanches called him Backeca-cho, but he had once answered to the name Clinton Smith. The boy spoke the Comanches' language fluently, and he didn't seem to realize that he wasn't one of them. The hunter knew better than to try to talk to him in English or win his sympathy. White boys who'd spent much time with the natives had a reputation for being crueler to their fellow Anglos than the Indians were.

After they left the camp, the Comanches and their prisoner rode swiftly across the plains, never stopping to rest. When they reached their village, the women and children ran up, pulled the buffalo hunter off Clinton's horse, and bound his legs. Then the Comanches put on a show to terrify him. Some of them rushed toward him brandishing spears and axes, threatening to split open his head, then diverting the blows at the last instant. He mustered his courage and stood firm, even managing to smirk at their theatrics.

Finally, they used sign language to let him know that they were going to execute him. They produced three pistols and loaded them with cartridges. The prisoner didn't know that his captors had removed the lead from the shells. Next, the Comanches chose three adolescent boys and handed the pistols to them. The boys pointed the weapons at the man's head. He didn't flinch. Then they fired the blanks at close range. The powder blackened his face. He calmly wiped it off without a word.

The Comanches' leader let out an impassioned yell of admiration and ran up to the hunter. He slapped the white man on the back, loudly praising his courage. Others undid his bonds. After passing the test, he was welcomed into their camp. Later, the Comanches let the man escape with one of their horses and didn't try to recapture him.

The three boys chosen to fire the pistols at the buffalo hunter's head were all captives themselves. One was Clinton Smith. Another was a Mexican captive, whose name is unknown. The third was Ca-choco, my uncle Adolph Korn.

The buffalo-hunter incident was the second recorded sighting of Adolph Korn after his capture in January 1870. He'd been seen in captivity once before, in the late summer or fall of 1870,[1] and his be-havior at that time had been markedly different. A group of Apaches had stopped beside a watering hole to relax for a few days. Among them was the white captive from Loyal Valley, Herman Lehmann. Be-fore long a party of Quahada Comanches happened along and joined them. The two tribes were on good terms at the time, and for the next three days, the Apaches and Comanches conducted horse races, plac-ing bets and enjoying the friendly competition.

Meanwhile, Herman was surprised to see his "old friend Adolph Korn" among the Quahadas. The two boys had grown up only ten miles from each other. They had a good deal in common besides their Mason County roots. They were both eleven by then, only a month apart in age, and they were able to speak with each other in German. Eventually, their captors, who were unable to understand what they were saying, grew suspicious and separated them. Another German Indian, Rudolph Fischer of Fredericksburg, was reportedly present at this gathering.[2] By then Rudolph, who was eighteen, had spent five years with the Comanches and was a full-fledged warrior. Despite his ethnicity and his Hill Country origins, he no longer had much in common with the two adolescent white boys.

Adolph had been with the Comanches at least seven months when he and Herman saw each other at the watering hole. According to Herman, the two boys talked about their predicament and "would have devised some means of escape" had they not been separated. Adolph had not yet come to prefer the Comanche way of life; like the Babb siblings at that stage, he still wanted to go home. When he met Clinton Smith the following spring, his outlook had changed radi-cally.

The captives who wrote about their time with Native Americans didn't say exactly when they started thinking of themselves as members of the tribe. Most likely they weren't aware of the change. But at some point—in Adolph's case, apparently no more than fourteen months—almost all of them experienced it. As Clinton Smith stated simply, "I considered myself an Indian, and an Indian I would be."

Adolph Korn would become even more of an Indian. His pal Clinton Smith described him as "the boldest boy I ever knew" and "about as mean an Indian as there was in the tribe at that time." Adolph and Clinton rode together across the Panhandle of Texas and the prairies of Indian Territory and eastern New Mexico with a mixed bunch of Quahada and Kotsoteka Comanches. Their group included about eighteen Anglo and Mexican captives, ranging in age from ten to eighteen. Clinton didn't identify them in his narrative, except for Uncle Adolph. However, among these were Temple Friend, the only unredeemed captive from the Legion Valley raid, and Rudolph Fischer.

Clinton Smith recorded the only tales that have survived about Adolph Korn's life as a Comanche warrior. According to his narrative, my white-Indian ancestor wasn't just bold; he was a daredevil who pushed the limits, a juvenile horse thief who wasn't content to play it safe if he could set off a hair-raising chase or a little gunplay. That sort of bravado wasn't uncommon among the Comanches. Stealing horses under especially dangerous conditions was a surefire way for a young man to establish his reputation and gain prestige among his peers.

One time Adolph, Clinton, and about twenty-five Comanche men were raiding in Texas when they approached a small town in a valley. All day long they kept watch over the settlement from the hills, waiting for nightfall. Once the valley became dark and still, the Comanches left their horses tied in the woods and slipped into town on foot. They found a stable and took a few horses. Adolph counseled Clinton, "Now go slow, and don't be afraid." Then he boasted, "I will get their horses."

Inside the quiet houses, a few candles and kerosene lanterns were still burning. The Comanches crept cautiously through the shadows.

Finally, the adult men decided it was too risky. They whispered to the boys not to go any farther.

Adolph ignored them. He slipped into another stable, cut the ropes, and brought out a horse. Then he went back inside for more. One of the animals got skittish and started snorting. Still, Adolph didn't let go of it. He wouldn't settle for less than all the horses, even if he woke the whole town.

He was a risk taker even when the Comanches weren't observing him. One night during this same trip, Adolph and Clinton both felt famished. The Comanches ate little while they were on a raid, and this must have been torture for the adolescents. The two boys asked the leader of the party if they could kill a cow from a herd they'd seen near camp. Their leader gave them permission to go shoot one with arrows. However, he told them not to fire their pistols, since the noise would alarm any cowboys or soldiers in the area.

Cachoco and Backecacho set out in search of their prey. They tried to get close enough to the herd to shoot their arrows. However, the moon was bright and the cattle were easily spooked, so the boys weren't able to sneak up on them. They decided to try to rope a cow instead. Clinton missed his first throw. However, Adolph's rope caught a calf by the hind foot. He held on. Clinton jumped off his horse and stabbed the animal behind the shoulder. The calf started to bellow, filling the night with deep, loud cries of distress. Clinton said, "We should leave her and go back to camp." Adolph refused. Let the white men come firing their rifles; he was determined to get his midnight meal. Finally, the calf died, and the boys butchered it.

It wasn't unusual for captives such as Adolph Korn to take greater chances than the natural-born Comanches. This may have been a matter of conversion zeal. Herman Lehmann, for instance, proudly proclaimed that he was the "wildest of the wild" when he was with the Apaches. The white Indians were also said to be crueler in initiating newly abducted captives than were their fellow tribesmen.

Risk taking was also a way for captives to increase their status in tribal society. Adopted Comanche captives got to keep the horses they stole during raids.[3] They weren't treated as second-class citizens; in fact, they might even become chiefs or headmen. That wasn't just an abstract possibility. In the summer of 1868, the Kotsoteka Comanche chief Mowway visited the Indian agency and admitted that he had nine captives in his camp, but pointed out that two of them had become chiefs.[4] The white boys living among the Quahadas— Rudolph Fischer, Adolph Korn, and Temple Friend—saw living proof of what the future could hold for them. A half-white warrior named Quanah, son of Comanche captive Cynthia Ann Parker, was rapidly emerging as a war leader. He was only a few years older than these three boys, and he undoubtedly served as a role model. My uncle Adolph, who had watched his white family work strenuously without ever getting ahead, saw unlimited opportunities dangling before him for the first time. If he performed well in battle, he might become the next Quanah.

At first the captives had no choice but to travel with the warriors. According to Clinton Smith, "All of the boys over twelve years old were compelled to go with them on their stealing raids." The younger captives, like the Comanche boys their age, rode with the party to take care of the horses and perform the menial chores. It was part of their apprenticeship. Every male Comanche was expected to become a warrior; there was no other career path.

At some point, they were forced to take part in the stealing and even killing, usually against their will at first. Herman Lehmann recalled, "I was among [the Apaches] about a year before I began to steal." (It was probably less than a year; the captives typically overestimated the passage of time.) During Herman's first raid near Fort Concho, Texas, his Apache father, Carnoviste, told him to go steal a large black horse that was staked near a tent in a meadow. Herman hesitated. Carnoviste drew his gun on the boy and ordered him to go. Then he gave Herman a pistol in case he got in trouble. Herman crept toward the horse, crawling through the grass part of the way. Just as he cut the rope, a white man threw aside the tent flap and fired a shot-gun at him. Herman wasn't hit, but the smoke and fire blinded him, and the blast knocked him flat. The boy, the man, and the horse, each as frightened as the others, all took off running in different directions. Herman, in his mad scramble, dropped the pistol. He told the Apaches that the white man had shot the gun out of his hand and grabbed it, so that they wouldn't make him go back for it.

Sometimes Clinton Smith was able to get out of going on raids. Once when the Comanches were getting ready to attack a camp of In-dian enemies, he went to his adoptive father, Tosacowadi, put his arms around his neck, and said: "Potaw, I am begging you not to send me out this time, for I have a big boil on my neck and I can hardly ride." Tosacowadi took his pipe from his mouth and replied, "Backe-cacho, you may have your wish." That day Clinton got to stay home with Tosacowadi's son, Monewostuki, whom he described as "almost a brother to me." Another time when Clinton asked Tosacowadi not to send him with the warriors, "The old black rascal said if I would kiss him I could stay in camp. Bless your soul, I smacked him in the mouth and hugged him, too." After a while, however, Tosacowadi started to push his adopted son to the front when a raiding party was preparing to leave camp. He knew that if Clinton didn't make a name for himself on the warpath, the other boys his age wouldn't respect him.

Of all the chores that a warrior-in-training might be ordered to do, the most disagreeable was carrying the scalps that the adult men took. Clinton Smith complained that "they began to stink and the hair began to come off." During one raid, Clinton stood firm and re-fused to carry the scalps of four trappers. The leader of the party was furious and threatened to kill him. Adolph Korn intervened, saying he would take revenge on the man if he dared touch Clinton. Later, Clinton proposed that they kill their leader that night, but Adolph said he was a good guide who knew the country well. They decided to let him live.

Within a few months, most of the boy captives no longer had to be coerced to take part in raids. They fought the Indians' battles, too. Adolph Korn even commanded a group of Comanches in a desperate fight with some Texas Rangers. On another occasion, the Comanches were being pursued by a posse and decided to set a trap. Adolph and a fellow warrior named Twovanta had the best horses, so their leader chose them to go challenge the white men. The two cocky boys rode straight toward the posse, taunting them and daring them to come fight. The white men accepted their invitation, charging at full speed. Adolph and Twovanta turned and retreated. The posse chased them— right into the trap. Eight other Comanches suddenly appeared and launched an attack. The battle lasted until sundown, and the white men got the worst of it. The following day, the Comanches cut the arms and legs off the dead enemies and strung them from trees.

Clinton Smith reported that the Comanches called Uncle Adolph "Cachoco," but he didn't say what that meant. Comanche nicknames typically described a noteworthy trait or an event that happened either to the bearer or someone else. Naturally, I wanted to believe that "Cachoco" referred to something lofty, like "Eagle's Heart" or "Runs from No Fight." On the other hand, given Adolph's known physical characteristics, I realized it might mean something derogatory, such as "Walks with a Limp" or "Scar on His Chin."

I got in touch with three Comanche language experts. The first, Barbara Goodin, is a historian and an enrolled member of the Comanche Tribe. She invited me to ask some elders at a meeting of the Comanche Language and Cultural Preservation Committee in Lawton, Oklahoma, who informed me that *cachoco* does not seem to be a Comanche term, at least not anymore. The word, like many, may have disappeared from the language since the 1870s. It's also possible that Clinton Smith remembered it imperfectly, or that his editor transcribed it incorrectly. In fact, "Cachoco" must be an approximation of Adolph's actual name, for the Comanche language has no true "ch" sound.

Tom Kavanagh, an anthropologist and author who has studied the Comanches for three decades, suggested that the *choco* component might be a corruption of *tsukuhpu?,* a Comanche word for "old." The *Ca* prefix could be a variant spelling of *ke,* which means "not." Thus, his name might translate simply as "Not Old."

Dan Gelo, a professor of anthropology who has also delved into the language and culture, reached the same conclusion independently: "Not" plus "Old Man." "It is impossible to know the precise meaning," he informed me, "but it is probably something like 'youngster' or 'not one of the elders.'"

That was not what I was hoping for. But it fits; several observers thought Uncle Adolph looked young for his age. Furthermore, Not an Old Man is no more prosaic than Herman Lehmann's name: White Boy. Or Rudolph Fischer's: Gray Blanket. It's not as enigmatic as Clinton Smith's: End of a Rope. Or as demeaning as Dot Babb's: Tired and Give Out. Or Jeff Smith's: Horse Tail. And it's not nearly as derisive as Banc Babb's: Smell Bad When You Walk.

The Plains Indians conferred nicknames spontaneously, and the ones they came up with were seldom heroic. In fact, some of them seem to have been intended as ribald jokes, memorializing a humiliating incident or characteristic. Anthropologist E. Adamson Hoebel, who interviewed many Comanches in the 1930s, quoted tribal members with sobriquets as inglorious as A Big Fall by Tripping, Breaks Something, Face Wrinkling Like Getting Old, Not Enough to Eat, She Blushes, and She Invites Her Relatives. In the nineteenth century, Southern Plains tribesmen rose to influential positions despite having been saddled with epithets such as Always Sitting Down in a Bad Place, Dog Eater, and Coyote Vagina. I was pleased to find that the Comanches I met in Oklahoma maintained a healthy sense of humor about their ancestors' nicknames. They assured me that I shouldn't feel disappointed to be a lateral descendant of a young warrior with a name as ordinary as Not an Old Man.

The Comanches' nicknames weren't nearly as merciless as some of their practical jokes. They didn't just play pranks on one another. Occasionally, the victims of their raids were good for a few laughs.

On one trip into Texas, the raiding warriors emerged from the woods and unexpectedly found themselves at a clearing on the edge of a farm. The homesteaders looked up and were just as surprised to see the painted horsemen. Terrified, they sprinted for their log shanty. Adolph, Clinton, and the other raiders all let out war whoops just to watch them run faster. The Comanches also managed to startle a team of mules hitched to a wagon. When the mules tried to flee, a wagon wheel got caught against a tree, and the animals struggled and kicked so hard they almost uprooted it. The Comanches laughed uproariously at the commotion they'd caused. Finally, they decided to leave before the trapped family started shooting at them.

During another raid, Adolph, Clinton, and several Comanche men infiltrated a community of destitute farmers after dark. The people in that region lived like moles in pitiful underground dugouts covered with sod. They didn't have any horses, cattle, or anything else worth taking. Disgusted, the Indians quietly withdrew. However, Adolph wasn't going to let the sodbusters off that easily. To have a little fun, he fired his pistol at the night sky and gave a war whoop, leaving the families quaking as they huddled in their dark hovels.

Another time, Adolph and Clinton went with a large party of Comanches on a raid into north Texas. They traveled many miles along the Red River until they sighted a campfire. The leader of their party sent a few young men, including Adolph, to investigate. When Adolph and the other spies returned with four horses, they reported that they'd found a wagon and tent. As Clinton Smith remembered, "We did not disturb the camp, but went on our way leaving the campers to discover as best they could that they were left afoot." Perhaps those unlucky travelers were able to look back one day and also laugh at the Comanches' joke—if they survived on the waterless prairie.

The raiding party moved south and followed the Concho River. One day they came upon a log cabin and saw a white man outside. They galloped toward the house. By the time they got there, the man had fled and hid. The Comanches looked around the farm and helped themselves to a few horses and mules.

This homestead along the river must have reminded Adolph of the Korn family's place near Castell. It should have brought back warm memories of his mother and stepfather, his twin brother, and their German-American neighbors in the village. Adolph stepped into the deserted cabin. He grabbed a burning log from the fireplace and set the house on fire. Then he took the log outside to a haystack and set it ablaze.

The battles and horse-gathering raids were the high points of their adventures, but the boy captives didn't spend the majority of their days terrorizing settlers. For the most part, Adolph Korn, Clinton Smith, Herman Lehmann, Rudolph Fischer, and Temple Friend simply enjoyed the pampered, leisurely life of teenage males in the Indian camps. They were expected to do their share of the work, of course. However, most of their chores weren't unenjoyable. For boys their age, the primary responsibilities were learning to hunt, ride, fight, and make weapons. As Indian men, they would be expected to be good protectors and providers so they wouldn't shame their families.

The boys enjoyed the sport of the hunt. Sometimes they disguised themselves to get closer to their prey. Clinton Smith recalled one occasion when his Comanche pal, Moniwoftuckwy,[5] and Uncle Adolph dressed him like a bush, tying leaves and limbs to his body. That day Clinton killed his first elk, and his father, Tosacowadi, greatly praised his marksmanship.

When they weren't hunting or breaking horses or making bows and arrows, the boys did pretty much as they pleased. Although the captives had been forced to carry water and gather wood at first, no manual labor was required of them as they grew older and became Indianized. Nor was there much parental supervision. Clinton said, "The Indian boys and I would go in bathing every day, run horse races, rope buffalo calves and ride them, and take wild horses out into deep sand and ride them." They also played ball and held shooting contests and footraces. They ate whenever they were hungry, and if they wanted anything, they just asked and usually got it. Some nights the boys would take their fathers' best horses and go racing across the plains. The adolescent Indians got to live in their own tepees—a far cry from the cramped, one- or two-room log cabins the white boys had shared with their former families.

Now and then, they got drunk. Clinton Smith gave a particularly vivid account of his first experience with whiskey:

> [W]hen it came my turn to drink I poured about a half a cupful and proceeded to swallow it. Great guns! I thought I would never get my breath. The Indians all laughed at me, and seemed to take great delight in my discomfiture. . . . In just a little while it began to get pretty warm in the wigwam and everything said sounded funny to me; then everything seemed to be going round and round. They were all laughing at me, so I told them to clear a place and I would show them how the Americans danced, and I began to sing, "Old Dan Tucker Came Too Late for His Supper." They got me quieted down, and passed around the big pipe. When I got still everything was whirling around me. I got up and went over to the chief, threw my arms around his neck and tried to help him smoke the pipe. . . . Next morning I was still drunk, and awful sick. . . . [A]s I went along it looked to me as if all the hills had been moved, and were still gradually moving.[6]

That wasn't the only time the Comanches got to hear "Old Dan Tucker." Sometimes Clinton agreed to entertain the Comanche men by singing the tune repeatedly if they would help him burn the lice out of his buckskin clothes. It was the only English song he could remember. Eventually, the Comanches got tired of "Old Dan Tucker" and asked him to sing something else. Stumped, Clinton told them, "That is the only song the Americans ever sing."

Herman Lehmann thought the Apaches were "morose" compared with the Comanches, whom he described as "a fun-loving people." Nonetheless, even the somber Apaches occasionally held drinking festivals when someone prepared a batch of home brew.[7] Herman Lehmann described these parties:

> All would get drunk, and even I'd get "tipsy." Gambling and fighting would be the next thing on programme. . . . [I]t was no unusual sight to see braves, squaws and squatters all in a bloody pile, gnashing their teeth and swearing vengeance on each other. . . . After a week's debauchery we would lie around and sleep and grieve over the death—maybe brought about by our own hands—of some loved one. . . . It was not unusual for an intoxicated warrior to murder his wife and children, or outrage his own daughter. . . . [8]

The communities in which the captives grew up rewarded cleverness as well as bravery. One day an old woman spied Clinton Smith at a spring eating a hard biscuit he'd swiped the night before. It wasn't the first time he'd done that. The woman reported the theft to Clinton's father, Tosacowadi. He summoned his adopted son to his tepee and demanded: "Backecacho, I want you to tell me how you managed to steal those cakes, with all of us near, and you have no clothes on which to hide them, after we have been trying for so long to catch you."

Unshaken, Clinton replied, "I stuck them under my arms." He then demonstrated how he hid the stolen biscuits.

Tosacowadi was greatly pleased. "You will never starve," he said. "Give him two more for being so wise."

The Southern Plains Indians and their captives lived in societies that imposed few rules and punishments. Young men learned how to behave by observing their elders, not by being taught a moral code. As long as the tribe had enough to eat and wasn't being threatened by enemies, camp life was relaxed and unfettered. The Indians gave their young free rein when it came to pleasures such as eating, drinking, sleeping, and gambling.

And sex.

As if adapting to a strikingly different culture weren't hard enough, the boy captives watched helplessly as their adolescent bodies underwent confusing changes. The youngsters may have been fearsome-looking warriors, but when they let out a bloodcurdling yell, their voices occasionally squeaked and broke. They started sprouting facial hair, which the Comanches found repulsive. Clinton Smith remembered, "They would get me down, and, with a pair of tweezers, pull out every hair they found growing on my face. It was very painful to me, but I had to bear it."

The boys were also encountering unfamiliar new feelings and desires. The Comanches didn't encourage premarital sex, but if it happened, they didn't take it very seriously, either. Teenage boys normally weren't the aggressors. Quite bashful, they stayed in their own tepees at night and weren't disposed to go carousing. It was slightly older girls who took the initiative, slipping into the boys' tents after dark. If the lovers were discovered, they would be the subjects of amused gossip and razzing around camp the next day.

Those of us with captives in our families wonder whether we might have blood relatives among the Indians today. It's possible, although I suspect that Adolph Korn, Clinton Smith, and Temple Friend were too young to have experienced this part of Comanche life. Clinton said that a Navajo once promised him a friendly, pretty girl if he ever got to be a Comanche chief, but Clinton wasn't interested at the time: "I did not want any Indian girl." Dot Babb, captured at age fourteen, was old enough to have been an object of the Comanche girls' affections. If he was, however, he was too discreet to mention it.

Only Herman Lehmann wrote frankly and unapologetically about his amorous adventures, first among the Apaches and later with the Comanches. As he explained, "With the Indian, all nature took its course, and we had none of those abnormal hugs on the sofa in a dimly-lighted parlor." At the same time, he was careful to point out, "There was virtue among the Indians and it was rigidly maintained." Ordinarily, the Apaches were shyer and more prudish about sex than the Comanches. In their system of beliefs, premarital sex was an offense against the girl's family. Most couples were too bashful to attempt it, anyway. Even after marriage, some mortified newlyweds asked their cousins to stay with them and sleep between the couple for a while to ease the awkwardness.

Herman chose a mate when he was about seventeen. She was a Comanche girl named Topay; they met while they were skinning a buffalo together. Herman confessed that when her hand touched his, "I had passions that I didn't know I possessed." He started watching Topay and following her around camp. Topay's father didn't like Herman and tried to keep them apart.

One night Herman arranged to come see Topay at about eleven o'clock. He crawled inside her tepee and "found her awake ready to receive" him. He was "whispering sweet words of love and encouragement to her" when he felt a rough kick in his behind. Topay's father was standing in the doorway. Herman promptly bounded out through the tepee wall, "leaving a pretty considerable hole in the tent." As Herman circled the tepee, he came face-to-face with the girl's father, who shot an arrow that struck Herman's knee. Topay sprang from the tepee and took him in her arms. She rebuked her father for treating him that way. "He was behaving nicely," she scolded, "and you should not have disturbed us." Her father calmed down, apologized, and removed the arrow from Herman's knee.

Herman once referred to Topay as "my spouse."[9] He probably wasn't using the term literally, although it's not entirely clear whether he and Topay were considered married in the eyes of the Comanches. For many years after he returned home, an unconfirmed rumor persisted that Herman Lehmann had taken an Indian bride. One day the gossip would cause trouble between Herman and his white wife.

The captives didn't just come to love their Native American families; after a while, they also started to despise their own people. At first their hatred seems to have been born of fear—not so much fear of their captors but fear that the white settlers or soldiers they came across would mistake them for Indians, shooting first and discovering the error later. For the first time, the boys were on the receiving end of the white people's gunfire. Clinton Smith said, "We were all painted up, and no one could have told me from an Indian boy. . . . [M]y hair had grown long, and I was sunburned so I looked like an Indian, and naturally I was afraid the white people would kill me."

In some instances, their fear of being killed by whites almost materialized. Adolph Korn received a flesh wound in the arm during a battle with some soldiers. In another hard fight between the Comanches and a wagon train of settlers, Clinton Smith was struck in the face by a shotgun blast that knocked him off his horse. After the battle, the Comanches held him down and picked out most of the pellets. He wrote in 1927, "Some of these shot are in my face yet."

As time went by, the captives were subjected to the same fiery sermons as the Native American boys their age. The elders' rhetoric left a deep impression on them. According to Clinton Smith, "Our chief was preaching to us that every Comanche from ten years old must fight or lose our hunting grounds, saying the palefaces would brand us and make us work like they had the buffalo soldiers (negroes), and whip us. That inflamed us and we were determined to fight for our rights."[10] *Our* hunting grounds. *Our* rights. Those first-person pronouns, casually sprinkled throughout the captivity narratives, suggest how strongly the captives had come to identify with their new people after only a year or two among them.

Herman Lehmann remembered attending an Apache council when Victorio, the famous Eastern Chiricahua leader, said: "The white man is the Indian's enemy, and the Indians must quit fighting among themselves and all go together to fight the palefaces." At the same meeting, Herman listened while another Apache leader named Red Wasp railed against the whites:

> They have robbed us of our hunting grounds; they have destroyed our game; they have brought us disease; they have stirred up discord among our own race; they have bought out and in-

timidated our braves; they have made profligates of our children, reprobates of our wives and destroyed our traditions. They have wrought despair and desolation to our tribe, and for my part I am ready to fight until I fall.[11]

These tirades had their intended effect; they gave the captives a sense of purpose and justification for attacking their fellow whites. By then the boys stayed with the tribes by choice. Clinton Smith recalled that there were times when he could have escaped. However, he had become so attached to his "chief"[12] and other members of the tribe that he "could not muster courage enough" to make a getaway. Clinton had come to idolize his Comanche father, Tosacowadi, whom he described as "my best friend."

Herman Lehmann had even more opportunities to leave the Apaches. Several times they took him raiding near his old home in Mason County. Herman eagerly took part in these raids against the Texans, for they had become to him "the hated tribe of palefaces." One night the raiders wandered into Fredericksburg unnoticed and watched the German-American boys drinking beer in a saloon. They quietly made off with their horses. Then the Apaches headed north to Loyal Valley, where Herman's family lived. There, the raiding party stole his former neighbors' livestock. As Herman related, "We passed right by my old home, and the Indians tried to get me to go see my mother. They called me paleface and urged me to quit them." Herman refused.

Similarly, the Comanches took Rudolph Fischer on raids near his old home in Gillespie County. Crouched behind a split-rail fence on a moonlit night, he watched his former neighbors pass by within easy killing distance. Legend has it that Rudolph even sneaked up to the window of the Fischer family's house to catch a glimpse of his mother. Still, he had no desire to stay there.

The captives' hatred of the whites wasn't just a matter of indoctrination. They were also deeply affected by the things they saw. Herman Lehmann recalled one particularly horrible mistake on the part of the U.S. Army. His band of Apaches was raiding in Texas, and some soldiers from Fort Griffin were following them. The soldiers came across a camp of friendly Lipans and other Apaches and mistook them for the raiders. The Indians in the camp had no reason to be afraid and put up no resistance. According to Herman, the soldiers charged into the camp and "murdered men, women and children, and only a few escaped to tell the tale."

Another time, when Herman was raiding with some Comanches on the Texas plains in the spring of 1877, his party returned to their camp at Quemado Lake and found that soldiers from the Tenth Cavalry had attacked it. He wrote:

> I remember finding the body of Batsena, a very brave warrior, lying mutilated and scalped, and alongside of him was the horribly mangled remains of his daughter, Nooki, a beautiful Indian maiden, who had been disemboweled and scalped. . . . In our council we swore to take ten captive white women and twice as many white children, and to avenge the death of our squaws, especially Nooki; we vowed to kill a white woman for each year of her age (she was about 18 years old), and that we would disembowel every one we killed.[13]

The army had its reasons for these attacks on Indian villages: the guilty sought refuge among the innocent, and in the heat of battle, it was impossible to tell them apart, especially when the Comanche women and children joined in the fight. To the soldiers, any Indians who harbored raiders in their camps were accomplices and deserved to be punished. The Native Americans, on the other hand, thought the soldiers were waging a war of extermination and were looking for any excuse to kill off a few more civilians.

The captives were practically the only people who got to see the conflict from both sides. Eight-year-old Minnie Caudle watched Indians butcher her relatives; nonetheless, after spending merely six months with the Comanches, she developed a bitter taste for the U.S. soldiers who pursued Native American raiders, and it stayed with her for the rest of her life. "When the army raided the villages, the Indians didn't have a chance," her great-grandson, Damon Benson, remembers her saying. "They slaughtered them like you would a bunch of chickens. They poisoned some water holes. She said the cowboys were real hard fighters, but they didn't bother the Indian women and children like the army did." (Benson doesn't know whether Minnie actually witnessed an army attack on a Comanche camp or whether she just heard her captors' tales.)

Herman Lehmann reminded his audience that the Indian-white conflict was two-sided when he told an interviewer in 1906: "I have always found the Comanches to be my most devoted friends. Don't you believe that the Comanche is a bad man. You hate him and believe him to be a rascal, but the Comanches don't keep books and their side of history has never been written."[14]

Similarly, Jeff Smith, Clinton's younger brother and fellow captive, thought it was important to present the Apache viewpoint even though he came from a family of Indian fighters and was himself a victim of a raid:

> In their opinion, they were justified in taking vengeance on the settlers for what they termed theft of their hunting grounds. They were forced back and back, and we must admit that, even before they became hostile, the pioneers did not hold their lives of much value. So they may not have been wholly to blame for playing a fair game of tit for tat.[15]

Eventually, the captives' hatred of their fellow whites led them to commit murder. Like Clinton Smith, Herman Lehmann, and Dot Babb, my uncle Adolph Korn almost certainly killed people. The boy captives didn't just shoot and scalp other fighting men; many of their victims were civilians. Herman Lehmann, who murdered a white ox driver, came to think of killing as "sport." Clinton Smith said, "I saw so many people killed that I became used to it, and looked upon it as a common thing of no more concern than the killing of a cow."

The former captives who told their stories in later years didn't like to dwell on this aspect of their Indian life. Chances are they didn't record all the murders in which they participated. As Clinton Smith explained:

> I have been asked many times, "Did you ever kill anybody while you were with the Indians?" When asked this question I always hang my head and do not reply. It pains me greatly when this question is asked for it brings up memories of deeds which I was forced to do, taught to do by savages, whose chief delight was to kill and steal. It must be remembered that I was just a mere boy, and that I had, without choice, absorbed the customs and manners of a savage tribe. I was an Indian.[16]

In this candid but ambivalent passage, Clinton goes through an interesting progression as he grapples with his past, as if he were thinking out loud. First, he claims that he was "forced" to kill. Then he corrects himself: he was "taught" to kill, but it seems that he did it voluntarily. Clinton was "just a mere boy" at the time; but was his youth supposed to account for his thorough Indianization, his irresponsible acts of violence, or both? He admits that he had "absorbed" the Comanches' habits—apparently not under duress, although it did happen "without choice," i.e., unconsciously. As "an Indian," it never occurred to him to question the values of his new people, including the practice of killing anyone whom the tribe saw as its enemy.

Herman Lehmann wrote in a similar passage: "While I still love my old Indian comrades, the refining influences of civilization have wrought a great change in me. When I was a savage I thirsted to kill and to steal, because I had been taught that that was the way to live; but I know now that that is wrong."

Were the former captives genuinely remorseful over the murders they'd committed, or were they just trying to appease their largely white audiences in the early twentieth century? They explained their actions by blaming the Indians for having "taught" them to kill. However, the native people were not really the first ones to teach them that. Uncle Adolph was old enough to remember Grandpa Korn trying to shoot the Indian raiders who surrounded their cabin. Clinton Smith had heard his father's stories about battling Indians while he was with the Texas Rangers. Rudolph Fischer had been raised among settlers who lynched a Comanche teenager on the mere suspicion that he might have been a spy and therefore a threat to their community. These children of the Texas frontier had learned through observing their elders that killing hostile Indians was sometimes necessary to defend their own people. After they became Comanches and Apaches, what changed was not so much their moral views on taking an enemy's life as their perception of who was an enemy.

By the fall of 1872, Adolph Korn, Clinton Smith, Herman Lehmann, Rudolph Fischer, and Temple Friend were living with the Indians as Indians, fighting their battles and taking part in their raids, prepared to die in defense of the tribe if necessary. "I had by this time become to all intents and purposes a wild Indian," Clinton Smith wrote. Herman Lehmann insisted that he "did not want to go" back to the white world, explaining, "I had learned to hate my own people." The captives made it clear that they wouldn't return to their former families unless they were forced to do so. That, in fact, is what happened to all of them. They didn't know it, but their time with the natives was running out.

Chapter Seven

Searchers
and Quakers

On a warm spring evening, May 4, 1871, Auguste Buchmeier hurried along a wagon road, trying to find the army camp in the woods. Earlier that afternoon, she'd learned that the general was spending the night nearby, and he was one of the most powerful men in America. In Georgia, where he'd cut his path of destruction seven years before, people still spoke the name Sherman with a mixture of enmity and terror. Auguste wasn't afraid of him, however; this man could help her more than anyone, and she was desperate. It had been almost a year since her boy, Herman Lehmann, disappeared.

Gen. William T. Sherman, the commander of the U.S. Army, had just started an inspection tour of the Texas frontier. In Washington he'd been swamped with pleas from settlers begging for more protection against Indian raiders. Two days earlier, on May 2, he'd left San Antonio with Maj. Gen. Randolph B. Marcy, inspector general of the army, and an escort of seventeen soldiers. Sherman and Marcy rode north through the lonely Texas Hill Country, lush with new growth and speckled with wildflowers. The two men traveled in a military ambulance, a boxlike cart designed to carry wounded soldiers but also used by high-ranking officers for transportation.

Sherman's party was traveling from Fredericksburg to Fort Mason when they stopped for the night near Loyal Valley. The soldiers were surprised to see a respectable woman entering the army camp alone.

In her German-accented English, Auguste asked for an audience with the general. When he appeared, she lost no time imploring him to do whatever he could to find her son. The woman described the scene that was still vivid in her mind: the Indians approaching the farm, the children playing in the wheat field, the terrifying men grabbing two of her sons and tying them on horses. One of her boys, Willie, had escaped. But Herman hadn't been seen since.

General Sherman listened carefully. He asked Auguste which Indians had taken Herman.

She replied, "I suppose they were Comanches. He is still in their hands."

Until then Sherman had expressed nothing but contempt for the Texans. He hadn't seen any signs of Indians on his way north from San Antonio, and he suspected that the frontier settlers were just alarmists and complainers. Nonetheless, he was moved by Auguste Buchmeier's story. He promised her that he would do his best. Privately, Sherman knew he could do little to help. It would be pointless for him to send small parties of soldiers out to look for the boy, for the Plains Indians ranged over an enormous territory, and the risk to his troops would be unwarranted. Experience had taught him that trying to find an Indian captive was "worse than looking for a needle in a haystack, rather like looking for a flea in a large clover field." Still, he directed one of his officers to write to the Kiowa-Comanche agent, relating the facts of Herman Lehmann's disappearance. As influential as General Sherman was, that was the most he could do.[1]

The kind of anguish known only to parents whose children have been abducted probably hasn't changed over time. Still, it's difficult in the twenty-first century to appreciate the sense of isolation those parents felt in the 1870s. In rural Texas after the Civil War, it sometimes took them more than an hour to notify their closest neighbors that their child had been taken. Usually, there were no soldiers or sheriffs or Texas Rangers nearby. The parents might try to round up a volunteer posse to follow the kidnappers. One San Antonio journalist rhapsodized about these chases:

> There is something grand in the perseverance of frontier men, when in pursuit of kindred who have fallen into the hands of the savages. While life lasts, the pursuit never flags. Even those who are sordid and mercenary, abandon everything and seek the recovery of the lost ones, who, while in the hands of savages, are slaves in the most abject sense.[2]

That scenario was mostly wishful thinking. Many of the Texas settlers were too terrified or too busy with farm chores to help track down Indian kidnappers. Furthermore, these chases were virtually never successful. By the time the rescue party took to the trail, the raiders had too great a head start.

Once the posse abandoned the search, the parents' next step was to report the abduction to the nearest military post, either in person or by mail. Some parents, such as Gottlieb Fischer, were immigrants who didn't speak English and had to find a letter writer to help them. Other families were too poor to travel. To make matters worse, the parents had no photographs of their children and had to rely solely on verbal descriptions. By the time they made their report to the army, several days would have passed. Another week might go by before a regional newspaper announced that a child was missing.

After the initial flurry of activity, the parents and siblings of a captured child had to cope with their loss on their own. Their neighbors were too far away and too preoccupied with their own struggles to console them. When they did visit, they didn't always offer comfort. Auguste Buchmeier remembered, "My friends would come to me and say: 'Why do you keep worrying and thinking about that boy? He is dead long ago.' But I would tell them that I never could believe that he was dead."[3] At night, as the family huddled in a secluded log cabin, the parents were fearful that the Indians might return and take more of their children.

Most families on the Texas frontier had little knowledge of the world beyond their rural communities. They didn't know which branch of government to contact for information on Native Americans and their captives. If the parents wrote to a military post, the officers usually forwarded their letters to the civilian Indian agents, since the army wasn't in the business of finding stolen children. The Indian agents questioned the tribal chiefs and traders who stopped by their agencies. However, the agents had their hands full dealing with reservation politics and the distribution of rations. Besides, they usually didn't know for sure whether the tribes under their jurisdiction were holding particular children.

In desperation some parents went higher up the chain of command, contacting the Texas governor or the secretary of the Interior in Washington. Gottlieb Fischer even wrote directly to Pres. Andrew Johnson about his son, Rudolph. It usually took several weeks to get a reply. The letters they received typically contained nothing more than bland assurances that the government was doing everything it could. Sometimes the parents' letters went unanswered. Eventually, most families stopped writing.

My own family gave up fairly quickly. Shortly after Uncle Adolph was kidnapped, Grandpa Korn traveled a hundred miles to San Antonio and reported Adolph's capture to Bvt. Maj. Gen. James W. Carleton. Three days later, Grandpa's account was published in the *San Antonio Daily Herald*. By then Adolph had been missing nearly two weeks, and any chance of overtaking his captors was long gone. The authorities presumed that the Indians had "taken their human and other booty to some more northern trading post or reservation." The Korns' best hope was that a trader doing business with the Indians might see Adolph and barter for his release.

Two months later, still having heard no news, Grandpa Korn asked Texas governor Edmund J. Davis for help in locating the boy. The governor was sympathetic, but he pointed out that he "could do nothing further than . . . give publicity to the fact." In this case, "publicity" meant notifying the headquarters of the Fifth Military District in Austin and the commissioner of Indian Affairs in Washington.

The Texas secretary of state, James P. Newcomb, used a blatant ploy to enlist the "sympathies and aid" of the Reconstruction government in Washington toward a family from a former Confederate state that was "bereft of a child by a band of savages." He was careful to emphasize that Grandpa Korn had been "a loyal citizen throughout the late war" who had "suffered misfortune in consequence" of his support for the Union. The Korns, like most German-Americans in the Texas Hill Country, had opposed secession and remained unionists after the Civil War broke out. These first-generation Americans had felt no desire to separate from their newly adopted country, and they had also been afraid that the federal army would abandon its frontier forts and leave them unprotected if the nation divided.

Newcomb's letter to Washington got results. The commissioner of Indian Affairs, Ely S. Parker, directed his superintendent at Lawrence, Kansas, to instruct the Kiowa-Comanche agent "to make diligent inquiry among the Indians of his charge concerning the boy." The superintendent, Enoch Hoag, brought the matter to the attention of Indian agent Lawrie Tatum at Fort Sill, Indian Territory: "This is an appeal of such a nature as to enlist thy sympathies and stimulate to a diligent search. As soon as practicable thou will notify this office of the result of thy investigation and inquiry." Tatum, as agent for the Kiowas and Comanches, was practically the only civilian employee of the federal government who had any direct contact with the tribes believed to be holding most of the captives from Texas. However, he was unable to learn anything about Adolph from the chiefs who came to his agency.

After only one round of letter writing, Grandpa Korn quit. He moved his family out of the rural Texas Hill Country and returned to San Antonio, where he went back into the confectionery business. Believing Adolph was dead, Louis and Johanna Korn moved on with their lives.

From a farm only twenty-three miles northwest of San Antonio,

Henry M. Smith was working much more aggressively to find his stolen boys, Clinton and Jeff. Henry and his wife, Harriet, wrote a long series of impassioned letters to anyone who might help them. In one letter, Henry implored Indian agent Lawrie Tatum:

> I beg, aye pray you, in the name of humanity and the sufferings of my poor children to exert yourself to the utmost of your power and ability, to get them back for me, from these merciless, inhuman creatures, what shall I say to you sir, to press this matter upon you, shall I tell you of my own feelings: words would fail me, they have no meaning, shall I tell you of the mother! no Sir, I will make no such vain attempts, but I will appeal to you trusting to your own good sense and humane feelings in the matter.[4]

Henry Smith was a former Texas Ranger who was used to dealing with his problems by taking quick, decisive action. It must have tormented him that the most important matter in his life, the search for his boys, was in the hands of federal bureaucrats. Nothing Henry did could hasten the recovery of Clinton and Jeff. On another occasion, he wrote to agent Tatum:

> Imagine yourself for a moment, in my situation, my dear friend, and then pardon me for again pressing this matter upon you, you have power, I have none, with all my anxiety of mind, I have to sit here at home with my hands folded as it were and can do nothing, all the hope I have left is in your section.[5]

H. R. Clum, the acting commissioner of Indian Affairs in Washington, tried to reassure Henry—or at least pacify him. He wrote, "Sympathizing with you in your distress by reason of so great an outrage, this office will do all it possibly can to cause your sons to be delivered up by the Indians, and returned to their home." He ordered the Indian agents to inquire among the Comanches, Kiowas, and Kickapoos.

THE CAPTURED

Over time Henry Smith grew less confident that the federal officials were really doing much to find Clinton and Jeff. He put his case
before the Texas governor: "Perhaps my over anxiety of mind causes
me to come to wrong conclusions, but it seems to me that all but myself have forgotten that my poor little boys are still in the hands of the
merciless savage, and that no effort is now being made to recover
them."

After a few months, Henry Smith was no longer content just to
write letters and wait for unsatisfactory responses. He met personally
with Indian agent John D. Miles, who was traveling on government
business from Kansas to the Rio Grande. However, Miles was unable
to locate the Smith children among the Kickapoos in Mexico. Henry
also made at least one trip to the Kiowa-Comanche agency in Indian
Territory to ask about his boys.

However, the Smiths, like the Korns and the Buchmeiers, made
most of their inquiries from home. In contrast, the relatives of a few
captives left home to conduct extensive searches on their own. Temple
Friend's grandfather, a Methodist circuit rider named Leonard S.
Friend, traveled more than fifteen thousand miles and spent over
$5,000 of his own money looking for the boy. He visited the Kiowa-
Comanche agency, the Apache reservations in Arizona and New Mexico, and even the Office of Indian Affairs in Washington, D.C. On
July 18, 1868, Texas governor E. M. Pease appointed Reverend Friend
to be the state's agent for recovering captives,[6] under Texas legislation
appropriating $2,500 to be used "in procuring the release of children
or other persons, citizens of this State, who are now, have been, or
may hereafter be held as prisoners of war by the Indians."[7] Several
times Leonard Friend thought he was on the verge of finding his
grandson; but the Comanches would break up into smaller groups,
separate their captives, and head for the plains.

Roving traders sometimes stumbled upon captives in remote Native American camps and tried to buy them from their captors. One
of the most persistent searchers on the Southern Plains was a thirty-
one-year-old merchant named Marcus Goldbaum. A native of Ger-

many and a butcher by trade, he moved around Kansas, Colorado, New Mexico, and California, occasionally prospecting in Arizona.

In late April 1866, Goldbaum arrived at a Comanche and Kiowa camp in New Mexico, expecting to barter with the Indians for a few days before moving on. The trader soon discovered that the Indians in the village were holding about twenty captives. Goldbaum was deeply troubled by what he saw. Over the next two weeks, he tried his utmost to liberate the prisoners. Perhaps because of his own German roots, he felt "particularly attracted" to a fourteen-year-old German-American boy living with the Comanches. Goldbaum had several conversations with this captive and learned that his name was Rudolph Fischer. The youngster related the details of his kidnapping near Fredericksburg, Texas, nine months earlier. (Rudolph had already lost track of time; he told Goldbaum he'd been with the tribe about two years.) The trader wrote, "To see that boy a slave of the wild Comanches is heart-rending!"

Although Goldbaum perceived Rudolph as a "slave," it's unlikely that the teenager was still a menial of his Comanche owner after nine months with the tribe. Dot Babb became an active warrior in less time than that. Clinton Smith also indicated that his battle training began shortly after he was abducted. However, Goldbaum assumed Rudolph was being mistreated and was determined to get him away from the tribe. He tried everything he could think of to ransom the boy, but the Comanches weren't interested in giving up Rudolph. Before Goldbaum left the Indian camp, he did his best "to provide for the better treatment of the poor boy, by promising the Indians to see the great father and to get presents for them if possible."

Marcus Goldbaum immediately started planning another expedition into Comanche land for the express purpose of rescuing Rudolph. When the boy's father, Gottlieb Fischer, learned about this plan, he offered to put up money for Goldbaum to pay the Comanches if necessary. However, the trader wasn't any more successful on his second attempt. Much of Goldbaum's tale has been lost, and no information has surfaced about what happened during his trip in the summer of 1866. It's possible that the trader wasn't able to find the group that was holding the boy. If he did locate Rudolph, the Comanches may have still been unwilling surrender him. Or maybe Rudolph refused to go. Nonetheless, Goldbaum wasn't ready to quit. He kept searching for the youngster every time he traveled through Comanche territory. Four years would pass before he saw Rudolph again.

The federal Indian agents usually stayed close to their posts, waiting for the tribal representatives to come to them. Occasionally, however, the more intrepid agents went out into the field to visit the Native American camps—and in the process became active searchers for captives. In the summer of 1867, the agent at Santa Fe, Lorenzo Labadi, made a risky trip into Comanche country, taking only six men with him. Labadi believed it was safer to travel with civilians rather than a military escort, perhaps thinking the appearance of soldiers would alarm the Comanches and set off a skirmish. He sent his six employees in different directions, instructing them to invite all the Indians they saw to a council at a place in the Texas Panhandle called Quitaque.

Labadi was pleased with the results. Over seven hundred lodges of the Comanches and Kiowas showed up for the meeting. Fifteen-year-old Rudolph Fischer was with them. Labadi had no trouble identifying him, even though he was dressed in buckskin, his complexion darkened by two years in the sun and his black hair long and matted. The Comanches grudgingly allowed the Indian agent to speak with Rudolph and his fellow captives. Labadi reported that "they seemed afraid of the Indians and the Indians disliked it when they spoke to" him.

During the council, Labadi told the Indians they must give up Rudolph Fischer and all the other captives. They were surprised by his demand. At first they said nothing. Then they withdrew and held a conference among themselves. When they spoke with Labadi again, they assured him, rather cagily, they were willing to stop their raiding and deliver all the captives they were holding. There was one hitch, however. Their main chiefs were away from camp at the time, getting more horses and captives in Texas, and no one could conclude an agreement without their approval. The chiefs were expected to return at the full moon in October. The Comanches and Kiowas promised Labadi they'd deliver their captives at that time.

When Labadi got back to Santa Fe during the last week of August 1867, he reported that his meeting with the Comanches and Kiowas had been successful. He was confident that they would keep their word and give up their captives, including Rudolph Fischer, at the appointed time and place. However, when Labadi returned to Quitaque for the council in the fall, cholera had decimated the village. The Indians had fled, taking their captives with them.

In the latter part of 1868, President-elect Ulysses Grant started outlining a new peace policy toward the nation's native people. As part of his plan, he decided to ask religious organizations to choose the nation's Indian agents, most of whom had previously been military men. On January 25 and 26, 1869, two groups of Quakers met with Grant in Washington. They emphasized the importance of applying Christian principles in dealing with the Native American tribes. Grant reportedly told them, "If you can make Quakers out of the Indians, it will take the fight out of them. Let us have peace." Grant put the pacifist Quakers in charge of the central superintendency of the Indian Office, a region that was home to two of the country's most warlike tribes, the Comanches and the Kiowas. The irony was not lost on the Quakers. They described their mission on the Southern Plains as a "holy experiment."

To head the Kiowa-Comanche agency, the Quakers selected Lawrie Tatum, an Iowa farmer and civic leader in his late forties.[8] Tatum had studied law and had helped runaway slaves escape to freedom, but he had no previous experience working with Native Americans. A portly, avuncular man with a gentle but firm demeanor, he accepted the appointment out of a sense of duty. His job was one of the least enviable in the entire Indian Affairs bureau, for the Kiowas and Comanches were considered unmanageable and were on poor terms with the federal government at the time.

Lawrie Tatum had thought of himself as a pioneer in Iowa, where he was one of the early settlers of Cedar County. Still, he'd never seen anything quite as primitive as the conditions he found at Fort Sill and his new agency in the hinterland of Indian Territory. When he arrived in May 1869, the crude adobe building that would initially house his office was still under construction. The men he met at the military post were as unrefined as the facilities. Progress toward civilization was slow, and Tatum celebrated small victories. He was pleased when the soldiers finally "learned to eat with knives and forks, which were very much in their way at first." He also wrote to his wife, Mary Ann, that Fort Sill had "a very good surgeon," who had "taken off a good many toes the past winter, on account of being frozen."

The dedicated public servant who would later title his memoir *Our Red Brothers* was genuinely interested in getting to know the Plains Indians. Tatum was especially impressed by their hospitality, and he wrote a warm description of his visit to a Native American village with his interpreter, Matthew Leeper:

> We went to the lodge of the chief, who sent one of his wives to take care of our horses; another wife prepared some fuel for the fire in the tent, and a third wife prepared our supper. . . . She did not get nervous by having us sitting on the bed about four inches high on the opposite side of the fire watching her. When she had it cooked, she placed a board on the laps of her husband and visitors, spread her cleanest blanket on it, and placed the provision before us, and we had a sumptuous meal. Just as we got through eating an invitation came from another chief to eat with him. . . . So we accepted the kind invitation, supped a little more coffee, and partook of enough food to show that we were not above eating with him also.[9]

Not all of Tatum's encounters with Native Americans were that pleasant. Furthermore, his Quaker superiors in the Indian Office didn't fully appreciate what he was up against. They told him to make sure that "every member of each tribe under his care" who had "arrived at years of understanding" was "told the saving truths of the gospel." Tatum's Comanche and Kiowa charges were tough, independent men and women who had their own religious beliefs and were hardly amenable to friendly persuasion. He referred to them as "poor, ignorant creatures." They called him "Bald Head."

Of all the challenges that Tatum faced, none weighed more heavily on his mind than recovering the Indians' captives. He later recalled, with Victorian primness, "It was distressing to think of those savages having white captives, and especially women." Some parents told Tatum that "they would rather see their children killed than carried off in that way, and endure so much suspense and uncertainty of ever seeing them again." At first Tatum offered to pay the Indians $100 for each captive they brought to him. He later changed his mind, believing that this policy encouraged them to take more children. He started demanding that the Indians deliver their captives without ransom.

Tatum's only real bargaining chip was the government's rations. Every two weeks, the Indians came to his agency to receive beef, bacon, flour, cornmeal, coffee, sugar, salt, soap, and tobacco. Each chief would divide the goods among the women of his band, who sat on the ground in a circle around him. The Comanches and Kiowas were becoming increasingly dependent on these luxuries, which had been alien to their way of life only a few years earlier. Applying his legal training, Lawrie Tatum concluded that the Native Americans of his agency had forfeited their rights to annuities under the Treaty of Medicine Lodge by their frequent raids into Texas. He announced that he would cut off rations to those groups that refused to bring in all their captives.

Tatum also asked a friendly Apache chief named Pacer to go to the Indian camps and see if he could learn anything about the captives. Pacer inquired among some of the Comanches and Kiowas, but he didn't bother trying to locate the Quahadas. He knew it wouldn't do any good, for they were angry with practically everyone—the Texans, the army, Tatum, even their fellow Comanches who chose to cooperate with the whites. They were also the ones holding the most captives. Scornful of those Indians who lived on the reservation and the Quaker agent who treated them like wayward children, the Quahadas stayed mostly on the plains of the Texas Panhandle, far from the Fort Sill region. They were beyond the Indian agent's reach, and that rankled him. He knew he couldn't negotiate with them unless he had them at a disadvantage. Month after month, Lawrie Tatum waited for that opportunity.

In the fall of 1870, Marcus Goldbaum finally located Rudolph Fischer in a Comanche camp. The German-American captive was a strapping young man of eighteen, hard to distinguish from the other warriors. Goldbaum spoke with Rudolph and assured him that he would help him get away from the Comanches and return to his family. To the trader's astonishment, the young man refused to go with him. It was uncertain whether Rudolph's stubbornness resulted "from fear of being recaptured, or whether roaming life had gained such a charm for him that he preferred it to rejoining his parents and friends." Another factor may have influenced Rudolph's decision to stay: by then he was believed to have taken a Comanche wife.

Although Goldbaum was unsuccessful, his discovery led to a renewed effort to bring Rudolph Fischer back home. Lawrie Tatum's superiors in the Indian Office instructed him to ask about the young man when the Comanches came to his agency for rations. In March 1871, Tatum reported that a white youth matching Rudolph's description was living with one of the Comanche bands. However, Tatum added, "They say that he is married among them and not willing to leave." Tatum then put a thorny question to his bosses: "Will the department order that he be taken without his consent if it can be done without being likely to cause difficulty with the Indians? I think it would be best to remove him from the Indians if practicable, whether he is willing or not."

Rudolph Fischer presented a quandary for Tatum and the Quakers. Was it their duty, either moral or diplomatic, to rescue a captive who clearly didn't want to be redeemed? They referred the question all the way up to H. R. Clum, the acting commissioner of Indian Affairs in Washington. He waffled on the issue, replying:

> It is not perhaps advisable to take any step for compelling the young man against his will to leave his present associations, but if it be possible, he should be seen and persuaded to return to his relatives and friends in Texas. Should the only obstacle in the way of his return be the objection or unwillingness of the Indians to part with him, a demand positive and firm, should be made upon them, to deliver him up, as also any other captive in their possession.[10]

Clum also advised Lawrie Tatum to visit the Comanche band that was holding Rudolph "and by his utmost endeavors cause the captives to be released." Tatum's heart must have sunk when he read those words. What did his superiors in Washington think he'd spent the previous two years trying to do?

Clum's next instructions were even more impracticable, revealing the vast gulf that separated those who worked in Washington from those who actually dealt with Native Americans on the frontier. He forbade Tatum to offer the Indians any ransom for captives, not even "presents," the traditional token of goodwill in Indian-white diplomacy. Instead, he ordered the agent to demand the captives' release immediately and unconditionally. Nor would he allow Tatum to exchange Indian prisoners being held by the army for white captives. Essentially, he left the agent with no tools for negotiation except the withholding of rations—goods that the more hostile bands didn't especially want, anyway.

Tatum's report had failed to specify which Comanches were hold-ing the captives. Clum made one concession: "If they are distant and not likely soon to come in, and it be impossible for the Agent to go, it would be well to dispatch some trusty and influential Chief of the friendly Comanches living upon the reservation to effect the object desired."

Tatum didn't think that plan would work. He pointed out, "I tried several months ago to get chiefs to look for captives but have found none to be depended upon." However, he managed to engage a reliable envoy who was willing to venture into hostile territory and look for captives. This searcher was a Mexican whose birth name was Vincente de Demencio; but for most of his life, he had gone by the alias George Caboon, or sometimes by his adoptive name, George Chisholm. Caboon had been kidnapped by Comanches as a child and raised with the tribe. The trader Jesse Chisholm eventually bought him from his captors, adopting him as a son. Caboon still spoke the Comanches' language. He'd served as an interpreter for his brother, William E. Chisholm, a trader like their father.[11]

Lawrie Tatum didn't expect Caboon to be able to rescue the ab-ducted children single-handedly. Instead, Caboon's assignment was to visit the Comanche villages and surreptitiously find out which captives the different groups were holding. He planned to travel across the plains for about three months, spending enough time in each camp to quietly take inventory of the captives without putting the Comanches on guard.

George Caboon's journey during the summer of 1871 was suc-cessful in achieving its limited purpose. In August he returned to Tatum's agency and reported that the Quahada Comanches were holding three white captives. He was unable to learn their English names, but they were almost certainly Adolph Korn, Temple Friend, and a boy named John Valentine Maxey, who had been captured in Montague County, Texas, on September 5, 1870. In addition, Ca-boon learned that Mowway's group of Kotsotekas still had "the little captive taken last winter by the New Mexico Apaches," Clinton

Smith. In summarizing Caboon's report, Tatum noted: "There is another young man who is with the Quahadas a part of the time and occasionally with some of the other bands of Comanches. He is not willing to come to the Agency." This captive was apparently Rudolph Fischer, by then nineteen years old.

Tatum knew that the odds of recovering captives from the Quahadas were slim. He wrote, "This band of Comanches have never been into the Agency and I can have no control over them while this remains to be the case." The Indian agent also understood the urgency of rescuing the four young, impressionable white boys. He observed, "All the other captives have been with the Indians several years, are nearly or quite grown and from what I can learn are unwilling to leave the Indians." Tatum realized it was critical to recover Adolph Korn, Temple Friend, John Valentine Maxey, and Clinton Smith before those boys became as Indianized as Rudolph Fischer. Time was not on his side.

On May 12, 1871, Lawrie Tatum experienced one of the most galling incidents of his career, a confrontation that would prey on his mind for many months to come. The Kotsoteka Comanche chief Mowway (Shaking Hand) appeared unexpectedly at Tatum's office with several of his tribesmen. They had come to collect their annuity goods. Mowway was a striking figure with an angular face, wide mouth, and narrow eyes. Lawrie Tatum was pleasantly surprised to see the chief. He generally liked Mowway, whom he later described as "one of my best and most reliable of the Comanches." Mowway was the leader of "one of the most roving bands of the Comanches," and this was the first time he had reported to the agency in more than a year.

Tatum took the opportunity to ask whether Mowway had seen any captives among the Indians on the plains. Without hesitation the chief admitted that two months earlier, one of his own men had purchased a white boy captured in Texas by some New Mexico Apaches. From the description of the boy and the estimated time of the abduction, the agent knew that the captive was most likely one of the Smith brothers.

Tatum's welcoming expression vanished. In a fit of uncharacteristic anger, he told Mowway, "You cannot have the annuity goods for your people until that boy is delivered to me."

Mowway, taken by surprise, became just as indignant. He said, "The Comanches did not steal this boy. We only traded with the Apaches for him. We should not be required to give him up." For some time, Mowway had been trying to cooperate with the white people, but their way of thinking perturbed him. They spoke of ownership rights, so they should recognize that the Comanches had purchased this captive, fair and square. Bald Head had no right to take a man's property without paying for it.

Tatum stood firm, refusing to give them any goods that day. Mowway and his men were seething when they left the agency. As they rode off to their camp, one of the Comanches turned around and taunted the Indian agent, saying, "We will not bring in the boy."

Afterward, Lawrie Tatum couldn't stop brooding over his failure to recover a captive who'd been practically within his grasp. The next day, he discussed the matter with the friendly Comanche chief Tosawa (Silver Brooch). Tatum asked him to go visit Mowway and try to rescue the boy. Tosawa didn't think that was possible. He accurately predicted that Mowway would immediately return to the plains. Whoever this white boy was, he was already out of reach.

Later, Tatum wrote to Henry Smith to let him know that he thought he'd located one of his sons among the Comanches. When Henry learned that Mowway had been allowed to leave the agency without surrendering the boy, he exploded. He complained bitterly to Texas governor Edmund J. Davis: "Mr. Tatum allowed this chief to depart simply refusing him annuity goods, why did he not retain him as Hostage, until the captive was delivered up." When the Kiowas came to the agency that summer, they reported that Mowway had been traveling with them, and that he had reconsidered and decided to bring the white boy to Tatum after all. As the weeks passed, however, that never happened.

In desperation, the pacifist Indian agent eventually advocated the use of military force if necessary to recover the elusive boy in Mowway's group. He was also convinced that coercion was necessary to make the renegade Indians give up raiding and come live on the reservation under his care. General Sherman noted that the Quaker agent was "more fully convinced . . . that his humane efforts have been fruitless, and he now not only consents to, but advises extreme measures."[12] On August 4, 1871, Tatum wrote to Cols. Benjamin Grierson and Ranald Mackenzie, "I wish to have the captive recovered if at all practicable, and returned to its father whom I suppose to be Henry M. Smith." Throughout the remainder of 1871, Tatum would make "repeated but ineffectual efforts to procure the captive boy."[13]

Lawrie Tatum eventually obtained the release of twenty-six captive women and children, something that the private searchers hadn't managed to do. While the epic journeys of determined relatives such as Leonard Friend and adventurous traders such as Marcus Goldbaum and George Caboon lend a touch of romance to the story of the search for captives, the fact remains that they almost never recovered any stolen children. (Two exceptions were Brit Johnson and Jesse Chisholm, who reportedly ransomed several captives.) Even Tatum wasn't able to recover the captives through diplomacy alone. Most of them were finally released as a direct result of the army's campaign against the Comanches during the fall of 1872. In the end, the type of military action that Tatum reluctantly supported would prove to be as effective as it was ruthless. The federal government had bullied most of the Southern Plains Indians into complying with the Treaty of Medicine Lodge in 1867; between 1872 and 1875, Sherman's army would force the stragglers to obey.

Chapter Eight

Death on
the Red River

B y the early fall of 1872, those Comanches who still refused to walk the white man's road saw no reason why they couldn't continue their way of life forever. They hadn't seen any soldiers or Texas Rangers pursuing them as they made their way across the Texas Panhandle. They were far from Fort Sill, with its despised pauper's reservation and the annoying agent, Bald Head. The summer buffalo hunts had been successful. So had the horse-stealing raids the previous spring. These last Comanche holdouts had everything they needed to sustain their way of life, and that didn't include white people's houses or churches or schools for their children.

By September they had established their camp in a restful valley along the North Fork of the Red River. In the shade of large cottonwoods and oaks, they set up their tepees, which spread out several miles along the winding stream. The largest village was Mowway's camp on the south bank of the river, consisting of 262 lodges. Smaller camps were scattered nearby. Knee-high grass covered the prairie, providing ample grazing for the large herds of horses.

People from every Comanche division were staying in Mowway's village that fall. Among the young men lounging, eating, telling stories, and playing practical jokes were Adolph Korn and Clinton Smith. The Comanches' youngest white captive, eight-year-old John Valentine Maxey, was also staying with Mowway's people. Temple

Friend was in one of the camps, and Rudolph Fischer was probably in the vicinity, too.

Farther upstream was the village of Paruacoom (Bull Bear), a Quahada chief. Mowway and Paruacoom often traveled and hunted together, even though they didn't always see eye to eye. Mowway was tired of fighting; he simply wanted to enjoy his roving life and stay out of the cavalry's way. In fact, he had left for Washington that month to talk peace with the Great Father in his big white house. Paruacoom, on the other hand, was a war leader from the traditional mold. Described as "a great bear of a man" with curly hair, he had never attended a peace council or signed a treaty. He believed that the Comanches should fight until either they or the white invaders were finally conquered.

In this season of plenty, the Comanches were busy preparing for winter. Around the tepees, the women strung buffalo meat from scaffolds. They sliced the flesh into very thin strips so that it would dry quickly in the autumn sun. The women scraped and tanned the hides to make thick robes for their families. Some of the men were still out hunting.

They'd been lucky enough to find a large supply of grapes near the camps. Although the Comanches were mostly meat eaters, they liked to vary their diets with wild fruits and nuts. About seven miles downstream from Mowway's village, McClellan Creek emptied into the river. Along its banks grew thick vines loaded with grapes.

On September 29, 1872, a Comanche mother and her youngest son left home to pick grapes. The air felt warm and slightly breezy on their faces, and the sky was deep blue, with small patches of broken clouds. The mother and son rode their mounts several miles up McClellan Creek and stopped. They got off and thrashed the vines, then gathered the ripe grapes that fell to the ground. After they'd depleted the lower vines, the boy climbed a tree to reach those higher up. From his vantage point, he could gaze at the open countryside for miles around. What he saw made him freeze. In the distance, a long column of men in blue coats was crossing the prairie like an enormous serpent, heading straight toward them. The boy shouted to his mother as he scrambled down the tree. They jumped on their horses and started back toward camp. Their packs bounced all the way home, leaving a trail of purple grapes for the soldiers to follow.

Mowway had been away from his people's village for several weeks. Earlier that month, he'd gone to Leeper's Creek near the Wichita Agency in Indian Territory for a peace conference. At the meeting, the Indians told the federal commissioner that they weren't ready to come live on the reservation. Mowway said, "When the Indians in here are treated better than we are outside, it will be time enough to come in." Tabenanaka, who had once been Banc Babb's chief, was even blunter: "I would rather stay out on the plains and eat dung than come in on such conditions."

On September 26, Mowway boarded a train at Atoka, Indian Territory, bound for Washington, D.C. He was part of a multitribal delegation that had been invited to meet with President Grant and the commissioner of Indian Affairs. The Indian delegates traveled in a private car so that their fellow passengers from the plains region, whose ire had been fueled by tales of Indian raids, wouldn't harass them during the trip.

While he was away, Mowway had left one of the headmen, Kaiwotche, in charge of his people's village. Shortly after noon on September 29, Kaiwotche headed out on a mule to look around and make sure everything was all right. He followed the route that the mother and her son had taken, traveling twelve miles up McClellan Creek. He was returning to camp that afternoon when he caught a glimpse of the soldiers. By then they were approaching at full gallop. Goading his mule, he tried to get home to alert the villagers, but the warning would come too late. For one terrible half hour that afternoon, President Grant's peace policy was suspended.[1]

The advancing formation of soldiers looked endless: seven officers, 215 enlisted men, and nine Tonkawa scouts. Their commander was Col. Ranald S. Mackenzie, a thirty-two-year-old New Yorker who had graduated at the top of his class at West Point. Ulysses S. Grant called him "the most promising young officer in the Army." Ranald Mackenzie was on a difficult mission. For two months, he'd been riding across the plains of the Texas Panhandle and eastern New Mexico, trying to find and punish Native Americans whom his boss, General Sherman, considered "hostile"—that is, any Indians still living off the reservation. It was the army's duty to put an end to their wandering and raiding.

The Comanches living along the North Fork of the Red River had been enjoying the bounty of several successful raids. In June a young man named Tenebeka (Gets to Be a Middle-aged Man) and a few of his friends had daringly stolen fifty-four horses and mules from the corral at Fort Sill, while the army guard was taking shelter from a thunderstorm. The Comanches also had forty-three mules taken from a wagon train they'd attacked between San Antonio and El Paso the previous April. So far they'd stayed out of Mackenzie's path, and his expedition against them had been entirely uneventful.

At about one o'clock on the afternoon of September 29, his soldiers stopped to rest and eat some wild grapes they'd found along McClellan Creek. There, one of the Tonkawas discovered two fresh trails. One was made by two horses, the other by a mule. Mackenzie's men got back on their mounts and followed the tracks at a quick gait. Each time they lost the trail, they looked for the grapes, which led them all the way to Mowway's village.

Around four o'clock in the afternoon, the Comanches noticed a cloud of dust forming. Unable to see what was causing it, they assumed their hunters were chasing buffalo nearby. It was a lazy time of day in camp, and no one felt motivated to investigate. The prairie surrounding Mowway's village was deceptively open. With only a few patches of trees to break the sight lines, the Comanches could see tiny features on the horizon miles away. However, the knobby ridges nearby were high enough to hide the soldiers swiftly descending on them.

They were caught unprepared. The young boys minding the

horses on the outskirts of camp suddenly heard the roar of hooves and saw four columns of soldiers only half a mile away, charging the village. One company of cavalrymen started racing straight toward the boys. They tried to hurry the hundreds of horses to their camp for the fighting men to use. Mackenzie's troops were on them in no time. They charged right through the clusters of tepees at full speed. Then they fanned out, chasing the panicked villagers. Some Comanches fled on horseback or tried to find cover in the brush and ravines. Others, including women, grabbed bows and arrows, desperately trying to defend the village.

Clinton Smith had just stepped outside his tepee to start a fire when a volley of gunfire startled him. He looked around and saw smoke rising in the clear air at the end of the village. He called to his father, Tosacowadi: "Get up quick! Something is happening in camp." Tosacowadi rushed out of the tepee, clutching his gun. His wives were close behind him. He peered in the distance and hollered to Clinton, "This is an attack by white men!" Then he told everyone in his family to run for safety. One of his wives picked up her baby and headed for the river. Clinton's gray mule was staked nearby. Tosacowadi leaped on it. He grabbed his son, Monewostuki, and pulled the boy up behind him. Then he stuck out his foot and yelled for Clinton to climb on, too. The frightened mule took off but didn't get far. In his haste, Tosacowadi had forgotten to untie the animal. The mule jerked and fell, throwing all three riders into a heap. Tosacowadi sprang to his feet. He cut the rope. He and his two sons got back on the mule and fled.

The whole village was thrown into a frenzy of flashes, smoke, bloodshed, gunshots, shouts, and screams. Soldiers appeared from every direction. Clinton said they were "literally pumping lead into our badly demoralized camp." Tosacowadi finally gave up on the overburdened mule. He freed the terrified animal with a yell. Then he and his sons ran about four hundred yards to get out of the heat of battle. In the commotion, Tosacowadi deflected a bullet with his shield, causing it to strike his hip. The wound wasn't bad enough to cripple him.

Clinton and Monewostuki followed him, stumbling over dead horses in their path.

Adolph Korn had managed to jump on a horse and was shooting arrows at Mackenzie's men. Clinton recalled that Adolph never ran from the fight and "left several dead men to show for his brave stand."[2] While Tosacowadi and his two sons were escaping up the river, they saw Adolph's horse shot down in front of them. Adolph took cover in the bushes. He squatted there, waiting. As soon as Ranald Mackenzie drew near, Adolph shot an arrow that pierced the colonel's blue army jacket but somehow missed his flesh.

The Comanches in Mowway's village sent runners to the nearby camps to alert their neighbors and get reinforcements. One of the messengers was a white boy, eight-year-old John Valentine Maxey. As soon as the attack began, he mounted his pony and rode off to warn the other Comanches in the valley about the soldiers. Meanwhile, some of the Comanche men and boys circled around a small ridge, from which they watched the fight in terror. Clinton Smith, normally imperturbable, was enraged by what he saw that afternoon. He reported, "It seems that the soldiers tried to make a massacre of this attack, for they killed squaws, babies, warriors, and old white headed men."

The heaviest fighting took place near a long water hole in the river. About seventy-five Comanche men were trapped there, shooting at the soldiers from beneath the bank. Some of the warriors jumped into the water and took cover behind the long grass hanging from the edge of the stream. It was hard for them to hit their enemies, who were crouched in gulches and hidden from view. From time to time, a single Comanche horseman would rush the attackers, ride in a circle, and then return to the embankment, causing some of the soldiers to retreat momentarily. Twice a group of warriors tried to charge, but both times the cavalrymen drove them back, inflicting heavy losses. One warrior who made a run at the soldiers on foot was killed by a friend trying to give him cover. The Comanches threw the bodies of their dead comrades into the deep water, probably to save them from being scalped. During the combat at the water hole, the cavalrymen were startled to find a crippled Comanche woman hiding in a buffalo wallow very close to them. When they realized she was unarmed, they made signs for her to lie down and stay put until the shooting stopped.

Upstream, Paruacoom and his people heard the gunfire. The brawny Quahada chief shouted to his warriors in a booming voice: "Get all your good horses! Mount up! Get ready to fight!" Decades later his followers could still hear their chief's voice, which they said sounded "like the roar of a buffalo bull when angry." One of the young men preparing to lead the Quahadas' charge was a future chief, Quanah Parker, then in his early twenties. A shaman encouraged him and his cohorts, saying: "Many times you walk many miles to find an enemy. Today they are right before you." Quanah asked the medicine man to help make him invincible. Then Paruacoom, Quanah, and the Quahadas (who may have included Quanah's friend, Rudolph Fischer) gave the war cry and took off downstream.

They found the soldiers crouched in ravines, firing at the trapped Comanches along the river. At that distance, it would be hard for the reinforcements to attack the cavalrymen with bows and arrows. Paruacoom wasn't discouraged. He preferred hand-to-hand combat, anyway. To fire up the younger, inexperienced men, the chief made a short speech. He said, "When I was a young man like you, I met things straight ahead. I fight! I want you young men to do the same. Be brave!"[3] They charged straight toward the soldiers. The army's bullets cut down several of them, and before long the others were forced to pull back. The battle was lost.

Around the village, soldiers were trying to flush out the Comanches who were hiding. They were about to fire into a thicket when a woman came out waving a white flag. Ranald Mackenzie, through his interpreter, asked: "What do you want?"

She replied, "We do not want to be shot."

He told her, "Leave your weapons in the thicket. Come out and surrender to me. You will not be hurt."

A large group of women and children crawled out of the bushes with their hands raised. They surrendered to a captivity that would last seven months.

After only half an hour, Mowway's village was quiet once again. Campfires smoldered, meals sat half eaten, and strips of buffalo meat still hung from the drying racks, as if the villagers had all gone inside their tepees for an afternoon nap. In fact, the only Comanches who remained in camp were wounded, captured, or dead. Ranald Mackenzie's guide, Henry W. Strong, remembered that the fallen Comanches "were pretty thick on the ground."

Before long Mackenzie's Tonkawa scouts, who hated the Comanches, "were having a good time scalping and plunging their knives into the bodies," according to Strong. When Mackenzie ordered them to stop, they "said some very uncomplimentary things to him." One Tonkawa indignantly blurted out, "What fur you no lette me scalp heem Comanche?" The Tonkawas claimed they took eighty scalps that day, which was probably an exaggeration. Mackenzie's troops recovered the bodies of twenty-three dead Comanche men, but the colonel acknowledged that the actual number killed was probably higher. (He didn't mention how many women and children died in the battle.) The Comanches later reported fifty-two fatalities. Among the dead were the acting chief of the village, Kaiwotche, and his wife.

Mackenzie's men poured into the camp. Famished from their long ride, they helped themselves to some of the Comanches' dried buffalo meat. Sgt. John B. Charlton noticed a different type of meat of a lighter color on one rope and ate some of it. He handed it to the chief of the Tonkawa scouts and asked him if it was pork. The Tonkawa tasted it, and said, "Maybe so him white man." The Comanches weren't cannibals, and Sergeant Charlton must not have realized that the poker-faced Tonkawa was pulling his leg. He doubled over and vomited.

A few of the cavalrymen were taunting and baiting a blind woman, who made anguished, futile efforts to slash them with a knife as she cradled the body of her slain son. While the captured women and children looked on, the soldiers destroyed their homes, setting fire to the tepees. They also burned the Comanches' clothing and all their personal possessions, except for a few choice buffalo robes that the officers kept for themselves. The Comanches watched their store of food for the winter go up in flames.

Exactly what else happened in Mowway's camp that afternoon will never be known. According to Comanche lore, the soldiers plundered the tepees, murdered the wounded, and raped the captured women. Ranald Mackenzie, on the other hand, claimed that any injuries to the women and children were accidental, and that they received "the best care possible." Regardless of whose story is closer to the truth, the battle was a severe blow to the Comanches' morale. The commissioner of Indian Affairs later referred to Mackenzie's attack on Mowway's village as "righteous retribution for long courses of cruel and cowardly outrages."[4] Righteous or not, it was certainly effective. The free-roaming life the Comanches had known for as long as any of them could remember would vanish in less than three years.

Once the soldiers and their prisoners were gone, the Comanches who had escaped crept back into Mowway's burning village. Those who had been separated from their kin when the battle broke out searched anxiously for family members among the dead and wounded. Soon the mourning wails of the widows began. Clinton Smith walked to the riverbank where the heaviest fighting had occurred and was shocked by what he saw: "So many were killed and wounded in the water that it was red from hole to hole with blood." He recalled, "After what I had seen that day I was mad all over, and was willing to risk anything to get even with the soldiers."

By dusk men from the scattered Comanche camps had regrouped, determined to rescue their captives. That evening they headed for the army camp in the sand hills about two miles away. From a distance, they could see their women and children in the center of Mackenzie's camp, closely guarded by the soldiers. After darkness set in, the Comanches came within one hundred fifty yards of the army camp and began riding in wide circles around it, whooping and firing pistols. The soldiers returned the fire. Clinton Smith, who rode with the warriors, claimed that a few of the Comanche prisoners were able to escape during the confusion. He said, "Some of the Indians crawled out between the wagon spokes, and some even crawled through the soldiers' legs in getting away."

The Comanches failed to rescue their captured friends and relatives that night. However, they had better luck recovering their stock. The army had taken all of their loose horses and mules and corralled them in a sinkhole about a mile away from Mowway's village. The Tonkawas who were guarding them had rolled into their blankets and fallen asleep. Around midnight Clinton and the Comanches rushed the herd. The animals stampeded. The Comanches took many of the horses, including those of the Tonkawa guards. The following night, they attacked Mackenzie's next camp, about eighteen miles away, and recovered most of their remaining horses.

But this was a small victory. Ranald Mackenzie was making his way across the plains with 124 of their women and children. Eight would die during the march. The colonel sent the 116 surviving Comanche prisoners to Fort Concho, which he thought was the military post best suited for their long confinement.

The Quahadas had often sent taunting messages to Lawrie Tatum at Fort Sill, claiming that they wouldn't report to his agency and shake hands with him unless the soldiers came out to their camps and whipped them. The time for hand-shaking had finally arrived.

In the days after the battle, the Comanches were inconsolable. Every night the widows and mothers withdrew from the camp, gashing their faces, arms, and breasts with knives and wailing for their dead. The men grieved over their failure to rescue their friends and relatives taken by Colonel Mackenzie. They had no idea what the soldiers would do to them or whether they would ever see them again.

For the boy captives, life became increasingly difficult over the next six weeks. Antiwhite feelings ran high in the tribe, especially among the Comanche women who had lost husbands and sons. They made threats to kill the white boys if they ever caught them outside of camp. Clinton Smith's Comanche mother warned him to be on guard if these women approached him while he was alone in the woods. His father, Tosacowadi, even advised him to shoot anyone who refused to keep away from him after fair warning.

Before long the white boys faced another threat, one that terrified them even more than the vengeful widows. Indian visitors to their camp began to relay a message that the army would not release the women and children prisoners until the Comanches gave up all of their captives. That rumor was true. Both the army and the Indian agency had agreed that the Comanche prisoners would remain at Fort Concho until every captive was returned.

Captives had always been commonplace in the Comanche villages, but now their presence divided the tribe. Clinton Smith said that his father, Tosacowadi, put the question to his group and "could not get a one to say that they would" take the boy captives to Fort Sill. Nor was Clinton willing to go. He considered himself an Indian, and he had no desire to leave Tosacowadi and his Comanche brothers, not even if his departure would help the tribe as a whole. However, the army was holding 116 Comanche people, and all the tribe had to do to get them back was surrender a handful of stolen children and a few horses. There was no other choice. The captives would have to be hauled in.

Tosacowadi had once announced that when he died, his sons Monewostuki and Backecacho (Clinton Smith) would inherit all of his horses. "Sometimes I thought he would never die," Clinton joked. However, Tosacowadi did die sooner than anyone expected, from the hip wound he received in the battle.[5] His grieving family wrapped his body in a red blanket. They carried him up a hillside, placing the corpse on a scaffold to protect it from wild animals. The wives and children laid Tosacowadi's quiver and bow by his side. Then they departed. Clinton was devastated. He wrote, "With a heavy heart and bowed head I followed the wailing squaws back to camp, until my grief became too great to silently bear when I, too, joined in the wailing."

The boy also felt vulnerable, for there was no longer anyone to protect him from those Comanches who wanted to turn him over to Bald Head. One day an Indian showed up at camp with some tinned fruit and peach brandy. He told Clinton that his father, Henry Smith, had been to Fort Sill and had sent these gifts to him. He tried to get Clinton to go there and see him. Clinton refused to accept the goods. Still mourning Tosacowadi, he said, "My father was killed. I have no father."

Another time, two Indians lured Clinton away from camp on the pretense of helping him look for his horses. They hadn't gone far before one of the men pulled a pistol on the boy. After disarming him, they made him travel with them toward Fort Sill. During the night, he managed to escape and go back to his family.

The third attempt was successful. Some Comanches told Clinton that they would take him to Fort Sill and pretend to exchange him for some of their prisoners being held at Fort Concho. After the Comanche women and children were released, they said, he could steal some horses from the white people and return to them. They even promised to make him a chief. Clinton couldn't resist that offer. The boy thought it would be easy to fool the whites and soon resume his normal life on the plains. He didn't realize that his days as a Comanche were over.

Mowway still didn't know that his village had been destroyed. On the afternoon the battle was fought, he was attending a formal council with several other chiefs and government officials at the Everett House, a hotel on Fourth Street in St. Louis. The following day, the Indian delegation toured the city, then proceeded by train that night to Cincinnati, where they toured the Annual Industrial Exposition.

Mowway arrived in Washington, D.C., on the afternoon of October 2, 1872, with a group of "fifty-two scalpers," as the *Washington Evening Star* described them.[6] It was the largest and most important

Indian delegation that had ever visited the city. Members of these delegations usually stayed in comfortable suites at an upscale hotel called the Washington House, conveniently situated on the northwest corner of Third Street and Pennsylvania Avenue.

Two days after their arrival, the Indians toured the capitol. Some of them went out on the dome. Looking out over the city's whitestone buildings, straight-lined avenues, and congested walkways, a far cry from the unobstructed prairie they loved, they must have realized more than ever that they were dealing with an alien people who could never accept their way of thinking.

Many of the Indians had their photographs taken by Alexander Gardner, Matthew Brady's associate. They were given large silver medals and were invited to see other sights of the city, including the printing plant where the government produced paper money. A Comanche chief named Quirtsquip (Chewing Elk) joked, "They could give me some if they wanted to." The Indians didn't enjoy Washington, however, finding it noisy and crowded. A young Yamparika Comanche chief named Howea (Gap in the Woods) is said to have tried to count all the white people he saw, astonished by their numbers.

Mowway and the Indian delegation met briefly with President Grant and four members of his cabinet in the East Room of the White House on October 11, 1872. One by one, the Indians shook hands with the president. Newspapermen described them as dressed in "full savage costume, with their faces heavily painted." The president was not impressed by their native finery. In blunt terms, he explained that the government was trying to advance them in civilization. The white people were becoming so numerous that the Indians could no longer lead a nomadic life. They must settle in one place. The sooner they understood that, the better for them and their children. President Grant told them he had no more to say except through the secretary of the Interior. The Indians were not invited to respond. They left the White House after examining the gilded rooms.

The delegation also held a series of meetings with Francis J.

Walker, the commissioner of Indian Affairs. He told them that they must establish their homes within ten miles of Fort Sill by the middle of December. Otherwise, they would be considered "hostile." The Indians listened impassively. They still didn't know about Mackenzie's attack on their people, but they had seen how the army treated "hostiles." One of the chiefs assured the commissioner, "We came in to do what our Great Father wants us to do." However, the Indians had been admonished in this manner before and didn't really take the commissioner's speech seriously. They were probably bored. So was one journalist, whose attention was easily diverted. He reported:

> While the conference was in progress one of the dusky maidens amused herself by sticking a pin in the end of a stick and occasionally "prodding" one of the warriors near her. It is said that this is a delicate way of making love in some Indian tribes, and the fact that the warrior did not appear to be annoyed by the prodding would seem to give color to the statement.[7]

By then a telegram describing Colonel Mackenzie's victory over the Comanches in the Texas Panhandle had already appeared in newspapers across the country. Commissioner Walker decided to delay announcing the news to the delegation, as "it was not desired to stampede the Indians" while they still had business to conduct. It was during Walker's final meeting with the Indians on October 24 that he told them what had happened on the North Fork of the Red River. Walker read the telegram announcing that the soldiers had killed twenty-three Comanche men and captured their women and children. The Comanches in the room were shocked and grief stricken by the news. Walker warned them, "Those who remain outside the reservation may be similarly treated."

The following day, Mowway and the Indians left Washington for Baltimore. From there they proceeded to Philadelphia and then to New York, where they had to wait a few days for their connecting train.

In the interim, they roamed the streets of Manhattan, shopped for trinkets on Broadway, and studied the wildlife in Central Park. Most of the city's sights "they viewed with positive disdain." Everywhere they went, New Yorkers gawked at them. According to the local press, the Southern Plains delegates were "more to the prairie born than any of their race" than the people of the city had seen in some time. Therefore, they "excited rather more curiosity than cosmopolitans have recently manifested in the terrible race of tomahawkers." Most of the Indians were "profoundly indifferent to the staring." Some "preserved their equanimity with a horrible scowl and a malicious silence."

The Indians stayed at the luxurious Grand Central Hotel on the southwest corner of West Third Street and Broadway. The other guests were startled when they stepped out in the hotel corridor and saw men in buckskin and feathers and women in blankets and beads. Inquisitive New Yorkers hung around the hotel, some climbing the stairs to the fourth floor to get a better look at the "mild savages." One well-dressed man tried to steal an arrow from the quiver of Esihabit, Dot Babb's rescuer. The thief nearly set off a row with the Indians and quickly gave it back.

On October 30, the delegation visited the Church of Our Savior on East Twenty-fifth Street, where the Episcopal Board of Missions was meeting. The Indians were decked out in feathers and paint; some carried their arrows and tomahawks into the sanctuary. The Episcopalians, excited to have such exotic potential converts in their midst, serenaded them with the missionary hymn "From Greenland's Icy Mountains":

> *From many an ancient river,*
> *From many a palmy plain,*
> *They call us to deliver*
> *Their land from error's chain.*
> *Can we, whose souls are lighted*
> *With wisdom from on high,*
> *Can we to men benighted*
> *The lamp of life deny?*

Louis Jacob Korn, Adolph Korn's step-father, was a small, gentle patriarch, but he ensured that his children followed a strict regimen of hard work and religious observance.

PHOTOGRAPH COURTESY OF PEGGY LAVERTY.

The Korn family, like the other settlers of the Texas Hill Country, lived miserably in a primitive log cabin such as this one, built near Castell in 1869.

PHOTOGRAPH BY GLENN HADELER.

The Comanche-German peace council of 1847 established a brie[f] rare period of warm relations between the Penateka Comanches and the German settlers in the Texas Hill Country. Painting by Lucy Marschall, daughter of German negotiator John Meuseback 1928. COURTESY OF GILLESPIE COUNTY HISTORICAL SOCIETY, FREDERICKSBURG, TEXAS.

Scenes of the last major peace conference between the Southern Plains Indians and the U.S. government at Medicine Lodge, Kansas, as depicted by artist John Dare Howland in Harper's Weekly, *November 16, 1867.* COURTESY OF PRINTS AND PHOTOGRAPHS DIVISION, THE LIBRARY OF CONGRESS, WASHINGTON, D.C. USZ62-92503.

A Comanche camp in the early 1870s, photographed by William S. Soule.
PHOTOGRAPH COURTESY OF PRINTS AND PHOTOGRAPHS COLLECTION, THE CENTER FOR
AMERICAN HISTORY, UNIVERSITY OF TEXAS AT AUSTIN. CN 00478.

*John Friend's notice concerning the abduction of his son, Temple, and Minnie
Caudle from Legion Valley appeared in the* Daily Austin Republican *on June 1,
1868.* COURTESY OF CENTER FOR AMERICAN HISTORY, UNIVERSITY OF TEXAS AT AUSTIN.

Taken by the Indians !

TAKEN from my house by the Indians, in
Legion valley, Llano county, Texas, on
Wednesday, Feb. 5th, 1868, my son LEE
TEMPLE FRIEND, aged eight years, black
eyes, light hair and fair complexion; also,
my neighbor's daughter, MALINDA CAUDLE,
aged seven, blue eyes, fair complexion and
light hair. All Indian agents or traders, or
any person having an opportunity, are requested to rescue the above named children;
and delivering them to me or notifying me of
their whereabouts, will be liberally remunerated. Arizona and New Mexico papers please
copy.   Feb. 22.   JNO. S. FRIEND.

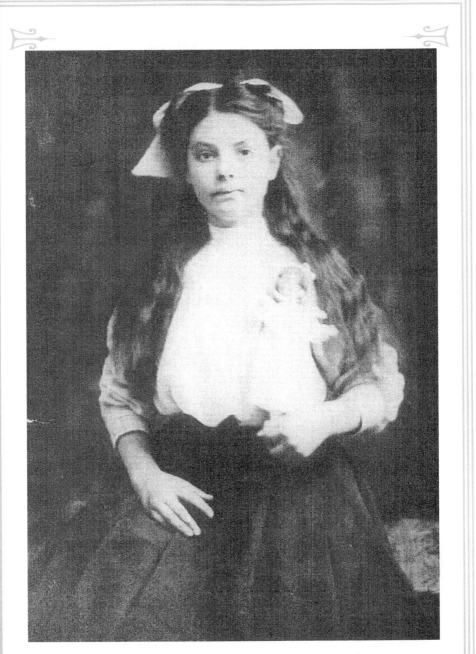

Minnie Caudle shortly after her recovery from the Comanches in 1868, clutching a doll given to her by the Wynkoop family at Fort Larned, Kansas. PHOTOGRAPH COURTESY OF DAVID JOHNSON.

Esihabit (Milky Way), a Penateka Comanche chief who promoted peaceful relations with the whites and negotiated Dot Babb's release from the Comanches in 1867. He was photographed by Alexander Gardner in October 1872 while visiting Washington, D.C., with an Indian delegation. PHOTOGRAPH COURTESY OF PANHANDLE-PLAINS HISTORICAL MUSEUM, CANYON, TEXAS. 1241/3103.

Mowway (Shaking Hand), the Kotsoteka Comanche chief whose warriors included Clinton Smith, and whose village was destroyed by Colonel Mackenzie's troops on September 29, 1872. PHOTOGRAPH COURTESY OF PANHANDLE-PLAINS HISTORICAL MUSEUM, CANYON, TEXAS. 2120/41.

Quanah Parker (right page), the last Comanche leader to use the title "chief." The son of a white captive, he was closely associated with two other white Indians. Herman Lehmann lived with Quanah's family in 1877-1878, and two of Quanah's sons married daughters of Rudolph Fischer. PHOTOGRAPH COURTESY OF PANHANDLE-PLAINS HISTORICAL MUSEUM, CANYON, TEXAS. 1612/20B.

Terheryaquahip (Horseback), principal chief of the Nokoni Comanches, delivered several captives to Fort Sill, including Clinton Smith, Adolph Korn, and Temple Friend.

PHOTOGRAPH COURTESY OF CALDWELL (FRANK) COLLECTION, THE CENTER FOR AMERICAN HISTORY, UNIVERSITY OF TEXAS AT AUSTIN. CN 04869.

Col. Ranald S. Mackenzie steadfastly pursued the Quahada Comanches across the Texas Panhandle and finally forced them to surrender in 1875.

PHOTOGRAPH COURTESY OF PANHANDLE-PLAINS HISTORICAL MUSEUM, CANYON, TEXAS. 1612/107.

John S. Evans's trading store at Fort Sill, Indian Territory (right foreground), around the time the Comanches brought their captives there. PHOTOGRAPH COURTESY OF PRINTS AND PHOTOGRAPHS COLLECTION, THE CENTER FOR AMERICAN HISTORY, UNIVERSITY OF TEXAS AT AUSTIN. CN 01373.

Camp of Nokoni chief Terheryaquahip (Horseback) north of Fort Sill during the winter of 1872-1873, around the time he delivered four white captives to Indian agent Lawrie Tatum. The man in the buffalo robe is Horace P. Jones, the interpreter. PHOTOGRAPH COURTESY OF PRINTS AND PHOTOGRAPHS DIVISION, THE LIBRARY OF CONGRESS, WASHINGTON, D.C. USZ62-19816.

Temple Friend (seated) and fellow captive John Valentine Maxey at Fort Sill, shortly after their recovery from the Quahada Comanches in the fall of 1872. Their long hair was cut off and their Comanche gear was taken away from them. PHOTOGRAPH COURTESY OF BUTLER COUNTY HISTORICAL SOCIETY, EL DORADO, KANSAS.

Main Plaza in downtown San Antonio was bustling and congested when Adolph Korn and Clinton Smith were brought there in January 1873, after several years of roaming the plains of the Texas Panhandle with the Comanches. PHOTOGRAPH COURTESY OF GRANDJEAN COLLECTION, DAUGHTERS OF THE REPUBLIC OF TEXAS LIBRARY, SAN ANTONIO, TEXAS. MMP S-297.

Beef issue day on the reservation; a pathetic substitute for the Comanches' glorious buffalo hunts of bygone years. PHOTOGRAPH COURTESY OF PANHANDLE-PLAINS HISTORICAL MUSEUM, CANYON, TEXAS. 1986-11/28.

Rudolph Fischer (left) and his adoptive Comanche father, Black Crow, in 1878, shortly after Fischer ran away from his Texas family and returned to Indian Territory to live the rest of his life with the Comanches. PHOTOGRAPH COURTESY OF HUGH CORWIN COLLECTION, MUSEUM OF THE GREAT PLAINS, LAWTON, OKLAHOMA. 72-P14: 18.

Former "Apache" Herman Lehmann met former Texas ranger James B. Gillett at an Old Trail Drivers Association reunion, San Antonio, November 1924. This was their first encounter since they fought each other on the Staked Plains in 1875. PHOTOGRAPH COURTESY OF ESTHER LEHMANN.

Former Indian captives gathered on the roof garden of the Gunter Hotel, San Antonio, at an Old Trail Drivers Association reunion, November 1924. They included Jeff Smith (third from left), Herman Lehmann (third from right, in regalia), and Clinton Smith (second from right). PHOTOGRAPH COURTESY OF HALEY MEMORIAL LIBRARY AND HISTORY CENTER, MIDLAND, TEXAS.

Clinton Smith and some of his boyhood Comanche pals renewed their friendship at an Old Trail Drivers Association reunion, San Antonio, October 1927. PHOTOGRAPH COURTESY OF EDDA RAYE SMITH MOODY.

Clinton Smith (left) and Jeff Smith (right) posing in the 1920s. A number of journalists interviewed the Smiths, who were billed as "the only two brothers ever known to endure the same hardships of captivity and get back alive." PHOTOGRAPH COURTESY OF CARLENE AND TOM SMITH.

Jeff Smith, clutching arrows, made his last public appearance at the San Antonio premiere of the film Geronimo *at the Texas Theater, March 8, 1940. Jeff died the following month.* PHOTOGRAPH COURTESY OF CARLENE AND TOM SMITH.

Banc Babb Bell, wrapped in a buffalo robe, with her grandson, Daniel Crooks, 1945. PHOTOGRAPH COURTESY OF ANNA CROOKS.

Dot Babb and his horse, Old Coley. A convert to the Comanches' free-roaming way of life, he later worked out-doors as a cowboy and trail driver. PHOTOGRAPH COURTESY OF HALEY MEMORIAL LIBRARY AND HISTORY CENTER, MIDLAND, TEXAS.

Adolph Korn spent his last years as a lonely misfit in the home of his stepsister, Hannah Korn Hey (Granny Hey), in Mason, Texas. The house, built around 1880, was torn down in 1971, disappearing along with most other traces of Adolph Korn's unusual life. PHOTOGRAPH COURTESY OF PATTY POLK.

Diamond Holes caves on Rocky Creek, Mason County, Texas. PHOTOGRAPH BY JAMIE SMITH JACKSON.

Interior of Diamond Holes caves, where former "Comanche" Adolph Korn lived as a hermit during the latter 1890s. PHOTOGRAPH BY JAMIE SMITH JACKSON.

Adolph Korn is buried, facing east, beneath this mesquite tree in the Gooch Cemetery, Mason, Texas. PHOTOGRAPH BY JAMIE SMITH JACKSON.

Bishop Henry Niles Pierce of Arkansas, the overseer of the church's mission to Indian Territory, welcomed the delegation. Through an interpreter, he told them that the Great Spirit had sent his son into the world to teach them how to be good and to take the bad thoughts out of their hearts. The Indians grunted at his remarks. When he had finished, their response wasn't as spiritual as the Episcopalians had hoped. Esihabit and the other chiefs assured Bishop Pierce that they were ready to live like white people, if only the government would build the houses it had promised them.

That afternoon the Indians attended the circus on East Thirty-fourth Street. Unimpressed, they scowled throughout the performance. Although the Comanches loved to laugh, they found the clown's tricks entirely unfunny. That night they saw a Broadway show at Booth's Theatre; the press reported that they "conducted themselves in a Christian-like manner, never applauding and being very silent." They had more important things to think about.

On the evening of November 1, the Indians began their trip back to the plains by way of Chicago and Lawrence. As the train rolled through the long nights across an America that no longer had a place for its native people, Mowway and his fellow Comanches had plenty of time to wonder which of their friends, brothers, sisters, parents, wives, and children had been killed or taken prisoner. And to worry about how the rest of the tribe would survive the winter ahead with their homes and provisions destroyed.

Chapter Nine

The Long Way Home

Standing outside John Evans's trading post near Fort Sill on October 24, 1872, the soldiers, Indians, and travelers who did business there saw the long line of horses trudging across the veld long before they could identify who the riders were. As the horsemen drew closer, they could make out the figures of Comanche plainsmen in buckskin, some carrying bows, arrows, and shields. No one at the trading post was surprised to see them coming, even if it wasn't ration day. Most people around Fort Sill knew what was going on. The Comanches, once haughtily independent, were now contrite, ready to do whatever it took to get their captured women and children back from Texas. All their hopes were in the hands of their agent, Lawrie Tatum—and he knew it.

Even Paruacoom and his wild Quahadas had voluntarily moved their tepees to the banks of Cache Creek, close to the Indian agency. Winter was coming on, and it would be a hard season for any Comanches still living away from the reservation. Colonel Mackenzie's men had destroyed most of their food supply and their warm clothes. For the first time, they needed the provisions doled out by their agent. However, Paruacoom couldn't quite bring himself to shake hands with Bald Head. Instead, the leader of the procession approaching Fort Sill that day was Terheryaquahip (Horseback), the main chief of the Nokoni Comanches. A tall, thick-bodied man in his fifties, he wore a single eagle feather on his head.

As powerful as he looked, Horseback was no longer a fighting man. He suffered from tuberculosis, and his weak lungs had kept him from traveling to Washington with Mowway and the Indian delegation the previous month. In fact, he was one of the few friendly Comanche chiefs who had remained behind in Indian Territory. The warring Comanches depended on him to plead for the prisoners' release, and Horseback had a personal stake in his mission as well. Among the women and children incarcerated at Fort Concho were his mother-in-law, his former wife and her daughter, and another close relative and her daughter.

Horseback had brought his bargaining chips with him that day. Halfway down the line of Comanches rode the two youngest warriors. Only twelve and eight years old, they stood out from the others, even if they might pass for Comanches at first glance. As the party approached Fort Sill, the stone buildings, corrals, and sheds looked as strange and foreboding to these white boys as the tepees of the Comanche camps had once seemed. The people they saw there scared them as well. The only non-Indians they'd encountered in recent years had been soldiers, Texas Rangers, and settlers—all of whom had tried to kill them.

Horseback and the Comanches stopped their horses at Evans's trading post, a barnlike frame building with large front windows. When the shopkeeper came out to greet them, he handed the two white boys some candy. As soon as the Comanche party left the trading post, the boys threw it away, suspicious that the white man was trying to poison them. The Comanches then headed toward Lawrie Tatum's office in one of the Indian agency's white-frame warehouses. Bald Head was waiting for them.

When they arrived, Horseback made the two white boys dismount beside the neat picket fence surrounding the agent's narrow strip of yard. Then he ushered them forward so Lawrie Tatum could examine them. The Comanches assured their agent, "These are all the white children in our camps." Bald Head wasn't convinced. He led the two captives into his office. The boys, used to the freedom of the outdoors, didn't feel comfortable in this room with its hard walls, glass windows, plank floors, and doors that locked. They wondered what this white man was going to do to them.

Tatum interviewed the boys privately, while Horseback and the Comanches waited outside. The older boy was tall and slender. He had a round face, long, tangled hair that was sun-bleached almost white, and large, dark eyes. He could speak some English and remembered his former name. Tatum was elated to learn that the boy was Clinton Smith, the captive from Mowway's group whom he'd tried to locate for more than a year. Clinton told Tatum that he thought the Apaches were still holding his brother, Jeff. The Smith brothers had seen each other a few times during captivity.

The younger boy had a long, narrow face and was darker complexioned. He couldn't speak any English. Tatum gently questioned him through his interpreter.

What was his name?

The boy identified himself as Toppish.

Toppish who?

He thought his full name might be Toppish Smith.

What did he remember about his capture?

The boy said that his father and mother were both killed at the time.

What were their names?

He didn't know.

How long had he been with the Indians?

Three winters, he thought.

Where was he captured?

In Texas.

Which part of Texas?

He didn't know.

That didn't give the Indian agent much to go on. Tatum had one final question for both boys: *did they know of any other white children among the Comanches?*

They admitted that they did. The boys told Tatum about two others in the Quahada camps.

The agent went outside, where Horseback and the Comanches were waiting. He told them, "I am not yet ready to talk about your women and children in Texas. You must deliver to me all the white children you have. Then I will talk about your captives." After he had spoken, Tatum turned around and went back into the building.

The Comanches were disappointed, but they said nothing. Horseback probably thought it was bad manners for Bald Head not to release at least a couple of his relatives in exchange for the two boys he'd delivered from the Quahadas. However, he was in no position to make demands. He and his fellow Comanches climbed on their horses and left the Indian agency.

Once the Comanches were gone, Lawrie Tatum stood in his office facing the two young savages, who eyed him suspiciously with the wild, nervous look of cornered animals. Tatum pitied the boys, but he also knew that this pair would like nothing better than to drive an arrow through his breast, slice off his scalp, and escape to the plains with their friends. For the time being, they would need the restraining influence of armed guards.

The quickest way to restore them to civilization, Tatum decided, would be to enroll them in the nearby mission school for Native American children until he could make arrangements for their return home. First they needed a thorough scrubbing. Tatum turned the boys over to some soldiers from Fort Sill, who promptly stripped the pair of their weapons and ornaments. Clinton Smith watched his whole identity being taken from him one piece at a time: a big silver ring, two brass bracelets, a pair of beaded moccasins, a six-foot bow, a decorated quiver, and about forty arrows.

After that the soldiers marched the boys to the stone guardhouse and locked them up in a cell. Before long a man appeared with some large sheep shears and snipped off their unruly locks. As warriors, their long hair was a source of pride. They watched helplessly as it fell to the floor in thick clumps. Next, the soldiers carried a tin tub into the cell and filled it with water. Puzzled, the boys stood by and watched. Comanches rarely bathed except for ritual purification.

Clinton recalled, "We thought the soap was to be eaten and the water was for us to drink." The soldiers started ripping off their breechcloths and buckskin leggings and made signs for Clinton and Toppish to step into the tub, one at a time. Then their tormentors began scrubbing the paint and grime off their bodies, none too gently. Afterward, the boys were forced to dress in pants, shirts, suspenders, and jackets. The new clothes felt strange against their skin and restricted the movement of their arms and legs. Finally, the soldiers led Clinton and Toppish out of the guardhouse and motioned for them to climb into an army wagon, which took them to the Quaker school a few miles away. There, they began their rehabilitation.

That evening Lawrie Tatum wrote to Henry Smith in Texas, relaying two bits of thrilling news. Henry's older son had been safely recovered from the Comanches, and his younger one was still living, probably with the Apaches. The agent encouraged Henry to come to Fort Sill and get Clinton. He wrote, "I think there will be no danger from Indians in coming here for thy son past Red River Station."

Tatum still hadn't identified the other boy, Toppish. The boy's answers to Tatum's questions didn't match the information he'd received from any of the parents who had visited or written to the agency. The agent, who had his hands full dealing with the Comanches and Kiowas, didn't want the extra burden of restoring Toppish to his family. He even encouraged Henry Smith to "take the other boy also if practicable, especially if his people can't be found." Meanwhile, Tatum placed advertisements in the major newspapers in Texas and Kansas, trying to locate the boy's relatives. He hoped that some of them were still alive and were residing in one of those states. And that they'd be willing to claim an orphaned savage.

On November 14, 1872, three weeks after Clinton Smith and Toppish had arrived at the Indian agency, another procession of Comanche men approached Fort Sill. Once again the Nokoni chief Horseback was in the lead, and he brought two more white captives with him. Winter had set in early, and the boys were shivering from the cold—or maybe from fright. They were twelve and thirteen years old. The Comanches told Lawrie Tatum that these were the last two white captives in their camps. Based on the intelligence he'd received from George Caboon the previous year, Tatum believed them. He knew that Rudolph Fischer was still living with the Quahadas, but the agent no longer thought of him as a captive.

Horseback made it clear to Bald Head that he was very anxious to get his relatives home from Fort Concho. Tatum couldn't make any promises, since the military, rather than the Indian agency, had the final say on the Comanche prisoners of war. Nonetheless, the agent agreed to write to Brig. Gen. Christopher C. Augur, commander of the Department of Texas, praising Horseback's good faith in securing the captives' release.

After Horseback left, Tatum tried to talk with the two white boys. The younger one had dark eyes and light auburn hair. Even in his savage state, he had an alert, intelligent expression. The older boy had blond hair, a broad face, a high forehead, and a scar on his chin. He could speak some German and English. Tatum understood his name to be Adolph "Kohn." The agent knew he could locate Adolph's parents, because the Office of Indian Affairs had received correspondence concerning him in 1870. However, the other captive had been with the Indians so long that he had lost all his English. Tatum tried to question the boy.

What were his parents' names?

John and Sarah, he thought.

How was he captured?

He said his mother was killed when he was taken. His father and sister were away from home at the time.

Where did it happen?

He didn't know. He vaguely remembered a military post on the south side of a river and some mountains not far from his family's house.

Was anyone else captured with him?

He recalled that the Indians who captured him killed several people. They took no other captives.

When was this?

The Comanches told him it was ten years ago.

That wasn't much help. Tatum sent the two boys to be stripped, deloused, groomed, clothed, and enrolled in the Indian school alongside Clinton Smith and Toppish. Two days later, he wrote to Louis Korn about Adolph's recovery, saying, "Please come or send for him. I think there will be no danger in coming here at present Post, Red River Station." He also described Toppish and the other unidentified captive, adding: "If thou knowest anything of these homeless children please inform me."

Once again Tatum placed notices in the major Texas and Kansas newspapers. He also wrote to the Friend family in Kansas, thinking one of the unidentified boys might be Temple Friend. Not many of the details matched, however. "Toppish" looked too young to be Temple, and he said that both his father and mother had been killed when he was captured. The older boy said that his mother's name was Sarah, not Matilda, and that the Indians had killed her. Also, the boy indicated that the Indians took no other prisoners at the time they abducted him. If this boy were Temple Friend, surely he would have remembered his playmate and fellow captive, Minnie Caudle. Maybe he meant that the Indians were no longer holding any other captives from the Legion Valley raid. But it was unlikely that he would have known that Minnie, who had gone with a different group of Comanches, had been recovered and sent home. Was he trying to protect her, afraid that Minnie, like himself, would be taken from her Indian family by force? Was this "bright intelligent looking boy," as Tatum described him, deliberately trying to mislead the Indian agent?

On November 21, 1872, a week after Horseback surrendered the last of the four boy captives to the Indian agent, Mowway arrived at Fort Sill from his trip to Washington. Soon he was reunited with the remnants of his people—those who had survived the attack on his village and hadn't been captured. Before long he started lobbying for the prisoners' release. In early December, Mowway called on Lawrie

Tatum, accompanied by two other Comanche chiefs. One was Tabenanaka, a Yamparika leader whose camp had once been home to Banc Babb. The other was Mowway's friend Paruacoom; the fearless Quahada war chief was about to have his first meeting with Bald Head.

Tatum welcomed the three chiefs but remained firm in his demands. Once more he told them that they must move their people onto the reservation by the middle of December. Otherwise, they could expect another drubbing by Ranald Mackenzie and the cavalrymen. The three Comanche chiefs, even Paruacoom, meekly agreed to do whatever the agent said. They told Tatum that they'd had their fight with the soldiers and had been whipped. They said they were ready to move to the reservation, send their children to the Quaker school, and even try farming. Later, the Quahadas delivered twenty-five horses to Tatum in partial payment for fifty-four that had been stolen from the quartermaster at Fort Sill the previous June. It appeared as though they were prepared to grovel if necessary.

Actually, they were just biding their time. Once the Comanches got their people home from Fort Concho, Bald Head would have no more power over them. They wouldn't need his government handouts when springtime arrived and the buffalo hunts resumed. Furthermore, they welcomed a chance to get even with Mackenzie and his blue-coated devils if he dared come after them in Texas. The Quahadas knew that Tatum and the army wouldn't be able to stop them from going back to the plains before long.

For the second time in their short lives, Adolph Korn, Clinton Smith, and the two other boy captives had their world turned upside down and were dumped into another disagreeable environment. Against their will, Lawrie Tatum introduced them to the discipline of the classroom. The boarding school for Native American children, part of the federal government's program to civilize the Southern Plains Indians, was housed near Fort Sill in a two-storied, rectangular stone building with a steeply gabled roof. The boy captives had never attended school before, and they weren't prepared for the torturous physical confinement. Most of their forty-eight classmates were Caddoes and Comanches. Clinton and Adolph must have held them in contempt—servile weaklings who took orders from the missionaries rather than helping their people fight the white enemies on the plains.

The school was run by two patient Quakers from Ohio, Josiah and Lizzie Butler,[1] and Clinton Smith recalled that they were very kind. Each school day began with a Bible reading in English, which sounded odd, even humorous, to the white Indians. After that the children learned letters and geography. Adolph and Clinton, accustomed to the chants of Comanche war dances, were taught instead to sing "There Is a Happy Land." At recess they got to play ball, a poor substitute for riding, stealing, and shooting. Although the Quaker school had a dormitory on the second floor, the white Indians, like the other Comanche children, were afraid to sleep upstairs. They spent the nights in tepees in a corner of the schoolyard. Even when the supper bell rang, the captives refused at first to go inside the dining hall that extended behind the classrooms. The Butlers brought their food outside on tin plates.

After a few days, Adolph, Clinton, and the other captives got used to the schoolhouse routine and learned to tolerate it. They didn't try to escape, probably because they were near Fort Sill and didn't want to fight any pursuing soldiers until they had a chance to get some good horses and weapons. Meanwhile, they didn't bother to hide their lack of interest in Mrs. Butler's lessons. When the bell rang, they dashed for the table, grabbed all the food they could carry, and headed outside to gobble it down.

One day a white man from Fort Sill arrived at the school in a buggy. He took out a boxlike contraption and set it up in the yard. The Indian children crowded around, curious and apprehensive. To the Comanches, the apparatus looked like a funeral scaffold. Adolph said to Clinton, "Somebody is dead. They are going to bury him right here in the yard." The Butlers took the white boys by their hands and led them toward the odd platform. The man covered the box with a black cloth and stuck his head underneath, which made the boys uneasy. Then the man turned the box around and pointed it straight at them. Adolph let out a yell. He and the other captives scattered and hid. The photographer would come back another day, when the captives were calmer, and take the photographs that Lawrie Tatum would send to their parents to identify them.

Patient though he was, Lawrie Tatum must have been put out with the parents. For three years, he'd been subjected to curt letters insinuating that he hadn't been diligent in searching for their kidnapped children. Now that he had at last succeeded in rescuing four boys and identifying two of them, their fathers, Louis Korn and Henry Smith, seemed to be in no hurry to come claim them.

Finally, Tatum decided that if the boys' parents weren't going to take any initiative in the matter, he would send the young rascals home the slow, cheap way. On November 20, 1872, Capt. Joseph Rendlebrock of the Fourth Cavalry arrived at Fort Sill with thirty-six enlisted men and seventeen wagons. The military caravan was on its way to San Antonio. Tatum arranged for Adolph Korn and Clinton Smith to travel with them.

Captain Rendlebrock was ready to leave Fort Sill by November 26. Shortly before the army convoy departed, the soldiers let Adolph and Clinton reclaim their Comanche gear, which had been confiscated when they arrived at the post. The two boys were overjoyed to hold their bows and arrows in their hands again. They knew they were one step closer to making their escape.

Their teacher, Josiah Butler, wrote in his diary that day: " 'May God bless them,' is my sincere prayer, for the dear boys have had a rough life so far." The "dear boys" were hellions during the trip home. Late the first night, they tried to run away to the Wichita Mountains, but the soldiers apprehended them and made them spend the rest of the night in Captain Rendlebrock's tent. When he invited the young troublemakers to breakfast the next morning, Adolph and Clinton scooped butter out of the dish with their fingers and ate it with no bread.

The trip from Fort Sill to San Antonio took exactly six weeks. During the days, Adolph and Clinton passed the time by shooting arrows at objects beside the road and investigating every hole and hollow they saw. At night they climbed into trees and imitated owls, coyotes, and squirrels. They hated sleeping near the soldiers. The wagon train moved slowly, and the troops had to perform various duties at several military posts along the way. As the army wagons crossed the Staked Plains of Texas, the soldiers stopped for a few days at Fort Concho and set up camp along the river. Adolph and Clinton tried once more to escape, fleeing some distance upriver before the soldiers overtook them. After that they were guarded more closely.

The medical officer at Fort Concho examined the captives. Although he described the boys as "quite stout and healthy looking," they must have been small for their ages. The doctor guessed that Clinton was nine and Adolph was seven. Actually, they were twelve and thirteen, respectively. It seems that their growth had been stunted while they were with the Comanches. The doctor also noted that Adolph had "lost his native language." It's not clear whether he meant German or English. What's odd, however, is that the Quakers at Fort Sill recorded that Adolph could speak some German, English, and Spanish at the time Horseback delivered him to Lawrie Tatum. Adolph must have learned a few English words from the Butlers while he was at the Indian school, but now he spoke only his tribal tongue. The entry in the medical records at Fort Concho was the first in a series of reports suggesting that Adolph became less communicative and more resentful during the trip home.

While they were staying at Fort Concho, Adolph and Clinton were allowed to visit the Comanche prisoners from Mowway's village. The two white boys knew all of them. According to Clinton, the women "came running to us and grabbed us around the neck." Classified as prisoners of war, they had arrived at the post in October "in a very destitute condition" after their long march from the Texas Panhandle. The fort didn't have a jail large enough to house all of them, so they were herded into a large stone stable. The post's commanding officer, Maj. John P. Hatch, immediately issued them bed sacks, blankets, and a few flannel blouses and socks. He also ordered that they receive full rations of flour, beef, salt, and rice, and half rations of coffee, sugar, and soap. Major Hatch took great pains to make sure his prisoners got what they needed.[2] His letters suggest that he was motivated both by compassion and by his awareness that these captives played a key role in the federal government's negotiations with the tribe.

After they were released from the stable, the prisoners set up camp outdoors in the stone-walled corrals. To prevent escape, the perimeters were lined with broken glass. Otherwise, security was minimal. The soldiers assigned to look after them brought huge quantities of meat in army wagons. They threw it over the walls to the Comanches, who grabbed it and ate it raw. Since the women got little exercise, some of them started putting on weight.

The presence of the unusual prisoners broke the monotony of life at Fort Concho. Now and then, the Comanche women and children drew curious visitors. The officers' wives were especially fascinated by them. The Comanches looked forward to their visits, because they brought food and candy. The Comanches and the white women also exchanged babies during these occasions. However, when the officers' wives left the corrals, they were horrified to find that they and their children were infested with lice. Some of the soldiers, taking a fancy to the women, asked a local dressmaker to sew bonnets for them. The Comanches balked and refused to wear the ridiculous headdresses.

Many people, Indian and non-Indian, were wondering how long the women and children would stay at Fort Concho. Both Lawrie Tatum and the Comanche chiefs assumed that the prisoners would return to their families as soon as the tribe met the government's demands. However, the army's commander, Gen. William T. Sherman, complicated matters by submitting a proposal that caused an uproar in Washington. He wanted to take the Comanche children away from their parents, recommending that they "be provided for by the Indian Bureau at some asylum in the Indian country, where they can be raised with habits one degree nearer civilization than they now possess." Sherman thought it was essential to force the youngsters onto the white man's road in their formative years. He wrote, "These Comanche children are as wild as coyotes, and unless taken in hand early must grow up like their fathers, unqualified savages."

When the commissioner of Indian Affairs, Francis Walker, learned of Sherman's plan for a Comanche orphanage, he exploded. Walker wrote to his boss, the secretary of the Interior: "I gravely doubt whether the law of the land or the public sentiment of the country would justify parents being permanently deprived of their children, even for the sake of saving the children from the life of savages." In the end, cooler heads prevailed. The secretary of the Interior agreed with Walker that "the children captured must be returned to their parents as soon as the restitution of white captives and Govt. stock is made by the Indians."[3] Until that time, however, the Comanche women and their young would remain camped in the corrals at Fort Concho, entertaining visitors while yearning for their families and friends far away.

In December 1872, as a reward for the Comanches' good faith in returning Adolph Korn, Clinton Smith, and the two unidentified white boys, Gen. C. C. Augur ordered the release of Horseback's relatives from Fort Concho. He also wrote to Lawrie Tatum, "I will release one, or two, as you may recommend, of the Indian prisoners, for every white captive returned to you by the Indians, from whatever tribe they may be obtained." The captive whom Augur most eagerly sought was Clinton Smith's younger brother, Jeff, possibly because their father had been so persistent in asking about him. Augur promised that he would "give double that number for the return of Mr. Smith's son—understood to be with the Apaches."[4]

Eventually, the army released the rest of the Comanche women and children once Tatum was satisfied that the tribe had surrendered all its captives. The prisoners were reunited with their people in Indian Territory on June 10, 1873, after a march of seventeen days.

* * *

Louis Korn was ecstatic that Adolph, the son he'd given up for dead, was on his way home. In his excitement, he took Lawrie Tatum's letters to the offices of the *San Antonio Express* and the *San Antonio Herald*. The *Express* congratulated him "upon the near prospect of the recovery of his son from a condition worse than death." The *Herald* also announced the thrilling news but used the occasion for political commentary, stating that Tatum's letter was "one more powerful appeal for protection to the frontier."

Why didn't Grandpa Korn go to Fort Sill to get Uncle Adolph? Family history provides no clues. He may have been too poor to buy the stage fare, or to close his confectionery shop for the amount of time it would have taken to get there and back. Perhaps he was afraid of meeting Indian raiders along the way.

Henry Smith, on the other hand, didn't let the danger or the distance deter him. As he put it, "I wish to get [Clinton] home immediately . . . for days are months to me now." Money was a problem, though. Smith wrote to Texas governor Edmund J. Davis:

> [M]y means are limited, and I wish to know if it is necessary that I go for him, and if so, are there any funds in the hands of the Government for defraying expenses of returning Captives if so, I beg your assistance in the matter. . . . [I]f it is necessary that I should go I will be compelled to go by stage as I have not the means to supply myself an outfit for such a trip at this season of the year. . . . [5]

In response to Smith's letter, Governor Davis wrote, "I will order the payment of the actual traveling expenses for bringing the youth home."

Henry Smith made the long journey by train and stagecoach. He arrived at Fort Sill on December 5, 1872, only to learn that Clinton had left with the army caravan nine days earlier. This disappointment was too much for him, and he broke down. The Quaker teacher Josiah Butler observed, "He has one more son with the Indians—poor man, how I felt for him as he sat and wept."

Late that night, a Mexican-American captive named Martina Diaz escaped from the Quahada camp near Fort Sill and sought sanctuary at the Indian agency. Martina, about eighteen years old, had been captured near San Antonio two years earlier and was anxious to return to her family. Lawrie Tatum found a way to make Henry Smith feel that his long trip hadn't been for nothing. He asked Henry to escort Martina back to San Antonio and help her find her people. The following evening, the stagecoach pulled up to the Indian agency. Tatum's whole household watched while Henry Smith, only twenty-four hours after he'd arrived, started back to Texas without his son. He would have to wait another month to see Clinton.

Four days later, on December 10, 1872, Rev. Leonard Friend arrived at the agency from El Dorado, Kansas, to find out if the older of the two unidentified white boys was his grandson, Temple. The Quakers at the Indian agency had become attached to the bright twelve-year-old boy. He seemed happy staying with them and had started speaking a little English. Late in the day, Lawrie Tatum and his wife, Mary Ann, took Reverend Friend to the Indian school. The boy ran up to Mary Ann Tatum and greeted her affectionately. The agent's wife was a tender, plain-looking woman who was popular with the Indians for her acts of charity.

The boy ignored Leonard. Mary Ann told him, "Speak to the gentleman."

He seemed confused. Leonard Friend gently put his arm around the boy and drew him near, recognizing his grandson at once. He tried to say something, but started weeping instead. When he finally got his emotions under control, he looked at the boy and said, slowly and distinctly: "Temple Friend."

Temple stared at him, bewildered. The Tatums thought the boy seemed to recognize the sound of the words. He replied, "Yesh."

Then the old man spoke his sister's name: "Florence Friend."

Again, Temple said, "Yesh."

Leonard kept talking to him. Eventually, Temple started to answer questions about his capture in Legion Valley nearly five years before. It took Leonard several hours to convince him that his stepmother, Matilda Friend, had survived the attack. Not long afterward, the preacher and his grandson started home in a buggy.

That left only Toppish unaccounted for. Eventually, he was identified as John Valentine Maxey. His father arrived at the agency to claim him on January 4, 1873.

Adolph Korn had never seen a city that he could remember. He'd grown up in the isolated village of Castell and the wilderness of the Saline Valley. The largest settlements he'd ever visited were the small towns along the frontier where he'd stolen horses with the Comanches. As the army wagon train slowly made its way toward San Antonio, the towns got larger. The caravan passed through Gillespie County, whose population had grown to over 3,500. In Fredericksburg, the county seat, Captain Rendlebrock and the soldiers stopped to purchase supplies. News soon spread that two of the white boys recovered from the Comanches were in town. Curiosity seekers flocked to the store and crowded around the boys, who spoke to each other in Comanche and still looked wild even with their clipped hair and schoolboy clothes. Captain Rendlebrock had grown fond of Adolph and Clinton during the trip. When he saw what was happening, he decided to let them have a little fun. He handed Adolph an ax, indicating that he should sound the Comanche war whoop and start at the crowd. Adolph did so, and the townspeople scurried.

The two captives and their military escort finally entered San Antonio on January 7, 1873. Nothing they'd seen along the way, not even the pesky crowd in Fredericksburg, could have prepared the boys for what they were about to experience. San Antonio was Texas's second-largest city, only slightly smaller than Galveston, and it was as cosmopolitan a gathering place as the Southwest had to offer. The town appeared abruptly on the mesquite plain. The adobe Mexican huts on the outskirts soon gave way to sturdy limestone houses with latticed balconies. As the wagon train got closer to the city center, the streets and plazas were packed with canvas-covered wagons, buggies, burros laden with firewood, and pedestrians.

To Adolph and Clinton, the people in the streets looked as strange as the buildings. The American poet Sidney Lanier, who was visiting San Antonio that winter, was fascinated by the mix of cultures in the city, "the queerest juxtaposition of civilizations, white, yellow (Mexican), red (Indian), black (negro), and all possible permutations of these significant colors." A sign at the Commerce Street Bridge warned in English, German, and Spanish: "Walk your horse over this bridge, or you will be fined." Around the plazas, hard-drinking cowboys, high-rolling cattlemen, and grizzled Indian fighters jostled with perfumed dandies, Mexicans adorned in silver, and recent European immigrants wearing the garb of their homelands. Lanier was charmed by these "characters," "a perfect gauntlet of people who have odd histories, odd natures, or odd appearances."[6]

Since Lanier came from the comparatively quiet town of Macon, Georgia, he was shocked to learn that Indian raids still occurred not far from San Antonio. After reading a local newspaper's account of the capture and recovery of Adolph Korn and Clinton Smith, Lanier wrote to his father back home: "[T]o think of children being carried into captivity by Indians, *in the year 1869,* [sic] and within a few miles of a town of near twenty thousand inhabitants! How far removed we all are, from even the remote appreciation of such a thing, at home!"[7]

And how far removed those two boys were from even the remote appreciation of a bustling American city. Adolph and Clinton gaped in fear and confusion at everything they saw. Clinton wasn't quite as much of a bumpkin as Adolph; he'd driven sheep to San Antonio in his boyhood and was familiar with the city. Still, it had been a long time since he'd seen so many non-Indians in one place.

The boys didn't slip into town quietly. News accounts of the white Indians had preceded their homecoming, stirring up much anticipation. When the wagon train stopped, a large crowd gathered to gawk at the two freakish youngsters. Reporters from three local news-papers covered the event.

The news articles noted that Adolph could speak no language other than Comanche, and that Clinton had to act as his interpreter. The *Herald*'s man reported that Adolph was "quite stout and healthy looking, having enjoyed good health since he was captured some three years ago." However, the *Express* estimated that the thirteen-year-old boy was "only about nine or ten years of age," again suggesting that his physical development had been arrested while he was with the Co-manches, even though he seemed healthy. Clinton was described as "older and more manly appearing than the other boy," although he was actually a year younger than Adolph. The *Herald* concluded, "The boys look wild out of their eyes, and it is doubtful if they will feel at home for some time to come."

Word of the boys' arrival soon reached the Korns' confectionery shop on Market Street. Louis Korn left his business and hurried to find the army caravan. The reunion of father and son took place in full view of the crowd. Louis Korn carefully examined the boy to make sure he was really his son. His skin was much darker after three years in the sun, and he now walked with a limp. Nonetheless, he still had his childhood scar in the middle of his chin.

Uncle Adolph showed no emotion. The German newspaper *Freie Presse für Texas* reported that Grandpa "cried like a baby, while the boy, looking on somewhat wildly, could not quite comprehend what was taking place." According to the *Express,* Adolph "did not recog-nize his father." He didn't smile; he didn't cry; he just acted irritated and uncomfortable.

Captain Rendlebrock brought the two boys to Louis and Johanna Korn's house, and the crowd followed them there. The captain in-structed his men to unload the boys' bows, arrows, buckskins, moc-casins, and ornaments. As people pressed closer, trying to get a better view and hear the boys' strange chatter, souvenir hunters stole all of their Comanche gear. According to the *Herald,* Adolph's reunion with his mother and siblings "was very affecting; he recognized them all, and was apparently glad to reach home." Clinton Smith remembered things differently. He recalled that Louis and Johanna Korn "both cried, and hugged and kissed their boy, but he manifested great indifference to their caresses. He looked wild and stubborn, and sat down on the bed."

Johanna Korn fixed the boys a big meal. Adolph and Clinton ate heartily, even though they were nervous with so many white people surrounding them. Afterward, Louis Korn led the pair to his shop and gave them as much candy as they wanted. They took what was offered to them and ate it, but the old man's gestures of kindness didn't make them like him any better. Adolph wasn't ready to recognize the Korns as his people. For three years, Louis and Johanna Korn had prayed that someday they might be reunited with their son. That day had arrived, but instead of bursting with unbridled joy, they felt the onset of a new kind of heartsickness. Their boy was back, and he hated them.

The next morning, the reporter from the *Express* tried to interview Adolph and Clinton. The boys were uncooperative, ignoring him. Miffed, he concluded:

> Doubtless owing to their youthfulness, severe treatment, and the habit of two years life among the dirty thieves and murderers, they have become more or less insensible to the vast difference between savage and civilized life. There was manifested little disposition or ability to communicate such facts as might have gratified the inquisitive.[8]

When Henry Smith learned of the two boys' arrival, he went to get his son. Clinton recognized his father instantly. Henry hugged the boy and then burst into tears, his happiness mingled with frustration that Jeff was still missing. Clinton, who was "a bit timid at first," described his return to the Smith farm and his first meeting with his stepmother and siblings as "a happy reunion." After a few weeks of herding sheep and doing ranch chores, however, he "was not satisfied."

* * *

Lawrie Tatum's newspaper advertisements describing the two unidentified white boys at Fort Sill were widely read and discussed throughout Texas and Kansas, raising the hopes of all the parents of captured children. On December 3, 1872, Phillip and Auguste Buchmeier wrote to Tatum to find out if one of the children might be their son, Herman Lehmann. Phillip, unlike his wife, wasn't entirely confident that their boy was still alive, for he told Tatum, "I am or was his stepfather." They'd heard nothing about him since his kidnapping more than two years before.

They soon got some exciting news. Shortly after Adolph Korn returned to Texas in January 1873, he met with the Buchmeiers and told them that Herman was still living with the Apaches. For the first time, the Buchmeiers realized that Herman was with Apaches rather than Comanches, Kiowas, or Kickapoos. They enlisted the help of Henry C. King, a Texas state senator, to plead their case to the Indian agency.

Their perseverance paid off. On April 2, 1873, a man who was passing through Loyal Valley delivered some marvelous news. He said that Herman had arrived at Fort Sill and would be sent home as soon as possible. Phillip Buchmeier immediately wrote to the Indian agency, asking for a response "*by return*" giving him "*all* particulars, saying *when* and by *what conveyance*" he could expect to see his stepson.

As it turned out, the traveler's report was only half-true. Herman's group of Apaches did spend about six months on the Kiowa-Comanche reservation near Fort Sill in 1872–1873. The Kiowa chief Kicking Bird told Lawrie Tatum that he'd seen a white boy among them. Tatum mistakenly assumed the boy was Jeff Smith (who was actually in Mexico at the time). When soldiers from Fort Sill went to the Apache camp to investigate, Herman hid beneath some blankets while they searched the tepee. The Apaches left the reservation not long afterward, and Herman slipped out of the Indian agent's reach.[9]

When the Buchmeiers finally received a letter dated April 23, they were told that the prisoner exchange with the Indians was already completed. The last five captives recovered had left Fort Sill for their homes on April 5. None of them matched the description of Herman; in fact, they were all Mexican boys. The agent wrote, "I am not able to learn of any more captives being held by the Indians of the Agency."

The Smith family was luckier. Only four months after Clinton's return, Henry and Harriet Smith got their younger son back. In early April 1873, William Schuchardt, the U.S. commercial agent at the American consulate in Piedras Negras, Mexico, learned from a Mexican trader named Alejo Santos Coy that Jeff was living in a camp of over three hundred Indians in San Rodrigo Canyon, about sixty miles from the Texas border. The group consisted of Lipan Apaches, Mescalero Apaches, Kickapoos, and Comanches who had been conducting swift raids into Texas and then dashing back to safety across the international boundary. Shortly afterward Albert Turpe, the district clerk in Eagle Pass, Texas, just across the Rio Grande from Piedras Negras, got this same information. Schuchardt and Turpe were certain the captive boy was Jeff Smith, for Santos Coy reported that he had been kidnapped two years earlier on Cibolo Creek while he was looking after his father's sheep. The trader also learned that Jeff's captor was willing to sell the boy. Schuchardt commissioned Santos Coy to return for the captive, and Turpe gave security for the ransom money.

Santos Coy soon ransomed Jeff Smith from his Lipan captor for $150 in gold. The U.S. government later reimbursed him, for, as consul Schuchardt noted, the boy's father was "unable to pay the ransom money, being very poor." Jeff was placed in the custody of special Indian agent Thomas G. Williams on May 1, 1873.

As it turned out, Jeff's Lipan captor had unwittingly made a wise bargain when he agreed to sell the boy. On May 18, 1873, about three weeks after Jeff was ransomed, Col. Ranald Mackenzie and the Fourth Cavalry crossed the Rio Grande at night and attacked the Indian villages at Remolino just before sunrise. Mackenzie carried out this quick and daring raid with the secret approval of his military superiors but in flagrant violation of Mexican sovereignty. At least nineteen Indians were killed, and forty women and children were taken captive. If the Lipans hadn't sold Jeff when they did, it's likely that Mackenzie's raiders would have taken the boy without payment.

In Eagle Pass, Texas, ten-year-old Jeff Smith found himself a prisoner once more. His new captors cut off his long hair and made him put on constricting clothes. He didn't understand their language. They served him a good meal, but the boy was too frightened to enjoy it. He worried about what was going to happen to him. His captors, thinking he might try to escape, guarded him closely. Jeff wondered if they were going to brand him, as the Apaches had done. He refused the bed they offered him, finding the floor more comfortable. On May 2, 1873, his guards placed him on a stagecoach bound for San Antonio.

Like his brother before him, Jeff Smith drew a large crowd when he arrived in the city. Inquisitive onlookers gathered on a Sunday morning, May 4, to gawk at the white boy who had lived with the Apaches. As Jeff put it, "The wild life I had led the past few years had made me afraid of white people. They almost scared me to death, asking questions and crowding close around me." A San Antonio reporter who saw him that day noted that he seemed "to have forgotten all his early language, and would not or could not respond to questions either in German or English. He appeared very much interested in the formation of the Turners for parade, and in listening to the music."

That evening a man named Steeneken took the boy by horse and buggy to his father's farm north of San Antonio. Jeff, who still couldn't figure out what was happening, assumed he'd been sold to yet another owner. He didn't understand what the man was saying to him. However, as the buggy drew closer to the Smith farm, he gradually began to recognize places near his old home. Grunting, he pointed down the road.

When Jeff and Mr. Steeneken arrived at the Smiths' house, Henry came out to the yard and wrapped the boy in his arms, hugging

him close. Jeff didn't respond. He recalled, "I had run wild too long
for such expressions of joy." His stepmother, brothers, and sisters
poured out of the house to see him. Henry Smith was "all unstrung,"
according to Jeff. For the rest of that afternoon, he walked the floor
and exclaimed, "Mama, isn't that a God blessing that we got them
boys back."

The only family member who kept his distance was Clinton. The
Smiths had been watching him closely, afraid that he would run off.
He peeped shyly over the fence at Jeff, then ducked behind it and hid.
Although the two white Indians longed for each other's company, they
were afraid to talk with each other when anyone else was around. Jeff
and Clinton Smith remained scared of white people for a long time.

At the time Jeff came home, a federal Frontier Commission was
visiting San Antonio to investigate Indian depredations in Texas and
report to Congress. Several former captives were paraded before the
commission to testify, and the men from Washington were shocked
by the "many acts of positive outrage" the witnesses described. Clinton Smith gave the wide-eyed commissioners an earful. He testified:
"The Comanches are very rough with their captive boys and whip
them terribly, sometimes killing them if they cry over the beating."
(Clinton made no such wild claims in his memoir; the shy adolescent
may have been responding to leading questions or simply been afraid
to contradict the white men.) Jeff Smith also appeared before the
commissioners; however, "being too young to understand an oath,
and his mind somewhat clouded by ill treatment, he was not examined."[10] Nor did Adolph Korn testify, even though he was living in
downtown San Antonio and was well known in the city. It seems that
my stubborn ancestor was still unwilling to talk about his life with the
Comanches.

The trouble had started the night after the pair left Fort Sill, long before they got to Kansas. While the old man was setting up camp,
Temple Friend tore off his school clothes and put on his buckskin and
moccasins. Then he got out his war paint and began decorating his

face. His grandfather, Leonard Friend, was horrified. The Methodist preacher tried to make his grandson understand that these practices were heathenish. Unable to make any headway, Reverend Friend finally threw away the paint. Temple, who had always been quick-tempered, was furious.

Traveling by buggy, Leonard and Temple passed through several towns on their way to El Dorado. Their story made good newspaper copy, and journalists were eager to talk with them. The *Wellington Banner* reported:

> The boy is rather small of his age and seems to have forgotten almost all the reminiscences of his early childhood. He remembered his name, and when recovered could talk a few words of English. His grand-father says that he picks up words in English very rapidly. Notwithstanding his long captivity, he is a bright, intelligent looking boy in the face, his walk and actions being those of an Indian, and he talks Comanche like a native brave. He being young it will require but a short time to bring back to his memory the recollections of the past, and to divest him of the actions and habits he has acquired by his long residence with the savages.[11]

During the trip, Reverend Friend tried to teach Temple the English names for the things they saw. However, by the time the boy finally got to El Dorado in late December 1872, a local correspondent reported, "He cannot speak a word of English." Temple, like Adolph Korn, seems to have become more taciturn and uncooperative as he reached his journey's end.

Leonard took his grandson to the Friend family's farm. Temple refused to believe that the woman who welcomed him was his stepmother. She finally had to show him the scars on her head to prove she'd survived the Indians' attack. Matilda Friend still dressed and bandaged her head every day to soothe the scalp wounds she'd endured the night Temple was taken and her women friends were murdered.

The morning after he got home, Temple put on his buckskin clothes again. Before long he became a familiar, if peculiar, sight in the streets of El Dorado. A local newspaper described him as "quite a lively young man." So lively, in fact, that he shot arrows through all the ducks around his parents' farm. Temple played rough sports with the other children in town and taught them how to make bows and arrows. One playmate recalled, "He could hit a penny on a stick at ten yards with his bow and arrow and wing a bird in the top of the tallest tree." He also brought children to the Friend farm, where he enjoyed showing them his stepmother's scalp wounds. (Rumor has it he charged a fee for this privilege.) However, he never liked to speak English. When he talked, he used few words.

His parents enrolled him in the local school. Temple hated it. Learning the alphabet and playing childish games such as Red Rover were beneath his dignity. At recess he usually stood apart from the other children, solemn and silent. After a while, his schoolmates started making fun of Temple's odd behavior. He was miserable. John Friend finally allowed his son to quit school. That still didn't cure his melancholy. He became more withdrawn and started disappearing in the woods for several days at a time.

Despite a good diet and plenty of exercise, Temple's physical health began to fail, and his physique declined. He seemed to lose interest in life. His parents and the local doctors didn't know what to do for him. They watched helplessly as he withered away, giving up without a struggle. Two and a half years after he was restored to his family, Temple Friend died at age fifteen on June 2, 1875—coincidentally, the same day that the last of his fellow Quahada Comanches finally surrendered to the army at Fort Sill.

"No one seemed to know exactly what his ailment was," his younger half sister, Carrie Friend Dwire, recalled in a 1961 interview. "There was a theory that he ate so much salt that it killed him. The Indians often were deprived of salt, and when they found a source of the mineral they gorged themselves on it." Some doctors speculated that he died from the ill effects of his sudden transition from Comanche life. Perhaps. Even if it were possible to pinpoint the exact cause of Temple Friend's death, the medical explanation wouldn't be satisfactory. It seems that he had all the symptoms of a more elusive malady, a broken heart.

While Temple Friend's readjustment to white society was unusually traumatic, all of the former captives had a difficult time during their first couple of years back home. The four other white boys who were recovered in 1872–1873—Maxey, Korn, and the two Smith brothers—kept their Indian habits for several months, even years, after they were reunited with their families. Old-timers in Montague County, Texas, remembered that John Valentine Maxey was "very rude" when he came back. Like his close pal, Temple Friend, he tried to kill all the chickens and pigs on his family's farm.[12]

Adolph Korn was even more antisocial. Even though he dressed like any other white boy in San Antonio, his demeanor was strange enough to make him stand out. In February 1873, a month after Adolph returned home, the poet Sidney Lanier wrote about him as one of the "odd personages and 'characters' " he saw on the streets. Adolph was described as "absolutely uncontrollable" during his teenage years. He reportedly committed so many offenses in San Antonio that the local law enforcement officers told Grandpa Korn he'd have to do something with the boy. There is no record of the nature of Adolph's crimes,[13] but it's likely that he got on the wrong side of the law by helping himself to whatever he fancied, especially horses. In addition, like the other white Indians, he probably got his target practice by shooting animals he thought were useless, such as fowl and swine. When Adolph saw Clinton Smith in San Antonio one day, he tried to talk his old raiding partner into running away with him and going back to the Comanches. Clinton refused; by that point, he was content with his white family. Besides, after Tosacowadi's death, Clinton may have felt he had no home within the tribe.

No doubt the Korns were embarrassed by Adolph's misdeeds in San Antonio. They must have also worried that he would get into more serious trouble as he grew older, perhaps ending up in prison or on a hangman's scaffold. In the spring of 1876, when Adolph was seventeen, the family finally addressed the problem by moving back to Mason County and putting Adolph to work on an isolated ranch. The move helped, but it didn't completely solve the problems. Adolph is rumored to have resumed his old habit of stealing horses once he got to Mason. Three years after his recovery, he still hadn't been reconciled to European-Americans' ideas of property ownership and acceptable behavior.

The Smith brothers didn't cause quite as much trouble as Adolph, although they both had a hard time readapting. At first neither was happy on the Smith farm. Jeff sized up the situation best when he remarked, "Everything seemed mighty tame by comparison after I got back home." It wasn't long before the former captives missed their adventurous years on the plains. Jeff said, "We two boys were pretty wild at first, and had no manners of any kind except those which we had learned from the Indians, and that did not fit very well in polite society." Their stepmother had to teach them how to use a knife and fork; the boys preferred to eat with their hands. They also struggled to relearn English. Jeff recalled, "We kept hammering away until we could make ourselves understood, without embarrassment, in friendly conversation."

It took Clinton and Jeff about a year to get used to being around white people and to lose their fear of them—much longer than it had taken them to feel comfortable with the Indians. The two brothers were curiosities among the children of their neighborhood. One of those neighbors reminisced in 1934:

> Sometimes these boys showed us Indian dances, and how they catch horses, and some of their tricks and stunts they had to learn by the Indians, but when it came to riding wild horses, well, these boys were not to be beaten, the more they bucqed, [sic] the better they liked it. They told us the signs of birds and animals, such as that of an owl, hoo-hoo, or that of a chicken or

turkey, or that of a horse, or other animals, what they meant, they said at nights they used these signs of animals, or fowl, that of an owl, hoo-hoo-hoo, meant look out, so every sign had its meaning.[14]

Within a year or two, the former captives more or less settled down and learned to curb the extremes of their unconventional behavior. Nonetheless, a part of them would always belong on the other side. They had spent their formative years in two very different cultures, Native American and European-American. The tension between those competing ways of looking at the world—both of which were deeply engrained in their characters—would cause more problems for the former captives attempting to reconnect with their own people than for their Indian friends who tried to walk the white man's road for the first time.

Chapter Ten

Resisting
the Reservation

A fter the Comanches got their women and children back from
Fort Concho, many of them promptly forgot the promises their
chiefs had made to President Grant, the army officers, the commissioner of Indian Affairs, their federal agent, and even the Episcopal bishop in New York—namely, to settle down on their reservation
and act like white people. The wounds they'd suffered in the battle on
the North Fork of the Red River had healed. Now they needed to
cleanse from their memories the humiliation of subsisting on government rations at Fort Sill while waiting for their captive families to return, of supplicating themselves like docile children in front of the
agents of the Great Father. Before long the defiant Quahadas and
other Comanches who had chosen to affiliate with them returned to
the plains. There they tried, for the last time, to resume the only life
they'd ever known, following the buffalo and raiding settlers' farms to
get more horses.

But as they rode silently in long lines across the Texas Panhandle,
the Comanches were deeply troubled by what they saw. The large
herds of grazing animals eluded them. Instead, they found the
skinned carcasses of thousands of buffalo rotting on the prairie. A
new breed of white enemy had arrived, one that was far more dangerous and aggressive than the hapless sodbusters of earlier years who
had encroached timidly on their hunting grounds. The brief and
profligate era of commercial buffalo hunting was under way.

Across the Southern Plains, the buffalo herds had been declining for several decades. Still, neither Indians nor non-Indians seriously believed that these shaggy beasts would disappear altogether from the American landscape. That assumption was shattered during the 1870s. After America's transcontinental railroad was completed in 1869, it became profitable to ship buffalo hides east. Two years later, the American leather industry developed new tanning processes that made the hides more valuable.

The number of animals killed on the plains in the course of a single decade was staggering. A professional hunter could shoot as many as seventy-five buffalo per day. He hardly even had to move; buffalo usually wouldn't run from the sound of gunfire. They recognized danger only when they could smell it. Standing downwind, a hunter began shooting the beasts on the outside of the group, leisurely working his way through the herd. Skinners traveled with the hunters, stripping off the hides and leaving the meat behind. In 1872 and 1873, traders shipped about 1.5 million hides east each year. The slaughter escalated after that. During the winter of 1877–1878, the stack of buffalo hides at Fort Griffin, Texas, was said to be as long as a city block. By 1881 commercial buffalo hunting on the Southern Plains was over. The herds were wiped out.

The army saw the hunters as allies in their campaign against Native Americans living outside the reservations, since the hunters were destroying the Indians' food supply. Texas ranchers also approved of the hunting, because the buffalo competed with their cattle for grass. Not all Texans quietly assented to the butchery, however. Even in Mason County, where settlers still lived in fear of Comanche and Apache raiders, one citizen wrote: "Would it not be in the interest of the frontier people to petition Congress . . . to prevent the wholesale slaughter of this noble animal for the hides alone? . . . At the present rate of destruction the species will soon become extinct."[1] Nonetheless, a few individual conservationists were no match for the combined power of the eastern leather industry, the Texas ranchers, and the U.S. Army. In 1874 Pres. Ulysses

Grant refused to sign a federal act to protect the buffalo. The following year, a bill was introduced in the Texas legislature to stop the hunting. Gen. Philip H. Sheridan personally appeared to testify before the lawmakers in Austin, arguing that the extermination of the buffalo was necessary to drive the Indians out of Texas and stop their depredations. The bill quickly died.

The buffalo hunters set off a new round of hostilities in the Indian wars. For the Comanches, the mass killing of these animals has been described as "death—physical and spiritual."[2] Between 1874 and 1877, the Comanches and their Indian allies at that time—Apaches, Kiowas, and Cheyennes—attacked several isolated hunting camps on the Texas plains. Two of the buffalo hunters' most dedicated enemies were German-Americans from the Texas Hill Country, Rudolph Fischer and Herman Lehmann.

While Ishatai the prophet spoke of better days ahead, Asewaynah (Gray Blanket) stood in the crowd brooding over every sentence. Just like the other young men who pressed close around him, he was fired up by the shaman's promises. Unlike them, he was white. The twenty-two-year-old Quahada had been raised a Christian, but for the past nine years he'd followed a different spiritual path, one that he hoped would lead him to success in battle. Asewaynah no longer answered to his baptismal name, Rudolph Fischer.

It was May 1874. The charismatic Quahada medicine man, Ishatai (Coyote Vagina), had gathered a large group of Comanches and Cheyennes for a religious revival in Indian Territory at the junction of Elk Creek and the North Fork of the Red River, about forty-five miles west of Fort Sill. His followers were receptive to what he said, for Ishatai told them what they wanted to believe. Even middle-aged men with sons old enough to fight were swayed by his message.

Look at the peaceful Indians, the Caddoes and Wichitas, Ishatai pointed out. *Their numbers are declining. They live like paupers ever since they took up the white man's road.* For the Comanches and the

Cheyennes, however, it was not too late. Ishatai offered a way out. *If you want to be powerful again, as in the days of yours fathers and grand-fathers, you must go to battle and kill as many white people as you can. After you do that, the buffalo will return to the plains in great numbers. Things will be like they once were.*

The reactionary preacher, only in his late twenties, couldn't have attracted a serious following a few years earlier, when the world of the Southern Plains Indians was still in balance. However, by the spring of 1874, they were desperate for a messiah. The Comanches living on the reservation were discontented and unruly. Heavy rains had kept the freight wagons from reaching the agency, so the government's promised rations fell short. The Indians had to kill their horses and mules for food.

Word spread among the Comanches that Ishatai had performed miraculous feats. Some claimed he had belched forth a wagonload of cartridges, then swallowed them again. In battle, according to his fellow fighting men, the bullets of his enemies fell harmlessly from their guns. Ishatai even told the Comanches that he had ascended above the clouds and communed with the Great Spirit. When he accurately prophesied a drought and the disappearance of a comet, many believed him. Ishatai also promised the congregation that he could create war paint that would deflect bullets.

Like all the men at the gathering, Rudolph Fischer was primed for battle. The commander of a squad of Comanche warriors, he had selected the heart of a bird known as a blue darter as his "medicine," the material object associated with his source of supernatural power and protection. In Comanche religion, certain animals represented guardian spirits who could bring success in war and hunting.

Another war leader who put his faith in Ishatai was Quanah, then in his midtwenties. He was a son of the Comanches' most famous white captive, Cynthia Ann Parker, and Fischer was his right-hand man. At Ishatai's revival, Quanah came forward and suggested that the first white people they killed should be a group of buffalo hunters camped along the South Fork of the Canadian River in the Texas Panhandle. The hunters had set up their headquarters near the ruins of William Bent's old trading post, known as Adobe Walls.

Ishatai gave his blessings to the plan. He and Quanah left the medicine dance with Rudolph Fischer and a group of Comanches and Cheyennes estimated to have numbered between 200 and 250. Day after day, they rode hard with little rest. Along the way, Ishatai kept the religious fervor high by encouraging the men to dance every night. He announced, "God tells me we are going to kill lots of white men. We will kill them all, just like old women."

They found the buffalo hunters where Quanah had said they'd be. During the predawn hours of June 27, 1874, the Comanches and Cheyennes gathered on a butte near the camp and gazed down on the makeshift settlement of Adobe Walls. Twenty-eight men and one woman were sleeping there in three separate buildings. No one was moving about. Nor had the hunters posted a guard.

The Comanches and Cheyennes prepared themselves for the attack. They formed battle units around their leaders—respected fighters such as Quanah and Rudolph Fischer. Ishatai painted his naked body yellow. Just before daylight, the Indians launched the assault. Whooping and firing their rifles, the first wave of fighters swept down from the plateau and dashed across the meadow, their horses' hooves as loud as thunder. They raced their mounts at full speed and started circling the buildings.

Inside the crude shacks, the hunters crept cautiously to the windows. Some were still in their underwear. Brandishing long-range rifles, they appeared at the openings just long enough to fire at their attackers. They'd had plenty of shooting practice, and their aim was deadly.

For half an hour, the Indians hurled lances into the compound, shot bullets and arrows through the windows, leaped onto the roofs, and beat on the doors with the butts of their rifles. They killed two German brothers and their black Newfoundland dog, then scalped all three. They also looted the hunters' wagons and drove off their livestock. However, they were surprised that the battle wasn't as quick and easy as Ishatai had promised. Even though the Indians greatly outnumbered their enemies, the hunters were experienced marksmen. Huddled in the buildings, they were also better protected. By the time the Indians retreated from the first attack to rest and regroup, the hunters had killed two Cheyennes and one Comanche.

Throughout the day, the Indians made several more charges, but the fight became a drawn-out, disheartening stalemate. Unable to overrun the settlement, the Indians suffered unexpectedly heavy losses in their attempts. The anticipated triumph turned out to be a costly fiasco. The Indians were amazed by the accuracy of the hunters' shots. A Comanche named Cohayyah remembered, "Sometimes we would be standing way off, resting and hardly thinking of the fight, and they would kill our horses." Even Quanah's horse was knocked out from under him. For much of the day, Quanah was disabled by a blow from a ricocheted shell. "They killed us in sight and out of sight," he said in later years.

Ishatai watched the debacle from the plateau. Too late his followers realized that they'd put their trust in a charlatan. One Cheyenne told him bitterly, "If the white man's bullets cannot hurt you, go down and bring back my son's body." Another Cheyenne named Hippy grabbed the bridle of Ishatai's horse and tried to use it as a quirt on him. Then came the medicine man's greatest humiliation. A stray shot killed Ishatai's horse, which he had coated with his special protective paint.

Around four o'clock, the Indians gave up. Three white men were dead, and the hunters had killed thirteen Comanches and Cheyennes. The bodies of some of the Indians were lying too close to the settlement for their friends to recover them. Later, the hunters cut off their heads and used them to decorate the gateposts of the corral.[3]

The defeat at Adobe Walls shook the confidence of the Comanches and Cheyennes, who had thought they would teach the buffalo hunters a lesson. Moreover, the attack on the hunters would lead to the abandonment of President Grant's peace policy toward the Indians, setting off a military campaign known as the Red River War. During the remainder of 1874, Col. Ranald Mackenzie kept the Quahadas on the run. He had resolved to drive them onto the reservation and force them to surrender. That fall the weather was unusually wet, and the Comanches referred to the miserable pursuit as the "Wrinkled Hand Chase."

Finally, Mackenzie and his cavalrymen wore down their adversaries. The Kotsoteka chief Mowway, whose village had once been defended by Adolph Korn and Clinton Smith, arrived at the reservation with a group of about 175 destitute Comanches on April 18, 1875. On April 23, Mackenzie sent four messengers to negotiate a truce with Quanah and the remaining Quahada holdouts. One of the emissaries was Jacob J. Sturm, who had recovered Banc Babb from the Comanches eight years earlier. On June 2, 1875, Quanah and over four hundred of his exhausted followers arrived at Fort Sill and surrendered to Colonel Mackenzie. Rudolph Fischer was most likely among this group.

Quanah's surrender in 1875 is often said to mark the end of the Comanches' free, nomadic life. That's not exactly true. About forty to fifty Comanches, still refusing to walk the white man's road, ran away from the reservation and remained at large over the next two years.[4] This small group of renegades would eventually include the last white captive living on the Southern Plains, Herman Lehmann.

In the summer of 1875, after the Comanches had given up the fight, scattered bands of Apaches were still raiding in western and central Texas. Among their warriors was Herman Lehmann. By then he was sixteen and had lived with the Apaches for five years. With his fair skin painted red and black and his long hair that had turned bright red, the white teenager looked like a supernatural terror to his enemies, both Indian and non-Indian.

That August Herman was raiding not far from his old home in Mason County with a party of twelve Apaches and their Mexican captive. Herman and the Apaches had stolen over forty horses in Kimble,

Mason, and Menard Counties. Once they were satisfied with their loot, they started driving the herd northwest.

Meanwhile, the local ranchers, helpless to stop the horse thefts, complained about their losses to some Texas Rangers stationed at Los Moras Camp in Menard County. On August 20, 1875, Capt. Dan Roberts, with a patrol of twelve men, left Los Moras in search of the raiders. They found the Apaches' tracks on Scalp Creek, a tributary of the San Saba River in Menard County.

By that time, the Apaches thought they were safe. They planned to hunt for a couple of weeks around Kickapoo Springs. However, their scouts soon discovered that the "hateful Rangers," as Herman called them, were on their trail. Herman wrote, "We well knew how sleepless and restless those Rangers were and how unerring their aim when they got in a shot, so we out-rode them." They quit hunting and headed for the plains at full speed. For three days and nights, the Apaches rode without eating or sleeping. When their horses got tired, they roped fresh ones and kept riding.

By August 23, the fourth day of the chase, the Apaches had reached open country, far from any settlement, with nothing in sight for miles around but a few scattered mesquites. They finally stopped to butcher a donkey they came across. After building a fire, they roasted the meat and ate it leisurely while they rested and let their horses graze. Later, they killed and ate a mustang. As Herman remembered, "We thought we were out of danger, so we became a bit careless." One of the raiders assured the others, "No white man will ever come here." Then he added boastfully: "If they do, I can whip ten of them." That evening they stopped and slept about sixty-five miles west of Fort Concho.

The Apaches broke camp at daylight on the morning of August 24, 1875.[5] They'd ridden about half an hour when they realized they'd been fooling themselves. Only five hundred yards away, the rangers were charging them in single file from the east. The rising sun had blinded the Apaches, and they didn't see the enemy approaching until they were almost on them. When the rangers started shooting and yelling, the Apaches panicked. Some of them began rounding up the herd. Others jumped on fresh horses, not stopping to take the saddles off the mounts they abandoned.

The rangers jumped off their horses and leveled their rifles. The Apaches' leader ordered his men to stand close together. He told them they had no choice but to fight, for it was too late to escape. But the men didn't obey him. The line of Apaches broke up when the shooting started. Herman recalled, "Everything was on the run and we were scattering like a flock of quail." The Apaches grabbed their Winchesters and took off at a gallop. The rangers got back on their horses and chased them, singly or in pairs. The two sides were evenly matched in numbers. A few of the Apaches rallied on a small plateau, where they opened fire on the rangers, giving their comrades cover while they caught fresh horses. Then they all took off again. The running fight went on for three or four miles.

The rangers shot and killed the horse of an Apache named Nusticeno. He started running west on foot. Herman rode up beside him on a big stallion the Apaches had stolen a few days earlier. Several rangers started after them. Herman leaned over and shot a few arrows from under his horse's neck. He missed, although two of the arrows struck a ranger's saddle. He shouted at Nusticeno, "Get up behind me." His fellow warrior jumped on Herman's horse.

They took off and tried to catch up with their friends. The rangers cut them off, firing at least a dozen shots at them. Several bullets smashed into Herman's shield, knocking it against his forehead. He could hear bullets striking Nusticeno's shield as well. Herman kept shooting arrows at the rangers in front of them. Nusticeno fired his Winchester at those in the rear. When he ran out of cartridges, he threw down his rifle and started shooting arrows. Herman's horse was slowing down under the weight of the two young men. He and Nusticeno couldn't get close to any fresh ones. They started to circle, a maneuver the Apaches used when they were cornered.

A ranger named Jim Gillett dismounted to fire at the stallion and its two riders. Gillett was only eighteen; this was his first Indian fight, and he later admitted he was "awfully nervous." In spite of his anxiety, he managed to fire a bullet that struck Herman's horse in the head. The stallion fell and slid forward twenty feet, pinning Herman to the ground beneath it. The horse's body also broke Nusticeno's bow during the fall. Nusticeno grabbed Herman's bow and ran, holding his shield over his back for protection. Herman cried out to Nusticeno not to leave him. But his friend, in a panic, abandoned Herman to fend for himself.

Two rangers, Jim Gillett and Ed Seiker, ran up to Herman. Gillett pointed his six-shooter at Herman's head. Herman closed his eyes just before he heard the shot. The bullet grazed his temple, and the gunpowder burned his face. He didn't think he was badly wounded. He heard the rangers talking with each other. Herman didn't understand English, but Seiker was shouting at Gillett: "Don't shoot him! Don't you see that he is a white boy?"[6] Terrified, Herman opened his eyes. The boy warrior saw two frightened boy rangers staring down at him. Gillett lowered his pistol. Then the rangers took off running after Nusticeno. Herman couldn't see anything from beneath his horse, but he heard several shots.

Herman finally managed to free himself from the body of the dead stallion. He crawled on his belly through the green grass, which was only seven or eight inches high in places. He remained motionless near a small mesquite tree. The young rangers came back to look for him. Several others joined them in a search that lasted at least an hour. The rangers covered every patch of ground for a mile around, examining each bush and tuft of grass. Twice they rode within a few feet of Herman. Finally, the rangers gave up. They stripped the bridle and saddle from Herman's fallen stallion. Then they left, heading east.[7]

Herman waited until they were long gone before he stood up. Neither the rangers nor the Apaches were anywhere in sight. He walked to the lifeless body of his horse and saw that the rangers had taken all of his weapons. A few hundred yards away, he found his friend Nusticeno, who had been "butchered terribly." In their zeal, the novice rangers had shot the Apache countless times, carved the skin off him, and even decapitated him. Herman couldn't find Nusticeno's head anywhere. The rangers had also taken Nusticeno's bow, quiver, shield, and moccasins as trophies.

Herman was completely unnerved by the gruesome sight. Apaches were afraid of the spirits of the dead under any circumstances, and the horrible condition of Nusticeno's corpse made things worse. Herman couldn't even turn the body facedown, in accordance with his people's burial custom, for there "was no face on which to turn him." He stared in disbelief. Then he turned and started running across the plains as fast as he could. He kept running until he fell to the ground, exhausted. Recalling the scene more than two decades later, Herman wrote: "I can see that headless form yet when I close my eyes."

He soon realized his Apache friends had given him up for dead. With no horse or weapons, Herman headed west on foot. He walked for five days through barren country, living on grasshoppers, lizards, bugs, roots, prickly pear, frogs, weeds, and anything else he could find. Water was scarce, and he nearly died of thirst. One time he ate mud to get some moisture. After a while, he became delirious. By the time Herman finally found his people's village, his toenails had come off his blistered feet. The Apaches were overjoyed to see him. The women cooked him a big meal, fixed him a comfortable bed, and showed him "every consideration." Having assumed Herman was dead, the Apaches had already killed all his horses so they might accompany him to the next world. They'd also destroyed his personal possessions in mourning.

It took two months for Herman to regain his health. One of his nurses was Ete, a sister of Herman's adoptive father, Carnoviste. Ete was a kindhearted, modest girl about Herman's age. They had been close friends since they were adolescents; as teenagers, they became even more intimate. She made him some moccasins and a new buckskin jacket decorated with red beads. He, in turn, lavished all his "love and affections on her." Herman wanted to impress Ete, as well as his other Apache friends, and when he told them about the fight on the

Staked Plains of Texas, he stretched the story a bit. He said he had buried Nusticeno facedown and had covered his grave with rocks, so the wolves would not disturb his body.

Over the course of more than five years, Herman Lehmann had plenty of occasions to prove himself to the Apaches. They, in turn, rewarded his loyalty and ability. He rose to the position of petty chief under his foster father, Carnoviste. By age sixteen, he was the leader of a small band of men. Herman's memoirs suggest that he would have been content to remain with the Apaches forever. However, an unexpected crisis in the spring of 1876[8] changed the course of his life.

One of Herman's few enemies in his tribe was a medicine man who "never lost an opportunity to torment" the captive boy. Shamans could use their mystical power for either good or evil; thus, the Apaches feared as well as respected them. Herman had always hated this man. One day they got into a quarrel. After a short cat-and-mouse chase around a rock, Herman shot an arrow through the man's stomach and another into his side. After the medicine man fell, Herman sent a third arrow through his heart. His eyes rolled up, and he died with a faint groan.[9]

Herman realized at once that he would have to run. Although the Apaches didn't punish a murderer at the tribal level, they also didn't stop the victim's family from torturing and killing the murderer in revenge. Herman stayed in hiding the rest of that day, waiting until after midnight to slip into the village. Before he left, he wanted to see Ete one more time.

That night they had a long talk. Ete told Herman she loved him and admired him and was grateful for their friendship. "I will never forget you," she said. For his own safety, however, she urged him to flee. Ete encouraged Herman to go back to his white family, for she thought he would be happy with them.

Herman told her, "I will not go unless you go, too."

Ete replied, "I will not be well received among the whites, while you will be perfectly at home." She also told him that she didn't have the stamina for the rigorous journey ahead of him. The girl finally convinced Herman that he must leave the village alone. They made no false promises to wait for each other; both knew they were parting ways. Ete gave Herman some blankets, ammunition, and dried meat for the trip. They were both weeping when he drew her to his breast, and they held each other for a long time. Then Herman gathered the provisions Ete had given him, crept toward a gray horse, and took off.

Throughout the night, Herman rode east across a vast, deserted plain covered with cactus and sagebrush. For the first time in his life, he was completely alone. The teenage fugitive had no family, Indian or white. By then Carnoviste and his wife, Laughing Eyes, had both died, and Herman no longer thought of his relatives in Loyal Valley as his people.

After an exhausting ride, he came to a deep, narrow canyon watered by a small stream. He camped there for a long time and lived as a hermit, always fearful of being discovered and killed. "I regarded all men as my enemies," he wrote. Often, he thought about the happy times he'd known with Ete. However, he hardly ever reminisced about his German-American family. He never considered going back to Loyal Valley, as Ete had encouraged him to do, for he still remembered how hard his parents had labored on their farm. Herman wrote, "How could I who was as free as a bird be cramped up in a house and forced to toil for a livelihood?"

Herman eventually left his hideout in the canyon and roamed the prairie, living off the land. By the winter of 1876,[10] the seventeen-year-old warrior had become despondent over his solitary existence. One morning he discovered that he was sharing the range with a party of renegade Comanches. All day long, Herman followed them at a distance. That night he watched the Comanches sitting around their campfire. They were eating and laughing and talking about the things they'd seen and done that day. Herman was cold and hungry, and he envied them. Deciding he had nothing to lose, he mustered his courage and walked into their camp unannounced. The sudden appearance of this wild-looking, redheaded youth with a drawn bow startled the Comanches. They let out loud whoops and yells, then disappeared into the darkness.

When they cautiously returned and surrounded him, Herman made signs for peace, since he didn't speak much of their language. A Comanche woman approached him, scowling and chattering. Herman couldn't understand her, but he later learned that she was encouraging the men to kill him. She warned, "He will bring us trouble." A young Comanche man stepped forward and rebuked her. He walked up to Herman and said to him in Apache, "You are with Comanches, and if you prove to be all right, you will be among friends and will be protected."

Through this interpreter, Herman explained to the group that he had been separated from his people by misfortune. He said that he was an Apache by adoption and that he "loved the Indian and hated the white man." He also showed them his shield with the scalps of his white victims. Finally, he told them, "I want to become a Comanche." The Comanches listened to Herman's story and showed their interest "by many explosive grunts." When he was finished, they told him he was welcome to stay with them as long as he pleased. Herman recalled, "How good, free, easy and at home I did feel!"

They allowed him to choose the family with whom he would live. Herman selected the head of the group, Cotopah, who spoke Apache. The Comanches gave the teenage boy a new name, Montechema.[11] Without hesitation Herman severed his ties with the Apaches, just as he'd long ago done with the German-Americans. From that night until the end of his life, he considered himself a Comanche.

During the early months of 1877, Herman and the Comanche renegades hunted on the plains of the Texas Panhandle as they'd always done. The small party found enough wild game to meet its modest needs. Although they had to be on the lookout for soldiers and Texas Rangers, their most serious threat was the buffalo hunters. Nothing gave the Comanches more satisfaction than destroying their camps. "The plains were literally alive with buffalo hunters," Herman recalled many years later. "We would often see great wagon loads of hides being hauled away, and would find the carcasses of thousands of slaughtered buffalo. It made us desperate to see this wanton slaughter of our food supply." The Comanches were wary of launching full-scale attacks on hunters' camps, however, for some of them had fought in the disastrous battle at Adobe Walls.

One morning in February 1877, Herman was riding with a large group of Comanches when they spotted a buffalo hunter named Marshall Sewell. He was working by himself, away from his camp near the headwaters of the Salt Fork of the Brazos River. The Comanches watched in silent fury as Sewell brought down the enormous beasts one by one. Finally, he ran out of ammunition. Buffalo hunters were notoriously careless; Sewell had failed to save a few cartridges for self-defense. The Comanches swooped down on the lone hunter and started circling him. They shot him in the thigh. Panicked, Sewell struggled to get back to his camp. He was close to it when the Comanches finally killed him. Meanwhile, Sewell's two skinners, known as Wild Skillet and Moccasin Jim, had started from camp in a wagon to collect the hides. The Comanches began chasing them. The skinners turned their wagon around and fled, heading for a small, brushy ravine. The wagon plunged over the steep bank, and the two men escaped on foot through the brush.

The Comanches headed for the hunters' abandoned camp and took anything they fancied: guns, ammunition, skinning knives, axes, bedding, and tin utensils. Whatever they didn't want, they destroyed. They even slashed the buffalo hides with knives and set them ablaze so the hunters couldn't sell them. As they left the area, Herman Lehmann and the Comanches passed by Sewell's body. They stopped to take two pieces of his scalp. They cut a gash in each temple, thrust a sharp stick through his stomach, and set fire to his wagon, delivering a potent warning to all buffalo hunters on the plains.

Word of Marshall Sewell's grisly death reached a settlement called Rath City (also known as Camp Reynolds), where buffalo hunters congregated. On March 4, 1877, a group of forty-six men, mostly hunters, left Rath City to pursue the Comanches who had killed Sewell. In the meantime, Herman and his party continued to plunder the camps of other hunters.

The buffalo hunters' guide accurately predicted that the Comanches would be camped in Yellow House Canyon, near present-day Lubbock, Texas. The "canyon" was just a small depression on the grassy plain, but the dense cover of trees and cactus gave the Indians a natural hiding place. On the bank of a small stream, the Comanches had camped with some Apaches who were trading with them.

Just after sunrise on March 18, 1877, the buffalo hunters charged the Indians' camp, taking them by surprise. The Indians thought the men shooting at them were either soldiers or Texas Rangers. At first a few Indians raised a white flag, but once they realized their attackers were few, they rallied and fought back. Some of the Comanche women jumped on their horses and headed out of camp to round up the rest of the herd grazing nearby. Other women grabbed bows, arrows, guns, and spears. They scrambled to the top of the canyon, firing pistols at the advancing hunters. Although the buffalo hunters were good shots, they weren't trained as fighters, and they were terribly disorganized. Some retreated after the Comanche women's first volley. Others shot at their fellow hunters rather than the Indians.

Herman Lehmann and the Indian men took refuge under a hillside northwest of camp. There, they managed to hold the hunters at bay for about three hours, firing at them with long-range rifles. Neither side made much headway. Finally, Herman Lehmann and one of his companions got tired of waiting and decided to charge the hunters. Herman's friend went first. He goaded his horse and rode out from his hiding place into the open. For a while, he dodged the hunters' bullets by circling. Eventually, his horse was hit and fell to the ground. The man continued to fight on foot until he, too, was shot dead. That only increased Herman's rage. He charged next. Before long his brown horse was shot down. Crouching behind its body, he continued to shoot at the hunters. Finally, the gunfire "got too hot" for the lone white Indian. He ran about fifty yards toward a bluff. While the hunters watched, Herman stopped for a moment and put his hand on his hip. Then he disappeared over the edge. Herman had been hit in the right leg, and his wound would cripple him for a long time.

After several hours, the buffalo hunters called it quits and retreated. The Indians chased them briefly, then pulled back. Gathering their families and horses, they moved camp. Neither the hunters nor the Indians could claim victory in the battle at Yellow House Canyon. In fact, the incident was significant only in hindsight. None of the participants knew at the time that they had taken part in the last major fight between Indians and non-Indians on the high plains of Texas. During the months after this battle, the skirmishes between the Comanches and the buffalo hunters became progressively inconsequential.[12]

Nonetheless, the raids did not go unpunished. On April 19, 1877, Capt. Phillip L. Lee left Fort Griffin to track down and punish the raiders. With him were ten Tonkawa scouts and more than forty African-American troops from the Tenth Cavalry. They trailed the Comanches for two weeks. At around two o'clock on the afternoon of May 4, they found the women, children, and wounded men camped at Quemado (Silver) Lake, a small salt lake in northern Cochran County, Texas, near the New Mexico border. Most of the able-bodied men, including Herman, were out hunting or raiding. Those in camp were still recovering from the injuries they'd suffered the month before at Yellow House Canyon.

Captain Lee gave the order for his soldiers to charge. By official counts, the cavalrymen killed four Comanches and captured four women and two children. Herman Lehmann maintained that "all of our women had been killed or captured except ten and all the men but two Indians and a Mexican who had married one of our women." When Herman and his group got back from raiding buffalo camps on the Brazos River, they found the mutilated corpses of their family members. "The bodies presented a revolting sight," Herman wrote. "Our rage knew no bounds."

After this massacre, the Comanches vowed to take wholesale revenge on the people of Texas as soon as they could consolidate their forces. They never got that chance.

Col. Ranald Mackenzie had succeeded in driving almost all the Comanches to their reservation in 1875. In the summer of 1877, he decided it would be wiser and easier to bring in the few stragglers from the plains through diplomacy rather than force. In early July, Mackenzie and Indian agent James M. Haworth arranged to send Quanah to locate those Comanches who had never surrendered or had run away from the reservation.

On July 12, 1877, in the middle of a sweltering summer, Quanah left Fort Sill with three women, three men, and several government pack mules loaded with supplies. As testimony to their peaceful intentions, Quanah's party carried a white flag and a stern letter from Ranald Mackenzie warning anyone they encountered not to harm them or interfere with their mission. Mackenzie was justifiably concerned about their welfare, and these precautions would be crucial during the dangerous journey. Any Texans who had suffered from Indian raids—and they were many—would have been delighted to take Quanah's scalp.

Quanah found Herman Lehmann and the runaway Comanches along the Pecos River in eastern New Mexico, where they had set up camp with about six Apache families. He met with the men in council for four days. Urging them to come to the reservation, he tried to convince the renegades that their roaming way of life was finished. "It is useless for you to fight longer," he said. "The white people will kill all of you if you keep on fighting. They will come in on you from every side." Although the Indians in the camp trusted Quanah, some of them thought they should try to hold out on the plains a while longer. They argued about this a great deal before they finally agreed to leave with Quanah. Some, including Herman, went reluctantly.

After Quanah persuaded the runaways to surrender, he still faced the challenge of moving them across the Texas Panhandle without getting shot by soldiers or buffalo hunters. On the evening of July 29, they started their trip under cover of darkness, leaving behind nearly two hundred horses and mules so they could travel more quickly. They abandoned over one hundred more head of stock at their campsite the next night. During the daytime, Quanah kept lookout with a pair of army field glasses, trying to keep the group as far away from the buffalo hunters as he could.

Once Quanah's party entered Indian Territory and got close to Fort Sill, the men started having second thoughts. They held a council, and fifteen of them, including Herman, took a new oath never to surrender or submit to white dominance. As they were about to flee to the prairie, Quanah succeeded in talking them out of it. Against their better judgment, they continued with Quanah toward the fort.

That night their leader, whom Herman called High Shorty, had a disturbing dream. The next morning, he called his men together, inviting Quanah to listen. After describing his dream, he told Quanah that he had done wrong by breaking his oath. "Quanah, I am not afraid of you," he said, "but I dread the white men."

Quanah assured him that they would be protected at Fort Sill and would not be punished. Although High Shorty knew Quanah was a man of his word, he doubted whether he had much influence over the army officers. Growing philosophical, he said to Quanah, "You are one of us, but where did we lose our warriors? Did we lose them in battle? No, we weakened and submitted to the whites and they transported many warriors far away from their wives and loved ones." High Shorty was referring to nine Comanche men who were accused of various crimes and sent to prison at Fort Marion, Florida, after they surrendered in 1875.

Quanah's reply was an appeal for pragmatism. "I have ridden on the black horse and seen white people by the thousands and thousands," he said. He convinced them that it would be foolish for fifteen Comanches to try to whip the U.S. Army. "You are too near akin to me for me to let the soldiers hurt you or any of your men," he said. "So come on and don't be killed."[13]

The renegades kept riding with Quanah. On August 20, 1877,

fifty-seven Indians and one white warrior finally arrived at their new, permanent home.[14] When they were within fifteen miles of Fort Sill, they noticed a cloud of dust and saw the soldiers coming to meet them. Suddenly, Herman panicked. He turned his black mare around and started riding as fast as he could toward the Wichita Mountains. Quanah took off after Herman and caught up with him after three or four miles. "There is no need to be afraid," he said. "You will not be hurt." Herman stopped and listened in silence. Still, he refused to go back. Finally, Quanah gave up trying to reason with the hardheaded German Comanche. He told Herman to go hide in his camp, giving directions how to find it.

Twenty-one men surrendered that day, along with their families. They were believed to be the last Comanches living off the reservation. The soldiers, after confiscating the horses and weapons, locked up the men in the guardhouse. True to his word, Quanah spoke to Ranald Mackenzie on the renegades' behalf. Although he couldn't prevent them from being classified as prisoners, Quanah was "very anxious that they be kept in confinement" with their families and friends at Fort Sill rather than being sent to Florida.

The colonel was sympathetic. He had come to respect, even like, his most dedicated enemies, the Quahadas. He once wrote, "I think better of this band than of any other on the reservation. . . . I shall let them down as easily as I can."[15] On account of Quanah's "excellent conduct in a dangerous expedition," Mackenzie recommended to his superiors that Quanah's request be granted. Noting that the prisoners surrendered "with no trouble whatsoever," he opined that "the good conduct in this matter of the Comanches entitles them to consideration." The colonel thought a lenient confinement at Fort Sill for one year would be a sufficient check on their propensity to run away and raid.

Ranald Mackenzie didn't know that one Comanche was still at large. Herman Lehmann, now a fugitive of sorts, was hiding in the Wichita Mountains near the fort. He followed Quanah's instructions and found his camp on the reservation. For several months, Herman lived in the mountains near the post. During the fall of 1877, he took his meals with Quanah's family, herded Quanah's horses, and hunted a lot. For the first time in seven years, Herman had to worry about his skin color. Neither the Apaches nor the Comanches had treated him differently because he was white, but he knew that the authorities at Fort Sill might send him away if they noticed him. He tried to disguise his race and avoided white people as much as possible.

The fall of 1877 was an unhappy time in Herman's life. Although he remained unfettered, he couldn't enjoy his freedom after his closest friends lost theirs. He grew sullen and resentful as he watched his fellow Comanches adjust to the drudgery of reservation life. "I did not like to see my comrades so badly treated," he wrote. They "were made to grade the roads all around the post and to do farm work, with which they were not familiar." Distressed by what he saw, Herman made up his mind to remain a true Comanche, even if he was the last one.

In May 1877, three months before the last free Comanches surrendered, preparations were under way for another white Indian's return to his family in the Texas Hill Country. For nearly two years, people around Fort Sill had noticed the wavy, auburn hair of a Comanche man known as Asewaynah. When questioned, he revealed his birth name, Fischer. He no longer remembered his parents' names or the place of his birth (or else pretended not to), but he admitted to having heard of Austin, Texas. On that slim clue, an advertisement was published in an Austin newspaper. That was how Gottlieb and Sophie Fischer of Fredericksburg, who had heard nothing about their son for six years, learned that Rudolph was still alive. Rudolph's mother was "said to be almost frantic with joy at the recovery of a son, whom she believed dead already."

Although it didn't take long to locate Rudolph on the Kiowa-Comanche reservation, the arrangements for his trip to Texas dragged on all summer. The main problem was not where but how to send him. William Nicholson, the Indian Office's superintendent in Lawrence,

Kansas, didn't want the government to spend much money on Rudolph's trip home. Nicholson specifically rebuffed a suggestion to hire an interpreter to accompany the young man to Fredericksburg:

> In the first place, if he was 13 years of age when captured, he must have been able to speak English very well and he can scarcely have so far forgotten his knowledge of it as not to be able to make himself understood on his journey homeward. Moreover, if it were really the case that he has lost all knowledge of English he would need an interpreter quite as much after getting home as on the way thither. Finally he is of sufficient age to take care of himself and if he remains with the Indians it must be because he prefers to do so and not from necessity.[16]

Nicholson's insensitivity was stunning. Rudolph Fischer, a German-American, spoke only a little English prior to his capture. More significant, a captive often lost his mother tongue after living merely a year or two with a Native American tribe; Rudolph had spent twelve years with the Comanches. Nicholson's observation that Rudolph would need an interpreter after he got to Fredericksburg was beside the point. The Indian Office still had an obligation to get him there safely. It seems that the superintendent didn't really care whether the young man's parents ever saw him again or not. Indian agent James M. Haworth, who was directly responsible for Rudolph while he was on the reservation, didn't expend much effort on the Fischer family's behalf, either.[17] In June he did manage to recruit a character known as Mexican Jim Guadalupe, who was willing to take Rudolph home if his expenses were paid. However, Haworth appears to have taken no further steps to hire him.

For Gottlieb Fischer, the wait that summer was unbearable. He spoke no English and had to ask friends in Fredericksburg to write letters for him. In August he solicited the help of a local gunsmith named Engelbert Krauskopf. On August 8, 1877, Krauskopf sent a telegram to Fort Sill asking how much Mexican Jim would charge to bring Rudolph home. The military officers at the post asked agent Haworth to obtain an estimate. Still, the matter languished.

Exasperated, Fischer and Krauskopf contacted their U.S. congressman, a fellow German-American named Gustav Schleicher, to see if he could move things along in Washington. Gottlieb Fischer also asked whether the Indian Office would cover the expenses of sending his son to Fredericksburg. Congressman Schleicher contacted the commissioner of Indian Affairs, John Smith. Finally, the Fischers' pleas fell on a sympathetic ear. Smith wrote to Superintendent Nicholson in Kansas: "From the statements made in the case I think it calls for favorable action, and *one hundred dollars*, or so much thereof, as is found actually necessary to pay the expenses of the young man's transportation from Fort Sill, where he now is, to his fathers home in Texas, will be allowed for the purpose indicated." The commissioner further directed that agent Haworth place Rudolph "in charge of some reliable person, or transportation company, to be taken to his home in Texas."

Once the money matters were resolved, the Indian agent faced the more daunting challenge of convincing Rudolph Fischer to leave his Comanche family and go live with people in Texas whom he barely remembered and no longer cared about. Rudolph was twenty-five years old by then. He was married and reportedly had fathered two children.[18]

In August Rudolph was brought to Fort Sill and was kept there while awaiting his return to Texas. According to a letter published in the *San Antonio Daily Express,* he would be leaving the Comanches "against his protest, for he is said to have not only forgotten his native tongue, but has become a stranger to all civilized customs, and is really of Indian nature." Even before Rudolph got to Texas, the writer declared that he would be opposed to his parents "in all their principles of living and in all their ideas of civilized life—an Indian warrior, the husband of a squaw, and the father of two young savages."

On September 3, 1877, Gottlieb Fischer's friend Engelbert Krauskopf received a letter from Jonathan Richards, a Quaker agent who had served at the Wichita agency. Richards reported that he had talked with Rudolph several times about returning to his people, but had not been able to obtain his consent. The letter suggested that Rudolph was not entirely opposed to traveling to Fredericksburg for a visit. Either his feelings about seeing the Fischer family were mixed or else he was placating the agent while dragging his feet. According to Richards, Rudolph

> states that he would like to see his people very much, but does not know enough about white people's ways to make a living with them. He has become accustomed to the Indian life, and is well contented, being well treated by them. He would like to re-main and go with them on their usual buffalo hunt this winter. I have thought it would be as well not to press the matter further for a while.[19]

Gottlieb Fischer had waited on the Indian agents long enough. Immediately, he left Fredericksburg to retrieve his son, arriving at Fort Sill on September 12, 1877. According to a telegram sent to several Texas newspapers, he recognized his grown son instantly and was overcome with joy. Rudolph was less enthralled to see Gottlieb:

> His embraces and caresses were received by the son with stoic in-difference and imbecile smiles, and nothing would induce him to recognize his father or consent to go home with him, until Gen-eral McKenzie [sic] interfered and authoritatively told him he had to go. Profuse promises of horses, guns, etc., dear to the In-dian's heart, made no impression on him, and he seems to feel the parting from the Indians very keenly.[20]

Indian agent Haworth confirmed this account, reporting: "The young man could not be prevailed upon to go before the arrival of his father, and only then by compulsion."

Meanwhile, as word of Fischer's imminent return spread throughout Texas, newspapers followed the story closely. Several years had passed since journalists had had an occasion to write about an Indian captive, and they made the most of the opportunity. The headlines announced: "A Redeemed Captive: He Spends Twelve Years with the Savages, and Learns to be Like Them." "Rudolf Fisher the Indian Captive: He refuses to Return to His Parents." "A Frontier Romance—Recovery of Young Fisher After Thirteen Years with the Indians—Meeting Of Father and Son."

People in Fredericksburg were anxious to see the young man whom the newspapers said "had grown wild and savage from his long intercourse with the blood-thirsty reds." One day a rumor broke out that Rudolph had arrived at Engelbert Krauskopf's gunsmith shop. The locals rushed there to get a glimpse of "the boy who had been with the savage reds." As it turned out, Krauskopf had only received a package of photographs from Fort Sill. The *San Antonio Daily Express* reported that in the portraits, Rudolph was dressed as a white man, except that a blanket was tied around his waist. His hair was "long and parted in the middle like an Indian's."

Gottlieb Fischer left Fort Sill with Rudolph on September 16, 1877. Ranald Mackenzie arranged transport for father and son as far as Fort Griffin in a military ambulance "sent especially for their benefit." Colonel Mackenzie also provided them with food for the trip. He noted that Gottlieb Fischer was "a very worthy man," but that he spoke "very little English." Mackenzie asked the commander of Fort Griffin, Phillip L. Lee, to "give them transportation to help them along beyond that post" if he could. The Indian Office's appropriation of $100 for the Fischers' trip home turned out to be an empty gesture; agent Haworth was not allowed to pay the transportation costs until after their travel was completed and the receipts were presented.

Rudolph clearly wasn't pleased to be going back to Fredericksburg with his white father. Still, Ranald Mackenzie must not have been too concerned that he would try to escape, for he didn't order a guard to accompany the Fischers. It appears that the young man grudgingly agreed to go with his father and not cause any problems. His close friends Quanah and Black Crow may have convinced him this was necessary. Or perhaps he had already made up his mind that his journey to Fredericksburg wouldn't be a one-way trip.

On December 17, 1877, in the middle of a heavy rainstorm, Ranald Mackenzie left Fort Sill on an overland march to Texas with six companies of the Fourth Cavalry. Once again the colonel was being sent to put an end to Indian depredations along the Texas-Mexico border. He and his men traveled south by way of Fort Griffin and Camp Colorado. They stayed overnight in Mason in January 1878. When Auguste Buchmeier's friends learned that he was nearby, they sent word to her that the colonel would pass through Loyal Valley the next day on his way to Fredericksburg. She had heard rumors about a white boy living with the Indians near Fort Sill and wanted to find out more about him.

By the time Auguste got the message the following day, Mackenzie had already left Loyal Valley and was well on his way to Fredericksburg. Auguste and her husband, Phillip, hitched a team of fresh horses to their carriage and tried to overtake him. They found his camp three miles north of Fredericksburg. The soldiers led Auguste to the colonel's tent. She described her son to him, mentioning that he would be eighteen by then.

Mackenzie replied, "There is one white boy there. But from the description you give, I don't think he is your son, for he is not that old."

Auguste wasn't able to hide her disappointment. Mackenzie studied her for a moment and then said, "Madam, I'll tell you what we'll do. We'll go on to Fredericksburg and telegraph the soldiers to bring him down, and if he is your boy I will be very glad. But if he should prove not to be your son, I will have him taken to San Antonio and place him where he can learn a trade. He has no business with the Indians."

When Colonel Mackenzie got to Fredericksburg the next day, he sent a telegram to Fort Sill asking about the white boy who stayed with Quanah's family. The answer that came back on January 28, 1878, brought Herman's mother both elation and frustration: "Buckiers [sic] boy out on the hunt with the Indians, Agent has been informed, matter to be attended to on boys return." A young man that they thought might be Herman was living there, but he was off hunting. After more than seven years without seeing her son, Auguste Buchmeier would have to wait a little longer. She recalled, "These were the longest three months I ever spent."

In the eyes of the federal government, Herman Lehmann was still a prisoner of war, even though he considered himself a Comanche by choice and by adoption. As a captive, his recovery was primarily the responsibility of the Indian agent who dealt with the tribe holding him. Yet when Herman got back to the reservation after hunting with the Comanches, the Kiowa-Comanche agent, James M. Haworth, apparently took no steps to send him to Texas. Haworth's indifference in this matter would put him at odds with Lt. Col. John W. "Black Jack" Davidson, the blustery, hot-tempered officer who had replaced Ranald Mackenzie as commander at Fort Sill.

Davidson finally took the initiative in returning Herman to Texas. In the early part of 1878, he got Quanah to bring Herman to Fort Sill. When they arrived at the post, the soldiers surrounded Herman and tried to prevent him from leaving. Davidson told Quanah that Herman's people were still living in Texas and that he should be sent to them.

Quanah said to Herman, "Your mother and folks are still alive. Do you want to go to them?"

Herman replied, "No. The Indians are my people. I will not go with the whites."

Quanah saw no easy solution. Finally, he told Herman, "I am going to leave you here at the post with the soldiers."

Herman became angry, thinking Quanah had deceived him. He said, "You are no man at all to bring me here when you knew these soldiers would try to keep me."

Quanah protested, "I did not know it. Besides, I often go into Texas to see my people, and always have a pretty good time."

Herman grew petulant. He said, "If you are getting tired of me, I am of you, too. I will leave you."

Quanah decided to take Herman to talk with Horace Jones, the veteran interpreter at Fort Sill. Jones, perhaps more than any other white man, could understand what Herman was going through. An adopted Comanche himself, Horace Jones had spent a great deal of time among the tribe and had a deep affinity for their culture. Jones also realized the trauma Herman would face once he was separated from his Comanche family. The interpreter had been present when Quanah's mother, Cynthia Ann Parker, was recaptured by Texas Rangers in 1860. Over the years, he had dealt with several bewildered captives shortly after their release, including Dot and Banc Babb.

Jones told Herman, as gently as he could, "You will have to go to your people."

Herman said, "I will never consent to go."

Jones replied, "They will have to take you anyhow."

In one swift motion, Herman drew his bow, fitted an arrow, and aimed it at the interpreter. Jones ducked under a table.

Quanah stopped Herman. He said, "I will see that they do not take you. I am going back to my tepee with you."

Herman turned around, intending to kill Jones anyway. He had slipped out of the room. Herman said, "I never got another chance at Jones, or he would have been a goner." He didn't explain why he chose to vent his rage on the well-liked interpreter. Maybe he just needed to kill someone, and he thought a nonmilitary man was an easy target. Herman went home with Quanah. That night they discussed his situation a long time. Quanah finally persuaded Herman that he couldn't fight the whites any longer.

Meanwhile, Herman's former friends and neighbors in Texas were eager to see him. On March 12, 1878, Engelbert Krauskopf, the Fredericksburg gunsmith who had helped get Rudolph Fischer home, wrote once more to U.S. Congressman Gustav Schleicher on the Buchmeiers' behalf, pleading with the legislator to use his "best endeavours to have the child returned to his parents." According to

Krauskopf, the Buchmeiers were "too poor to do anything for him." Oddly, Krauskopf remarked that "the Agent at Fort Sill would have to be paid for his assistance." He may have been referring to agent Haworth's offer the previous fall to hire a man to bring Rudolph Fischer home if his family would pay the cost.

Congressman Schleicher forwarded Krauskopf's letter to the commissioner of Indian Affairs in Washington. The acting commissioner, William M. Leeds, immediately wrote to agent Haworth, instructing him to "report the facts in the case, so far as you know them, or can obtain them, and do so at as early a date as practicable." Still, Haworth procrastinated. The following month, Black Jack Davidson, the gruff commander of Fort Sill, finally decided something had to be done. On April 12, 1878, he sent a tersely worded telegram to Fredericksburg, announcing that he had recovered Herman. He also indicated that he was fed up with agent Haworth:

> Bucksheimer [sic] son has been taken by me from the Indians, which the Agent here had failed to do. He is now at my Indian farm, and will be sent, when I get the orders of the Department Commander.[21]

In later years, Herman recalled that he voluntarily gave himself up at Fort Sill. However, the earlier records indicate otherwise. Quanah and some of his tribesmen gave an affidavit stating that Herman "was taken from us forcibly by the soldiers at Fort Sill."[22] Lieutenant Colonel Davidson also indicated that he had to go get Herman. He wrote to his superiors in the army's Department of the Missouri:

> I have the honor to report that I have taken from Quanah (a Comanche who occupies a prominent position among his people) a captive boy about eighteen years of age, a German by birth and whose parents are living near Fredericksburg Texas, east of Fort McKavett. He was captured some ten [sic] years ago and has

been with the Apaches and Comanches ever since. He was taken
by Quanah from the Apaches. I write to know if I shall send him
via Griffin and McKavett to his people with a safeguard. Two
soldiers and a pack mule will be sufficient.[23]

No guard had been ordered to accompany Rudolph Fischer the previous September, but Herman apparently posed a greater flight risk.

Davidson received a letter from the army's Department of the
Missouri on April 24, ordering him to return the captive boy to his
parents in Texas. Before Herman left, Quanah told him how to find
the way back to his camp. He promised to take care of Herman's
horses while he was gone to Texas. Quanah said to Herman, "I will be
a brother to you. If you do not have any people, you should come back
and live with me." Herman would always remember that invitation.

News spread through the Hill Country that Herman Lehmann
was on his way home. The peculiar young man, only a month shy of
his nineteenth birthday, was traveling in a military ambulance drawn
by four mules, with an escort of five soldiers—three more than Lieutenant Colonel Davidson had originally proposed. After they passed
through Mason and crossed the Llano River on May 12, 1878, they
started meeting people who had come to get an early glimpse of the
celebrated white Indian. Meanwhile, his mother and her friends were
preparing a huge feast at the small hotel she'd established in Loyal
Valley. Herman and the soldiers didn't reach the village until after
dark. About three hundred people were waiting at Auguste Buchmeier's hotel to witness the family reunion.

Nothing looked familiar to Herman. He had grown up on Squaw
Creek, four miles to the west, and had never lived in Loyal Valley. The
soldiers made signs for him to climb down. One of them said, "Get
out and kiss your mother!" At first Herman refused to step down from
the ambulance. When he finally alighted, Auguste ran up to him,
threw her arms around his neck, and started weeping. He didn't know
her and grunted in disdain. To him, "she was no more than a white
squaw." The crowd spoke excitedly in German and English, languages

Herman couldn't understand. Some were laughing, some crying, some shouting praises to God and singing hymns of thanksgiving. Their emotional outbursts irritated him. "Pshaw!" he wrote. "I did not approve of such conduct, so I broke away from them." He tried to walk off, but the soldiers stopped him.

Someone kept saying, "Herman. Herman." The name had a familiar sound. All at once he realized, to his horror, that he really was among his own people. "But," he explained, "I was an Indian, and I did not like them because they were palefaces." He lay down on a blanket in the yard, drowning out the noise of their church music by singing Indian songs to himself.

His sister insisted that he come eat. Herman finally went inside the hotel. He was about to sit down grudgingly with his family and neighbors when he saw a ham on the table. He flew into a rage, kicking over chairs and tables and heading for the door. Herman pointed to the pork and finally made them understand that it offended him. As he recalled, "The thought of having to eat with hog-eaters choked me." He wanted nothing but roasted beef. He said, "All those sweetmeats and delicacies disgusted me, and I despised so much effeminacy." Later that night, Herman wouldn't sleep in the featherbed his mother fixed for him, but made a pallet of his own blankets on the ground. His brother Willie slept in the yard to keep him company.

The summer of 1878 was the most miserable period of Herman Lehmann's life. Even his first weeks as an Apache captive hadn't been as traumatic. He recalled, "I was mad all of the time. In fact, nothing pleased me." His family humored him and treated him gingerly, for Herman wasn't easy to be around. He'd been spoiled and pampered by the Native American women for many years. When he returned from hunting, he would leave his horse at the front door of his mother's hotel with a slain deer still tied to it. He expected the women of the household to skin and clean the deer, as well as feed and stake his horse. Although his mother and sisters tried to do everything he wanted, he flew into a rage if they failed to roast the short ribs or tenderloins to his satisfaction.

About a year after Herman came home, his mother enrolled him in the local school. He hated it. Herman was twenty years old and couldn't stand being confined. Finally, he told his mother that he was going to tear down all the lattice in the schoolhouse so he could see out. She never made him go back. His teacher at Loyal Valley, John Warren Hunter, wrote, "As one in prison, he pined for the companionship of his Indian friends, and their manner of life."

Herman recalled only one moment during that trying period when he thought he could reconcile with his white mother and win her admiration. One day he asked her if she remembered seeing fires on House Mountain on a cold winter night several years before.

"Yes," said Auguste. "I remember the time. There was snow on the ground, and the Indians made a raid and got off with a large number of horses."

Herman's face lit up. "Me got heem!" he shouted. "Me got heem!"

Then he squatted and traced in the sand the brands of the horses he had taken. All of them had belonged to his neighbors around Loyal Valley. Herman couldn't understand why his mother didn't seem proud of his accomplishment.

Gottlieb and Sophie Fischer were well aware that their son was dissatisfied in Fredericksburg. Gottlieb tried to persuade Rudolph to bring his Comanche wife and children to Texas, thinking that would make him content. However, Rudolph refused to send for his family. He said, "The white people would always look upon my wife as a squaw, and she would not be happy here."

Unlike most recovered captives, Rudolph does not appear to have caused any trouble when he returned home. The news items and letters describing his time in Fredericksburg do not indicate that he stole horses or killed swine or fowl. Perhaps he thought those sorts of juvenile pranks were beneath his dignity as an adult warrior. Or maybe he was just biding his time.

Only two months after Rudolph arrived in Fredericksburg, rumors of his departure started to circulate. At Fort Sill, Indian agent James

M. Haworth heard that some cowboys had seen Rudolph at their camps south of the Red River in the latter part of November 1877. Rudolph was supposedly traveling with one of the Indian hunting parties on the way back to the reservation. This report turned out to be false; Rudolph was in Fredericksburg throughout the fall and winter. (The young man the cowboys saw was probably Herman Lehmann.)

Still, the rumors seemed plausible, for many people suspected that Rudolph wouldn't stay in Fredericksburg very long. On the one hand, the locals admired his decorum and his efforts to get along with them. In March 1878, the gunsmith Engelbert Krauskopf sent a photograph of Rudolph to Gustav Schleicher, the congressman who had helped arrange his return, noting that "the boy" was "very well disposed" and would "make a good citizen." At the same time, people knew that Rudolph was making other plans; he didn't keep his intentions secret. According to a news report from Fredericksburg dated April 14, 1878: "Rudolf Fisher, the Indian captive, is talking of paying a visit to his Indian friends at Fort Sill this spring, but the general opinion is that he will never return to his family again if he gets with the Indians."

Meanwhile, Rudolph condescended to take a job for wages. A local man named Crocket Riley hired him to help drive a herd of horses to Nebraska Territory. They left Fredericksburg near the end of May 1878, just a couple of weeks after Herman Lehmann was reunited with his family in nearby Loyal Valley. The trip across the plains that spring proved to be too great a temptation for Rudolph, who was starting to think he'd done his duty by his German-American family. According to Fredericksburg lore, he called his employer's attention to some piles of rock they passed along the way, saying they were signs left by the Comanches. That evening he and Riley set up camp north of Fort Concho. Rudolph was very restless and pensive all night. Around four o'clock in the morning, he got up, discarded his whiteman's clothes, painted his face, and selected one of Riley's best horses. With a Comanche war whoop and a quick wave good-bye, he disappeared into the darkness, heading for the reservation.

A year later, Engelbert Krauskopf once again wrote to the Indian agent at Fort Sill, asking what had become of Rudolph Fischer. The young man had promised to return to Fredericksburg in the spring of 1879, once he had completed his "visit" to Comanche country. By that summer, his father was anxious to find out what had happened. The new agent, P. L. Hunt, wrote back:

> I have to say that he is here and last Fall I told him he must go home, but he asked me to let him remain and go Buffalo hunting with the Indians and then he would go after he came back. I consented to it, but he did not comply with his promises, and I said no more to him, thinking every week that I would. Black Crow with whom he lives is now in the office, and I sent word for him to come in. Black Crow says he is now married and wants to remain.[24]

Rudolph Fischer was finally home. He wouldn't return to Fredericksburg for twenty-one years, and then only for a short visit.

When Herman Lehmann left Fort Sill in April 1878, he was the last white Indian of the Kiowa-Comanche reservation, and possibly the last Indian captive in North America, to be sent back to his former family. In June of the following year, the Quahada warrior Black Horse led the final Comanche raid into Texas. Although Indians and non-Indians continued to fight each other for a few more years in other parts of the country, the lords of the South Plains were conquered. By 1880 the people of Texas, Indian Territory, and Kansas, like their fellow Americans on the eastern seaboard, spoke of the Indian wars in the past tense.

The last major confrontation between Indians and non-Indians in the United States occurred on December 29, 1890, when the cavalry slaughtered a large group of Sioux men, women, and children at Wounded Knee. After that the Indian wars were officially over. In 1894 the U.S. Department of the Interior issued a report stating:

It has been estimated that since 1775 more than 5,000 white men, women, and children have been killed in individual affairs with Indians, and more than 8,500 Indians. History, in general, notes but few of these combats. . . . The Indian wars under the government of the United States have been more than 40 in number. They have cost the lives of about 19,000 white men, women, and children, including those killed in individual combats, and of the lives of about 30,000 Indians. . . . The actual number of killed and wounded Indians must be very much greater than the number given, as they conceal, where possible, their actual loss in battle, and carry their killed and wounded off and secrete them. The number given above is of those found by the whites. Fifty percent additional would be a safe estimate to add to the numbers given.[25]

The federal government had finally established a boundary between Comanches and non-Indian settlers, but it wasn't the line across Texas envisioned in the 1840s by the Penateka chiefs who met with Sam Houston and made a peace treaty with the German immigrants. Instead, it was the boundary defining the Kiowa-Comanche reservation in Indian Territory. The Comanches' life in Texas was over.

Part Three

Redemption

Chapter Eleven

Once and
Always Indians

T hey couldn't stay cooped up indoors.

Their love of nature kept most of the former captives from getting even a basic education. They simply couldn't tolerate the confinement of the classroom. As a result, Herman Lehmann and Jeff Smith remained illiterate throughout their lives. Herman even signed his name with an *X* for most of his life. Clinton Smith's daughters eventually taught him to read and write—"not very well, but it was legible," says his granddaughter, Edda Raye Moody.

Most of the male white Indians became cowboys. Adolph Korn broke horses for a neighbor near Castell, his boyhood home. Jeff Smith's two years with the Apaches had also increased his love for horses. "We couldn't content ourselves to stay indoors and naturally went to working cattle," he said. The captives' teenage years and early adulthood coincided with the great cattle drives of the 1870s and 1880s. Trail bosses hired youngsters such as Dot Babb and the Smith brothers to help take their herds to markets north of Texas.

When Clinton Smith was about seventeen, he tried to join a group of trail drivers. After he succeeded in riding their wildest horse, the boss hired the gangling teenager. Clinton was careful not the let his fellow cowboys know about his past life with the Comanches, for the Indian wars had not quite ended in Texas. Whenever they passed places he recognized from raiding with the tribe, he kept his mouth shut.

One day a large party of Comanches rode up to the trail boss and asked if he could spare a few beeves. The boss granted their request, and they took the animals to one side and butchered them. Suddenly, one of the Comanches recognized Clinton. He walked up to the teenager and called him by his old name, Backecacho. Clinton was horrified. He shook his head, pretending not to understand.

Cattle herding got the boys back out on the plains, but it couldn't give them the same thrills they'd known as Indians. Jeff Smith told an interviewer in 1930, "Trail driving and cattle work is all so much of a sameness." Captivity had clearly been the high point of their lives.

They couldn't settle in one place.

The former captives weren't content just to spend their days outdoors; they also needed to roam and see new country. Even after he married and had children, Clinton Smith traveled across Texas to rodeos, parades, and old settlers' reunions. He was especially proud of the Angora goats he raised, which won him several trophies at livestock shows. "The Indians moved around a lot, and I suppose Clinton never got over it," says his granddaughter, Edda Raye Moody. "My grandpa never could settle down when he came home. He was gone a lot."

For Banc Babb, the most annoying aspect of captivity had been moving camp every few weeks. Nonetheless, the habit stayed with her. She and her husband, Jefferson Davis Bell, an abstractor of land titles, moved from town to town across north Texas, California, and New Mexico. Her grandson, Daniel Crooks, says, "Grandmother had the Indian travel fever in her, because she was always buying a new house and moving. She said a person gets tired looking at the same old things all the time." Minnie Caudle's great-granddaughter, Neoma Benson Cain, sums up her ancestor's nomadic half year with the Comanches by saying, "I guess that was kind of a wild, carefree life. The house got dirty, you just packed up and moved on."

They couldn't hold a regular job.

"I would not work at first," Herman Lehmann said when he recalled his reintroduction to white society. Eventually, however, he "began to want to possess property like other people." Initially, he hired out to do hard manual labor. He also tried raising cattle, but no steady career seemed to suit him. In 1890 he went into business, opening a beer saloon and dance hall at Cherry Spring, near Loyal Valley. The tavern made good money, and his customers had a fine time. So did Herman. "I got too fat and drank too much," he said. He sold the business around 1895. Before long he'd squandered all the proceeds.

"That was the story of Uncle Herman's life," says his niece, Esther Lehmann. She and her sister, Gerda Lehmann Kothmann, grew up with Herman in the 1920s.

"Uncle Herman wasn't very good at cowboying or raising livestock or any other business," Gerda confirms.

"I don't remember him doing any kind of work," says Esther. "He wasn't successful at anything." She adds, "They should have brought him back and let Grandma know he was all right and left him with the Indians. He would have been happier."

Clinton Smith spent many years as a cowpoke before he bought a ranch near Rocksprings, Texas, in 1910, where he raised his family. "My grandmother told me that Grandpa never would work," says his granddaughter, Edda Raye Moody. "Both of them would be plowing in the field, and if a neighbor rode up on a horse, Grandpa would throw down the plow-horse reins, go over to the fence, and talk a while. In a few minutes, they would go to the house and play checkers and drink coffee the rest of the day. My grandmother had to do the plowing by herself. He had no value of money, so why would he work to support anybody?"

Rudolph Fischer chose to continue his relaxed way of life among the Comanches in Oklahoma. When his granddaughter, Josephine Wapp, visited her Fischer relatives in Fredericksburg in 1996, the family talked about how hard the German-Texan children worked on the farms. She recalls, "Someone made the remark, 'I guess that's the reason Rudolph didn't stay.' Everybody laughed. We always say he went back to the Comanches for an easier life."

They couldn't stay married.

The extreme cultural differences that separated Native Americans from other Americans sometimes led to severe problems when the white Indians married and tried to raise families. My ancestor, Adolph Korn, never experienced marital problems, because he never married. No one would have him, even if he were interested. People say he was just too strange.

When Herman Lehmann was twenty-six, he fell in love with a young woman in Loyal Valley, identified in the marriage records as N. E. Burks. They were married by a Baptist preacher at her parents' home on July 16, 1885. Herman had been back in white society for seven years, and it seemed that he was finally getting his life in order. However, the union was unhappy and short-lived.

Herman claimed that he left his first wife because she spent all his money, flirted with other men, and was eventually unfaithful. However, Willis Skelton Glenn, a buffalo hunter who knew Herman in Oklahoma, told a different story. He reported that Herman's wife sought a divorce after someone told her that he had once been married to an Indian. (As far as anyone knows, that rumor was false, although it followed Herman all his life.) In all likelihood, neither version of the story fully explains the quick collapse of Herman's marriage, and it's safe to assume that his wife wasn't entirely to blame. Herman was still an Indian in many ways. He undoubtedly wanted his bride to conform to his expectations of a Native American wife.

Once he was single again, Herman "drank some and fought a great deal." He "gambled and ran horse races and was turned out of" the Methodist church. Herman was a brawler in those days, although he never carried a grudge after he'd fought. "I loved beer and other strong drinks," he said, "and when a man did anything I didn't like, I never quarreled with him, but I would knock it out with him. We would be the very best of friends afterwards until some other trouble arose."

Herman wed again on March 4, 1896. He and his second wife, Fannie Light, stayed married until Herman's death in 1932. However, they didn't get along very well. In 1926 Herman left his family in Oklahoma, where they had resided since 1900, and returned to Texas to spend the rest of his life with his brother Willie in Loyal Valley.

Clinton Smith also weathered a turbulent marriage for forty years. On August 29, 1889, he wed an industrious woman named Dixie Alamo Dyche, named for the Mason-Dixon Line and an ancestor who died at the Alamo. Their granddaughter, Edda Raye Moody, recalls, "My grandmother worked night and day. She raised her children almost by herself. She took in washing and ironing and sewed for her kids at night. When I was growing up, I could tell that she resented it that Grandpa never was home to help her much. She hardly ever mentioned him at all, and if she did, it wasn't very good."

Although the Smiths spent much of their adult lives together, they separated when Clinton was sixty-three. After threatening to leave for many months, he finally walked out in the early part of 1924. Dixie eventually filed for a divorce, which was granted on February 16, 1929. In her petition, she complained that ever since their separation, Clinton had "not contributed to the support of herself or her children" and had not "intimated any desire to do either of these things." Despite the strife they'd known during their four decades together, Dixie's demand for a divorce hit Clinton hard. When the court papers were served on him, he sat down and bawled.

"He never supported any children after that," says Edda Raye. "Not that he ever did before."

Although several of the white Indians had difficult relationships with their spouses, they managed to hold the affection and admiration of their children. The same traits that caused problems in their marriages—their generosity, indulgence, and easygoing manner—may have also endeared them to their young. Herman Lehmann's daughter May recalled, "He was wonderful to us . . . the best father there ever was."[1] Similarly, Edda Raye Moody says, "All the Smith kids seemed to have great regard for both parents." She adds, "About seven out of ten Smiths are named Clinton."

The marital problems that Herman Lehmann and Clinton Smith suffered didn't come close to the domestic turmoil that followed Minnie Caudle. One of the three survivors of the Legion Valley raid, she married a man named James M. Benson around 1874, when she was no more than fifteen. They had three children. By the time of the 1880 census, Minnie was enumerated as a "widow," a common euphemism for a divorced woman. On May 17, 1883, she married her second husband, William F. Modgling. They had one son. The Modglings divorced on October 6, 1890, and the judge, without explanation, ordered Minnie to "pay all costs."[2] Her descendants don't know the reason for her second divorce, and no court papers have survived. She then married James Benson—again. Afterward, she placed her son by her second husband in a home for orphaned or indigent children, reportedly because of friction between the boy and her first family. Minnie's fourth and final marriage was to Will "Doc" Dane, a salesman of patent medicines. They traveled through Texas and New Mexico in a wagon. Wherever he sold his miracle cures, she played music on a wind-up phonograph to lure the crowds.

Minnie Caudle Benson Modgling Benson Dane spent only six months with the Comanches. It would be presumptuous to link her difficulties on the home front to her brief immersion in a foreign culture if it weren't for two things. First, divorce seems to have been much more pervasive among former captives than within the general population of their time. Second, Minnie's behavior in many other ways suggests that she retained a surprisingly large amount of what she'd learned during her short stay with the Comanches.

Consciously or not, they held fast to their Native American teaching.

"She never would sleep with her head to the east," Neoma Benson Cain says. Her great-grandmother, Minnie Caudle, lived part-time with Neoma's family on a farm north of Rising Star, Texas, during the 1920s and early 1930s. "When she was going to come stay with us, Mother and Daddy moved the bed to suit Grandma," says Neoma. In the Comanche camps, all the tepees opened to the east. The beds were placed against the opposite wall, so that the occupants, their heads to the west, faced the rising sun when they woke.

"Mother had this little quirt, and when we kids would disobey, we got spanked with it," Neoma continues. "Grandma got Mother's quirt and threw it in the fireplace. She didn't want us to get whipped." The Comanches were indulgent toward their children and seldom punished them.

"She could stop blood. We had a colt that ran into a barbed fence and cut itself. Mother came into the house and told Grandma about it. Grandma wanted to know what color and how old the colt was. And she stopped the bleeding." Comanches were skilled at stemming the flow of blood from an arrow or bullet wound, often using a soft buckskin thong as a tourniquet.

Like the Comanches, Minnie understood the behavior of horses. Neoma remembers, "In the spring of the year, there came a dark cloud. Mother said, 'Grandma, that old silly mare has taken the baby colt and gone right out in the middle of the field.' Grandma told her, 'You get the kids in the house and shut all the windows and doors. That's going to be a bad cloud.' She knew there was going to be a big wind. If the mare had gone to the brush, the wind would have broken down the trees and hurt the colt. She knew a lot of Indian things like that."

The boy captives were even more like Native Americans in their behavior. In 1910 one of Rudolph Fischer's neighbors in Oklahoma wrote about him: "He is certainly Indianized. He not only acts like an Indian, but he looks like one, and at a short distance you would judge him to be one." That's not surprising, considering that Fischer had been living with the Comanches since 1878. However, even the returned captives who lived far from their former tribesmen in Oklahoma kept their Native American traits.

According to one news article, Dot Babb "retained many of the Indian characteristics through his life. He had the reticence of the red man among strangers, but once his friendship was gained, he talked freely." Similarly, a journalist who interviewed Jeff Smith noted, "It took a three-year acquaintance with him to induce him to say anything. . . . [A] habit contracted from association with the Indians has stuck tight. He keeps his eyes busy and sees much, says little and tells the truth."

Even among their immediate families, they were reserved. Minnie Caudle's grandson, Frank Modgling, recalls, "She didn't talk a whole lot." Similarly, Banc Babb's granddaughter, Claudia Crooks, says, "Grandmother did not talk much. I cannot remember a single time when she spoke directly to me." One of Rudolph Fischer's granddaughters, Teresa Parker, also remembers, "He didn't talk very much." When he did speak, it was usually in Comanche.

Adolph Korn's stepsister, my granny Hey, recalled: "Throughout his life he retained many of the habits and customs of the Indians. Always restless, he would sometimes take up his gun, leave home and be gone for days in the woods. When he came back he said little about where he had been."

The habit of wandering off into the woods was common among white Indians. Herman Lehmann's niece, Esther Lehmann, tells me, "He would take off and go out in the pasture. He'd be gone a couple of days. When he got back, he'd sit out beside the house with his legs crossed, and you could tell his mind was way off somewhere."

"We never worried about him," her sister Gerda says of his absences. "That was part of his routine."

Esther adds, "One morning I heard some strange noises when I was out in the woods. I got pretty scared. I kept asking my brother Gus what it was. He'd just laugh. It was Uncle Herman. The Indians could imitate wild animals."

Like Native Americans, the returned captives were more closely attuned to the natural world than most non-Indians. Jeff Smith's son, Bert, recalled in a 1979 interview, "When we'd be out in the woods, he was so good at doing things that it was obvious he knew the ways of the Indians."

Sidney M. Whitworth, whose grandfather knew Jeff Smith, reported, "After Jeff 'came home,' he still lived as an Indian in many respects. . . . I recall hearing Grandpa Tom tell stories of Jeff always sleeping outside under a big tree—winter, summer, spring or fall, he slept under that tree when he came to visit. Sometimes, if it was raining or real cold, he would come indoors, but even then, he would only sleep on the hard floor with only his blanket. Jeff followed the Indian customs in many ways, sometimes making folks uncomfortable, but my grandmother didn't pay any attention to it and just went along with it. He didn't like to sit at their table to eat, choosing instead to sit 'Indian style,' eating in the corner or outdoors."

Throughout their lives, the former boy captives continued to make their own bows and arrows and sometimes used them to hunt. When they brought home wild game, they expected the women to do the rest of the work. M. J. Lehmann, Herman's great-nephew, recalled in 1983: "If he shot a deer, it was left for someone else to clean and prepare."

Both Adolph Korn and Herman Lehmann still liked to eat raw meat after they returned home. Even toward the end of his life, Herman enjoyed raw venison ground with onion, salt, and pepper. (That habit may be attributed to conversion zeal. The natural-born Plains Indians ate raw meat mostly out of convenience or necessity, not preference.)

They were tougher than the average person, and they had no taste for luxuries. Herman Lehmann's hands were so hardened that he could grab a coal out of a fire and use it to light a cigarette. One journalist noticed that Banc Babb Bell, at age eighty-two, preferred to sit on a hassock, scorning soft cushions and easy chairs.

When Jeff Smith recalled his trail-driving days, he remarked: "As far as I was concerned, the usual occurrences that sometimes upset the other boys in the outfit had no weight with me. I had gone through so many worse things that they were scarcely noticeable. . . . If we ran short of chuck on a stampede hunt or anything, I had the advantage of the others, for I had gone hungry so much in my Indian life that I just pulled my belt a little tighter and forgot it."

They also didn't fret over anything. Herman Lehmann's nephew, Maurice J. Lehmann, reminisced shortly after his uncle's death: "He was always carefree and happy and refused to let any inconvenience of any kind worry him. I remember on one occasion while fishing on

Beaver Creek, he ran out of tobacco and without a word of complaint, reached over, picked up some dry live oak leaves, crushed them in his hand, tore off a piece of paper from a bag and rolling a cigarette, smoked it with as much content and satisfaction as if it had been a Turkish blend cigarette or an expensive Havana cigar."

Their Indian habits stayed with them until the end of their lives. Edda Raye Moody was born a year before the death of her grandfather, Clinton Smith. "The family told me that he used to rock me and sing an Indian lullaby," she says. "Whatever that is."

Eventually, some of them drifted back to the Indians.

During the last two decades of the nineteenth century, Herman Lehmann made several trips to see his old friends in Indian Territory. When Herman was having marital problems in the mid-1880s, he "rode back to the Comanches at Ft. Sill, and spent several weeks with Quanah Parker." He went to see Quanah at least two other times, including a visit during the summer of 1900. In the spring of 1898, he renewed his friendship with one of his Apache captors, Chiwat (Chebahtah), who was then living among the Comanches.

Even though the various white Indians had been through similar experiences that set them apart, they didn't seek each other's company. Between 1878 and 1900, Herman Lehmann and Adolph Korn lived only a few miles from each other in Mason County. Minnie Caudle also resided there during part of that time. Yet none of the family stories or published articles suggests that these former captives had much contact with each other.

Sometimes the Comanches made trips to Texas, although not specifically to visit their former captives. Around 1884, when Dot Babb was living in Wichita Falls, he ran into Quanah Parker and a large group of Comanches on their way to a cowboy reunion in Seymour, Texas. Quanah was traveling with Tonarcy, his trophy wife who accompanied him on his diplomatic junkets to Washington. (The white folks thought her name was "Too Nicey.") The Comanches started chasing a large group of antelope, and Dot joined them. Tonarcy asked for his pistol, and another Comanche woman borrowed his rope. The rope proved useless, but Tonarcy, who was riding a good horse, succeeded in running down and shooting five bucks.

This chance meeting with the Comanches, along with several subsequent encounters with his former tribesmen, whetted Dot's appetite for his old life with them. In 1887 he moved his family to the Kiowa-Comanche reservation at the invitation of his Comanche friends, whom he claimed "contended that I was by captivity and adoption a Comanche Indian, and had as much right in the Territory as the rest of the tribe." The Babbs built a house on a creek near Fort Sill and raised livestock. The Indian agent at that time, Lee Hall, permitted Dot to stay on the reservation once he learned that the Comanches had asked him to come there.

Agent Hall was replaced by Eugene E. White in October 1887. The new agent was suspicious of any white people living on the Indians' land, and for good reason. Since 1878 the Kiowa-Comanche reservation had become a haven for white rustlers, murderers, gamblers, and thieves, mostly from Texas. In addition, Texas cattlemen drove their herds across the border to take advantage of the free grazing. Agent White decided to get tough on these unsavory characters. On May 19, 1888, he directed the chief of police to make a tour of the reservation with twelve martial policemen and "notify Mr. Babb, Graham Bro and Acum who are reported to me as holding cattle horses and sheep without authority to remove from the Reservation on or before the 15th of June with all their horses cattle sheep and other effects under pain of forcable [sic] removal, toll and penalties."[3] Although the Comanches had encouraged Dot Babb to move to Indian Territory, he was swept off the reservation as part of the new agent's attempt to purge the Indians' land of nearly all non-Indians. Dot suffered several more personal setbacks shortly after he left Indian Territory in 1888. He was defeated in his election bid for sheriff of Wichita County, Texas, in 1890. He also lost his parents' farm in Wise County to foreclosure in 1891.[4]

Despite having been forced off the reservation, Dot continued to visit Comanche country periodically. In the early 1920s, he was talking in English with some Native Americans in Cache, Oklahoma, when he noticed his adoptive mother crossing the street. He called to her in Comanche. One of the Indians looked at him in amazement and asked, "Where in the hell did you learn that?"

While Dot eventually became more successful in the ranching business than most of the other former captives, the only white Indian who truly prospered throughout his life was Rudolph Fischer. It's probably no coincidence that he was also the only one who went back to the Comanches to stay. Rudolph spent most of his life on a farm about four miles south of Apache, Oklahoma, where he raised cattle and cultivated a fruit orchard. A judge who lived in Apache noted in 1910, "Fischer is quite well to do and considered a good citizen, despite his Indian ways."

Like many prosperous Comanche men, Rudolph took more than one wife. He married two sisters named Tissychauer and Kahchacha. The women's father, Hoascho, was a Mexican; their mother, Tooene, was Comanche. Consequently, Rudolph's children were only one-fourth Comanche by blood, although they were accepted as full members of the tribe. It was reported that Rudolph sat between his two wives at the dining table and that their household was peaceful and content.

When the Fischer family converted to Christianity, the missionaries pressured Rudolph to give up one of his wives. At some point between 1897 and 1901,[5] Rudolph and Kahchacha divorced, apparently amicably, and she remarried. The census records indicate that the minor children of Rudolph and Kahchacha spent time in the homes of both parents during the early 1900s.

Rudolph became a devout Catholic. His farm was a favorite gathering place for the local priests and nuns. He was adamant that his children and grandchildren receive a good education, and he sent them to a Catholic boarding school in Anadarko, Oklahoma. Unlike many of the white Indians, Rudolph learned to read.

Rudolph's father, Gottlieb Fischer, died in 1894, leaving his oldest son an interest in the family farm near Fredericksburg. It took several years for the Fischer family to settle the estate, because Rudolph wanted nothing to do with the property in Texas and was uncooperative. Finally, in the summer of 1900, Rudolph's brother Arthur took a train to Indian Territory to visit with him. Rudolph, finally persuaded that he could relinquish his part of the property to the estate so that it could be divided among his white siblings, reluctantly returned to Fredericksburg with Arthur. It is said that he climbed into the buggy wearing his old work clothes, bringing nothing for the trip. On September 1, 1900, he sold his interest in his father's farm to Arthur and a brother-in-law, Otto Rabke, for $150.[6] Rudolph remained in Fredericksburg for a few days, visiting his mother and siblings. Then he returned home to Indian Territory.

People in the Texas Hill Country remained fascinated by Rudolph Fischer's story and were curious about his life among the Comanches. In 1892 a man from Kerrville named Charles Morris was riding a train from Fort Worth to Pecos. Across the aisle from him sat Quanah Parker and one of his wives. Morris introduced himself to Quanah and asked, "Do you know a German in Indian Territory by the name of Fischer?"

"Fischer?" Quanah responded. "A German named Fischer." He repeated the name several times. Finally, he said, "You mean a Dutchman, don't you? A Dutchman by the name of Fischer? Oh, yes, I know him. He is well fixed, has fine farm, much cattle. Oh, he is all right."

Quanah was being cagey. He didn't let on that he actually knew Rudolph quite well. In fact, two of Quanah's sons, Len and Thomas, eventually married two of Rudolph's daughters by Kahchacha, Bertie and Helen. Some people in Indian Territory even described Rudolph as Quanah's right-hand man. Quanah didn't mention that Rudolph had also helped him battle buffalo hunters and soldiers in the early 1870s. Memories of the Indian wars in Texas were still too fresh.

Many of the former captives struggled financially throughout their adult lives. Some felt they deserved compensation from the federal government for having been held in captivity. The idea wasn't all that far-fetched. Frontier settlers who lost livestock or other property to Indian raiders could file federal Indian depredation claims and, if they succeeded in proving their cases, receive payment. However, the former captives and their families were frustrated to discover that they had no similar recourse. The law authorized payment only for losses to property, not personal injuries.

In 1894 the U.S. Court of Claims finally awarded John Friend $897 for property taken or destroyed by Indians during the raid on his home in Legion Valley in 1868. By the time the Friend family had its day in court, John's son, Temple, had been dead for nearly two decades. Although John recovered damages for the goods he'd lost, the court denied his claim for injuries to his wife, Matilda, and for Temple's five-year captivity. John's lawyer argued that the Friend family should be compensated under a federal treaty provision entitling a U.S. citizen to be "reimbursed for his loss" caused by Indian depredations. Amazingly, the judge wrote in his decision: "The words 'reimbursed for his loss' are not apt words to describe damages for personal injuries to one's self, or for scalping his wife, or carrying off his son and detaining him in captivity for some years."[7]

Having failed on the personal injury counts in the Court of Claims, John Friend sought direct relief from Congress. In 1896 the House Committee on Indian Affairs recommended approval of a bill to pay him $6,500. However, the bill never passed.[8] Similarly, Dot Babb persuaded Congressman John H. Stephens to introduce a bill in the House of Representatives to recover the value of his family's property that was destroyed. However, Stephens warned Dot that the Babbs could not recover "for their personal injuries or imprisonment or for the death of other members of the family, as there is no precedent for such action of Congress, and at this late date [1911] it would be utterly useless to ask for such damages."[9]

Some former captives tried unsuccessfully to collect payment until the end of their lives. In 1929 Clinton Smith wrote to the General and Special Claims Commission in Washington to find out if he could either recover damages for his captivity or receive a pension as an adopted Comanche. The commission dismissed his request, replying that these matters were not within its jurisdiction.[10] As late as 1935, Clinton's brother, Jeff, submitted an application to receive federal money. The commissioner of Indian Affairs said he knew of no way a person could recover damages from the government by reason of having been captured by Indians. Nor could Jeff's adoption by the Apaches entitle him, that many years later, to any benefits that tribal members received.[11]

A few former captives sought satisfaction in another way: they applied for allotments of farmland in Indian Territory as adopted Comanches. In 1887 Congress bowed to the popular opinion that Native Americans controlled too much land and weren't doing enough with it. Under the Dawes Act, the legislature authorized the president to unilaterally modify the Treaty of Medicine Lodge by breaking up the Indians' reservations if he thought their land was "advantageous for agricultural and grazing purposes."[12] The Dawes Act forced Native Americans to accept individual allotments of one hundred sixty acres of farmland. Once the allotments were granted, the federal government proposed to buy the rest of the reservation land from the tribes and open it to non-Indian settlers.

The Jerome Commission, appointed by Pres. Benjamin Harrison, dealt with the Kiowas, Comanches, and Apaches in Indian Territory. The commissioners arrived on the reservation in September 1892. They found the Indians unwilling to sell any of their land. The native people thought that allotments of one hundred sixty acres were too small to support a family in most areas of the reservation, and they voted to reject the Jerome Commission's offer. However, the commissioners made it clear that the terms they proposed were not really negotiable. They used a combination of threats, pressure, and promises to force the Indians to sign the contract. During the decade that followed, Quanah Parker and other Comanche leaders still refused to accept this arrangement, lobbying to delay Congress's ratification of the agreement.

Banc Babb Bell wandered into this political hotbed in the spring of 1897, when she arrived in Indian Territory seeking to be adopted by the Comanches. She called on the family of Jesse G. Forester, a Methodist missionary, to see if they could help her locate her Comanche people. Banc and the Foresters went to visit some Comanches who were camped around Fort Sill, waiting for a payment from their grazing leases. From them Banc learned that her foster mother, Tekwashana, had died. However, she found her Comanche uncle and a Mexican captive who had lived with Tekwashana's family thirty years earlier. They remembered Banc and promised to help. She submitted a formal application for adoption in the fall of 1899.

Banc's determined campaign to be accepted as a Comanche does not appear to have been motivated solely by the promise of free land. The allotments were located at least seventy miles from Banc's home in the north Texas town of Henrietta, and she expressed no intent to move her family there. A one-hundred-sixty-acre tract would have provided little rental income to an absentee owner.[13] Nor could she have sold it; the federal government planned to hold title to the allotted land in trust for twenty-five years. "She wouldn't have wanted land in Oklahoma," says her grandson, Daniel Crooks. "When she was there, land was free. She said only the white man used land for money." Even if Banc had desired land in that area, it would have been much less trouble and expense for her to have waited and applied for it when the reservation was opened to non-Indian settlers in 1901. Instead, she made several trips to the Fort Sill area and wrote numerous letters over a three-year period in an effort to earn the land as a genuine Comanche rather than claim it as a white homesteader.

Banc, it seems, felt a need for some sort of official acknowledgment of the extraordinary experience she had endured as a child. She also thought that she was being unjustly denied something that was rightfully hers. In another letter to Indian agent James F. Randlett, she stated, "I honestly believe that my self and children are entitled to a right in that Country. The Indians did me a great wrong, murdered my mother, took me captive and destroyed or stole every thing that my Father possessed. They can partially recompense me for loss of property by adopting me, and I believe if they now had an opportunity that they would do so." Banc's letter indicates that she held a lingering grievance over her family's misfortune; but at the same time, she was on cordial terms with the Comanches she knew in Indian Territory. Her brother, Dot, also believed that the Babbs were "entitled to something on account of our having been captured by the Comanche Indians."

Both Banc and Dot returned to Indian Territory and attended the general council meeting of the Kiowas, Comanches, and Apaches in October 1899. On the second day, October 10, they "asked to be adopted into the Comanche tribe in consideration of what they had suffered at the hands of those Indians." A Comanche named Mihecoby, himself an adopted Mexican captive who had been granted full tribal rights, spoke in favor of the Babbs' request, relating the story of their capture. The council decided to delay action until the following day. Meanwhile, the Indians discussed the matter privately. On October 11, the council reconvened. All of its members, including Quanah Parker, voted to reject the proposal to adopt the Babb siblings. The council entered no explanation in the minutes.

Before the Babbs left Indian Territory, Quanah privately encouraged Banc not to give up. He said, rather cryptically, that certain things stood in the way of their adoption, but that those obstacles might be overcome in the future. He assured her that the Indians were in favor of adopting her, but were afraid that her adoption would adversely affect their ongoing efforts to repudiate the Jerome Agreement. It's hard to pinpoint exactly what Quanah was thinking. He was trying to keep more land for Native Americans and may have been worried that adopting some white people would risk opening the door to many others. It's also possible that Quanah and his fellow council members thought Banc wasn't Comanche enough to be adopted, but were too polite to tell her. Unlike her brother Dot or Herman Lehmann, she'd had virtually no contact with the tribe since her ransoming in 1867.

After Congress ratified the Jerome Agreement on June 6, 1900,

Banc contacted agent Randlett to find out "what seemed to be the general feeling of all concerned" regarding her petition. He replied, "I sympathize with you most heartily and would be glad if the Indians could be induced to adopt you." However, in December 1900, Randlett informed her that the council had never reversed its decision the previous year declining to adopt her. Then he dealt the final blow to her case: "Since the Act of June 6, 1900 ratifying the Jerome Treaty of 1892, the Honorable, the Secretary of the Interior has decided that as the Indians have relinquished their rights to all lands not required for allotments to Indians, such surplus lands revert to the United States and that no further adoptions can be approved that convey any rights to lands that have become landed property of the United States." In short, the Kiowa-Comanche reservation no longer existed, and the Comanches had no unclaimed land that they could give Banc.[14]

When he closed Banc Babb Bell's case at the end of 1900, Indian agent James Randlett thought he'd seen the last of the white Indians trying to obtain land. Less than a month later, however, the case of Herman Lehmann landed on his desk. In the summer of 1900, Herman had returned to Indian Territory to visit Quanah Parker and ask if he could be formally adopted into the tribe. Two other events that happened near Herman's home in the Hill Country that summer may have rekindled his desire to go back to the Comanches. In July his fellow white Indian, Adolph Korn, who was only a month older than Herman, died in Mason. Herman must have realized that time was passing him by; he knew he shouldn't wait too long to give Indian Territory a try. Then, in early September, Rudolph Fischer visited Fredericksburg to settle his father's estate. Although it is unknown whether the two white Indians saw each other at that time, Herman, who lived only twenty-five miles away in Loyal Valley, certainly would have heard the fantastic tales about his fellow German-American who had grown wealthy among the Comanches.

Later that year, Herman moved his family to Duncan, Indian Territory, east of Fort Sill. On December 15, 1900, he began the long process of applying for an allotment as an adopted Comanche. When his petition reached Washington, the commissioner of Indian Affairs asked agent Randlett to investigate Herman's case. In the early part of 1901, Herman and Quanah Parker called on Randlett in person. During their meeting, Quanah did something he had never done for Banc Babb Bell: he recommended that Herman be enrolled as a Comanche. Quanah may have acted differently in Herman's case because the Jerome Agreement had already been ratified and he had given up trying to save the reservation from being broken up. Or maybe he simply believed that Herman, a proven warrior and Quanah's foster son, was more deserving.

The legal obstacle, however, was that none of the Comanches could say exactly when Herman had been adopted. Herman gave an affidavit in which he swore that he had considered Quanah Parker to be his adoptive father since 1878. Although Randlett thought Herman's claim was credible, he wanted more testimony from Native Americans, especially Quanah Parker, confirming that they truly accepted Herman as one of them. During an Indian council held on April 10, 1901, the chiefs and twenty headmen of the Kiowa, Comanche, and Apache tribes, on Quanah's recommendation, voted unanimously that Herman "be enrolled with the Comanche tribe of Indians and given full rights with them to all benefits pertaining to their lands and annuities."

Shortly afterward, Herman's case went back up the chain of command all the way to the secretary of the Interior, where his application hit its first real barrier. On May 1, 1901, the secretary determined that Herman's petition for enrollment and tribal rights by adoption could not be approved: "He claims to have been adopted by the Indians in 1878, but there is no record of such adoption; it was never reported to the Agent, nor approved by [the Kiowa-Comanche agency] and the Department." Herman, of course, had panicked and fled shortly before he got to Fort Sill in August 1877, so his name wasn't entered on the Comanche rolls at that time.

As Herman feared, his lengthy absence from Indian Territory also weighed against his claim. The secretary further pointed out, "He is now about 42 years of age; he returned to his mother in Texas when about 18 years old, and has therefore for over 20 years resided off the reservation." Then the secretary, in a cranky fit of parsimony, voiced his concern that claims such as Herman's—for a mere one-quarter of a square mile of prairie land—would reduce the amount of territory that the federal government had wrested from the Indians under the Jerome Agreement to be redistributed to non-Indian homesteaders. He wrote: "[I]f any increase of tribal membership is allowed, it would practically be modifying the agreement made and entail a loss to the United States, as each individual, not a party to the agreement, but now to be enrolled or adopted, reduces the amount of land to be received by the United States from the Indians for the price fixed in the agreement."

Herman got a lawyer, who asked that his case be heard again. The controversy over his land rights turned on a single legal issue: whether Herman had actually been adopted when he lived with Quanah's family in 1877–1878. If so, then he was entitled to an allotment as a bona fide Comanche. Herman's lawyer couldn't find much proof in the records. However, he astutely observed that the Comanche census of 1878[15] showed that Quanah had three wives, one daughter, and one son. He contended that Quanah had no son of his own at that time; therefore, the unnamed boy listed with Quanah's family must have been Herman.

The secretary of the Interior still wasn't convinced. He countered that the Indian council had voted to adopt Herman when it met on April 10, 1901. If Herman was already a Comanche, why would they have felt a need to readopt him at that time? The secretary offered one small concession, however: Herman could be enrolled as a member of the Comanche tribe, even though his adoption in 1901 had occurred too late for him to receive land.

Herman and his friends in Indian Territory weren't pacified. On August 26, 1901, Quanah Parker gave an affidavit in support of Herman's claim. Recalling the events of 1877–1878, he stated, "The boy wanted to live with me and I took him to my camp and he was called my boy. . . . While he lived with me he drew rations with my family. After he was sent home he returned three times to visit my people." Quanah was doing all he could to help Herman, but the additional information he volunteered in his affidavit muddled the issues. While Herman had said that he always thought of Quanah as his "foster father," Quanah stated under oath that he never considered Herman "as adopted by deponent as one of deponent's children, but while Lehman lived with deponent the Indians called him deponent's captive boy." Furthermore, Quanah was "unable to state positively if Lehman was ever taken up on the rolls or census of deponent's family or not." More damagingly, Quanah identified the unnamed boy enumerated with his family on the 1878 census as his own son, Harold Parker. Finally, Quanah said that when Herman came to see him in the summer of 1900, he "wanted to be adopted into the tribe, and I told him I was willing for him to be adopted if it was not too late for him to do so." This statement cast even greater doubt on Herman's claim that he was a full-fledged Comanche as far back as 1878.

The officials in Washington weren't persuaded by Quanah's affidavit. The secretary of the Interior allowed Herman to be enrolled as a Comanche, which entitled him to any monetary benefits bestowed on tribal members. However, in the government's view, Herman had not been adopted until 1901, too late to receive an allotment of land. Since the Comanches had already surrendered their surplus lands to the government under the Jerome Agreement, they no longer had the power to grant allotments to newly adopted members. Herman, still disgruntled, was enrolled as a Comanche on September 16, 1901.[16]

While the former captives were unable to seek reparations from the federal government, some of their most hated enemies—the buffalo hunters—were allowed to do just that. One of them was Willis Skelton Glenn, who filed an Indian depredation claim for damages that Herman Lehmann and the Comanche renegades had done to his hunting camps in 1877. In the spring of 1903, Glenn traveled to Lawton to collect the testimony of witnesses in his case, including

Herman. Shortly beforehand, he had seen a photograph of Herman and recognized him as the "Comanche" who shot him at close range in early May 1877. At first Herman was suspicious that Glenn had come to take revenge for Herman's attacks on his camps twenty-six years earlier; before long, however, they became friends. When the depositions were taken on April 28, 1903, Glenn introduced Herman to John Stansbury, the defense attorney representing the federal government, by saying, "This is the Indian that shot me and broke my leg and helped fire my wagons."

Stansbury looked at Herman disapprovingly, and said, "So you are the man, are you? The state of Texas will take you up for attempted murder and break your neck."

Herman wasn't intimidated by the threats. He replied, "I am going to tell the truth." Then, sadly, he acknowledged his inability to provide for his family: "I expect they will send me to jail, but I expect that squaw and papoose will be better off."

When he testified that day, Herman kept his promise to Glenn and Stansbury. He gave a full, candid, and unapologetic account of raiding Glenn's camps: "We destroyed everything that was there, corn, flour, sugar, and buffalo hides; we burned the wagons and buffalo hides, put fire to them. We done that because we thought the men was killing our game. . . . We destroyed everything at every camp as near as we could."

On cross-examination, John Stansbury attempted to discredit Herman's status as an adopted Comanche by asking: "The Comanche Indians each secured an allotment here some time ago, didn't they?"

Herman said, "Yes, sir."

"You being a white man couldn't get any, could you?"

"No, sir, I didn't get any."

"You made an application . . . then you made a second application, did you not?"

"Yes, sir."

"Both of those applications have been thrown out by the secretary of the Interior, have they not?"

"Yes, sir."

Stansbury needled Herman by dwelling on a sore subject, but Herman kept his cool that day. Glenn, the claimant, had promised Herman that in exchange for his testimony, he would do all he could to help him get an allotment. Some white citizens of Lawton also circulated a petition in support of Herman's application. After eight years of legal wrangling, Herman finally got his land. On May 29, 1908, Congress authorized the secretary of the Interior "to make an allotment to Herman Lehman (Montechema), an enrolled member of the Comanche tribe of Indians, who did not get an allotment, of one hundred and sixty acres of unappropriated and unallotted land."[17] Herman selected a tract nine miles west of Grandfield, close to some of his Native American friends, and moved his family there sometime after 1910. Ever generous in the Comanche manner, he gave some of his property for the construction of a school.

Although he won his battle at long last, Herman Lehmann never found the contentment he was seeking in Oklahoma. His relatives have suggested several reasons—he didn't like farming, he didn't care for the flatlands, he missed his brother Willie and the Texas Hill Country. More significant, Herman waited too long to go back to the Indians. By the time he moved to Indian Territory in 1900, the manner in which his Comanche and Apache friends were living bore little resemblance to the adventures he had shared with them on the plains in the 1870s. They toiled in their fields and sent their children to schools and fretted about money. The carefree days were only a memory.

Both Herman Lehmann and Rudolph Fischer had been seduced by the unadulterated culture of the Southern Plains Indians before their way of life was forever changed by their confinement on the reservation. Unlike Fischer, however, Lehmann decided not to accompany his Comanche brothers as they learned to walk the white man's road—that rocky path to assimilation into mainstream American society. He tried to forge his own way, acquiring livestock and going into business in Texas. It never worked for him. Had he moved to

Indian Territory earlier, Herman, like Rudolph Fischer, probably could have adjusted to modern life alongside his Comanche friends. Most important, he would have had a guide. Like Fischer, Lehmann could have followed the example of his friend and mentor, Quanah Parker.

Instead, the changes Herman found when he arrived in Indian Territory in 1900 bewildered him, and the twentieth century soon left him behind. After spending twenty-six years in Oklahoma during its boom days, watching the children of his Comanche brothers marry outside the tribe and move away from their relatives while more white people poured in, Herman grew disillusioned. He returned to Texas in 1926 to live out his remaining years on Willie's ranch. An anachronistic figure, he had spent his whole adult life moving irresolutely between two peoples, both of whom had embraced him but had also moved on without him. His incomparable experience had come at a heavy cost. Herman's niece, Esther Lehmann, says, "He died a broken man."

Chapter Twelve

In the Limelight

Hollywood called on Dot Babb in 1920. The movie people caused a stir in his hometown. The front page of the *Amarillo Daily Tribune* announced the impending production of "a great drama of the early days," depicting the life of the former Comanche captive. By then his story was well known in Texas. Dot's 1912 memoir, *In the Bosom of the Comanches,* would serve as the source for the film's scenario. The production outfit was the Oklahoma Motion Picture Company, which had a studio in Los Angeles and an office in Oklahoma City.

Dot, who had moved to Amarillo from Clarendon in 1906, had just retired and leased his ranch at the time the motion picture project was announced. In the summer of 1920, he spent several months helping with preproduction in Oklahoma. He was also signed to appear in the film, which would be shot in the Wichita Mountains near Lawton, using five to six thousand Indian extras. By that time, the Comanches and Kiowas were no strangers to film work. In 1908 the Oklahoma Natural Mutoscene Company had recruited Quanah Parker for a cameo role in *The Bank Robbery,* the earliest two-reel western. That picture, one of the first to cast real-life participants in the recreation of historical events, starred a former bank robber, Al Jennings, and was directed by a popular lawman, William Tilghman. Cattleman Charles Goodnight invited Native Americans from Oklahoma to his Texas ranch to reenact a buffalo hunt for the 1916 film *Old Texas.* In 1920 two of Quanah's children, White and Wanada, were cast as principals in *The Daughter of Dawn,* a six-reel melodrama filmed around Lawton with an all–Native American cast.[1]

The shooting of the Dot Babb story was expected to begin in October 1920 and last sixty days. However, the project appears to have died before the film ever went into production. No trace of it remains. It's possible that the producers couldn't raise enough money or that their company folded. Or they may have decided that the market for this type of picture was saturated. By 1920 Hollywood studios had already made more than sixty films about Indian captivities.[2]

Even though *In the Bosom of the Comanches* never made it to the screen, the announcement of the project marked the beginning of a decade in which the former Indian captives of Texas, whose lives had been characterized mostly by failure and discontent, enjoyed a brief reemergence as regional celebrities. Their stories were featured in popular history magazines such as *Frontier Times,* which began publication in 1923 to preserve the recollections of elderly pioneers. The same year, a Dallas publisher issued a second edition of Dot Babb's book, which became even more widely circulated than the first.

The 1920s would also be the last decade in which the myth and the reality of the American West substantially overlapped. Although the early western pictures gave audiences a biased view of the time and place, they were peopled with authentic cowboys, Indians, and lawmen. To audiences in the silent era, these old-timers on screen were quaint curiosities, as far removed from the Jazz Age as Huckleberry Finn or Natty Bumpo.

The first westerns told the stories the way the white pioneers wanted them to be remembered, glorifying the courage and fortitude of the settlers along the frontier. Their tales needed cruel, terrifying antagonists, and Native America's public image didn't benefit from many of the photoplays. Nonetheless, the film shoots gave the Plains Indians a chance to put on their feathers and war paint, race their best horses, and launch arrows at their former enemies once more, if only in make-believe.

Something else happened during the 1920s that would have seemed unthinkable half a century earlier. Aging white settlers and aging Native Americans, who had once tried to kill one another on the plains of Texas, now eagerly looked forward to meeting one another at reunions and parades. They enjoyed comparing their experiences from the old days and solving some lingering mysteries. These long-ago combatants had more in common with one another than they did with their own grandchildren, who played "Oh, Lady, Be Good!" on phonographs, drove automobiles to dance halls and speakeasies, and decorated their faces with cosmetics rather than ceremonial paint. Old cowboys and old Indians became strange bedfellows in a world that had long since left them behind.

By the age of radio and silent screen stars, the white men and women who had lived with the Indians already belonged to the realm of legend. Every year the living legends of the Texas frontier gathered at their own convention. In 1915 a former trail driver and livestock commission agent named George W. Saunders helped found an organization called the Old Trail Drivers Association. Its purpose was to perpetuate the memory of the early cowboys who had taken the herds to market in the 1870s and 1880s. Each fall the association hosted a weekend reunion at the Gunter Hotel in San Antonio, a gathering place for cattlemen.

The three-day event in 1924 began on November 6.[3] The press promoted it as "a great gathering, old frontiersmen and cowboys, Indian fighters, freighters and rangers coming from different sections of the country to once more greet their old comrades." President Saunders also promised a special treat: "At the reunion this year will be quite a number of men who spent years in captivity among the Indians."

Jeff Smith was living in San Antonio at the time. He showed up.

Clinton Smith arrived in town from his ranch at Hackberry. His son, Allen, drove him to the reunion. The *San Antonio Light* interviewed the Smith brothers, and they posed for a publicity photo with their pistols drawn.

Frank Buckelew came from Bandera to relive the old days, even though he'd hated his time with the Lipan Apaches.

Herman Lehmann traveled all the way from Grandfield, Oklahoma. His picture appeared in the *San Antonio Express* as one of the "Veteran Trail Drivers." That must have amused him. He'd never gone up the trail, although he'd stolen horses from a number of those who had.

The white Indians were the center of attention at the gathering in 1924. Herman Lehmann, dressed in a buckskin suit and a buffalo-horn headdress, performed Native American dances for the crowd. At age sixty-five, he was still strong and agile. Later, in the lobby of the Gunter Hotel, he spoke to the old-timers, many of them former Indian fighters, about his experiences as a warrior in Texas. He told the well-worn story of his close call with the Texas Rangers on the Staked Plains in August 1875.

In the audience sat a well-dressed gentleman three years older than Herman. He stood and announced, "I was with the Rangers who attacked those Apaches." The man was James B. Gillett, who had joined the Texas Rangers at age eighteen and fought against Herman shortly afterward. In front of the audience, the two men discussed all the particulars of the battle.

"You shot me in the temple after my horse had fallen on my leg, but I wasn't hurt very much," said Herman.

Gillett replied, "I remember shooting your horse out from under you, but I don't think I fired at you after you were down."

"Yes, you did. And you and another Ranger left me lying there while you chased an Indian who had been riding behind me on the horse." Then Herman tossed off a seemingly casual remark that must have chilled Gillett: "I later found where you caught my pal." The reference went right past the audience, for Herman spared them a description of the headless, mutilated corpse of his Apache friend, Nusticeno. However, the former Texas Ranger must have remembered the sight very well. Later, when Lehmann and Gillett shook hands for a photographer, neither looked entirely at ease.

During the 1920s and early 1930s, the former captives were often asked to put on shooting and riding exhibitions at all sorts of community gatherings—county fairs, rodeos, reunions, parades, grand openings, and so forth. "When he wasn't at a goat show, he was at a rodeo as a participant, even when he was up in years," says Edda Raye Moody, Clinton Smith's granddaughter. "Or some place would be celebrating the one hundredth anniversary of its establishment, and they would ask Clinton and Jeff to dress in Indian clothes and ride in the parades."

Jovial and outgoing, Clinton Smith became a very popular figure in Texas, and he relished the attention. None of the former captives matched the public's image of a cowboy more perfectly. With his lanky frame, droopy white moustache, wide-brimmed hat, and easy-going manner, Clinton would have been an ideal find for a Hollywood casting agent.

His brother, Jeff, was slightly smaller and darker, with an intense, serious expression. Jeff also participated in many public events as a featured guest, but he seemed less comfortable in the spotlight. Sidney M. Whitworth recalled seeing the Smith brothers at the fairgrounds in Bandera, Texas, in the late 1920s. Jeff was dressed in a black suit and a large felt hat, with a shiny gold watch chain hanging across the front of his vest. Whitworth said, "He just sat on a bench under a tree and looked at his pocket watch, turning it over and over in his hand, never saying a word. . . . Even then, you could see him reliving his years with the Indians. Every now and then, he would stare out in the crowd as though he were trying to put all the pieces of his life back together."

None of the white Indians enjoyed performing more than Herman Lehmann. No longer content to limit his exhibitions to Oklahoma, he started making more frequent trips to the Texas Hill Country in the early 1920s. For many years, he was the headline attraction at county fairs in Fredericksburg, Comfort, Llano, Mason, and Burnet.

"I've never seen anything like it in my life," says Carlos Parker, ninety-one, who saw Herman perform in Fredericksburg during those years. "He'd make that gray mare run as fast as she could go, riding bareback, with no bridle. Then he'd lean over on one side, pull the bow, and shoot a calf. He'd never miss a shot."

This was Herman Lehmann's trademark act. He appeared suddenly on his horse, wearing a headdress of eagle feathers, a buckskin suit, a breastplate of white bone, and a beaded belt and moccasins. While the crowd cheered wildly, Herman started chasing a calf, grabbing arrows from the quiver on his back and shooting them at the calf's hooves to get it running full speed. Occasionally, he let out a war whoop. Before long he would kill the calf, jump off his horse, cut out the liver, and eat it raw. People who saw these performances say that the audience didn't recoil at the bloody spectacle; instead, the crowd treated Herman with immense respect. They were in awe of his considerable prowess.

One night at the Gillespie County Fair in August 1925, Herman told his life story to a spellbound crowd of hundreds. Afterward, he joked, "I had a letter from my son in Oklahoma who says they are about to strike oil on our land and maybe I'll have some money yet."

Some money yet. That would never happen for Herman. The public's adoration may have shored up his self-esteem, but he was still a financial failure.

Cowboys weren't the only old-timers gathering at events in Texas to celebrate the frontier days. In the spring of 1926, some special guests from Oklahoma arrived in San Angelo, Texas, to appear at the fairgrounds. The visitors were Comanches who had traveled by automobile to take part in the Wild West show of Hackberry Slim Johnson, a promoter described as a "squinty-eyed, one-legged, would-be Buffalo Bill."[4] Two of the Comanches, Mamsookawat and Haykobitty Millet, paid a visit to Fort Concho and were interviewed by a reporter.[5]

Mamsookawat, a prominent Indian council member who had fought under Paruacoom in the Battle of the North Fork of the Red River, was rumored to own oil-producing land in Oklahoma worth approximately $100,000. One cheeky local asked him, "Did you ever do a day's work in your life?" He grunted and looked disgusted. His interpreter explained that Mamsookawat had better ways to spend his time; he "smoked, talked, and ate lots of beef."

The two Comanches made the trip to the Staked Plains of Texas because they wanted to see the country their people had once roamed. Mamsookawat said it "made him sad to look about and see this country which once was the Comanche's, now in the hands of others." He promised that someday the young Comanches "would know the white man's ways—and would appeal to the President to give them back their property." The elderly Comanche visitors were also anxious to meet and "smoke the pipe of peace" with old pioneers in the area. Half a century after Ranald Mackenzie drove them to their reservation, the Comanches were gradually drifting back to Texas, where they were now treated as celebrities.

One significant event that happened at the Old Trail Drivers reunion in November 1924 went unnoticed at the time. Herman Lehmann renewed his acquaintance with J. Marvin Hunter, a journalist and publisher of *Frontier Times*. Hunter, born in Loyal Valley in 1880, had known Herman since early childhood. In fact, Hunter's father, John Warren Hunter, had briefly been Herman's teacher at the Loyal Valley schoolhouse in 1879 and had interviewed him for a newspaper article in 1906. As a child, J. Marvin Hunter had been afraid of Herman. His mother used to threaten that if he didn't behave, "that Indian" would get him.

Hunter knew that Herman Lehmann had published a memoir in 1899, written by a Mason County schoolteacher and future county judge named Jonathan H. Jones. Herman and Jones called their collaborative work *A Condensed History of the Apache and Comanche Indian Tribes for Amusement and General Knowledge,* but it was more commonly known by a different title printed on the cover, *Indianology.* Jones took great liberties with both style and content, confusing the chronology of Herman's tales, littering the narrative with ludicrously inappropriate word choices, and supplementing it with sentimental verses and superfluous extracts from other works. Herman's first venture in publishing was a commercial failure. When he traveled to New Braunfels, Texas, to peddle *Indianology*, his buggy flooded in a creek crossing, and many of the copies floated downstream. In the Mason County census of 1900, Herman listed his occupation as "book dealer," although that brief career was as unsuccessful as all his others.

The prospects for a Lehmann autobiography seemed brighter in the 1920s. As a publisher, J. Marvin Hunter was aware of the resurgence in popular histories about Indian captivities. The second edition of Dot Babb's memoir, *In the Bosom of the Comanches,* was selling briskly despite its purple prose and florid style—the handiwork of Dot's ghostwriter, Amarillo entrepreneur Albert Sidney Stinnett. Twenty-five years had passed since *Indianology* appeared, and Herman had never really liked it, anyway. He and Hunter were thinking along the same lines. It was time to bring Herman's story to a new and larger audience.

A month after the reunion in 1924, *Frontier Times* announced the impending publication of a new book, to be called *Herman Lehmann, The Indian.* It would be edited by the magazine's publisher, J. Marvin Hunter. He planned to work quickly, scheduling publication for March 1925. In the early part of 1925, Herman Lehmann returned to Texas from Oklahoma and spent more than a week at Hunter's home in Bandera, relating the story of his life while the publisher took notes. Hunter later recalled that Herman "in many ways expressed himself as an Indian."

Herman had been displeased with the liberties Jonathan Jones took in *Indianology,* and told Hunter, "I want you to write my book the way I tell you, so the young people of this country will know what we went through." Hunter didn't exactly follow Herman's instructions. Much of the manuscript he compiled was taken word for word from *Indianology*. (In his introduction, Hunter stated that he had "obtained valuable material" from Jones's book, although he indicated that Herman had related most of the facts during their meetings.) Even though most of Hunter's work wasn't original, he performed a great deal of much-needed editing. He deleted large chunks of extraneous material, corrected the personal names of the Apaches and Comanches, and weeded out most of Jones's odd phrases, clichés, and digressions. (He also toned down the racier passages, perhaps at Herman's urging.) Herman was satisfied with the results.[6]

By the time of the Gillespie County fair in August 1925, *Herman Lehmann, The Indian* still wasn't in print. When J. G. Burr, a writer for the *Austin American-Statesman,* tried to interview Herman during the festivities, he protested, "I've been having too much publicity already. My life has been written and the people will not buy the book if the papers publish everything in advance."

"Why not?" said Burr. "You have been telling these stories for years and the same people are as anxious as ever to hear them again. If we write about you, it will only serve to create more interest in your book."

As it turned out, there would be plenty of time to generate publicity. Herman's autobiography wasn't published until 1927, two years after it was written. The reason for the delay is unknown, but the problems may have been financial. J. Marvin Hunter's magazine press, *Frontier Times,* was originally going to publish the book, but those plans fell through. Herman's nephew, Maurice J. Lehmann, eventually financed publication and paid Hunter for his work as editor. Maurice sent the manuscript to another firm, Von Boeckmann-Jones Company in Austin.

The new publisher gave Herman's memoir a more descriptive title, *Nine Years Among the Indians 1870–1879.*[7] Due to some editorial carelessness, the title on the cover appeared as *Nine Years* with *the Indians,* and the book has been known by both titles ever since. Either is a slight overstatement, for Herman actually spent eight years among the Apaches and Comanches. The publisher also added an inaccurate paragraph describing how the Apaches made flint arrowheads, apparently without Herman's knowledge.[8] Despite these minor glitches, Herman's book was a publishing triumph. The clothbound volume, which sold for three dollars, was accurately advertised as the "thrilling life story of a white man who was an Indian. . . . He tells his story simply and without frills or flourishes, or exaggeration."

Herman Lehmann wasn't the only white Indian whose memoir appeared in 1927. Clinton Smith had decided to write an account of "the only two brothers ever known to endure the same hardships of captivity and get back alive," as the book was billed. That description also appears to have been accurate. Clinton and his brother, Jeff, collaborated on the narrative over a long period of time, working at the kitchen table by the light of a coal-oil lamp. Using a lead pencil, Clinton scribbled the manuscript, appropriately, on pages of Big Chief writing tablets. When he finished each page, he tore it off and placed it in a cardboard box. The brothers took the box full of handwritten pages to J. Marvin Hunter in Bandera. Hunter published the narrative, with a fair amount of judicious but unobtrusive editing,[9] under the title *The Boy Captives*.

As memoirists, Clinton and Jeff Smith had one major advantage over Herman Lehmann: Clinton was able to transcribe their story himself. Consequently, their personalities came through unfiltered on every page. For the Smith brothers' audience, reading *The Boy Captives* was like listening to a good campfire tale, well told by two masterful storytellers. The narrative was also permeated with their quick sense of humor, and they didn't hesitate to crack jokes at their own expense.

In the fall of 1927, Hunter announced that the Smith brothers' book would be off the press and available for purchase at the Old Trail Drivers reunion in October. He promoted the book in *Frontier Times,* stating: "The story is told in pleasing style, and is a true recitation of the hardships endured and the cruelties visited upon helpless white captives. . . . When they were restored to their people they were almost as wild as the Indians with whom they had been associated." The first edition was paperbound and sold for two dollars. In one advertisement, Hunter pitched the book, rather pitifully, as somewhat of a charity case, noting that the Smith brothers were "old men now" and "have lived a hard life, have had to toil, and still have to toil, for the necessities of life."

Actually, Clinton's wife, Dixie, was the one who'd had to toil. She had resented the time her husband spent on the book while she did all the "real" work for the family. Nonetheless, by the time *The Boy Captives* appeared in print, even Dixie Smith was excited. She said, "Oh, he is going to make so much money out of it!" However, Clinton ended up giving away most of the copies to his many friends. He was a popular fellow, and he refused payment from anyone he knew, even mere acquaintances. "Just like an Indian," his granddaughter jokes. "He had no idea of the value of money." The former captives could barely make a living for their families, and to compound their financial troubles, they had acquired the Comanches' generosity to a fault.[10]

The thirteenth annual reunion of the Old Trail Drivers Association got under way on October 6, 1927, and it would prove to be the humdinger of them all.[11] More than one thousand members registered at the ballroom of the Gunter Hotel in San Antonio, while the Cockle Burr Band played lively fiddle tunes. Three of the association's members—Hermann Lehmann and Clinton and Jeff Smith—were hawking their new books.

Everything on the program that year was larger than life. The association was trying to raise $100,000 for a huge bronze sculpture to be erected in honor of the trail drivers in San Antonio.[12] The reunion featured a spectacular event to raise money for the monument—a Wild West pageant at Garrett Field on North Flores Street depicting a battle between cowboys and Indians. The casting couldn't have been more realistic. A local journalist noted that almost all the roles would be played by "persons who participated in such actual events a quarter of a century or more ago." About twenty-five aging trail drivers came from southwest Texas to play the cowboys, wearing the rough, homespun clothes that some of them probably still had hanging on nails in their doors at home, along with their spurs, chaps, six-shooters, and high-heeled boots.

That wasn't all. As one San Antonio newspaper announced, "Real Comanche Indians were brought here for the show." Thirty-seven Comanches traveled all the way from Oklahoma to portray the antagonists. After the long, dusty road trip, they "prowled the city trying to find a place to have the car washed and polished." Many were more than seventy years old. They were described as "giants of men, six feet and over and weighing 200 pounds." The former warriors wore their hair in two tightly wound braids, and they were decked out in deerskin suits and headdresses made of eagle feathers. Among them were "a dozen or so old men who opposed with rifle and bow the advance of the wagon trains across the Southern Empire."

Every day local reporters attended the rehearsals for the pageant. They noted that the Comanche men talked with one another in their own tongue unless a white man joined the group: "Then, in politeness to him, they speak in halting, jerky English, in phrases incomplete." The former trail drivers were "frequently found engaged in earnest conversation with ex-warriors—each man gesturing valiantly, using the one language known to both." During one rehearsal, a young Comanche horseman rode around the field "wearing a war bonnet, which looked absurdly out of place with his white shirt and blue trousers." He finally tore off the headdress, exclaiming, "That darn thing's too hot!" One of the tribe's elders, dressed in full regalia and leaning against a touring car, glared at him with contempt.

The show featured an attack on a wagon train by the Comanches. They captured a white girl, played by Edith Kelley, the daughter of a trail driver. She told the local press, "I know one thing—that it's not any fun to be an Indian captive. I feel like I've been scalped a dozen times." The newspaper identified the Comanche who played her captor as, preposterously, "Idaho, Heap Big Brave." In the show, he hoisted Edith off the ground and onto a galloping horse.

The production was a big hit, even though one newspaper critic groused that the attack "would have been better if more space had been available and better light provided." Nonetheless, "[t]he Indians in their circling of the camp mounted bareback displayed some marvelous horsemanship." The cowboys, unlike the real-life pursuers of Native American raiders half a century earlier, managed to track down and kill all the Indians, rescuing the captives.

Clinton and Jeff Smith attended the pageant. While they were waiting for the show to start that night, they noticed three Comanches around their age gearing up to attack the wagon train and then get killed by cowboys. They wore feathers and elaborate buckskin outfits. Clinton stared at them, with his hand cupped over his mouth. He nudged Jeff and murmured, "Look! Look at those old bucks over there! Ain't them . . ."

The Comanches glanced their way. They studied the Smiths.

A moment later, the Comanches let out loud whoops of joy. They called Clinton by his old name, Backecacho. He answered them in Comanche. The three Comanches hadn't seen Backecacho since he was taken from their camp and delivered to Fort Sill in 1872. In full view of the crowd, he and the Comanches rushed toward one another, hugging and pounding one another on the backs.

It's doubtful whether Clinton, the three Comanches, or the audience in San Antonio fully appreciated the bizarre irony of the moment: Comanches traveled to Texas to reenact the kidnapping of a white child, only to be reunited with a real captive their fathers had abducted and brought to their village. A few years later, a meeting like that could no longer take place. As one newspaper noted sadly, each year a few more folks such as these went "up the trail from which there is no return."

Even though Jeff had lived with the Apaches, he was almost as excited as Clinton to be back in the company of Comanches his own age. That night he asked his son, Bert, to drive him to the Comanches' camp. "We were there all night," Bert recalled. "He was like a young man again, smoking their pipes, chanting and dancing with them. I don't think I'd ever seen him so happy."

* * *

Herman Lehmann, Dot Babb, and the Smith brothers actively sought publicity. Some former captives did just the opposite: they stubbornly resisted talking about their time with the Indians. My granny Hey said that Uncle Adolph never told the family much about his experiences. Only a few boyhood friends around Castell got to hear his tales. Rudolph Fischer refused repeated requests to tell his story. "We respected his privacy," says Josephine Wapp, his grand-daughter. "I'm sorry I didn't ask him more questions. We just left it alone." Consequently, very little is known about Fischer's prereservation life with the Comanches.

Minnie Caudle liked to tell her grandchildren and great-grandchildren stories about her time in the Comanche camps. However, she never seemed to want her tales to go beyond the family. Nor did Minnie want to leave any traces of her Comanche life after she was gone. When her daughter-in-law started writing down her stories, Minnie found the notebook and burned it. She also told her family that when she died, she wanted them to destroy her Comanche paraphernalia—her beaded pantaloons, belts, vest, moccasins, and quiver that she'd kept through the years.

By their silence, the captives who refused to tell their stories unwittingly gave birth to some fantastic local legends. The public filled in the gaps, and wildly inaccurate tales were passed from one generation to the next. It is said, for instance, that a contingent of ten soldiers took Rudolph Fischer from Fort Sill to Fredericksburg with his hands bound. That's not true; Rudolph returned to his former home grudgingly but voluntarily, accompanied only by his father. Also, some accounts state that Rudolph was abducted with another boy named Johnson, who later went with a band of Comanches on a raid into Mexico and never returned. Yet there is no documented evidence that "Johnson" ever existed. In fact, Rudolph told one of his neighbors that no one else was captured with him.

According to another legend, Temple Friend refused to leave Fort Sill without his fellow captive and close companion, Toppish (John

Valentine Maxey). Leonard Friend took both boys back to Kansas, where they were inseparable. After Temple died, Toppish disappeared into the woods and was never seen again. This romantic story is entirely unfounded. Toppish's father came to get him at Fort Sill a few weeks after Leonard Friend left with Temple.

In 1935 my granny Hey told one interviewer a completely fallacious version of how Adolph Korn was recovered from the Comanches. She said that the Indians "finally traded him to a white man for a barrel of crackers. In some way, this man heard that my father was in San Antonio and offered to sell my stepbrother to him for $100. This was the way father got his son back." How Granny came up with that tale, I'll never know. What's even stranger is that the same story was told about another Mason County captive named William Hoerster. It wasn't true in his case, either.

In 1926 Herman Lehmann left his wife and grown children in Oklahoma to spend the last six years of his life in the home of his brother, Willie, at his ranch in Loyal Valley, Texas. Herman was as popular in Texas as he had been in Oklahoma. His nephew, Maurice J. Lehmann, said, "I recall when I was a boy at home, Uncle Herman visited us often, and as soon as neighbors for miles around heard of him being there, they would come to see him and would have him talking continuously about the experiences he had with the Indians."

"He'd really get kids interested," says Esther Lehmann, Willie's daughter. "Then he'd let out his Indian war whoop and scare the daylights out of them."

Herman never held a job while he lived with Willie. (His death certificate listed his occupation as "retired stockman."[13]) He hunted and fished a great deal. He also made lots of bows and arrows out of dogwood and mulberry, giving away many of them. Sometimes, he peddled his books. He learned to operate a Model T, but he was never a very good driver. Instead, he walked most places. Herman wore white-man's clothes, saving his Comanche regalia for special occasions. Unlike Adolph Korn and Jeff Smith, he didn't mind sleeping indoors.

In the wintertime, Herman sat in front of the fireplace in a rocking chair, smoking his cigarettes. "You could tell his mind was way off somewhere," says Esther. "I think he really missed the Indian life." He never left his old life completely behind him. Herman continued to visit his Comanche friends in Oklahoma every year, traveling by bus, never taking anyone with him.

Eventually, Herman developed a heart condition. Toward the end of his life, he was bedridden. He died at Willie's home on February 2, 1932, at the age of seventy-two. According to the Fredericksburg newspaper, "A large concourse of mourning relatives and friends attended the funeral and covered his last resting place with beautiful flowers, as a token of the high esteem in which he was held by his fellow citizens." In the end, Herman left nothing to his name except his many friends. He died trusting that Willie would pay for his burial.

Unlike Herman Lehmann, Clinton Smith didn't make repeated trips to Oklahoma. Nonetheless, he kept in touch with some of his Comanche friends there. His granddaughter, Edda Raye Moody, reports, "While I was digging through his papers, I came upon a letter written to Grandpa from an Indian in Oklahoma, stating that he would like to come to Texas to visit and talk about old times. He also asked if there was any peyote around here. I do not know if Grandpa Smith replied to this letter, but I feel sure that the Indian did not make the visit or my dad would have told me."

After Clinton and Dixie Smith divorced, Clinton became a nomad, living with one of his children for a while and then another. He was staying in Rocksprings with his daughter, Zona Mae, when he died suddenly on September 10, 1932, probably of a heart attack. In a span of only seven months, Texas had lost two of its most famous white Indians, Herman Lehmann and Clinton Smith. Like Herman, Clinton was seventy-two when he died.

His funeral at the Rocksprings Baptist Church was huge, for Clinton had been an enormously popular figure. According to his obituary, he "was known and loved by the ranching fraternity over the

broad scopes of Texas as well as New Mexico. . . . Beautiful floral of-
ferings were laid beside his casket at the church by a large gathering
who knew Mr. Smith to love him, and his remains were followed to
the cemetery by a large gathering, who were brought to tears as his remains were laid beneath the sod."

As well known and well liked as Clinton was, he suffered from low
self-esteem, perhaps because he hadn't been more successful in business. Many years after his death, his granddaughter, Edda Raye
Moody, displayed in her house the photograph of Clinton and his
three Comanche friends at the 1927 Old Trail Drivers reunion. Her
mother looked at it, and said, "You cannot realize how proud your
grandpa Smith would have been if he only knew you had his picture
in your living room."

Edda Raye said, "Really?"

Her mother replied, "Oh, yes, he would have been so flattered
that somebody thought that much of him."

Minnie Caudle's fourth and final marriage ended with the death of
Will "Doc" Dane, the purveyor of miraculous medicinal cures.
Afterward, she went from the home of one of her children to another,
staying several months at each place.

"Grandma was pretty easy to get along with," says her great-
grandson, Damon Benson, who grew up on his parents' farm near
Rising Star, Texas. "She did have her little contrary spells, though.
When she got peeved at us, she'd threaten to run off and go back to
the Indians. She said if she just knew a good Indian tribe somewhere,
she'd go to them."

Minnie started losing her eyesight before she was thirty, possibly
from hereditary macular degeneration. She was completely blind by
age fifty-seven. "Her eyes were just as white as snow," says Damon
Benson. "No color to them whatsoever."

Minnie sometimes stayed with the family of another son, Henry
Modgling, in Artesia Wells, Texas. Henry's widow, Bertie, recalled in
1984, "When she stayed with us, she'd talk on and on and tell us sto-

ries about the Indians and what happened when she was captured. She would talk about her life and how she lived, and about how brave her mother was. After a while, we'd just listen *at* her, not to her."

Minnie was staying with her son Mose Benson in Marble Falls, Texas, when she died on March 11, 1933. She was seventy-three. Her obituary stated, "She was converted in early life and united with the Baptist Church. . . . Loved the Lords House and his work and was formerly a beautiful singer." For many years, "Grandma Dane" had been the last survivor of the Legion Valley raid of 1868. Her playmate and fellow captive, Temple Friend, had been gone since 1875. Temple's stepmother, Matilda Friend, who had given birth to a healthy daughter after being shot with two arrows and scalped, had finally succumbed to a stroke in 1909.

As Dot Babb grew older, he became even more devoted to his adoptive people. At age sixty-six, he embarked on a strange, quixotic campaign to prove that the Comanches had been wrongly accused of stealing cattle from Texas ranchers, arguing that white thieves were really responsible for the thefts. (He was almost certainly wrong about that.[14]) Between 1918 and 1925, he sent out questionnaires and collected testimony from several veteran cattlemen, including Charles Goodnight.[15] Dot's motive in sending the questionnaires remains a mystery, although he wrote in 1922, "It is never too late to do right." He apparently held a grudge against some of the well-known ranchers of the Texas Panhandle, whom he thought had filed bogus Indian depredation claims to recover losses from alleged cattle thefts by Native Americans. Dot went to great lengths in his unsuccessful attempt to clear the Comanches' name, hoping the tribe could recover the federal money awarded to the white ranchers.

Around five o'clock on a Saturday evening, February 21, 1931, Dot collapsed in the yard of his home in Amarillo. The local newspaper announced that he had suffered a stroke and was not expected to live through the night. However, the white Indians were tough. Dot was released from the hospital the next morning, and his condition had improved rapidly by Sunday night. Nonetheless, he was confined to a wheelchair for the rest of his life. By 1934 he left home only occasionally.

Dot Babb remained one of the Texas Panhandle's best-loved characters. He took great interest in the development of the Panhandle-Plains Historical Society. In 1935 Dot made a special trip to the Panhandle-Plains Historical Museum in Canyon, Texas, to present a gift. It was a sinew necklace strung with copper ornaments, bright beads, dried berries, pierced buffalo teeth, and a charm. One of his Comanche brothers had given it to him when he left the tribe in 1867. Dot said, "I knew exactly what it meant when that necklace was placed around my neck. It was a bond of eternal friendship between us. It was his dearest possession. I've kept it all these years. I want you to take care of it."

Dot died on August 10, 1936, at age eighty-four. The *Amarillo Globe*'s eulogy for him applied just as readily to all the other white Indians of his generation: "It cannot be said that the death of Dot Babb closes a chapter in the history of Texas and the Panhandle. The chapter which his life epitomizes was closed long ago, and Dot Babb became, as it were, a carryover into a new and strange order of things. . . . Dot Babb is gone, and with him almost the last link of a modern, fenced West, with a West preserved only by the legends and writings that have been spared by the erasure of the years."

Dot had been a cowboy and a rancher nearly all his life. Inexplicably, his death certificate listed his occupation as "Indian Scout."[16]

Jeff Smith spent his latter years in San Antonio, where he tilled gardens and small plots of land for families who kept milk cows in the area. After his wife, Julia, died in 1933, he stayed with different relatives for a few months at a time. In the 1930s, "he would still hunt with a bow and arrows that he made himself," says grandson Tom Smith.

On March 8, 1940, Jeff made his last public appearance as a special guest at the San Antonio engagement of the film *Geronimo* at the

Texas Theater. In an interview with the *San Antonio Light*, he referred to Geronimo as a "nice" Indian—perhaps the first time that adjective had ever been applied to the Apache leader by either his defenders or detractors. The article was mostly about Jeff, however. It stated, "He attributes his longevity and present hardy condition to the rigors of Indian ways. . . . All in all, he was not treated much worse than were the Indians' own children, and presently he forgot that he was not actually one of them. . . . He still carries the brand of ownership placed there by the tribes on each cheek."

Grandson Charles Smith recalled, "He was a fun-loving man who loved to go to dances." One Saturday evening, April 20, 1940, Jeff's son and daughter-in-law dropped him off at a family-style tavern while they went to the movies. Jeff played the fiddle for hours while people danced. When his son returned for him later that night, Jeff was having the time of his life and wasn't ready to leave. Instead, he rode home with some friends and spent the night at their place about seven miles outside of San Antonio on the Pleasanton Road. Around noon the next day, he was sitting in a rocker, clutching his cane, when he died of an apparent heart attack. He was seventy-seven.

The *San Antonio Light* reacted to the passing of the city's last white Indian with this understatement: "Smith was born in Texas when it was still part of the frontier and he endured more than the usual share of hardships that went with life at the time."

At age eighty-three, Rudolph Fischer finally developed an interest in his family in Texas. In 1935 his grandson took him to Fredericksburg to visit his brother, Arthur. The two brothers' families hunted deer and spent several happy days together. The Fredericksburg newspaper noted that Rudolph was "still hale and hearty and enjoying life very much. He still attends to his ranch chores personally, being in the saddle every day."

He made his last trip to Fredericksburg in 1939 to attend Arthur's funeral. Rudolph himself died at age eighty-nine on Easter Sunday, April 14, 1941. His first wife, Tissychauer, had passed away in 1933.

Her sister, Kahchacha, the wife whom Rudolph had divorced at the missionaries' insistence, stayed by his bedside and attended him during his last illness. He was buried from the Catholic church in Apache, Oklahoma.

J. Marvin Hunter, writing in *Frontier Times* magazine, reflected that Rudolph was probably the last of the Indian captives from the Texas Hill Country, a group that had once included Adolph Korn, Herman Lehmann, Minnie Caudle, and Clinton and Jeff Smith. "Now Rudolph Fischer has passed on to join his companions in the Great Hereafter," he concluded.

That left only Banc Babb Bell. Like Jeff Smith, Banc had lived most of her life in the shadow of a more famous older brother, Dot. She didn't seem to mind. Banc didn't avoid publicity, but she didn't seek attention, either. When one journalist asked her in 1939 why she'd never published an account of her life, she seemed genuinely surprised by the idea. "Write a book?" she replied. "Well, maybe I should, but I've never thought much about it. No, I don't mind talking about my experiences as a captive, but I suppose I've just taken those early experiences as a matter of course and haven't thought that others were much interested."

At age eighty-two, Banc was a guest of honor at the opening of a new opera, *Cynthia Parker,* at North Texas State Teachers College in Denton on February 16, 1939.[17] It was the first opera premiere ever held in Texas. The composer, Julia Smith, was a Juilliard graduate who later became Aaron Copland's first biographer. The libretto was written by Jan Isbell Fortune. Leonora Corona, formerly a soprano with the Metropolitan Opera, flew from New York to sing the title role. Banc sat in the same row with one of Quanah Parker's sons, Rev. White Parker, and Quanah's last surviving wife, Topay,[18] who was wearing shells and beads. During an intermission following the prologue, the college president, W. J. McConnell, introduced Banc, noting: "She knew Quanah when he was a boy. Her capture was six years after Cynthia Ann's recapture by the whites."[19]

Widowed since 1934, Banc spent her last years living in comfortable obscurity in a neat brick house in Denton, Texas. A family friend, Bette S. Anderson, recalls, "I was aware that Mrs. Bell had been captured by Indians as a child. But I did not hear her say anything about the Indians." Few people who met the nice, quiet old lady were aware that she had once hunted buffalo, attended war dances, and shared a tepee with a woman named Tekwashana, who bundled her in buffalo robes on cold winter nights.

Banc died at her home on April 13, 1950, at age ninety-three. An abbreviated account of her remarkable childhood experience appeared in the Denton and Fort Worth papers, but her death didn't even make the news in nearby Dallas. No one seemed to realize that her passing marked the end of an extraordinary era, for Texas had lost its last Comanche captive. In fact, by 1950, Banc Babb Bell may have been the last white Indian in America.

Chapter Thirteen

The Trail Fades

ncle Adolph finally got a proper headstone in 2000, a century after he died. My grandmother's cousin, Lora Hey, paid for the monument. It's an inconspicuous block of gray granite resting flat on the ground. The tablet states his name and life span, then adds, matter-of-factly: Lived with the Comanches Jan. 1870–Nov. 1872. Each year at Christmas, another relative, Susie Hey Ellison, and her daughter, Debbie, place a small poinsettia by his stone. He's part of our family again.

When April arrives, the old section of the Gooch Cemetery in Mason reverts to nature. If there's been enough rain, a few bluebonnets and fire red Indian paintbrushes sprout between the crevices in fallen tombstones and the rods in wrought-iron fences. Unruly native grass grows out of control like wool over a sheep's eyes, almost hiding the headstone. Even in death, Uncle Adolph resists discovery.

He was staying with his stepsister, my granny Hey, when he died at three o'clock on the afternoon of July 3, 1900, at her rambling frame house on the Fredericksburg Road in Mason. Uncle Adolph was only forty-one. No one remembers the cause of his premature demise. His obituary mentioned "an illness of several months," adding that until then he had been "the very picture of vigorous, rugged manhood." As a former Comanche warrior, Uncle Adolph wouldn't have feared death or even fought it. Instead, having missed his chance to die gloriously in battle, he would have welcomed the opportunity to avoid the indignities of old age.

His obituary was barely noticeable at the bottom of the third page of the Mason newspaper. It explained briefly that Adolph Korn had been captured by Indians and eventually recovered, noting that he had "imbibed many of their customs and mannerisms that remained with him till his death." Uncle Adolph was a private man who made others uncomfortable, and not many people were interested in the details of his strange life at the time it ended. His contemporaries must have shaken their heads, thinking how sad it was that he'd ended up a failure, a misfit, and a loner.

He didn't have enough personal property to pay the debts he left, which included $209.20 he owed to Granny Hey. The administrator of his estate had to sell the land that Uncle Adolph had bought a few years earlier, before he stopped trying to fit in and decided to live in a cave.[1]

Granny saw to it that he was buried with proper rites. The mourners—a small group, no doubt—gathered at his graveside in the Gooch Cemetery to pay their respects the evening after he died. The date of the funeral happened to be the Fourth of July, but that didn't matter; the events of the American Revolution meant little to people on the Texas frontier who had fought their own war against Indians. Afterward, Granny had a death announcement, "To the Memory of Adolph Korn," printed in gold letters on black cardboard. For the few friends and kinfolk who cared about him, the card would be their only memento of his short and seemingly insignificant life. Granny couldn't read, and she may not have realized how inappropriately the sentimental, stock verse on the announcement marked his passing:

One precious to our hearts has gone,
The voice we loved is stilled,
The place made vacant in our home
Can never more be filled.
Our Father in His wisdom called
The boon His love had given;
And though on earth the body lies,
The soul is safe in Heaven.

Other circumstances of his burial are more fitting. Uncle Adolph is facing the rising sun, as is proper for a Comanche. Above his remains grows a lone mesquite, a tree highly valued by the Southern Plains Indians as a source of food during hard times. Across the fence from his grave, a neighboring landowner keeps horses, the Comanches' dearest possessions. Even though Uncle Adolph is not with his tribesmen, I think he would have liked this site.

My chance discovery of his grave sent me in search of him, but I've come to realize that it's impossible to find the answers to all my questions. His trail has become too dim and broken to follow all the way to the end. The reality of his life has been supplanted by the legend, and even that has faded from most people's memories. That's probably the way he wanted it.

The family doesn't have even a single photograph of him. I wonder if no one thought it was important to preserve his image. Maybe he refused to go to a photographer's studio. Even the photograph of Adolph Korn that was taken when the Comanches brought him to Fort Sill in 1872 has never surfaced in any museum or private collection.[2]

He didn't leave many traces at the Korn homestead. In the spring of 1876, Grandpa Korn moved his family for the last time, leaving San Antonio and returning to Mason County. Only six years had passed since Adolph's capture, but the Hill Country was a different place by then. The U.S. Cavalry and the Texas Rangers had done their job well. The Indians were gone for good.

Louis and Johanna Korn bought a 640-acre ranch on the Llano River, where Uncle Adolph spent his late teen and early adult years. The Korns built a small, two-story sandstone house near a spring. They also put up rock fences to enclose the garden and the corral. Uncle Adolph probably helped haul the rock, chisel the corners square, and set the stones in straight lines to build the thick walls. Like Herman Lehmann, he must have despised that type of manual labor. He would have preferred the simplicity and portability of a tepee, anyway.

His toil was ultimately for nothing. The Korn house has been reduced to a pile of rocks and a few rotting timbers completely overgrown with persimmon, broomweed, and prickly pear. From the pasture road, it's hard to even see where it stood. Only the foundation is intact. The well, dug by hand and lined in sandstone, dried up long ago. Wild, native vegetation has reclaimed the fruit orchard. A hundred yards south of the remains of the house, the tiny, rectangular enclosure where Adolph's mother, Johanna, was buried beneath an oak tree in 1883 is hardly recognizable as a family cemetery.

Several crumbling rock fences, in various stages of decay, mark the boundaries of the Korns' ranch and subdivide the pastures. Eventually, those barriers will disappear. My ancestors tried to impose their European sense of order and permanence on these former Native American hunting grounds, but today the Korn place looks much the way it did when the Indians held it.

The families of Adolph Korn and Herman Lehmann tried similar ploys to help their white-Indian sons readjust. Herman's family gave him livestock to care for after he returned. Likewise, Adolph registered a cattle brand in 1877 and owned his own herd by 1879. He opened a charge account at a Mason dry-goods store in 1889. The same year, Adolph became even more deeply immersed in the American way of doing business: he was sued in a property dispute.[3] He lost the case, and his opponent recovered possession of the premises. Uncle Adolph couldn't find the words to explain to the white judge what he'd learned while he was away: the land didn't really belong to any single individual.

Just as Willie Lehmann looked after his brother, Herman, I suspect that Adolph's twin, Charlie Korn, tried to help him get back on his feet. The two boys had worked side by side before Adolph's capture, and they remained close after they both returned to Mason County in 1876. They were given county roadwork assignments together in 1879 and 1885. After that, Charlie Korn disappeared from Mason County records and from Korn family history; he drifted away and fell out of touch with the family. Adolph was alone once more.

During the 1890s, Adolph found work in Castell, near the site of his capture. He broke wild horses for a man named Jacob Bauer. One day Adolph and Bauer's young son, Frank, were following an old Native American trail when they came upon a pile of rocks. Adolph told Frank that the Indians had covered a spring with buffalo hides, then piled stones and soil on top to stop the water from flowing. He didn't explain why they did that. Perhaps it was a last-ditch effort to hold the white invaders at bay by cutting off their water supply.

Adolph also taught Frank how to make a bow. He cut a dogwood branch and covered it with cow manure for about ten days to soften it. The branch was then very pliable, and he could easily shape it.

That's the sum of the stories about Adolph Korn that have been handed down through the generations. If it weren't for Clinton Smith's narrative, Uncle Adolph's experiences among the Comanches would be entirely lost. Like Minnie Caudle and many other former captives, he seemed determined not to leave an Indian legacy.

On October 12, 1892, Uncle Adolph testified in the Indian depredation case of Adolph Reichenau, the Korns' former neighbor in the Saline Valley. Reichenau was trying to recover the value of more than fifty horses stolen by Indian raiders in 1868 and 1869. At the time Adolph gave his testimony, he was working as a well digger. The shy, reticent man must have been terrified of speaking before lawyers and a court reporter. The transcript of his deposition, taken in Mason, is the only surviving record of Adolph's hesitant, stilted way of expressing himself.

Reichenau's attorney was a boisterous and outspoken Englishman named Henry M. Holmes, a friend of Granny Hey and her family. When Holmes asked Adolph to state his age, he replied, "Thirty-three past."

After establishing that Adolph had lived in the Saline Valley at the time of the thefts, Holmes asked, "Did [Reichenau] lose any property or have any property destroyed on or about that time, and if so, what was it?"

"Yes, sir."

"What was it?"

"Horses and oxen." Then Uncle Adolph reconsidered. "I don't remember about the oxen, but he lost horses. He was running a big stock of cattle and used plenty of horses, which horses I often saw Mr. Reichenau ride."

"Who took that property?"

"As much as I know, the Indians at that time."

"How do you know the Indians took them?"

"I heard the Indians running the horses that night and found an Indian saddle there the next morning."

"Did you ever see any of these horses again?"

"I have seen those horses afterwards, that I had seen him ride before."

"Where did you see them?"

"With the Comanche Indians."

"State how you came to be with the Comanche Indians."

"I was herding sheep in Mason County for August Leifeste on the first of January, 1870, and the Indians come and got me and took me prisoner. These were the Apaches."

"State how you came to be with the Comanches."

"They took me up there after traveling with me ten days or over, and I stayed one day and a half with them at their camp. Then traveled me another half a day afoot, and then another half a day and then reached the Comanche camp. And then I was traded to the Comanches. I stayed with the Comanches nearly three years."

Under the federal plan for compensating victims of Indian depredations, a tribe could not be held liable if it was at war with the government at the time of the claimant's property loss. On cross-examination, the government's attorney, Thomas Ball, asked Adolph a standard question: "From 1865 on to 1876, did a condition of war exist between the Apache and Comanche Indians and the governments of Texas and the United States?"

Adolph's answer explodes off the page: "Yes, of course there was war! They killed one another whenever they got a chance."

Ball then asked, "Did you ever go with these Indians on their war party?"

Adolph replied, "I was too little."

"Where did they leave you?"

"They left me at their places of rendezvous of their woman and children, which was always being moved. I never stayed over fifteen days at one place."

Why did Adolph Korn deny his involvement in all the raids and battles that Clinton Smith documented in detail? Did he think he might still be prosecuted for horse thefts? Or hanged for treason, because he'd shot arrows at U.S. cavalrymen? Did he want to conceal the misdeeds of his Comanche youth from his family and neighbors in Mason? For whatever reason, Uncle Adolph kept his secrets. It's likely that Grandpa Korn and Granny Hey never knew that during Adolph's years away from home, he had not been a cowering, horsewhipped slave but an unholy terror.

In 1893 Adolph Korn was thirty-four years old and finally seemed to be finding his place in life. Once again he made some effort to become a regular property owner. He purchased several residential lots in the town of Mason, apparently as investments. Granny Hey, who was always interested in real estate, probably encouraged him to buy land, perhaps even lending him the money. Adolph also bought sixty acres a mile and a half north of Mason, suggesting that he planned to settle down, maybe build a house, and perhaps even marry and raise a family.[4]

No one knows what caused Adolph to revert to his Comanche ways and eventually become a hermit. He never built on his sixty acres north of town. Early in 1896, he sold one of his residential tracts in Mason for $500, the same price he had paid for it. In November of that year, he sold another lot for $130, a loss of seventy dollars.[5]

Some time after that, Adolph Korn dropped out of society altogether. He went to live in a row of small caves known as Diamond Holes on Rocky Creek, near the Mason County community of Hilda. His home in a bluff was located on Gustav and Emma Loeffler's ranch. It's not clear why he chose that spot, but the caves were believed to have been a Comanche lookout. A quarter of a century earlier, he may have even spent time there when he was raiding with the tribe.

Adolph hunted and lived off the land. Granny Hey worried about him. She sent the Loefflers cornmeal, sugar, coffee, and other provisions to deliver to her younger stepbrother. The Loefflers' son Otto, who was only nine or ten at the time, rode horseback to the crest of the bluff above the caves. Using a rope, he lowered the food in a basket. Adolph appeared and acknowledged the goods with a wave, but he said nothing. He didn't seem to want to visit with Otto. He didn't want to talk to anyone.[6]

If Uncle Adolph was so deeply alienated from his German-Texan kin, why didn't he go back to the Comanches in Oklahoma, like Rudolph Fischer and Herman Lehmann?

At first I wondered if it was because he thought the tribe had betrayed him by bringing him to Fort Sill and handing him over to the Indian agent. But that seems unlikely. Clinton Smith and Herman Lehmann held no grudges against the Comanches for coercing them to return to their white families. What's more, the captives' fellow warriors assured them that they were welcome to come back and live with the tribe any time they wanted.

When I was doing research at Fort Sill, I found a more plausible explanation. It came from the report of a federal Indian agent, Julian Scott, who visited the Comanche reservation in the summer of 1890. Scott stated, "There still remains one feature of Indian life on reservations which distinctly links the present with the most savage past. The beef issue is looked upon as a gala day." He described how the government agents provided the Comanches with five or six cows, which they chased and killed in a sort of mock buffalo hunt. The pathetic spectacle was a pale imitation of their rousing adventures on the plains. Scott sniffed, "This exhibition of savage cruelty, permitted as it is by a kind and indulgent government, is no credit to our civilization."[7]

I don't think Uncle Adolph wanted to live in a world where his fellow Comanches chased government-issued cows around an enclosed arena. He couldn't go back to the way of life he'd loved, for it no longer existed. Adolph found greater freedom in a cave in the Texas Hill Country than he would have known within the confines of the Kiowa-Comanche reservation. He preferred to live in the past, even if that meant living alone.

'I've waited three years to see this," I told the others as we got closer. All of us were looking for the Jeep tracks that led to Diamond Holes caves. My dad, Gene Zesch, was driving his four-wheel-drive pickup across rough, brushy ranchland. Jamie Smith Jackson, a family friend and photographer, was with us to take pictures of the cave.

As we crept down the last hill, the pickup lurching over each rock ledge, we discovered that we'd chosen the correct forks in the pasture road. In the valley below, the caves on Rocky Creek were easy to recognize by the series of diamond-shaped openings near the top of a steep limestone bluff. The dirt road led us through a shady grove along the creek to a rustic cabin. We stopped the pickup, walked to the water's edge, and stood in a thicket of post oaks, looking up at the bluff across the creek.

None of us was expecting Uncle Adolph's cave to be so high or inaccessible. From this vantage point, it seemed less like a home than a fortress, guarded by sotol plants with daggerlike spines and impenetrable stands of prickly pear cactus. It was obvious that he didn't want company. We all marveled at the multiple, near-perfect diamond shapes of the apertures in the cliff. "I believe it was man-made," my dad said. "I'll bet there were existing holes and the Indians shaped them like that."

"There's got to be some sort of spiritual implication," added Jamie. "There's a reason for that shape."

We stared in silence. Just downstream from where we were, the creek was dammed, forming a smooth, clear pool that reflected a perfect mirror image of the craggy face of the cliff. The intense sunlight of mid-June brought out the gray, white, and yellow strata of the limestone. At the top of the bluff, the holes looked mysterious. We couldn't see beyond the dark openings.

Jamie asked, "What do you think he did all day?"

I couldn't imagine. I was curious how he carried his water.

We climbed back into the pickup and found a way to coerce it partway up the rocky slope behind the cliff, driving over prickly pear and pushing through thorny shrubs when we had to. About halfway up the high hill, we parked the vehicle in the meager shade of a scrub oak. Then we got out and slowly picked our way around the cat's-claw and agarita bushes that grew in the shallow soil on the sharp incline. My long-sleeved chambray shirt was clinging to my back. Uncle Adolph probably climbed this same steep hill on hotter days, barely aware of the discomfort. I wondered if he wore any clothes.

When we reached the top of the bluff, directly above the caves, we found a cleft leading down into the main chamber. The path was probably the same one that Uncle Adolph used when he went out to hunt deer or to get water or firewood. As soon as we crawled across the threshold into the cave, the midday heat vanished. A steady breeze swept through the diamond-shaped holes, and the rock surfaces felt almost chilly against our hands.

"It's a wonderful place," my dad said. "I could live up here."

On the inside, the cave was much more hospitable than I'd pictured it. The room was just tall enough to stand up in. The floor was level, and the long, narrow gallery had several full-length windows that cooled and lighted the space. Thick, twisted limestone columns supported the arches above the wide openings.

I was hoping to see some pictographs, possibly even a few traces of Uncle Adolph's time in the cave. We found some graffiti on the wall, but it wasn't put there by Native Americans. *Otto Loeffler. Emilie Arhelger. Albert Reichenau. 1887. A. C. Eckert. HH.* Some of those names had already been carved or painted in the cave by the time Uncle Adolph came to live there in the latter 1890s.

I sat in one of the windows where he once must have rested. From this lofty perch, the view of the unspoiled countryside was breathtaking. For miles into the distance, successive ranges of stony, oak-dotted hills rose and then dropped off, until one seamless, bluish ridge finally met the sky. Hardly any signs of human civilization intruded on that landscape. If Uncle Adolph had wanted to meditate on his past life or just escape his present circumstances, he found the right place to do it.

At one end of the gallery, the gnarled trunk of a dead mesquite tree stretched across the floor. Jamie sat on it to take some photos. A moment later, we heard her shout. Dad and I got up and hurried to see what Jamie was looking at. On the rock above her was an ancient, stylized painting of the sun in dark red, with rays streaming out. "It's gorgeous! It's perfect!" She saw a linear figure beside it. "There's an arrow pointing outward!"

I looked behind her and found a painting that was even better preserved in a crevice that got no direct light. It was an abstract geometric shape outlined in red ocher, its interior filled in white. Uncle Adolph must have studied these same pictures. Maybe he understood what they meant.

Jamie noticed the blackened ceiling right over our heads. "Look, that's where the smoke went up when he was building his fire."

I ran my hand over the traces of smoke on the rough stone surface, trying to picture him with his long, wild, blond hair and callused hands, crouching by the fire on a frosty winter evening, stoking the coals with a stick. In the old days, aging Comanche warriors would gather around the campfire at night and entertain one another with tales of derring-do from their glory days—the raid when they risked their lives to get a particularly good horse, the death-defying prank they played on a friend, the dirt-poor immigrant family they terrorized for fun, the Indian enemies they whipped in battle, the hated buffalo hunters they ambushed and scalped. But Uncle Adolph, after he was back among the German-Americans of Mason County, had to relive his raids alone. There was no one he could tell his stories to. His neighbors would have called him a thief, a murderer, and a savage.

My ancestor's tracks were nearly impossible to follow, but this cave was one place where I could be certain I was occupying the same space he once inhabited. My reaction was unexpected. Even though he was long gone, I somehow felt like an intruder. I'd invaded a sanctuary, his private retreat from what he probably saw as a dull, sterile society filled with spiritless people who couldn't understand him and didn't try, people whose customs, values, and pretensions must have seemed both laughable and offensive.

I decided it was time for us to leave. That site belonged to his memory. As we took our last look around the cave, Jamie remarked, "It takes a really lonely, angry person to live in a place like this."

I agreed. Lonely, angry—or maybe just terribly sad. Every day he spent in that cave, with its commanding outlook of the distant hills where his people used to ride, my uncle Adolph kept a solitary vigil for Comanche brothers whom he knew would never return.

I think the Germans were cruel to their children," a friend of mine remarks. I've asked for her opinion because her husband grew up in Castell, and she's observed German-Texan life as an outsider.

"They couldn't show affection," her daughter agrees. "They thought that as long as they provided for the family, that was love."

The German children of the Texas Hill Country did seem to work harder than those of other ethnic groups, well into the twentieth century. Nor did their parents indulge them much. The children weren't paid allowances for doing farm chores, because that was simply what they owed the family. Even as they grew to adulthood, the parents found ways to block their independence. Sons worked for their fathers for promises of inheritance rather than wages; the fathers kept title to the land.

Our family history describes Grandpa Korn as a gentle fellow who loved sweets, music, and dancing. However, he could also be demanding and rigidly moralistic. He seems to have worn out two wives, both of whom died relatively young. It is said that later in life, he would have fired any cowboy working for his family who didn't attend Sunday school. The Comanches, on the other hand, placed few restrictions on their children, giving them a full measure of autonomy at adolescence. They rewarded cleverness and success, not hard labor or adherence to dogma.

I've often questioned whether the privation the Korn children suffered was due solely to the family's poverty or whether Grandpa was also parsimonious. The German-Texans were famously unwilling to part with their money. Grandpa Korn's wife and infant son died two decades before he did, and he never purchased headstones for the family cemetery at the Korn place. I wonder, too, if Grandpa was really too poor to go get Uncle Adolph when he was recovered at Fort Sill or if he was willing to let him come home with the army just to save the stage fare. The Comanches, in contrast, were renowned for their generosity. They would share everything they had with those they liked.

Uncle Adolph grew up herding sheep every day. He was never able to attend school or venture beyond his isolated community. The Comanches let him hunt and ride and see new country.

In the winter of 1870, Adolph suddenly went from living in a log cabin to a tepee. He was probably surprised to find that the tepee was more comfortable in Texas weather. Then his leg was injured when he was thrown from a horse, crippling him for life. Among the Comanches, he could still win respect, because he carried out his most daring feats on horseback. He rode one of their best mounts; he was sent on reconnaissance missions; he even commanded a band of Comanches in battle. When he got back to Mason County, he was just a peculiar recluse who walked with a limp. After he died, no one bothered to give him a real headstone for a hundred years.

Highway 29 runs through the spacious cattle ranches that lie between Mason and Llano, and from it a winding, unpaved lane called Bauerville Road heads south and leads to Castell the roundabout way. Its surface is corrugated like a washboard, swept by wind and rainwater. The road cuts through gently sloping pastures dense with undergrowth. Whitetail deer, turkey, and rabbits thrive in this unpopulated country. Otherwise, it's a lonely route; chances are a motorist won't meet any other vehicles. Several of the roadside farmhouses that were once home to generations of German-American families are now empty. The porches sag. Old tractors and livestock trailers sit idle in the weeds.

The road eventually turns east, and the last stretch runs beside the north bank of the Llano River, shaded by tall pecan trees. Down in the riverbed, a wooden waterwheel encased in a shell of stone and mortar stands strong against the current, even though it is no longer turning. Not far beyond the waterwheel is the land of August Leifeste, the man who hired the Korn boys to tend his flock.

I decided to commemorate the 133d anniversary of Uncle Adolph's capture by visiting the place where it happened. I'd seen the site from a distance but never had set foot on the land. That day I wanted to stand where Adolph and his twin brother, Charlie, were herding sheep and see what they saw. It was a cloudless morning in Mason County, unusually warm for January. I'd always assumed the weather was cold and overcast the day he was taken, but now I realized it might have been a gorgeous New Year's Day like this one.

Around noon, the time of day Adolph was abducted, I parked my car in front of a sturdy white farmhouse with a long veranda, its decorative tin roof now a shroud of solid rust. Many years ago, this was the home of August Leifeste's daughter, Wilhelmina. Now it's shuttered and locked. I made my way down the slope to the Llano River, passing through tall weeds and over the tops of pink granite outcroppings, their surfaces sparkling in the sunlight. The river bottom is wide at this point, and half of it is covered by a sand bar sprinkled with polished gravel. As I crossed it, I followed scattered tracks in the mud left by deer that drank there earlier.

I reached the water's edge and stopped directly across from the place. The older Castell natives say that Adolph Korn was captured beside an unusually large oak tree that stood on the south bank of the Llano. In the summer of 1935, that tree was uprooted and swept away during a violent flood; later, a windmill was erected just east of where it stood. As I stared at the site from across the river, the only sounds I heard were a few birdcalls and the steady grind of the rusty windmill, its blades turning lazily in the breeze.

The river looked wadeable. I removed my sneakers and socks, rolled up my jeans, and stepped in. Even though the air was warm, the water felt like ice as I started across. When I got to a limestone ledge in the middle, I stopped for a moment and warmed my feet in the sunshine. I debated whether to continue or do the sensible thing: go back to my car and drive around a few miles to the site. But it was so close; I couldn't wait.

I plunged ahead, only to discover that the clear water wasn't as shallow as it looked. I felt the coldness creeping up my thighs. Then I slipped on a mossy rock and was drenched to my chest. I'd been carrying my shoes to keep them dry, but they got submerged as I foundered in the water, trying to gain a foothold. Finally, I steadied myself. By the time I reached the other side, I was soaked. I made the steep climb up the south bank below the windmill, relieved to be out of the frigid water.

At the top of the riverbank, I stopped to catch my breath and look around. I'd finally reached my destination, and I wanted this place to be memorable, distinctive. However, I found myself fighting back disappointment. His capture site looked like any other bank on this stretch of the Llano River. Then I realized: *that's the point.* The abduction could have happened anyplace, anytime, to any child. The Korn boys had no reason to suspect they were in danger there. If the three Apaches had taken a slightly different route, they could just as easily have made off with an adolescent Leifeste or Bauer instead, and another family would be telling stories about its white Indian.

I walked upstream along the water's edge, tracing the path Adolph and Charlie must have used as they let the sheep drift upriver. In my mind, I could hear Adolph telling the story during his deposition: *I was herding sheep in Mason County for August Leifeste on the first of January, 1870, and the Indians come and got me and took me prisoner. These were the Apaches.* Most of the bushes around me were either leafless or thinly clad. I wondered how Uncle Charlie managed to hide from the Apaches. Maybe the grass was tall enough to cover him.

I paused to take in the landscape in every direction. According to family lore, the Korn boys first saw the Apaches riding across a distant hill. However, the land is level on both sides of the river; I could see no hill. Legend also has it that Adolph was going down into a ravine to eat his lunch when the Apaches appeared. I found no ravine as I ambled along the riverbank, only a slight depression in the ground near some granite boulders.

Maybe the ravine has filled in over the years.

Maybe the "hill" was just a low ridge.

Or maybe the stories have changed over time. Perhaps I wasn't even standing at the exact spot. At this late date, no one knows for sure.

Whether it was precisely the right place or not, I realized I'd followed Uncle Adolph's trail as far as I could. His story started for me at his grave; I'd finally reached the end of my search on the riverbank where his own journey began. I knew as much about him then as I was likely to ever know. The time had come to let him rest in peace.

The breeze kept reminding me that my shirt and jeans were dripping. I climbed back down the steep riverbank and plunged into the stream again, getting even wetter when I crossed this time. My sneakers were caked with sand by the time I scrambled up the grassy slope toward the road. As soon as I started my car, I put the heater on high, turned the vehicle around, and headed up the dirt lane, spraying gravel along the way.

The Apaches took me up there after traveling with me ten days or over, and I stayed one day and a half with them at their camp. Then traveled me another half a day afoot, and then another half a day and then reached the Comanche camp.

One hundred thirty-three years: only a few generations ago, this part of America was inconceivably wild and brutal. I was crisscrossing the path the three Apaches took when they left with Uncle Adolph. They moved nearly as fast on horseback as I could travel by car. Old-timers say the Indians tied a cloth across Adolph's eyes so that he wouldn't know where he was going and couldn't find his way back home if he escaped. It doesn't matter whether that story is true. Blindfolded or not, there is no way he could have seen what was ahead.

TABLE
DATES AND PLACES OF
BIRTH, CAPTURE, RECOVERY, AND DEATH

NAME	BIRTH	CAPTURE	RECOVERY	DEATH
RUDOLPH FISCHER	Jan. 12, 1852 Gillespie County, Tex.	July 29, 1865 near Morris Ranch, Tex.	Sept. 1877 Ft. Sill, I. T.	Apr. 13, 1941 Apache, Okla.
BANC BABB	Aug. 26, 1856 Lecompton, Kan.	Sept. 14, 1866 near Chico, Tex.	Apr. (?) 1867 Ft. Arbuckle, I. T.	Apr. 13, 1950 Denton, Tex.
DOT BABB	May 17, 1852 Reedsburg, Wis.	Sept. 14, 1866 near Chico, Tex.	June (?) 1867 Ft. Arbuckle, I. T.	Aug. 10, 1936 Amarillo, Tex.
MINNIE CAUDLE	Sept. 1, 1859 Llano County, Tex.	Feb. 5, 1868 Llano County, Tex.	July 27, 1868 Ft. Larned, Kan.	Mar. 11, 1933 Marble Falls, Tex.
TEMPLE FRIEND	May 21, 1860 Llano County, Tex.	Feb. 5, 1868 Llano County, Tex.	Nov. 14, 1872 Ft. Sill, I. T.	June 2, 1875 El Dorado, Kan.
ADOLPH KORN	May 8, 1859 San Antonio, Tex.	Jan. 1, 1870 near Castell, Tex.	Nov. 14, 1872 Ft. Sill, I. T.	July 3, 1900 Mason, Tex.
HERMAN LEHMANN	June 5, 1859 near Fredericksburg, Tex.	May 16, 1870 near Loyal Valley, Tex.	Apr. 1878 Ft. Sill, I. T.	Feb. 2, 1932 Loyal Valley, Tex.
CLINTON SMITH	Aug. 3, 1860 near Bergheim, Tex.	Feb. 26, 1871 near Bergheim, Tex.	Oct. 24, 1872 Ft. Sill, I. T.	Sept. 10, 1932 Rocksprings, Tex.
JEFF SMITH	Aug. 31, 1862 near Bergheim, Tex.	Feb. 26, 1871 near Bergheim, Tex.	May 1, 1873 Piedras Negras, Mexico	Apr. 21, 1940 San Antonio, Tex.

Notes

A Comment on the Sources

Historian T. R. Fehrenbach observed that "the type of white person drawn to the frontier, either as a settler or an Indian fighter, was one whose life was given to ceaseless action, rarely reflection or philosophy. . . . Only a handful of the thousands of Texans who battled Indians on the frontier ever bothered to write down their observations" (Fehrenbach, *Comanches,* 306). Fehrenbach's remarks explain the difficulty I encountered in searching for reliable information on the captives' experiences and the dilemma I faced in trying to create an unbroken narrative without sacrificing historical integrity. Sometimes, the only sources on particular events were thirdhand accounts, family legends, or popular histories of dubious scholarship. The white Indians' stories also contained numerous gaps and omissions. And if the Texas settlers didn't set down many written accounts, the Comanches and Apaches left virtually none.

My retelling of the events in this book represents a synthesis of the sources that I considered generally trustworthy, even if they contained some errors. In weighing the credibility of each source, I was guided by two inquiries.

1. Was the narrator an eyewitness to the incidents reported? If not, did he or she at least obtain the information from someone who was in a position to observe the events?

Even some eyewitness accounts are suspect. Many were written or dictated from memory decades after the events occurred. Others were tailored to meet audience expectations. Furthermore, the captives' published interviews and "as told to" autobiographies no doubt contain some inaccuracies and biases introduced by their interviewers and editors.

Consequently, I employed a second test:

2. Are the eyewitness's recollections either corroborated or contradicted by credible reports of the same events recorded shortly after they occurred?

Although some scholars have questioned the reliability of the captivity narratives I've cited, I found that they held up surprisingly well under the second test. For the most part, the captives' own recollections of their abduction and eventual recovery were consistent with the official reports, letters, and newspaper accounts written at the time those events occurred. That led me to believe that the captives' tales of their lives among the Indians (most of which cannot be checked against other sources) are generally credible. What's more, captivity narratives are among the very few accounts of prereservation Comanche and Apache life authored by insiders, since those tribes didn't use written languages (other than pictographs).

Some elderly Comanches gave interviews in the 1920s and 1930s, which provided valuable information on their captives and prereservation culture. Especially important are the 1933 Comanche Field Notes of the Santa Fe Laboratory of Anthropology research party, which will be published in a forthcoming compendium edited by Thomas W. Kavanagh.

As a rule, when two sources disagreed, I gave more credence to eyewitness testimony than hearsay, and to earlier rather than later sources. I decided against interrupting the flow of the story with analyses of the credibility of particular sources or the discrepancies among them. However, I discuss some of those finer points in the notes to the individual chapters.

In writing my account of the captives' experiences, I did not invent any of the dialogue, although I reconfigured a few lines of narrative prose taken from eyewitnesses' reports into direct speech. When necessary, I took the liberty of inserting information on what settlers and Indians ate, wore, rode, etc., that was gleaned from accounts handed down by people who lived during that period.

The English transcriptions of Comanche names vary widely from source to source. For the most part, I used the spellings found in the most recent political history, Kavanagh's *The Comanches,* which contains detailed information on the derivations and translations of prominent chiefs' names. The names of several other Native American individuals that were taken from the captives' narratives should be viewed as rough approximations. For transcriptions and definitions of Comanche words and phrases, I used the Comanche Language and Cultural Preservation Committee's excellent *Taa Numu Tekwapu?ha Tuboopu (Our Comanche Dictionary).*

Correspondence, articles, and interviews pertaining to each captive are cited in the Bibliography. Other sources specific to a particular chapter are mentioned in the chapter notes. I've used the abbreviations listed below when citing documents from the major archives I visited. However, many of the real "gems" collected during my search were tucked away in vertical files in small-town libraries and local history museums, especially those in Mason, Llano, Decatur, and Boerne, Texas; El Dorado, Kansas; Reedsburg and Baraboo, Wisconsin; and Lawton, Oklahoma. For background information, I relied on many fine articles in the journals *Southwestern Historical Quarterly, Chronicles of Oklahoma,* and *Prairie Lore.*

In all citations, Roman numerals refer to volumes and Arabic numerals to pages, unless otherwise indicated. No volume numbers are given for periodicals that are not consecutively paginated.

APSL   American Philosophical Society Library, Philadelphia, Pennsylvania

CAH   Center for American History, The University of Texas at Austin, Texas

FCML   Fort Concho Museum Library, San Angelo, Texas

FLNHS   Fort Larned National Historic Site, Larned, Kansas

FSMA   Fort Sill Musuem Archives, Fort Sill, Oklahoma

HML   Haley Memorial Library, Midland, Texas

KSHS   Kansas State Historical Society, Manuscripts Department, Topeka, Kansas

MGP   Museum of the Great Plains, Lawton, Oklahoma

NARA   National Archives and Records Administration, Washington, D.C.

NARA-CP   National Archives and Records Administration at College Park, Maryland

NARA-SW   National Archives and Records Administration, Southwest Region, Fort Worth, Texas

OHS   Oklahoma Historical Society, Archives and Manuscripts Division, Oklahoma City, Oklahoma

PPHM   Panhandle-Plains Historical Museum, Canyon, Texas

SINAA   Smithsonian Institution National Anthropological Archives, Suitland, Maryland

TSA   Texas State Archives, Austin, Texas

UTEP   University Library, University of Texas at El Paso, Texas

WHC   Western History Collections, The University of Oklahoma Libraries, Norman, Oklahoma

CHAPTER I: NEW YEAR'S DAY

1. The information in this chapter about the Korn family is drawn from: Hulda C. Wilbert, *Kernels of Korn: The Historical Events of a Pioneer Family* (Burnet, Tex.: Nortex Press, 1982); O. C. Fisher, *It Occurred in Kimble* (1937; reprint, San Angelo: The Talley Press, 1984), 113, 117, 133; and Scott Zesch, "The Two Captivities of Adolph Korn," *Southwestern Historical Quarterly,* CIV (Apr. 2001), 515–40. My discussion of living conditions in Castell during its early years relies primarily on Hazel Oatman Bowman, "Quaint Castell, Outpost of German Pioneers," *San Antonio Express,* July 26, 1936, D1, D3. The quotes by and stories

NOTES

about Granny Hey (Hannah Korn Hey) are taken from: *Frontier Times,* VI (Jan. 1929), 155–56; Fisher, *It Occurred in Kimble,* 133–35; *Colorado County* [Tex.] *Citizen,* June 11, 1936, Magazine Section, 2; *Mason County News,* Mar. 14, 1935, 8; Florence T. Hillard, "Tallow Candle Days," [*The Daily Oklahoman*], n.d., photostat of clipping in Hey family file, M. Beven Eckert Memorial Library, Mason, Texas; *San Angelo Standard-Times,* May 3, 1934, Section 3, 2; and Hannah Korn Hey to Hazel Oatman Bowman, Jan. [1935], copy of manuscript in the author's possession.

2. George W. Todd to N. G. Taylor, July 22, 1868, Microfilm Roll 375, FLNHS.

3. Clinton L. Smith and Jefferson D. Smith with J. Marvin Hunter, *The Boy Captives* (Bandera, Tex.: Frontier Times, 1927), 82.

4. Vol. H, page 353 (July 5, 1861), Deed Records, Gillespie County Clerk's Office, Fredericksburg, Texas.

5. Smith, *The Boy Captives,* 119.

6. *San Angelo Standard,* May 14, 1926, 2.

7. Alice Todd's fate was never determined, although there were periodic reports that she remained with the Kiowas, married a Mexican (probably a fellow captive), and had a daughter. Todd to Taylor, July 22, 1868; Dan Allen to Charles Lewis, July 25, 1869, Microfilm Roll M234/376, NARA-SW; and John Lee to H. Clay Wood, Jan. 24, 1870, Southern Plains Indian Agencies Collection, WHC.

8. Indian depredation claim of Rans [sic] Moore, Record Group 123, Case No. 5121, NARA.

9. The murders in the Saline community are described in: *Weekly Southern Intelligencer* [Austin], Aug. 18, 1865, 2; Fisher, *It Occurred in Kimble,* 49–50, 113–37; Thomas W. Gamel, *The Life of Thomas W. Gamel,* ed. Dave Johnson (Mason, Tex.: Mason County Historical Society, 1994), 5–11; J. W. Wilbarger, *Indian Depredations in Texas* (1889; reprint, Austin: Eakin Press, 1985), 644; Joseph Carroll McConnell, *The West Texas Frontier, or a Descriptive History of Early Times in Western Texas* (2 Vols.; Palo Pinto, Tex.: Texas Legal Bank and Book Co., 1939), II, 68, 218; *Mason County News,* May 1, 1985, 7, and May 15, 1985, 8; and Josephine Conaway Hunter to Elizabeth Mahill, 1942, copy of notes in the author's possession.

10. Affidavits of Adolph A. Reichenau, Sept. 4, 1888, Gus Reichenau, Dec. 19, 1889, and Charles Wartenbach (n.d.), Indian depredations papers, Mason County Clerk's Office, Mason, Texas.

11. Indian agent Lawrie Tatum reported that Adolph Korn's captors were New Mexico Apaches or Arizona Apaches. Lawrie Tatum to Enoch Hoag, Nov. 15, 1872, Microfilm Roll M234/377, NARA-SW; Lawrie Tatum, *Our Red Brothers and the*

Peace Policy of President Ulysses S. Grant (1899; reprint, Lincoln: University of
Nebraska Press, 1970), 139. Both designations probably referred to the
Mescalero Apaches. Frank D. Reeve, "The Apache Indians in Texas," *Southwestern Historical Quarterly*, L (Oct. 1946), 211. In 1915, when Indian depredation
claims were still being litigated, the federal government speculated that Adolph
was captured by Mescalero Apaches from New Mexico, which would have proven
that the Mescaleros were raiding in that area in 1870. Harry Peyton, an attorney
in Washington, D.C., didn't believe that was true: "My theory is that this location in Mason County was entirely too far removed from the natural habitat of
the Mescalero-Apaches to probably involve them in this capture and depredation.
I am led to assume that the Apaches who captured him were of those Apaches
that were affiliated with the Comanches and Kiowas on the reservation in the Indian Territory." Peyton hoped Uncle Adolph could answer this question defini-
tively, not realizing that he had died fifteen years earlier. Harry Peyton to Charles
Bierschwale, Jan. 15, 1915, Charles Bierschwale Collection, Box 2-22/994, TSA.
12. According to one version of Adolph's story, based on interviews with pioneer
citizens of Mason County who knew him, the Comanches were not motivated
by revenge: "When an Indian child died, the Indians buried their Guardian with
them. They did this in order that the child might not be lonely in his Happy
Hunting Ground. After they have buried the child for several hours, they will
not kill the Guardian." Alva Catherine Beach, "History of Events of Mason
County, Texas," in *Mason County Scrapbook and Obituary*, Archives and Manuscripts Collection, CAH.
13. Uncle Adolph did not specify which men wanted to kill him. Although anyone
could have expressed an opinion on this issue, an owner's decision to dispatch
his captive—or, for that matter, to adopt him and give him full rights as a
Comanche—would not have been made collectively; these choices did not re-
quire tribal consent. Recollections of Naiya (Slope of Land), Comanche Field
Notes, Waldo Rudolph Wedel and Mildred Mott Wedel Papers, Box 109, SINAA.
14. Circular, Office of Indian Affairs, Lawrence, Kansas, 1870, Microfilm Roll
KA42, OHS.

CHAPTER 2: GERMANS IN COMANCHE LAND

1. A. Irving Hallowell, "American Indians, White and Black: The Phenomenon of
Transculturalization," *Current Anthropology*, IV (Dec. 1963), 523.
2. Dorman H. Winfrey and James M. Day (eds.), *The Indian Papers of Texas and
the Southwest, 1825–1916* (5 Vols.; Austin: The Pemberton Press, 1966), II, 8.
3. Winfrey and Day (eds.), *The Indian Papers of Texas*, III, 62.

NOTES

4. The earliest accounts of the founding of Fredericksburg and the relations between the Comanches and the German settlers in the vicinity include: *Democratic Telegraph and Texas Register* [Houston], Dec. 7, 1846, 4, and Feb. 17,
1848, 3; Robert Penniger, *Fredericksburg, Texas: The First Fifty Years,* trans.
Charles L. Wisseman Sr. (1896; English ed., Fredericksburg: Fredericksburg
Publishing Co., Inc., 1971), 29–49, 73–78; Louis Reinhardt, "The Communistic Colony of Bettina," *Texas Historical Association Quarterly,* III (July 1899),
33–40; *Frontier Times,* VII (Aug. 1930), 514–16 (recollections of Katherina
Burrer); *San Antonio Express,* July 26, 1936, D1, D3 (interviews with the children of Castell's first settlers); *Mason County News,* Aug. 19, 1937, 4 (interview
with William Schmidt); Terry G. Jordan and Marlis Anderson Jordan (eds. and
trans.), "Letters of a German Pioneer in Texas [Franz Kettner]," *Southwestern
Historical Quarterly,* LXIX (Apr. 1966), 463–72; H. T. Edward Hertzberg
(trans.), "A Letter from Friedrich Schenck in Texas to His Mother in Germany,
1847," *Southwestern Historical Quarterly,* XCII (July 1988), 145–65; Brian J.
Boeck, "'They Contributed Very Much to the Success of Our Colony': A New
Source on Early Relations between Germans and Indians at Fredericksburg,
Texas," *Southwestern Historical Quarterly,* CV (July 2001), 81–91; and the
sources cited in Karl A. Hoerig, "The Relationship between German Immigrants
and the Native Peoples in Western Texas," *Southwestern Historical Quarterly,*
XCVII (Jan. 1994), 423–51.
5. The most comprehensive and objective eyewitness account of the German expedition into the Fisher-Miller Land Grant and the Comanche-German peace
council of 1847 is Ferdinand Roemer, *Texas, with Particular Reference to German Immigration and the Physical Appearance of the Country,* trans. Oswald
Mueller (1849; English ed., 1935; reprint, Austin: Eakin Press, 1983), 218–87.
Other eyewitness reports are found in: John O. Meusebach, *Answer to Interroga-
tories in Case No. 396, Mary C. Paschal et al., vs. Theodore Evans, District Court of
McCulloch County, Texas* (1894; reprint, Austin: Pemberton Press, 1964),
23–25; Robert S. Neighbors to William Medill, Apr. 24, 1847, Microfilm Roll
M234/858, NARA; and Penniger, *Fredericksburg, Texas,* 37–45 (report of two
unnamed Germans). Newspaper coverage is found in *Democratic Telegraph and
Texas Register* [Houston], Mar. 22, 1847, 3, Mar. 29, 1847, 4, May 3, 1847, 4,
May 10, 1847, 4, and June 14, 1847, 3.
6. Report of P. M. Butler and M. G. Lewis, Aug. 8, 1846, House of Representa-
tives, 29th Cong., 2d Sess., Doc. No. 76, 8; *The Civilian and Galveston Gazette,*
Weekly Edition, July 10, 1847, 2; *Frontier Times,* Jan. 1927, 24; and Phoebe S.
Allen, "The Double Exposure of Texas Captives," *Western Folklore,* XXXII (Oct.
1973), 250–53.

7. An English version of the peace treaty appears in Irene Marschall King, *John O. Meusebach: German Colonizer in Texas* (Austin: University of Texas Press, 1967), 175–76.

8. Roemer, *Texas,* 14.

9. The murder of the four surveyors is described in: John C. Hays to Robert S. Neighbors, July 15, 1847, and Robert S. Neighbors to William Medill, Aug. 5, 1847, Microfilm Roll M234/858, NARA; Winfrey and Day (eds.), *The Indian Papers of Texas,* V, 33–34; and *Democratic Telegraph and Texas Register* [Houston], July 26, 1847, 5, Aug. 9, 1847, 5, Aug. 30, 1847, 6, and Oct. 7, 1847, 4.

10. Don H. Biggers, *German Pioneers in Texas: A Brief History of Their Hardships, Struggles and Achievements* (1925; reprint, Austin: Eakin Press, 1983), 75.

11. *Western Texian* [San Antonio], Jan. 12, 1849, 2.

12. Winfrey and Day (eds.), *The Indian Papers of Texas,* III, 134.

13. Winfrey and Day (eds.), *The Indian Papers of Texas,* III, 181, and V, 127–28.

14. The story of the Comanche boy captured and lynched by the Germans was recalled by two eyewitnesses, Fernandina Ottmers Otte and Julius Kott. *Frontier Times,* May 1927, 1–2; *Frontier Times,* X (Dec. 1932), 117–18; *Fredericksburg Standard,* May 1, 1946, Section 5, 1, 6. Both were children at the time, and their accounts vary in several particulars.

15. G. W. Todd to D. N. Cooley, Oct. 14, 1866, Microfilm Roll M234/375, NARA-SW.

16. *San Antonio Daily Express,* Sept. 2, 1877, 2.

17. This assumption turned out to be correct. Rudolph Fischer later told his daughter, Lottie, that he had been captured by a Comanche warrior named Naahsueca. However, he was raised by another Comanche named Black Crow. Lottie Fisher to Arthur Lawrence, Sept. 14, 1958, Arthur Lawrence Collection, MGP.

18. Vol. D, pages 442–43 (Mar. 10, 1851), Deed Records, Gillespie County Clerk's Office, Fredericksburg, Texas.

19. Rudolph Fischer's grave marker states that he was born in 1850. However, the oldest sources, including those cited in the Mormon genealogy database, www.familysearch.com, indicate that he was born in 1852. Gillespie County census of 1860; A. Siemering to U.S. Secretary of State, Mar. 22, 1867, Microfilm Roll M234/375, NARA-SW; Rudolf Radeleff to Charles E. Morse, Nov. 22, 1869, J. Evetts Haley Collection, HML (copy of letter from NARA, Records of the War Department, U.S. Army Commands, Fort Concho, Texas).

20. The contemporary transcription is *esiwana.* Comanche Language and Cultural Preservation Committee, *Taa Nʉmʉ Tekwapʉ?ha Tʉboopʉ (Our Comanche Dictionary)* (Lawton: Comanche Language and Cultural Preservation Committee, 2003), 4.

CHAPTER 3: THE BOSOM OF THE COMANCHES

1. Most of Dot Babb's quotes in this chapter are from his autobiography, T. A. Babb, *In the Bosom of the Comanches* (1912; 2d ed., Dallas: Hargreaves Printing Co., 1923). Others are from his later writings and the numerous interviews he gave, cited in the Bibliography. Most of Banc's quotes are from her brief captivity narrative, "A True Story of My Capture by, and Life with the Comanche Indians," reprinted in Daniel J. Gelo and Scott Zesch (eds.), " 'Every Day Seemed to be a Holiday': The Captivity of Bianca Babb," *Southwestern Historical Quarterly*, CVII (July 2003), 35–67. The Wise County Heritage Museum in Decatur, Texas, maintains a comprehensive file on the Babb family, which includes another shorter, untitled memoir by Banc Babb. Contemporaneous sources on the raid through Wise County and the Babbs' capture, listed in the Bibliography, are scant and provide relatively little information. The Babb siblings' earliest accounts of their captivity are the affidavits and depositions they gave in 1887 and 1898 in the Indian depredation claim of Hernando C. Babb, Record Group 123, Case No. 4606, NARA. This case file also includes the depositions of eyewitnesses Robert G. Cates, Daniel Waggoner, Rufus Booth, George I. Morrow, and George B. Pickett, taken in 1900.
2. U.S. House of Representatives, Misc. Doc. No. 139, 41st Cong., 2d Sess., 8; and J. H. Leavenworth to G. W. Todd, Dec. 24, 1866, Microfilm Roll M234/375, NARA-SW.
3. J. H. Leavenworth to Thomas Murphy, Dec. 14, 1866, Microfilm Roll M234/375, NARA-SW.
4. *San Antonio Daily Express*, Mar. 3, 1871, 4. While there is very little contemporaneous documentation of Brit Johnson's journeys (which some historians dismiss as mere legend), his redemption of his family from the Comanches in exchange for seven ponies is substantiated in Samuel A. Kingman, "Diary of Samuel A. Kingman at Indian Treaty in 1865," *Kansas Historical Quarterly*, I (Nov. 1932), 447.
5. In researching *The Searchers*, novelist Alan Le May studied sixty-four Indian captivities from Texas in the 1860s and 1870s, including five discussed in this book: Dot and Banc Babb, Minnie Caudle, Temple Friend, and Herman Lehmann. Alan Le May to Agnes L. Tucker, May 8, 1957, Alan Le May Papers, Collection No. 880, Box 23, Folder 1, Manuscripts Division, Department of Special Collections, Charles E. Young Research Library, University of California, Los Angeles. However, his surviving research notes suggest that the only "searcher" whose story he followed was Brit Johnson. Le May Papers, Box 22, Folders 2 and 3.

6. E. L. Smith to Assistant Adjutant General, Department of the Arkansas, Apr. 3, 1867; also E. L. Smith to Jesse Chisholm, Apr. 3, 1867; Record Group 393, Part I, Department of the Missouri, Entry 2593, Box 32, NARA.
7. S. C. Morrow to S. V. Babb, Apr. 14, 1867, in the possession of Babb descendants.
8. I have not been able to verify McCleskey's identity. Dot elaborated: "[Charles] Goodnight loaned McCleskey twenty dollars one time and 'Mike' bought whiskey with it and got drunk. He struck out toward camp and froze to death." Dot Babb to J. A. Hill, June 17, 1926, T. A. Babb file, PPHM. I suspect that "Mike McCleskey" was actually Phillip McCusker, an interpreter who froze to death in 1885 while carrying messages from Fort Sill to Camp Augur. Wilbur Sturtevant Nye, *Carbine and Lance: The Story of Old Fort Sill* (1937; 3d ed., Norman: University of Oklahoma Press, 1969), 292 n.13.
9. H. H. Halsell, *Cowboys and Cattleland: Memories of a Frontier Cowboy* (1937; reprint, Fort Worth: Texas Christian University Press, 1983), 29.
10. Clinton Smith did not indicate when he first met Adolph Korn, who lived with a different Comanche division, the Quahadas. However, the chief of Clinton's group, Mowway, was known to have camped in the same region as the Quahadas as early as 1868 and had become closely associated with them by 1869. Nye, *Carbine and Lance*, 58, 104. Given Mowway's close connection with the Quahadas, it is highly likely that the two boys met shortly after Clinton's capture on February 26, 1871, at which time Adolph had been a captive for fourteen months.
11. James Axtell, "The White Indians of Colonial America," *The William and Mary Quarterly*, 3d Ser., XXXII (Jan. 1975), 82.

CHAPTER 4: LEGION VALLEY

1. *San Antonio Daily Herald,* Oct. 17, 1868, 2.
2. Of the fourteen raids described in this book for which I have specific dates, only four occurred within a period between three days before and three days after the date of a full moon, when the moonlight was brightest. Those were: the capture of Caroline McDonald and her children on August 8, 1865 (full moon was August 7); the murder of Frank Johnson on October 12, 1867 (full moon was October 13); the Legion Valley raid of February 5, 1868 (full moon was February 8); and the capture of the Lehmann brothers on May 16, 1870 (full moon was May 15). The other ten raids were those involving: the murder of the Parks family on April 2, 1862 (new moon); the capture of Alice Todd on January 7, 1865

(first quarter); the capture of Rudolph Fischer on July 29, 1865 (new moon); the theft of Rance Moore's cattle on August 8, 1866 (last quarter); the capture of the Babb children on September 14, 1866 (new moon); raids on Adolph Reichenau's farm on December 10, 1868 (last quarter) and March 10, 1869 (last quarter); the capture of my uncle Adolph Korn on January 1, 1870 (last quarter); the capture of John Valentine Maxey on September 5, 1870 (first quarter); and the capture of the Smith brothers on February 26, 1871 (new moon). Dot Babb also refuted the myth that the Comanches raided mostly on moonlit nights. He said they went on raids whenever they got ready. Jonnie R. Morgan, *The History of Wichita Falls* (1931; republication, Wichita Falls, Tex.: Nortex Offset Publications, Inc., 1971), 45.

3. William T. Sherman to J. J. Reynolds, May 10, 1871, "Early Fort Sill Letters" Box, FSMA.

4. *San Antonio Daily Herald,* Aug. 11, 1868, 2.

5. The raid on Legion Valley and its aftermath are extensively documented in a number of eyewitness accounts: affidavits of Matilda J. Friend and John S. Friend, Indian depredation claim of John S. Friend, Record Group 123, Case No. 3379, NARA; *San Antonio Daily Herald,* Feb. 19, 1868, 2 (report of Hardin Oatman); *Tri-Weekly State Gazette* [Austin], Feb. 14, 1868, 3 (report of E. R. Beeson); *Llano News,* Oct. 2, 1914 (recollections of John Oatman); *Frontier Times,* V (July 1928), 396–99 (recollections of Charles Haynes, a member of the posse); *El Dorado* [Kan.] *Times,* July 1, 1926, 3, 6 (interview with John S. Friend); *Frontier Times,* Jan. 1924, 20–22 (article based in part on interview with Minnie Caudle Benson); and *Dallas Morning News,* Nov. 26, 1922, Magazine Section, 6 (interview with Asa (Boy) Johnson). These accounts differ in some particulars. In resolving the discrepancies, I've relied on the statements of Matilda Friend and Hardin Oatman, which seem to be the most creditable. Secondhand reports include: *San Antonio Daily Herald,* Feb. 14, 1868, 3, and Feb. 19, 1868, 3; *San Antonio Daily Express,* Feb. 20, 1868, 2; *Frontier Times,* V (Nov. 1927), 49–52; and *Houston Chronicle,* Oct. 7, 1928, Automobiles and Highways Section, 10. Other valuable resources were the Betty Henning papers in the M. Beven Eckert Memorial Library, Mason, Texas, and the Legion Valley vertical file in the Llano Public Library, Llano, Texas.

6. The identity of the Indians who raided Legion Valley was never determined. Most of the evidence points to the Comanches, from whom both Minnie Caudle and Temple Friend were recovered. However, the Comanches later denied any role in the raid, claiming the raiders were Esaqueta Apaches, who sold Temple Friend to them. "Record of Indian depredations, return of provisions received, etc., at Fort Sill, etc.," Microfilm Roll KA6, OHS. The raiding party may

have been a mixed group. It is uncertain exactly who the Esaqueta Apaches were. The name properly referred to the Mescalero Apaches, although it was sometimes applied to the Kiowa-Apaches. James Mooney, "Calendar History of the Kiowa Indians," in J. W. Powell, *Seventeenth Annual Report of the Bureau of American Ethnology to the Secretary of the Smithsonian Institution, 1895–96* (Washington: Government Printing Office, 1898), I, 245. The Comanches also used the term to refer to the Lipan Apaches. Comanche Language and Cultural Preservation Committee, *Taa Numu Tekwapu?ha Tuboopu (Our Comanche Dictionary)* (Lawton: Comanche Language and Cultural Preservation Committee, 2003), 3.

7. Minnie Caudle's tale of the jokesters stampeding the horses was corroborated by two Comanches, Tasura (That's It) and Post Oak Jim, who recalled occasions when young pranksters pushed a wild colt into the elders' smoke lodge, where it kicked the men inside and tore things up. Comanche Field Notes, E. Adamson Hoebel Papers, Manuscript Collection No. 43, Series V, APSL; Comanche Field Notes, Waldo Rudolph Wedel and Mildred Mott Wedel Papers, Box 109, SINAA.

8. U.S. House of Representatives, Misc. Doc. No. 139, 41st Cong., 2d Sess., 8.

9. The date of July 27, 1868, comes from the diary of 1st Lt. Edward G. Mathey, in the possession of Cindy Gettelfinger. Mathey was at Fort Larned at the time.

10. Minnie Caudle's attachment to the doll the Wynkoops gave her lasted beyond her childhood. Around 1878, when she was married and living in Loyal Valley, Texas, a rumor broke out that Indians had been sighted in the vicinity, and that mothers should try to keep their children quiet. Minnie let her three-year-old son, Jay, play with the doll to keep him occupied. When she heard the doll's head crack on a rock, she was furious and scolded him severely. Her sister pleaded, "Oh, Minnie, don't make him scream. The Indians will come!" Even in her later years, she was still upset over the damage her son had done to the doll. Minnie told her daughter-in-law: "Jay, the little devil, broke my doll. I wasn't going to take no chances with the Indians, but that doll was dear to me." Bertie Oma Modgling to Johnie Lee Reeves, June 22, 1984, copy of notes in the author's possession.

11. E. M. Pease to Fort Arbuckle, Apr. 6, 1868, Record Group 393, Part V, Fort Arbuckle, Oklahoma, Entry 1, Vol. 1, NARA; Acting Governor of the Territory of New Mexico to E. M. Pease, May 18, 1868, Records of Governor Elisha Marshall Pease, Box 301–57, Folder 38, TSA.

12. *Atchison Daily Free Press*, Aug. 8, 1868, 1; Thomas Murphy to N. G. Taylor, Aug. 6, 1868, Microfilm Roll M234/59, NARA-SW; and Thomas Murphy to Chauncey McKeever, Oct. 31, 1868, Microfilm Roll 880, FLNHS.

13. J. Norman Heard, *White into Red: A Study of the Assimilation of White Persons Captured by Indians* (Metuchen, N.J.: Scarecrow Press, 1973), 2.

14. Dot Babb's theory wasn't exactly right; the Comanches raided for many reasons, but usually not to avenge thefts. Nor was his chronology accurate. The raid that culminated in his mother's death happened in 1866; white horse thieves didn't start to plunder the Indians' herds on any significant scale until about 1874. William T. Hagan, *United States—Comanche Relations: The Reservation Years* (1976; reprint, Norman: University of Oklahoma Press, 1990), 121–22.

CHAPTER 5: WARRIORS IN TRAINING

1. *San Antonio Daily Herald,* Oct. 17, 1868, 2.
2. Quoted in *San Antonio Daily Express,* Mar. 9, 1871, 4.
3. *New York Herald,* Aug. 8, 1868, 4.
4. *The New York Times,* May 10, 1870, 4.
5. As told to S. M. Barrett, *Geronimo: His Own Story,* ed. Frederick Turner (1906; rev. ed., New York: Meridian, 1996), 35.
6. Of all the Texas captives, Herman Lehmann's life is the best documented. He was the subject of two "as told to" autobiographies: Jonathan H. Jones, *A Condensed History of the Apache and Comanche Indian Tribes [Indianology]* (1899; reprint, New York: Garland Publishing, Inc., 1976); and Herman Lehmann, *Nine Years Among the Indians, 1870–1879,* ed. J. Marvin Hunter (1927; reprint, Albuquerque: University of New Mexico Press, 1993). Although *Nine Years* is more carefully edited and is the version that Lehmann preferred, *Condensed History* is franker in many respects and contains a significant amount of additional information about Herman's family and his return to white society. A third edition of Lehmann's *Nine Years* (San Antonio: Lebco Graphics, 1985) includes an informative essay by Garland Perry and Kitti Focke. A. C. Greene's *The Last Captive* (Austin: The Encino Press, 1972) is a synthesis of the two Lehmann memoirs, with footnotes and historical photographs. In addition to these various versions of Lehmann's autobiography, a buffalo hunter named Willis Skelton Glenn, who knew Herman Lehmann in Oklahoma, recorded his stories in an unpublished memoir, written around 1910. "Shelton Glenn [sic; Willis Skelton Glenn] Buffalo Hunt Manuscript," Ch. XIV, Microfilm Roll MF6, UTEP. Another valuable source is a 1906 newspaper article titled "Nine Years with the Apaches and Comanches," written by Herman's teacher, John Warren Hunter, and reprinted in *Frontier Times,* XXXI (July, Aug., Sept. 1954), 251–77.
7. The oldest accounts of the capture state that Phillip Buchmeier had arrived at the house shortly beforehand and was eating lunch. *San Antonio Daily Herald,* May 19, 1870, 2; affidavit of T. Buchmeyer [sic; Phillip Buchmeier], July 2, 1870, Southern Plains Indian Agencies Collection, WHC; Jones, *Condensed His-*

tory, 217. However, both Willie Lehmann and his younger stepbrother, Henry Buchmeier, recalled that Phillip was working away from home at the time, and that Auguste could not go for help for fear that the Indians would return and take her other children. Greene, *The Last Captive,* 5; Gerda Lehmann Kothmann to the author, Mar. 24, 2004.

8. Herman's memory of the events at the time he dictated his memoirs was quite good. He recalled that the Indians who captured him stole some horses at Moseley's Mountains. Later, they took a horse belonging to a Mr. Stone and finally passed by the Keyser ranch. Jones, *Condensed History,* 15; Lehmann, *Nine Years,* 4. The oldest news accounts confirm that the Indians stole eight horses from Moseley's ranch at about four o'clock that afternoon. An hour later, Christian Keyser saw them steal Stone's horse. The Indians hid in the bushes when they saw him. Keyser thought the reason they did not chase him was because they had "the captive boys along, and did not wish them to be seen." *San Antonio Daily Herald,* May 21, 1870, 2, and May 24, 1870, 2.

9. In his memoirs and interviews, Herman Lehmann did not specify which Apaches he was with, and his group has been variously identified in the literature as Esaqueta, Mescalero, Kiowa-Apache, Jicarilla, and Mimbres. However, Herman's captors Billy Chiwat and Pinero were both Lipan Apaches, which indicates that Herman was affiliated with the Lipans. Hugh D. Corwin, *Comanche and Kiowa Captives in Oklahoma and Texas* (Guthrie, Okla.: Cooperative Publishing Co., 1959), 129; Omer C. Stewart, *Peyote Religion: A History* (Norman: University of Oklahoma Press, 1987), 58–61. Nonetheless, some odd incongruities remain. In writing about one of his fights with the Texas Rangers, Herman seemed to distinguish his Apache group from the Lipans: "Captain Roberts and Captain Gillett both say the Indians they fought were Lipans, but I know they were Apaches, for I was with them." Lehmann, *Nine Years,* 104. When Herman met Captain Gillett in San Antonio in 1924, Gillett told him, "One of your boys we caught [a Mexican captive] said you were Lipans." Lehmann smiled and replied, "Maybe he lied to you." *San Antonio Evening News,* Nov. 6, 1924, 1. To confuse matters further, the name Lipan has been used carelessly to refer to other Apache groups of the Southern Plains, such as the Mescaleros and the Kiowa-Apaches. Frederick Webb Hodge (ed.), *Handbook of American Indians North of Mexico* (New York: Pageant Books, Inc., 1959), I, 768.

10. Willie Lehmann thought that this skirmish occurred on May 19, and that the Apaches lost between ten and fifteen horses. *San Antonio Daily Herald,* June 2, 1870, 2. The military reports do not mention any fatalities, suggesting that Sergeant Stance did not realize that his men had killed the leader of the Apache raiding party. Or perhaps the missing Apache escaped in a different direction,

and Willie Lehmann mistakenly thought he'd died in the fight. The Ninth Cavalry's participation in the search for the Lehmann brothers is detailed in: Special Orders No. 73, Fort McKavett, May 19, 1870, and Emanuel Stance to B. M. Custer, May 26, 1870, Microfilm Roll M929/2, NARA; post returns, May, 1870, Fort McKavett, Texas, Microfilm Roll M617/687, NARA; and *San Antonio Daily Herald,* May 26, 1870, 2.

11. A number of African-American volunteers received the Medal of Honor for their service in the Civil War. However, African-Americans were not allowed to serve as regulars in the U.S. Army until 1866.

12. According to an editor's note, "The cover painting on this issue does not portray an actual incident in our lead story, 'Nine Years Among the Indians.' However, this form of torture was practiced by the Apaches, the tribe with which Herman Lehmann spent so much time." *Frontier Times,* Mar. 1963, 4.

13. T. A. Babb, *In the Bosom of the Comanches* (1912; 2d ed., Dallas: Hargreaves Printing Co., 1923), 144.

14. *San Antonio Daily Herald,* Mar. 2, 1871, 2; *San Antonio Daily Express,* Mar. 7, 1871, 4.

15. Most of the quotes by the Smith brothers in this chapter are from their memoir, Clinton L. Smith and Jefferson D. Smith with J. Marvin Hunter, *The Boy Captives* (Bandera, Tex.: Frontier Times, 1927), which is one of the most delightful and least appreciated of the Texas captivity narratives. It's also the funniest. Some of Jeff Smith's remarks are taken from an article about him that was serialized in four issues of the *Semi-Weekly Farm News* [Dallas]: Nov. 4, 1930, 2; Nov. 11, 1930, 2; Nov. 18, 1930, 2; and Nov. 25, 1930, 2.

16. Captain Sansom reported that on Tuesday, February 28, the Indians killed a man named John McCormick and wounded his brother, Edward McCormick, in the leg. John W. Sansom to James Davidson, Feb. 28, 1871, Adjutant General, General Correspondence, Box 401-390, Folder 390-4, TSA. Although Clinton did not mention a second man, it is likely that John McCormick was the person whom the Smith brothers saw murdered.

17. Clinton's account of this skirmish was confirmed by Captain Sansom, who reported that two young men named Waldrope and Allhouse exchanged shots several times with the Indians, and that Allhouse thought he wounded one Indian badly. However, Sansom recorded that this battle happened on February 28, near the same place where the Indians attacked the McCormick brothers. Sansom to Davidson, Feb. 28, 1871.

18. *Tosa* is a Comanche prefix meaning "white." Comanche Language and Cultural Preservation Committee, *Taa Numu Tekwapu?ha Tuboopu (Our Comanche Dic-*

tionary) (Lawton: Comanche Language and Cultural Preservation Committee, 2003), 63. The name might be more accurately translated as "White Cat."

19. Both Clinton and Jeff Smith recalled that Jeff was sold to Geronimo (Goyathlay), the famous leader of the Chiricahua Apaches who inhabited southern Arizona and New Mexico. However, the oldest records indicate that Jeff was eventually recovered from a Lipan Apache, who claimed to have bought him from the Comanches. William Schuchardt to Hon. Second Assistant Secretary of State, Mar. 29, 1873, Microfilm Roll M299/T-1, NARA-CP. While it's possible that Jeff ended up with Geronimo's Chiricahuas at some point, I suspect that after the Smith brothers returned from captivity, they heard people speak of Geronimo as the leader of the Apaches and simply assumed that the man who had headed Jeff's Lipan group (possibly Costilietos, a principal Lipan chief) was Geronimo. Jeff visited with Geronimo when the latter was being held prisoner in San Antonio in the fall of 1886 and said that Geronimo recognized him instantly. Smith, *The Boy Captives,* 205. However, Geronimo was a shrewd operator and may have pretended to recognize Jeff, hoping that Jeff could help him and the Apache prisoners in some way.

20. Apparently, Clinton Smith still remembered the Comanche language fairly well at the time he published his memoir in 1927. *Pahki* is a Comanche word for "rawhide rope," and *katso* means "end" (Backecacho = Pahkikatso). Comanche Language and Cultural Preservation Committee, *Taa Nʉmʉ Tekwapʉ?ha Tʉboopʉ,* 9, 151.

21. A. Irving Hallowell, "American Indians, White and Black: The Phenomenon of Transculturalization," *Current Anthropology,* IV (Dec. 1963), 522.

22. Martin Symonds, "Victim Responses to Terror: Understanding and Treatment," and Thomas Strentz, "The Stockholm Syndrome: Law Enforcement Policy and Hostage Behavior," in Frank M. Ochberg and David A. Soskis (eds.), *Victims of Terrorism* (Boulder: Westview Press, 1982), 95–103, 149–63. The Stockholm syndrome took its name from a hostage crisis that began during a bank robbery in Sweden on August 23, 1973.

23. Erwin H. Ackerknecht, " 'White Indians': Psychological and Physiological Peculiarities of White Children Abducted and Reared by North American Indians," *Bulletin of the History of Medicine,* XV (Jan. 1944), 27, 30.

24. Dot Babb to J. A. Hill, June 17, 1926, T. A. Babb file, PPHM.

25. *Mason County News,* Aug. 19, 1937, 4 (interview with William Schmidt, who grew up near Castell).

26. J. Norman Heard, *White into Red: A Study of the Assimilation of White Persons Captured by Indians* (Metuchen, N.J.: Scarecrow Press, 1973), 13.

27. James Axtell, "The White Indians of Colonial America," *The William and Mary Quarterly*, 3d Ser., XXXII (Jan. 1975), 87.

CHAPTER 6: AS MEAN AN INDIAN AS THERE WAS

1. The meeting at the watering hole took place "some time after" the Apaches' second raid on Herman Lehmann's homestead, which occurred on July 18, 1870. Herman Lehmann, *Nine Years Among the Indians, 1870–1879*, ed. J. Marvin Hunter (1927; reprint, Albuquerque: University of New Mexico Press, 1993), 43.

2. *Frontier Times*, XXXI (July, Aug., Sept. 1954), 262–63. Both Adolph Korn and Herman Lehmann knew Rudolph Fischer while they were with the Indians. *Frontier Times*, XVIII (June 1941), 424.

3. Recollections of Naiya (Slope of Land), Comanche Field Notes, Waldo Rudolph Wedel and Mildred Mott Wedel Papers, Box 109, SINAA.

4. *The New York Times*, Aug. 14, 1868, 1. Ethnologist John R. Swanton studied fifteen male Indian captives from across America and found that three or four of them became chiefs, a proportion that he concluded "does not appear to be above what might have been expected." John R. Swanton, "Notes on the Mental Assimilation of Races," *Journal of the Washington Academy of Sciences*, XVI (Nov. 3, 1926), 501.

5. Clinton Smith remembered Comanche names fairly well at the time he wrote his memoir in 1927. In the 1879 Comanche census, "Monawuftakewa" was identified as a member of Mowway's band, the group with whom Clinton lived. It appears from Clinton's stories that "Moniwoftuckwy," as Clinton spelled his friend's name, was not the same person as "Monewostuki," his foster brother, despite the similarity of the two names.

6. Clinton L. Smith and Jefferson D. Smith with J. Marvin Hunter, *The Boy Captives* (Bandera, Tex.: Frontier Times, 1927), 114–15.

7. James L. Haley, *Apaches: A History and Culture Portrait* (1981; reprint, Norman: University of Oklahoma Press, 1997), 98, 159–60.

8. Jonathan H. Jones, *A Condensed History of the Apache and Comanche Indian Tribes [Indianology]* (1899; reprint, New York: Garland Publishing, Inc., 1976), 68–69.

9. Jones, *Condensed History*, 173. In his second autobiography, Herman said that he merely "had a passing fancy" for Topay, which "soon passed." Lehman, *Nine Years*, 176.

10. Smith, *The Boy Captives*, 122.

11. Jones, *Condensed History*, 63–64; Lehmann, *Nine Years*, 51–52.

12. Clinton Smith referred to his Comanche father, Tosacowadi, as "my chief." This title should not necessarily be taken literally, for the captives tended to use the term "chief" very loosely to describe any prominent man or head of a family.
13. Lehmann, *Nine Years*, 185–86. This attack, which is discussed in Chapter 10, occurred at Quemado (Silver) Lake in northern Cochran County, Texas, on May 4, 1877.
14. *Frontier Times*, XXXI (July, Aug., Sept. 1954), 269.
15. *Semi-Weekly Farm News* [Dallas], Nov. 25, 1930, 2.
16. Smith, *The Boy Captives*, 152.

CHAPTER 7: SEARCHERS AND QUAKERS

1. Auguste Buchmeier's meeting with General Sherman is documented in W. T. Sherman to "Dear Brother," May 18, 1871, "Early Fort Sill Letters" Box, FSMA, and J. E. Tourtellotte to Lawrie Tatum, May 27, 1871, Microfilm Roll KA42, OHS.
2. *San Antonio Daily Express*, Sept. 26, 1868, 2.
3. Jonathan H. Jones, *A Condensed History of the Apache and Comanche Indian Tribes [Indianology]* (1899; reprint, New York: Garland Publishing, Inc., 1976), 221.
4. Henry M. Smith to Lawrie Tatum, Mar. 14, 1871, Microfilm Roll KA42, OHS.
5. Henry M. Smith to Lawrie Tatum, July 16, 1871, Microfilm Roll KA42, OHS.
6. Dorman H. Winfrey and James M. Day (eds.), *The Indian Papers of Texas and the Southwest, 1825–1916* (5 Vols.; Austin: The Pemberton Press, 1966), IV, 266–68.
7. H. P. N. Gammel (comp.), *The Laws of Texas, 1822–1897* (10 Vols.; Austin: The Gammel Book Co., 1898), V, 960.
8. Background information on Lawrie Tatum and his service at the Kiowa-Comanche agency comes from several sources, including: Martha Buntin, "Beginning of the Leasing of the Surplus Grazing Lands on the Kiowa and Comanche Reservation," *Chronicles of Oklahoma*, X (Sept. 1932), 369–82; Aubrey L. Steele, "The Beginning of Quaker Administration of Indian Affairs in Oklahoma," *Chronicles of Oklahoma*, XVII (Dec. 1939), 364–92; Lee Cutler, "Lawrie Tatum and the Kiowa Agency, 1869–1873," *Arizona and the West*, XIII (autumn 1971), 221–44; T. Ashley Zwink, "On the White Man's Road: Lawrie Tatum and the Formative Years of the Kiowa Agency, 1869–1873," *Chronicles of Oklahoma*, LVI (winter 1978–1979), 431–41; and "Lawrie Tatum's Letters," *Prairie Lore*, IV (July 1967), 50–61, IV (Jan. 1968), 186–89, and V (Oct. 1968), 116–24.

9. Lawrie Tatum, *Our Red Brothers and the Peace Policy of President Ulysses S. Grant* (1899; reprint, Lincoln: University of Nebraska Press, 1970), 86–87.

10. H. R. Clum to Enoch Hoag, Apr. 4, 1871, Southern Plains Indian Agencies Collection, WHC.

11. Stan Hoig, *Jesse Chisholm: Ambassador of the Plains* (Niwot, Colo.: University Press of Colorado, 1991), 96–99.

12. W. T. Sherman to R. S. Mackenzie, May 29, 1871, "Early Fort Sill Letters" Box, FSMA.

13. Tatum first described the white boy in Mowway's band in Lawrie Tatum to Enoch Hoag, May 13, 1871, Microfilm Roll M234/377, NARA-SW. Subsequently, this captive was mentioned in numerous letters and reports: H. R. Clum [to Enoch Hoag?], June 8, 1871, Microfilm Roll KA42, OHS; Lawrie Tatum to Cols. Grierson and Mackenzie, Aug. 4, 1871, Microfilm Roll M234/377, NARA-SW; Lawrie Tatum to his wife, July 8, 1871, and Aug. 5, 1871, *Prairie Lore*, V (Oct. 1968), 116, 118; annual report of Lawrie Tatum, Sept. 1, 1871, in *Report of the Commissioner of Indian Affairs to the Secretary of the Interior for the Year 1871* (Washington: Government Printing Office, 1872), 503; and annual report of Lawrie Tatum, Sept. 1, 1872, in *Annual Report of the Commissioner of Indian Affairs to the Secretary of the Interior for the Year 1872* (Washington: Government Printing Office, 1872), 247–48.

CHAPTER 8: DEATH ON THE RED RIVER

1. The Battle of the North Fork of the Red River, described in this chapter, is difficult to reconstruct with precision because of the paucity of firsthand sources. Ranald Mackenzie summarized his attack on Mowway's village in his brief report to the assistant adjutant general, Oct. 12, 1872, transcribed and reprinted in Ernest Wallace (ed.), *Ranald S. Mackenzie's Official Correspondence Relating to Texas, 1871–1873* (Lubbock: West Texas Museum Association, 1967), 141–45. Other eyewitness accounts of the battle, recorded many years after the fact, include: Henry W. Strong, *My Frontier Days and Indian Fights on the Plains of Texas* [Waco, Tex.: n.p., 1926], 38–39, 117–18; Robert G. Carter, *The Old Sergeant's Story: Winning the West from the Indians and Bad Men in 1870 to 1876* (New York: Frederick H. Hitchcock, 1926), 82–90; and Robert G. Carter, *On the Border with Mackenzie, or Winning West Texas from the Comanches* (Mattituck, N.Y.: J. M. Carroll & Co., 1935), 376–93. Secondhand reports include: *Dallas Herald*, Nov. 16, 1872, 1; C. C. Augur to Assistant Adjutant General, Sept. 30, 1873, Fort Concho files, Secretary of War 1870s (photostat from Records of the War Department, U.S. Army Commands, Letter Sent, 1873–1874),

J. Evetts Haley Collection, HML; and Lawrie Tatum, *Our Red Brothers and the Peace Policy of President Ulysses S. Grant* (1899; reprint, Lincoln: University of Nebraska Press, 1970), 134–35. Accounts of the battle from the Comanche viewpoint are even harder to come by. The fullest published eyewitness report is that of Clinton Smith, found in Clinton L. Smith and Jefferson D. Smith with J. Marvin Hunter, *The Boy Captives* (Bandera, Tex.: Frontier Times, 1927), 127–32. Col. Wilbur S. Nye transcribed the recollections of two Comanches, Cohayyah and Mumsukawa (usually spelled Mamsookawat), in 1935. Excerpts from these interviews appear in: Wilbur Sturtevant Nye, *Carbine and Lance: The Story of Old Fort Sill* (1937; 3d ed., Norman: University of Oklahoma Press, 1969), 162; Wilbur Sturtevant Nye, *Plains Indian Raiders: The Final Phases of Warfare from the Arkansas to the Red River* (Norman: University of Oklahoma Press, 1968), 302; and Jo Ella Powell Exley, *Frontier Blood: The Saga of the Parker Family* (College Station: Texas A&M University Press, 2001), 220, 222–23. An account based on the recollections of Persuwiyeckwit George Maddox is recorded in J. Emmor Harston, *Comanche Land* (San Antonio: The Naylor Co., 1963), 168–69. In 1933 a Comanche named Post Oak Jim related stories about Quanah Parker's participation in the "Battle of Tipi Creek" or fight with the soldiers on the "North Fork River." Comanche Field Notes, E. Adamson Hoebel Papers, Manuscript Collection No. 43, Series V, APSL; Comanche Field Notes, Waldo Rudolph Wedel and Mildred Mott Wedel Papers, Box 109, SINAA. Other sources about the Comanches who participated in the battle include Thomas C. Battey, *The Life and Adventures of a Quaker Among the Indians* (1875; reprint, Williamstown, Mass.: Corner House Publishers, 1972), 86 (describing John Valentine Maxey's role in the battle), and Hugh D. Corwin, "Parra-o-coom, Comanche Indian Chief," *Prairie Lore,* III (Oct. 1966), 93–95 (stating that Paruacoom and Quanah Parker led the Quahadas in the battle).

2. "Several dead men" is an exaggeration. By official counts, this battle left one of Mackenzie's men dead and three seriously wounded, one of whom soon died.

3. Nye, *Plains Indian Raiders,* 302. In an earlier writing, Colonel Nye indicated that Paruacoom made this speech during a battle with Colonel Mackenzie's forces along the White River (Fresh Water Fork of the Brazos) on October 10, 1871. Nye, *Carbine and Lance,* 151. In fact, most of the Comanche accounts, as recorded in Nye, Corwin, and the Comanche Field Notes, seem to conflate the two fights, confusing the details.

4. *Annual Report of the Commissioner of Indian Affairs to the Secretary of the Interior for the Year 1872* (Washington: Government Printing Office, 1872), 94.

5. Clinton Smith indicated that Tosacowadi received his mortal wound in a different battle with the army. Smith, *The Boy Captives,* 161. This was probably an er-

ror, as I found no record of any other major fight between the army and Clinton's group of Comanches between the time of the Battle of the North Fork of the Red River on September 29, 1872, and Clinton's arrival at Fort Sill on October 24, 1872.

6. The visit of the Indian delegation to Washington, D.C., and other cities is described in: *Annual Report of the Commissioner of Indian Affairs 1872*, 128–33; *Evening Star* [Washington, D.C.], Sept. 28, 1872, 1, Oct. 1, 1872, 1, Oct. 2, 1872, 1, Oct. 5, 1872, 1, Oct. 11, 1872, 1, Oct. 15, 1872, 1, and Oct. 25, 1872, 1; *New York Herald*, Sept. 24, 1872, 4, Oct. 12, 1872, 7, Oct. 23, 1872, 6, and Oct. 31, 1872, 5; and *The New York Times*, Sept. 26, 1872, 5, Oct. 12, 1872, 4, Oct. 23, 1872, 1, Oct. 25, 1872, 1, and Nov. 1, 1872, 2.

7. *Evening Star* [Washington, D.C.], Oct. 15, 1872, 1.

CHAPTER 9: THE LONG WAY HOME

1. The Butlers' recollections of the captives' time at the school are recorded in Josiah Butler, "Pioneer School Teaching at the Comanche-Kiowa Agency School 1870–3," *Chronicles of Oklahoma*, VI (Dec. 1928), 518–21.

2. One writer contended, "At Fort Concho the women appear merely to have existed, although they did receive a small allowance of meat." J. Emmor Harston, *Comanche Land* (San Antonio: The Naylor Co., 1963), 169. I found no other source suggesting that the women were mistreated; in fact, practically all the other evidence is to the contrary. The Comanches' experience at Fort Concho is chronicled in: John P. Hatch to the Acting Comsry. of Sub., Oct. 21, 1872, and John P. Hatch to Assistant Adjutant General, Department of Texas, Oct. 24, 1872, Record Group 393, Part V, Fort Concho, Texas, Entry 2, IV, 147, 149, NARA; Wilbur Sturtevant Nye, *Carbine and Lance: The Story of Old Fort Sill* (1937; 3d ed., Norman: University of Oklahoma Press, 1969), 164; *San Angelo Standard-Times*, Aug. 29, 1954; and Jo Ella Powell Exley, *Frontier Blood: The Saga of the Parker Family* (College Station: Texas A&M University Press, 2001), 224.

3. Endorsement, W. T. Sherman, Oct. 30, 1872, F. A. Walker to C. Delano, Nov. 4, 1872, and C. Delano to the Honorable Secretary of War, Nov. 23, 1872, Microfilm Roll 19, FCML.

4. C. C. Augur to John P. Hatch, Dec. 5, 1872, and C. C. Augur to Lawrie Tatum, Jan. 16, 1873, Southern Plains Indian Agencies Collection, WHC; John P. Hatch to Commanding Officer, Fort Griffin, Dec. 11, 1872, John P. Hatch to Commanding Officer, Fort Richardson, Dec. 11, 1872, and John P. Hatch to

Lawrie Tatum, Dec. 12, 1872, Record Group 393, Part V, Fort Concho, Texas, Entry 2, IV, 166, 168, 169, NARA.

5. Henry M. Smith to E. J. Davis, Nov. 18, 1872, Records of Governor Edmund J. Davis, Box 301–82, Folder 268, TSA.

6. Sidney Lanier, "San Antonio de Bexar," in Charles R. Anderson (ed.), *The Centennial Edition of the Works of Sidney Lanier* (10 Vols.; Baltimore: The Johns Hopkins Press, 1945), VI, 202–46.

7. Anderson (ed.), *Centennial Edition,* VIII, 289.

8. *San Antonio Daily Express,* Jan. 9, 1873, 3.

9. Deposition of Herman Lehmann, Indian depredation claim of W. S. Glenn, Record Group 123, Case No. 1893, NARA; J. M. Haworth to Enoch Hoag, May 14, 1873, Microfilm Roll M234/378, NARA-SW; Jonathan H. Jones, *A Condensed History of the Apache and Comanche Indian Tribes* [*Indianology*] (1899; reprint, New York: Garland Publishing, Inc., 1976), 123; Herman Lehmann, *Nine Years Among the Indians, 1870–1879,* ed. J. Marvin Hunter (1927; reprint, Albuquerque: University of New Mexico Press, 1993), 116–17.

10. U.S. House of Representatives, Exec. Doc. No. 257, 43d Cong., 1st Sess., 27.

11. Reprinted in the *Wichita City Eagle,* Dec. 26, 1872, 2.

12. G. W. Cox, *Pioneer Sketches* ([Saint Jo, Tex.:] Montague County Historical Committee, 1958), 12.

13. I examined the criminal records of Bexar County, Texas, for the period 1873–1876 without finding any mention of Adolph Korn. However, the records that still exist are far from complete. Furthermore, unless Adolph's offenses were serious, they would not necessarily have been entered on the books.

14. *Boerne Star,* Sept. 20, 1973 (reprint of 1934 letter from Mrs. Peter Lex).

CHAPTER 10: RESISTING THE RESERVATION

1. *San Antonio Weekly Express,* Dec. 27, 1877, 4.

2. Wilbur Sturtevant Nye, *Carbine and Lance: The Story of Old Fort Sill* (1937; 3d ed., Norman: University of Oklahoma Press, 1969), 188.

3. Sources on Ishatai's uprising and the Adobe Walls fight include: G. Derek West, "The Battle of Adobe Walls (1874)," *Panhandle-Plains Historical Review,* XXXVI (1963), 1–36; J'Nell Pate, "The Battles of Adobe Walls," *Great Plains Journal,* XVI (fall 1976), 3–44; and *Amarillo Daily News,* Apr. 26, 1939, 1, 13 (interviews with two Comanche eyewitnesses, Yellowfish and John Timbo). Information about Rudolph Fischer's participation in the battle comes from: R. E. Moody to Robert H. Bostman, Jan. 10, 1938, Indian Pioneer History Collec-

tion, OHS, LXXI, 394; Lottie Fisher to Arthur Lawrence, Sept. 14, 1958, Arthur Lawrence Collection, MGP; Hugh D. Corwin, *Comanche and Kiowa Captives in Oklahoma and Texas* (Guthrie, Okla.: Cooperative Publishing Co., 1959), 170; and Josephine Wapp to the author, Feb. 27, 2001.

4. William T. Hagan, *United States—Comanche Relations: The Reservation Years* (1976; reprint, Norman: University of Oklahoma Press, 1990), 124. In 1933 a Comanche named Howard White Wolf confirmed that after the Quahadas' surrender, about twenty warriors and their families broke away and fled to "No Man's Land" (possibly the Llano Estacado of northwest Texas), where some of them died of thirst. Comanche Field Notes, Waldo Rudolph Wedel and Mildred Mott Wedel Papers, Box 109, SINAA. When the runaways returned to the reservation in 1877, Colonel Mackenzie reported that they consisted of "twenty-one [Comanche] men and their families." R. S. Mackenzie to Assistant Adjutant General, Dept. of the Missouri, Sept. 6, 1877, Box D62.137.118, FSMA. E. L. Clark, an agency interpreter at the time, described a "band of about 40 Comanches." Commissioner of Indian Affairs to James F. Randlett, July 24, 1901, "Section X—Comanche Indians—Captives—Herman Lehmann" (vertical file), OHS. However, Quanah Parker recalled that this group included "about six (6) families of Apaches" (including one of Herman Lehmann's captors, Chiwat [Chebahtah]). Affidavit of Quanah Parker, Aug. 26, 1901, Microfilm Roll KA1, OHS. Herman Lehmann referred to his group of warriors as the "famous fifteen," which may be the most accurate count of the adult Comanche men living away from the reservation. Jonathan H. Jones, *A Condensed History of the Apache and Comanche Indian Tribes [Indianology]* (1899; reprint, New York: Garland Publishing, Inc., 1976), 183.

5. The date of the battle was derived from Capt. Dan Roberts's earliest report, which states that on August 20 he "struck the trail of a party of Indians" and "after following them four days" overtook them on the Staked Plains about 150 miles northwest of Camp Los Moras, where he "had a round with them." D. W. Roberts to J. B. Jones, Aug. 26, 1875, Adjutant General, Ranger Records, Box 401-1158, TSA. Roberts indicated in a subsequent report that the fight occurred on August 7, 1875. Dorman H. Winfrey and James M. Day (eds.), *The Indian Papers of Texas and the Southwest, 1825–1916* (5 Vols.; Austin: The Pemberton Press, 1966), IV, 445–46. Ranger James Gillett later said that the battle occurred on August 25, 1875. *San Antonio Evening News,* Nov. 6, 1924, 1.

6. Herman Lehmann, *Nine Years Among the Indians, 1870–1879,* ed. J. Marvin Hunter (1927; reprint, Albuquerque: University of New Mexico Press, 1993), 111. This dialogue was recorded by another ranger in the party, Thomas P. Gillespie, who attributed it to Seiker. Two other ranger accounts indicated that

Gillett was the first to discover that Lehmann was white, and that he prevented Seiker from killing Lehmann. Dan W. Roberts, *Rangers and Sovereignty* (1914; reprint, Austin: State House Press, 1987), 73; and James B. Gillett, *Six Years with the Texas Rangers, 1875 to 1881* (1921; reprint, Lincoln: University of Nebraska Press, 1976), 43. Herman, however, later identified Gillett as the ranger who fired the pistol at him. *San Antonio Evening News,* Nov. 6, 1924, 1.

7. Herman Lehmann gave at least four accounts of the battle between his group of Apaches and the Texas Rangers on the Staked Plains: Jones, *Condensed History,* 45–50; *Frontier Times,* XXXI (July, Aug., Sept. 1954), 260–62; "Shelton Glenn [sic; Willis Skelton Glenn] Buffalo Hunt Manuscript," Microfilm Roll MF6, UTEP; and Lehmann, *Nine Years,* 96–105. Three of the Texas Rangers who participated in the battle also recorded their recollections of it: Lehmann, *Nine Years,* 106–12 (reprint of account of Thomas P. Gillespie, written in 1907); Roberts, *Rangers and Sovereignty,* 67–75; and Gillett, *Six Years with the Texas Rangers,* 33–45.

8. The date is approximate. After his fight with the Texas Rangers on August 24, 1875, Herman Lehmann returned to his people in New Mexico. He indicated that his Apache group remained in camp that winter, then resumed raiding in Texas the following spring. When Herman described his life as a hermit after his separation from the Apaches, he noted, "I was then in my sixteenth year." Lehmann, *Nine Years,* 139. If his recollection of his age was correct, then he left the Apaches after the spring raids started in 1876 but sometime prior to his seventeenth birthday on June 5, 1876.

9. Although most of Herman's stories remained consistent in the various retellings, his explanations for why he left the Apaches differed considerably. In both versions of his autobiography, he claimed that the Apache medicine man had murdered his adoptive father, Carnoviste, during a drunken brawl, and that he killed the shaman in revenge. Jones, *Condensed History,* 131; Lehmann, *Nine Years,* 126. In a 1906 interview, Herman indicated that the man he killed was Genava, the petty chief whom Herman's mother had wounded during the second raid on their farm and who always persecuted him after that. In this version, the "hated chief" flew into a rage when Herman let some of his horses stray, and Herman killed him in the confrontation that followed. *Frontier Times,* XXXI (July, Aug., Sept. 1954), 262–64. Willis Skelton Glenn, who knew Herman in Oklahoma, reported that the man Herman killed was a Comanche who was a member of a party that was attacking the Apaches. According to Glenn, Carnoviste was killed during this skirmish, and Ete warned Herman to flee because "it was customary to kill all that belonged to a warrior at his death." Glenn, "Buffalo Hunt Manuscript."

10. It is impossible to determine exactly when Herman joined the Comanches. The only clue he provided as to the time of year was that "the cold was so intense that I knew I would freeze to death before morning." *Frontier Times,* XXXI (July, Aug., Sept. 1954), 268. Herman probably became affiliated with the Comanches in the latter part of 1876, or early 1877 at the latest.

11. The meaning of Herman's Comanche name is uncertain. Willis Skelton Glenn, a buffalo hunter who knew Herman in the early 1900s, said that Montechema meant "Our Child in Common." Glenn, "Buffalo Hunt Manuscript." Vance Tahmahkera, a grandson of Quanah Parker, suggested that Montechema might be a variant of *maatuseni* (or *maatusinai*), which translates as "Onto Someone or Something in Different Ways." Sandi Tahmahkera to Esther Lehmann, Aug. 30, 1994, in the possession of Lehmann descendants; Comanche Language and Cultural Preservation Committee, *Taa Numu Tekwapu̱ʔha Tuboopu̱ (Our Comanche Dictionary)* (Lawton: Comanche Language and Cultural Preservation Committee, 2003), 16, 52. Tahmahkera thought the name could have referred to Herman's skill and cleverness in fighting for both the Apaches and the Comanches using various techniques.

12. The earliest sources on the battle of Yellow House Canyon include *Galveston Weekly News,* Apr. 9, 1877, 3, 6, and *The New York Times,* May 30, 1877, 1. Eyewitness testimony is found in the depositions of Willis S. Glenn, James W. Dobbs, and Herman Lehmann, Indian depredation claim of W. S. Glenn, Record Group 123, Case Nos. 1892 and 1893, NARA; Rex Strickland (ed.), "The Recollections of W. S. Glenn, Buffalo Hunter," *Panhandle-Plains Historical Review,* XXII (1949), 15–64; and *Lubbock Evening Journal,* Sept. 10, 1958, Section II, 2 (Herman Lehmann's comments). Secondary sources include: William C. Griggs, "The Battle of Yellowhouse Canyon in 1877," *West Texas Historical Association Year Book,* LI (1975), 37–50; and Sharon Cunningham, "Yellow House Canyon Fight: Buffalo Hunters vs. Plains Indians," *Wild West,* June 2003, 46–52.

13. The dialogue in this section, as recalled by Herman Lehmann, was recorded in Jones, *Condensed History,* 183–85.

14. R. S. Mackenzie to Assistant Adjutant General, Dept. of the Missouri, Aug. 21, 1877, and Sept. 6, 1877, Box D62.137.118, FSMA; J. M. Haworth to William Nicholson, Aug. 26, 1877, Microfilm Roll M234/382, NARA-SW.

15. Michael D. Pierce, *The Most Promising Young Officer: A Life of Ranald Slidell Mackenzie* (Norman: University of Oklahoma Press, 1993), 168.

16. William Nicholson to James M. Haworth, June 28, 1877, Microfilm Roll KA42, OHS.

17. When a lawyer in Fredericksburg later wrote to thank Congressman Gustav Schleicher for his help in arranging Rudolph's return, he added a thinly veiled

criticism of Haworth's inaction: "I do not believe [Gottlieb Fischer's] boy would have been sent away from the Indians, had the father not have gone after him. I have learned that this young man had been at Ft. Sill, on the reservation, for two or three years, and no attention paid to it." J. F. Estell to Gustav Schleicher, Dec. 23, 1877, Microfilm Roll M234/384, NARA-SW.

18. The Comanches claimed that Rudolph Fischer was already married by 1871. Lawrie Tatum to Enoch Hoag, Mar. 11, 1871, Microfilm Roll M234/377, NARA-SW. At the time of his recovery, he was said to have had two children. *San Antonio Daily Express,* Aug. 31, 1877, 2. However, neither Fischer family records nor the Mormon genealogy database, www.familysearch.com, indicates that Rudolph had a wife or child prior to 1879. Kenn Knopp, "The Fischer/ Fisher Family Tree," copy in the author's possession.

19. *San Antonio Daily Express,* Sept. 6, 1877, 4.

20. *Galveston Weekly News,* Sept. 17, 1877, 1; *Frontier Echo* [Jacksboro, Tex.], Sept. 21, 1877, 2.

21. J. W. Davidson to Engelbert Krauskopf, Apr. 12, 1878, Box D62.137.118, FSMA.

22. Jones, *Condensed History,* 233.

23. J. W. Davidson to Assistant Adjutant General, Apr. 14, 1878, Box D62.137.118, FSMA.

24. P. L. Hunt to Engelbert Krauskopf, June 16, 1879, Microfilm Roll KA8, OHS.

25. Census Office, Department of the Interior, *Report on Indians Taxed and Indians Not Taxed in the United States (Except Alaska) at the Eleventh Census: 1890* (Washington: Government Printing Office, 1894), 637–38.

CHAPTER II: ONCE AND ALWAYS INDIANS

1. Garland Perry and Kitti Focke, "A New Look at Nine Years Among the Indians," in Herman Lehmann, *Nine Years with the Indians, 1870–1879,* ed. J. Marvin Hunter (3d ed.; San Antonio: Lebco Graphics, 1985), 286.

2. *William Modgling v. Malinda Modgling,* Case No. 199, Mason County District Court, Minute Book 3, 586 (Oct. 6, 1890), Mason County Clerk's Office, Mason, Texas.

3. Eugene E. White to James W. Carson, May 19, 1888, Microfilm Roll KA16, OHS.

4. *The Canadian and American Mortgage and Trust Co. Ltd. v. Theodore A. Babb et al.,* Case No. 9399, 44th District Court, Dallas County, Texas (court papers in Dallas Public Library); Deed Records, Vol. 21, page 611, Wise County Clerk's Office, Decatur, Texas.

5. Both of Fischer's wives were enumerated in his household in the Comanche census of 1895. The youngest child of Rudolph and Kahchacha, Helen Fisher Parker, was born in 1897. On July 27, 1901, Kahchacha married William Tivis, a Comanche who had studied at the Carlisle Indian School in Pennsylvania and was active in reservation politics. Kenn Knopp, "The Fischer/Fisher Family Tree," copy in the author's possession; Barbara Goodin to the author, Mar. 28, 2004. Rudolph received annuities on behalf of his minor daughters by Kahchacha. A. C. Tonner to James F. Randlett, May 9, 1902, Microfilm Roll KA83, OHS. Rudolph and his family in Indian Territory anglicized the spelling of their German surname to "Fisher."

6. Deed Records, Vol. 7, pages 460–61, Gillespie County Clerk's Office, Fredericksburg, Texas.

7. *John S. Friend v. The United States and the Comanche Indians*, Indian Depredation Claim No. 3379, 29 Ct. Cl. 425 (Oct. 29, 1894).

8. U.S. House of Representatives, Report No. 1475, 54th Cong., 1st Sess.

9. John H. Stephens to A. S. Stinnett, Nov. 28, 1911, reprinted in T. A. Babb, *In the Bosom of the Comanches* (1912; 2d ed., Dallas: Hargreaves Printing Co., 1923), 32.

10. Clinton Smith to General and Special Claims Commissions, Dec. 18, 1929, and Donald S. Stormont to Clinton Smith, Jan. 2, 1930, in the possession of Smith descendants.

11. John Collier to Charles D. Bates, Apr. 1, 1935, in the possession of Smith descendants.

12. 49th Cong., 2d Sess., Ch. 119 (1887).

13. The Comanches leased their allotments at annual rates varying from $0.25 to $3.00 per acre. William T. Hagan, *United States—Comanche Relations: The Reservation Years* (1976; reprint, Norman: University of Oklahoma Press, 1990), 272.

14. Banc Babb Bell's petition for adoption is documented in a long series of her correspondence with the Indian agency: Bianca Bell to Frank Baldwin, Aug. 6, 1897, and Sept. 14, 1897, Bianca Bell to James F. Randlett, Oct. 15, 1899, June 12, 1900, June 24, 1900, July 21, 1900, Aug. 6, 1900, and Dec. 17, 1900, Microfilm Roll KA1, OHS; Bianca Bell to James Randlett, Sept. 23, 1899, and Sept. 27, 1899, and Report of the General Council of the Kiowa, Comanche, and Apache tribes, Oct. 9, 10, and 11, 1899, Microfilm Roll KA48, OHS; James F. Randlett to Bianca Bell, Sept. 29, 1899, Microfilm Roll KA33, OHS; James F. Randlett to Bianca Bell, June 22, 1900, July 31, 1900, and Aug. 14, 1900, Microfilm Roll KA56, OHS; and James F. Randlett to Bianca Bell, Dec. 20, 1900, Microfilm Roll KA57, OHS. An oral account of Banc's return to Indian Territory in 1897 is

found in Mary Alice Mount Huff to Hazel H. Harelson, May 12, 1937, Indian Pioneer History Collection, OHS, XXX, 101–03.

15. In 1878 an interpreter named E. L. Clark "took an enumeration of the band of about 40 Comanches (with whom Lehman [sic] was living) that surrendered to the military authorities." Commissioner of Indian Affairs to James F. Randlett, July 24, 1901, "Section X—Comanche Indians—Captives—Herman Lehmann" (vertical file), OHS. However, by the time Lehmann made his application, Agent Randlett noted that "no such record for the year named [1878] can be found preserved among the Agency records." James F. Randlett to commissioner of Indian Affairs, Aug. 5, 1901, Microfilm Roll KA61, OHS.

16. Information on Herman Lehmann's petition for adoption is drawn from voluminous correspondence with the Office of Indian Affairs: A. C. Tonner to James F. Randlett, Jan. 17, 1901, May 6, 1901, and Aug. 16, 1901, "Section X—Comanche Indians—Captives—Herman Lehmann" (vertical file), OHS; Herman Lehmann to James Randlett, Mar. 9, 1901, and Mar. 29, 1901, and affidavit of Quanah Parker, Aug. 26, 1901, Microfilm Roll KA1, OHS; James F. Randlett to Herman Lehmann, Mar. 16, 1901, Microfilm Roll KA59, OHS; affidavit of Herman Lehmann, Apr. 15, 1901, James F. Randlett to commissioner of Indian Affairs, Apr. 13, 1901, and Apr. 16, 1901, and James F. Randlett to Herman Lehmann, May 13, 1901, Microfilm Roll KA60, OHS; A. C. Tonner to James F. Randlett, Sept. 30, 1901, Microfilm Roll KA62, OHS; endorsement, James Randlett, Oct. 21, 1901, Microfilm Roll KA61, OHS; A. J. Burton to James F. Randlett, May 16, 1902, Microfilm Roll KA42, OHS; and Herman Lehmann to U.S. Indian Agent, July 20, 1908, "Captives" vertical file, FSMA.

17. 60th Cong., 1st Sess., Ch. 216, Section 28 (1908).

CHAPTER 12: IN THE LIMELIGHT

1. Leo Kelley, "The Daughter of Dawn: An Original Silent Film with an Oklahoma Indian Cast," *Chronicles of Oklahoma,* LXXVII (fall 1999), 290–99.

2. Ralph E. Friar and Natasha A. Friar, *The Only Good Indian . . . The Hollywood Gospel* (New York: Drama Book Specialists, 1972), 304–05.

3. Information about the 1924 Old Trail Drivers reunion was taken from: *Frontier Times,* Nov. 1924, 32, and Dec. 1924, 32; *San Antonio Express,* Nov. 2, 1924, 14A, Nov. 5, 1924, 6, Nov. 7, 1924, 10, and Nov. 9, 1924, 15; *San Antonio Evening News,* Nov. 6, 1924, 1, 2, 11, Nov. 7, 1924, 1, 2, and Nov. 8, 1924, 1, 2; *San Antonio Light,* Nov. 2, 1924, Part One, 9, Nov. 5, 1924, 1, Nov. 6, 1924, 16, Nov. 7, 1924, 24, and Nov. 10, 1924, 5; and *New York Herald Tribune,* Oct. 11, 1931, Magazine Section, 26.

4. *San Angelo Standard-Times,* May 17, 2000 (reprint of column by Rick Smith).
5. *San Angelo Standard,* May 14, 1926, 2.
6. Sources on the making of *Nine Years Among the Indians* include: *Frontier Times,* Dec. 1924, 32, Feb. 1925, 8–9, and Sept. 1927, inside back cover (advertisement); John H. Jenkins, *Basic Texas Books: An Annotated Bibliography of Selected Works for a Research Library* (1983; rev. ed., Austin: Texas State Historical Association, 1988), 336; and Gerda Lehmann Kothmann to the author, Feb. 20, 2001.
7. The title was borrowed from an article that J. Marvin Hunter's father, John Warren Hunter, wrote for the *San Angelo Standard* in 1906, called "Nine Years with the Apaches and Comanches." John Warren Hunter mistakenly thought that Herman had been captured in 1869 and recalled that he had returned to Loyal Valley in 1878—hence, his calculation of nine years. Herman's publisher knew from the details he related that he had been abducted in May 1870 but wasn't sure when he had come home. Thus, the publisher erroneously calculated the time span and inserted "1870–1879" into the title.
8. This paragraph appears on pages 93–94 of Herman Lehmann, *Nine Years Among the Indians, 1870–1879,* ed. J. Marvin Hunter (1927; reprint, Albuquerque: University of New Mexico Press, 1993).
9. Tom and Carlene Smith graciously provided me with a copy of Clinton's handwritten draft of Jeff's section of *The Boy Captives,* which I compared with the published version. Although Hunter corrected the spelling and grammar, inserted paragraph breaks, deleted or condensed some material, and made the run-on sentences flow more smoothly, he did not significantly change the content, structure, or vocabulary of the Smith brothers' manuscript.
10. The writing of *The Boy Captives* is described in: *Frontier Times,* V (Oct. 1927), 16, and June 1928, inside back cover (advertisement); Carlene Smith, "The Boy Who Lived with Geronimo: Jefferson Davis Smith," *Our Heritage* [San Antonio Genealogical and Historical Society], spring 1994, 28; and Edda Raye Moody to the author, Feb. 10, 2001.
11. Information about the 1927 Old Trail Drivers reunion was taken from: *Frontier Times,* V (Nov. 1927), 96; *San Antonio Express,* Oct. 4, 1927, 3, Oct. 5, 1927, 6, Oct. 6, 1927, 9, Oct. 7, 1927, 14, 15, Oct. 9, 1927, 10, and Oct. 10, 1927, 5; *San Antonio Evening News,* Oct. 5, 1927, 4, Oct. 6, 1927, 1, 6, and Oct. 7, 1927, 3, 5; *San Antonio Light,* Oct. 6, 1927, 1B, and Oct. 8, 1927, 1A, 2A; and *Claude* [Tex.] *News,* Oct. 9, 1931.
12. *The New York Times,* Dec. 20, 1925, Sunday Magazine, 11, 23. The fundraising drive wasn't successful. When the bronze sculpture was finally cast in 1940, it was only one-fourth its intended size. The artist was Gutzon Borglum, best known as the sculptor of Mount Rushmore.

13. Death Records, Vol. 5, page 103, Mason County Clerk's Office, Mason, Texas.
14. A. B. Norton, the superintendent of Indian Affairs in New Mexico, reported that "thousands of cattle stolen by the Comanches from the people of Texas were being traded for by Mexicans" in 1866–1867, the exact period when Dot Babb was with the tribe. At the time Indian agent Lorenzo Labadi visited a Kiowa and Comanche camp in the summer of 1867, he also reported that the Indians had "Texas cattle without number, and almost every day" brought in more. *Annual Report of the Secretary of the Interior 1867* (Washington: Government Printing Office, 1867), Part II, 194–95, 215.
15. The questionnaires that Dot Babb sent to Charles Goodnight (1919), James N. Browning (1918), W. A. King (n.d.), W. D. Reynolds (1925), C. B. Ball (1919), and W. H. Wiggins (n.d.) are contained in the T. A. Babb file, PPHM.
16. Office of Vital Statistics, City of Amarillo, Texas.
17. *Campus Chat* [North Texas State Teachers College (now the University of North Texas), Denton], Feb. 9, 1939, 1, 2, and Feb. 16, 1939, 1, 6; *Denton Record-Chronicle,* Feb. 15, 1939, 5, and Feb. 17, 1939, 1, 4; *Daily Times Herald* [Dallas], Feb. 17, 1939, Part 2, 2; *Dallas Morning News,* Feb. 17, 1939, Section I, 10; and *Fort Worth Star-Telegram,* Feb. 15, 1939, 18, and Feb. 17, 1939, 5, 7, 28.
18. "Topay" was also the name of Herman Lehmann's Comanche sweetheart. I was unable to determine whether Quanah's wife was the same woman. It's worth noting, however, that in Herman's first autobiography, which was published while Quanah was still living, he didn't reveal the name of his Comanche girlfriend. Perhaps he thought that discretion was the better part of valor.
19. "Cynthia Parker" files, University of North Texas Archives, Denton, Texas.

CHAPTER 13: THE TRAIL FADES

1. Minutes Probate Court, Book 3, pages 368–74, and Deed Records, Book V, pages 594, 597, Mason County Clerk's Office, Mason, Texas.
2. Clinton Smith's descendants recall seeing a portrait photograph of Adolph Korn as a young man in their family collection. In the image, his face was slender, and his blond hair was long and straight, like a woman's. However, even this photograph has vanished.
3. *G. Brandenberger v. Adolph Korn,* Case No. 150, Mason County District Court, Minute Book 3, pages 490–91 (Oct. 5, 1889), Mason County Clerk's Office, Mason, Texas. No court papers have survived describing how the dispute arose.
4. Deed Records, Book R, pages 234, 244, 311, 351, and Book Q, page 583, Mason County Clerk's Office, Mason, Texas.

5. Deed Records, Book T, page 581, and Book V, pages 26, 76, Mason County Clerk's Office, Mason, Texas.

6. Neil Fisher to the author, Nov. 26, 2002. In the summer of 1959, Neil, a young geologist, was mapping the Hilda area. During the evenings, he visited with Otto Loeffler, by then a lonely widower of seventy-one, who told Neil about his trips to the caves during his boyhood to deliver food to Uncle Adolph.

7. Census Office, Department of the Interior, *Report on Indians Taxed and Indians Not Taxed in the United States (Except Alaska) at the Eleventh Census: 1890* (Washington: Government Printing Office, 1894), 541.

𝓑𝓲𝓫𝓵𝓲𝓸𝓰𝓻𝓪𝓹𝓱𝔂

CORRESPONDENCE, ARTICLES, AND INTERVIEWS

Banc Babb: Report of Indian Depredations in Wise County, Sept. 1866, transcribed and reprinted in Dorman H. Winfrey and James M. Day (eds.), *The Indian Papers of Texas and the Southwest, 1825–1916* (5 Vols.; Austin: The Pemberton Press, 1966), IV, 115–16; Endorsement, J.J. Sturm to Fort Arbuckle, Dec. 12, 1867, and [?] D. Greene, Jan. 4, 1868, Record Group 393, Part V, Fort Arbuckle, Oklahoma, Entry 1, Vol. 1, NARA; E. O. C. Ord to Adjutant General, Jan. 10, 1868, Microfilm Roll M711/52, NARA; deposition of Bianca L. Bell, June 23, 1898, Indian depredation claim of Hernando C. Babb, Record Group 123, Case No. 4606, NARA; *Dallas Herald,* Oct. 6, 1866, 2, and Oct. 27, 1866, 3; *Reedsburg Free Press,* Feb. 19, 1914, 1 (Banc's letter describing her captivity); *Campus Chat* [North Texas State Teachers College (now the University of North Texas), Denton], Feb. 9, 1939, 1, 2; *Fort Worth Star-Telegram,* Mar. 5, 1939, Oil News and Classified Ads Section, 12; *Denton Record-Chronicle,* Apr. 14, 1950, 1 (obituary); Bette S. Anderson to the author, Sept. 20, 2001, and Nov. 17, 2001; Daniel Crooks to the author, May 14, 2002, and June 3, 2002; Claudia Crooks to the author, June 4, 2002; and Daniel J. Gelo and Scott Zesch (eds.), " 'Every Day Seemed to be a Holiday': The Captivity of Bianca Babb," *Southwestern Historical Quarterly,* CVII (July 2003), 35–67.

Dot Babb: Report of Indian Depredations in Wise County, Sept. 1866, transcribed and reprinted in Dorman H. Winfrey and James M. Day (eds.), *The Indian Papers of Texas and the Southwest, 1825–1916* (5 Vols.; Austin: The Pemberton Press, 1966), IV, 115–16; Mark Walker to Chauncey McKeever, May 14, 1867 (including William T. Sherman's endorsement), Microfilm Roll M234/375, NARA-SW; Mark Walker to the acting commissioner of Indian Affairs, Sept. 27, 1868, Microfilm Roll 375, FLNHS; Charles E. Mix to Mark Walker, Oct. 1, 1868, Microfilm Roll M21/88, NARA-SW; Mark Walker to Ely S. Parker, Aug. 11, 1869, Microfilm Roll M234/376, NARA-SW; depositions of Theodore A. Babb, Dec. 28, 1887, and June 23, 1898, Indian depredation claim of Hernando C. Babb, Record Group 123, Case No. 4606, NARA; T. A. "Dot"

Babb, answers to questionnaire, Oct. 7, 1922, Dot Babb, "Notes from Speech Made at Cowboy's Reunion, 1925," statement of Dot Babb, Mar. 16, 1926, Dot Babb to J. A. Hill, June 17, 1926, T. A. Babb to J. Evetts Haley, Nov. 27, 1926, and T. A. Babb to J. Evetts Haley, Feb. 27, 1927, T. A. Babb file, PPHM; Dot Babb to J. Evetts Haley, Oct. 27, 1927, and Dot Babb to J. Evetts Haley, June 9, 1935, J. Evetts Haley Collection, HML; *Dallas Herald,* Oct. 6, 1866, 2, and Oct. 27, 1866, 3; *Amarillo Daily Tribune,* Sept. 11, 1920, 1 (motion picture); *Amarillo Sunday News-Globe,* Feb. 22, 1931, 1; *Amarillo Daily News,* Feb. 23, 1931, 1, Oct. 1, 1934, 2, and Aug. 11, 1936, 1, 3 (obituary and interview); *San Angelo Standard-Times,* Oct. 2, 1934; *Amarillo Globe,* Aug. 11, 1936, 4 (editorial); *Wise County Messenger,* Aug. 13, 1936, 2 (obituary); *Frontier Times,* XIV (Nov. 1936), 76–80; and Leslie Hargus to the author, Mar. 28, 2001.

Minnie Caudle: E. W. Wynkoop to Thomas Murphy, Aug. 4, 1868, and Charles E. Mix to J. W. Throckmorton, Aug. 21, 1868, transcribed and reprinted in Dorman H. Winfrey and James M. Day (eds.), *The Indian Papers of Texas and the Southwest, 1825–1916* (5 Vols.; Austin: The Pemberton Press, 1966), IV, 269–70; Thomas Murphy to N. G. Taylor, Aug. 6, 1868, and Aug. 10, 1868, and E. M. Pease to Charles E. Mix, Sept. 1, 1868, Microfilm Roll M234/59, NARA-SW; Thomas Murphy to Chauncey McKeever, Oct. 31, 1868, and Thomas Murphy to N. G. Taylor, Nov. 24, 1868, Microfilm Roll 880, FLNHS; *Atchison Daily Free Press,* Aug. 8, 1868, 1; *New York Herald,* Aug. 14, 1868, 8; *The New York Times,* Aug. 14, 1868, 1; *New York Daily Tribune,* Aug. 14, 1868, 5; *San Antonio Daily Herald,* Sept. 13, 1868, 2; *Frontier Times,* Jan. 1924, 20–22 (article based in part on interview with Minnie Caudle); *Marble Falls Messenger,* Mar. 23, 1933, 2 (obituary); Bertie Oma Modgling to Johnie Lee Reeves, June 22, 1984, copy of notes in the author's possession; Damon W. Benson to Wayne Benson, Jan. 17, 1994, copy of notes in the author's possession; Frank Modgling to the author, Aug. 28, 2001; and Damon W. Benson and Neoma Benson Cain to the author, Sept. 1, 2001.

Rudolph Fischer: G. W. Todd to "Hon. Secretary U.S. America" [secretary of the Interior], Dec. 24, 1865, Gottlieb Fischer to Andrew Johnson, Dec. 26, 1865, Marcus Goldbaum to James H. Carleton, June 7, 1866, Gottlieb Fischer to Office of Indian Affairs, July 11, 1866, and A. Siemering to U.S. Secretary of State, Mar. 22, 1867, Microfilm Roll M234/375, NARA-SW; D. N. Cooley to Gottlieb Fischer, Jan. 20, 1866, Microfilm Roll M21/79, NARA-SW; summaries of letters of M. Goldbaum, June 7, 1866, and June 22, 1866, Microfilm Roll M1097/1, NARA; D. N. Cooley to Gottlieb Fisher, July 30, 1866, Microfilm Roll M21/81,

NARA-SW; Lorenzo Labadi to A. B. Norton, Aug. 28, 1867, Microfilm Roll M234/554, NARA-SW; Rudolph Radeleff to Charles E. Morse, Nov. 22, 1869, J. Evetts Haley Collection, HML (copy of letter from NARA; record group unknown); E. Degener to Ely S. Parker, Feb. 3, 1871, E. S. Parker to Lawrie Tatum, Feb. 10, 1871, E. S. Parker to Enoch Hoag, Feb. 10, 1871, Enoch Hoag to Lawrie Tatum, Feb. 15, 1871, H. R. Clum [to Enoch Hoag?], June 8, 1871, William Nicholson to James M. Haworth, June 28, 1877, Engelbert Krauskopf to John P. Hatch, Aug. 8, 1877, S. R. Whitall to James M. Haworth, Aug. 8, 1877, A. Bell to James M. Haworth, Dec. 6, 1877, and Engelbert Krauskopf to Indian Agent of Fort Sill, June 10, 1879, Microfilm Roll KA42, OHS; Lawrie Tatum to Enoch Hoag, Mar. 11, 1871, and May 12, 1871, Microfilm Roll M234/377, NARA-SW; H. R. Clum to Enoch Hoag, Apr. 4, 1871, and Enoch Hoag to Lawrie Tatum, Apr. 8, 1871, Southern Plains Indian Agencies Collection, WHC; John Smith to William Nicholson, Aug. 9, 1877, and John Smith to Gustav Schleicher, Aug. 14, 1877, Microfilm Roll M21/136, NARA-SW; Richard B. Hubbard "To whom it may Concern," Sept. 5, 1877, and Richard B. Hubbard to U.S. Officer in Command at Fort Sill, Sept. 5, 1877, Records of Governor Richard Hubbard, Box 301–102, TSA; Ranald S. Mackenzie to Phillip L. Lee, Sept. 14, 1877, Box D62.137.118, FSMA; James M. Haworth to A. Bell, Dec. 12, 1877, Microfilm Roll M234/382, NARA-SW; J. F. Estell to Gustav Schleicher, Dec. 23, 1877, and Engelbert Krauskopf to Gustav Schleicher, Mar. 12, 1878, Microfilm Roll M234/384, NARA-SW; P. L. Hunt to Engelbert Krauskopf, June 16, 1879, Microfilm Roll KA8, OHS; *Dallas Herald*, Sept. 2, 1865, 2; *San Antonio Daily Express*, Aug. 31, 1877, 2, Sept. 6, 1877, 4, and Sept. 27, 1877, 4; *Daily Democratic Statesman* [Austin], Sept. 6, 1877, 4; *Galveston Weekly News*, Sept. 17, 1877, 1; *Frontier Echo* [Jacksboro, Tex.], Sept. 21, 1877, 2; *San Antonio Weekly Express*, Apr. 25, 1878, 4, and June 6, 1878, Supplement, 2; *Frontier Times*, Jan. 1926, 2 (recollections of Charles Morris), and XVIII (June 1941), 423–24; *Fredericksburg Standard*, May 9, 1935, 6, and May 1, 1946, Section 5, 1; J. J. Methvin and H. M. Lindsay to Lillian Cassaway, Sept. 28, 1937, Indian Pioneer History Collection, OHS, CVII, 38–40; H. M. Lindsay to Lillian Cassaway, Oct. 14, 1937, Indian Pioneer History Collection, OHS, XXXIII, 280; R. E. Moody to Robert H. Bostman, Jan. 10, 1938, Indian Pioneer History Collection, OHS, LXXI, 394; *Lawton Constitution*, Apr. 14, 1941, 5 (obituary); Lottie Fisher to Arthur Lawrence, Sept. 14, 1958, Arthur Lawrence Collection, MGP; J. H. Sellars Jr., "Early Day Indian Neighbors, Comanche County," *Prairie Lore*, X (Oct. 1973), 76–78; Barbara Goodin, "The Fisher Family Indian Cemetery," *Prairie Lore*, XXVII (fall 1991), 93–103; Josephine Wapp to the author, Feb. 27, 2001; and Teresa Parker to the author, Mar. 25, 2003, and May 8, 2003.

BIBLIOGRAPHY

Temple Friend: Enoch Hoag to Lawrie Tatum, Feb. 15, 1871, and Leonard S. Friend to Lawrie Tatum, Mar. 18, 1871, Microfilm Roll KA42, OHS; Lawrie Tatum to Enoch Hoag, Mar. 11, 1871, Aug. 19, 1871, and Nov. 15, 1872, Microfilm Roll M234/377, NARA-SW; *Wichita City Eagle,* Dec. 26, 1872, 2; *Emporia News,* Jan. 10, 1873, 2; *Walnut Valley Times* [El Dorado, Kan.], Jan. 24, 1873, 2; *Daily State Journal* [Austin], Jan. 24, 1873, 3; *Wichita Beacon,* May 2, 1926, Magazine Section, 7; *El Dorado Times,* July 1, 1926, 3, 6 (interview with John S. Friend); *El Dorado Times,* Aug. 7, 1929, 1, 5; William A. White, *The Autobiography of William Allen White* (New York: The Macmillan Co., 1946), 24–25; and *Wichita Eagle and Beacon,* Mar. 26, 1961, Magazine Section, 18 (interview with Carrie Friend Dwire).

Adolph Korn: Louis Korn to James W. Carleton, Jan. 10, 1870, endorsement of H. Clay Wood on Korn's letter to Carleton, Jan. 24, 1870, and James P. Newcomb to J. J. Reynolds, Mar. 25, 1870, Record Group 393, Part V, Fort Concho, Texas, Entry 7, Box 1, NARA; James P. Newcomb to Ely S. Parker, Mar. 25, 1870, Ely S. Parker to Enoch Hoag, Apr. 11, 1870, and Enoch Hoag to Lawrie Tatum, Apr. 11, 1870, Microfilm Roll KA42, OHS; Lawrie Tatum to Enoch Hoag, Nov. 15, 1872, Microfilm Roll M234/377, NARA-SW; [Medical] Record for the Month of December 1872, Fort Concho, Microfilm Roll 38, FCML; affidavit of Adolph Korn (n.d.; c. 1889–1890), Indian depredations papers, Mason County Clerk's Office, Mason, Texas; deposition of Adolph Korn, Oct. 12, 1892, Indian depredation claim of Adolph A. Reichenau, Record Group 123, Case Nos. 3503, 3504, 3505, and 3506, NARA; *San Antonio Daily Herald,* Jan. 13, 1870, 2, Dec. 1, 1872, 2, and Jan. 8, 1873, 3; *San Antonio Daily Express,* Nov. 30, 1872, 2, Jan. 8, 1873, 3, and Jan. 9, 1873, 3; *Freie Presse für Texas* [San Antonio], Jan. 9, 1873, 2 (Al Dreyer, trans.); *Mason County News,* July 6, 1900, 3 (obituary); Alva Catherine Beach, "History of Events of Mason County, Texas," in *Mason County Scrapbook and Obituary,* Archives and Manuscripts Collection, CAH; *Frontier Times,* VI (Dec. 1928), 122–24, and XVIII (June 1941), 424; *Colorado County* [Tex.] *Citizen,* June 11, 1936, Magazine Section, 2; *San Antonio Express,* July 26, 1936, D1, D3; Scott Zesch, "The Two Captivities of Adolph Korn," *Southwestern Historical Quarterly,* CIV (Apr. 2001), 515–40; and Neil Fisher to the author, Nov. 26, 2002.

Herman Lehmann: affidavit of T. Buchmeyer [sic; Phillip Buchmeier], July 2, 1870, Rudolph Radeleff to Lawrie Tatum, Dec. 3, 1872, Phillip Buchmeier to Lawrie Tatum, Dec. 3, 1872, Rudolph Radeleff to Lawrie Tatum, Feb. 12, 1873, Texas Senate Chamber (no signature) to Lawrie Tatum, Mar. 20, 1873,

— *336* —

and Henry C. King to James M. Haworth, May 8, 1873, Southern Plains Indian Agencies Collection, WHC; J. E. Tourtellotte to Lawrie Tatum, May 27, 1871, Henry C. King to Lawrie Tatum, Mar. 20, 1873, Phillip Buchmeier to Lawrie Tatum, Apr. 3, 1873, and William M. Leeds to James Haworth, Mar. 27, 1878, Microfilm Roll KA42, OHS; H. R. Clum to R. Radeleff, Oct. 1, 1872, Microfilm Roll M21/108, NARA-SW; J. M. Haworth to Phillip Buchmeier, Apr. 23, 1873, and John O. Meusebach to John Hancock, Aug. 10, 1874, and accompanying news clippings, Microfilm Roll M234/379, NARA-SW; John A. Wilcox to Engelbert Krauskopf, Jan. 28, 1878, J. W. Davidson to Engelbert Krauskopf, Apr. 12, 1878, and J. W. Davidson to Assistant Adjutant General, Apr. 14, 1878, Box D62.137.118, FSMA; Engelbert Krauskopf to Gustav Schleicher, Mar. 12, 1878, Microfilm Roll M234/384, NARA-SW; affidavit of Herman Lehmann, Apr. 15, 1901, Microfilm Roll KA60, OHS; affidavit of Quanah Parker, Aug. 26, 1901, Microfilm Roll KA1, OHS; deposition of Herman Lehmann, Apr. 28, 1903, Indian depredation claim of W. S. Glenn, Record Group 123, Case No. 1893, NARA; *San Antonio Daily Herald,* May 19, 1870, 2, May 21, 1870, 2, May 24, 1870, 2, June 2, 1870, 2, and Aug. 4, 1870, 2; *San Antonio Daily Express,* May 28, 1870, 2; *San Antonio Weekly Express,* Mar. 21, 1878, 3, and May 16, 1878, 3; *Frontier Times,* Dec. 1924, 32; *Austin American-Statesman,* Sept. 13, 1925, Sunday Magazine, 2; *Fredericksburg Standard,* Aug. 15, 1925, 1, Feb. 5, 1932, 1, 2 (obituary), and May 1, 1946, Section 5, 1; *New York Herald Tribune,* Oct. 11, 1931, Magazine Section, 26; *San Antonio Express,* Nov. 21, 1932, 1D (interview with Willie Lehmann); *Houston Post,* Mar. 5, 1933, Magazine Section (interview with Maurice J. Lehmann); Howard Wheeler to Maurice R. Anderson, Apr. 12, 1937, Indian Pioneer History Collection, OHS, XI, 338; *Frontier Times,* XVIII (Mar. 1941), 277–88, and XXXI (July, Aug., Sept. 1954), 251–77; *Highlander* [Marble Falls, Tex.], Jan. 27, 1972 (interview with Mayfield Kothmann); *Fredericksburg Radio Post,* Nov. 16, 1972, 10 (interview with Esther Lehmann); *Boerne Star,* Mar. 10, 1983 (interview with M. J. Lehmann); Garland Perry and Kitti Focke, "A New Look at Nine Years Among the Indians," in Herman Lehmann, *Nine Years with the Indians, 1870–1879,* ed. J. Marvin Hunter (3d ed.; San Antonio: Lebco Graphics, 1985), 247–89; [Gerda Lehmann Kothmann], "Herman and Willie Lehmann Captured by Apache Indians May 16, 1870," Herman and Willie Lehmann historical marker file, M. Beven Eckert Memorial Library, Mason, Texas; Gerda Lehmann Kothmann to the author, Feb. 20, 2001, and Mar. 24, 2004; Esther Lehmann to the author, July 24, 2002; and Carlos Parker to the author, Nov. 25, 2002.

Clinton and Jeff Smith: John Mangold to James Davidson, Feb. 27, 1871, and John W. Sansom to James Davidson, Feb. 28, 1871, Adjutant General, General Correspondence, Box 401-390, Folder 390-4, TSA; H. M. Smith to Edmund Davis, Mar. 8, 1871, Henry M. Smith to Lawrie Tatum, Mar. 14, 1871, H. R. Clum [to Enoch Hoag?], June 8, 1871, H. M. Smith to Lawrie Tatum, July 16, 1871, H. M. Smith to Edmund J. Davis, Aug. 1, 1871, H. R. Clum to Enoch Hoag, June 10, 1872, and Edward F. Hoag to Lawrie Tatum, June 14, 1872, Microfilm Roll KA42, OHS; H. M. Smith and H. E. Smith to John Sansom, Mar. 8, 1871, John W. Sansom to Edmund Davis, Mar. 11, 1871, Edmund J. Davis to Lawrie Tatum, Mar. 17, 1871, H. R. Clum to Enoch Hoag, Apr. 4, 1871, Enoch Hoag to Lawrie Tatum, Apr. 8, 1871, and Edmund J. Davis to Lawrie Tatum, Aug. 11, 1871, Southern Plains Indian Agencies Collection, WHC; H. R. Clum to H. M. Smith, Apr. 13, 1871, Microfilm Roll M21/100, NARA-SW; Lawrie Tatum to Enoch Hoag, Apr. 15, 1871, and May 13, 1871, Lawrie Tatum to Cols. Grierson and Mackenzie, Aug. 4, 1871, John Hancock to secretary of the Interior, May 27, 1872, Lawrie Tatum to Enoch Hoag, Oct. 24, 1872, and Cyrus Beede to F. A. Walker, Dec. 13, 1872, Microfilm Roll M234/377, NARA-SW; Lawrie Tatum to Henry M. Smith, Oct. 24, 1872, and Henry M. Smith to E. J. Davis, Nov. 18, 1872, Records of Governor Edmund J. Davis, Box 301–82, Folder 268, TSA; [Medical] Record for the Month of December 1872, Fort Concho, Microfilm Roll 38, FCML; William Schuchardt to Hon. Second Assistant Secretary of State, Despatch No. 101, Mar. 29, 1873, Despatch No. 103, May 8, 1873, Despatch No. 105, May 17, 1873, Despatch No. 109, July 20, 1873, and Despatch No. 110, Aug. 28, 1873, Microfilm Roll M299/T-1, NARA-CP; William Schuchardt to Editor San Antonio Express, Apr. 7, 1873, and Thomas Williams to C. C. Augur, May 1, 1873, reprinted in the 2002 edition of *The Boy Captives*; J. M. Haworth to Enoch Hoag, May 14, 1873, Microfilm Roll M234/378, NARA-SW; U.S. House of Representatives, Exec. Doc. No. 257, 43d Cong., 1st Sess., 22–23, 26–27; *San Antonio Daily Herald,* Feb. 28, 1871, 3, Mar. 2, 1871, 2, Dec. 1, 1872, 2, Apr. 25, 1873, 1, and May 6, 1873, 3; *San Antonio Daily Express,* Feb. 28, 1871, 5, and Nov. 30, 1872, 2; *Semi-Weekly Farm News* [Dallas], Nov. 4, 1930, 2, Nov. 11, 1930, 2, Nov. 18, 1930, 2, and Nov. 25, 1930, 2 (interview with Jeff Smith); *San Antonio Light,* June 13, 1931, Mar. 8, 1940, 4A, and Apr. 22, 1940, 3A (Jeff Smith's obituary); *Claude* [Tex.] *News,* Oct. 9, 1931; *Rocksprings Record,* Sept. 16, 1932, 4 (Clinton Smith's obituary); *San Antonio Express,* Apr. 22, 1940, 1A (Jeff Smith's obituary); *San Antonio Evening News,* Apr. 22, 1940, 5 (Jeff Smith's obituary); *Dallas Morning News,* Aug. 6, 1979 (interview with Bert Smith, Jeff's son); Carlene Smith, "The Boy Who Lived with Geronimo: Jefferson Davis Smith," *Our Heritage* [San Antonio Genealogical and Historical Society], spring 1994, 26–28; Smith Genealogy Report, posted at http://lady3248.tripod.com/smithgenealogy.htm, visited May 24, 2004 (recollections of Sidney M. Whitworth); Edda Raye Moody to the author, Feb. 8, 2001, Feb. 10, 2001, Feb. 12, 2001, Mar. 25, 2001, and June 18, 2003; Tom and Carlene Smith to the author, June 11, 2001; and Allen Smith Jr. to the author, May 13, 2003.

BOOKS

Ashton, Sharron Standifer, comp. *Indians and Intruders*. 3 Vols. Norman: Ashton Books, 1998.

Babb, T. A. *In the Bosom of the Comanches*. 1912; 2d ed., Dallas: Hargreaves Printing Co., 1923.

Baker, T. Lindsay, and Billy R. Harrison. *Adobe Walls: The History and Archeology of the 1874 Trading Post*. College Station: Texas A&M University Press, 1986.

Banta, S. E. *Buckelew, the Indian Captive*. Mason, Tex.: The Mason Herald, 1911.

Battey, Thomas C. *The Life and Adventures of a Quaker Among the Indians*. 1875; reprint, Williamstown, Mass.: Corner House Publishers, 1972.

Bierschwale, Margaret. *A History of Mason County, Texas Through 1964*. Mason, Tex.: Mason County Historical Commission, 1998.

Biesele, Rudolph Leopold. *The History of the German Settlements in Texas, 1831–1861*. 1930; reprint, Austin: Eakin Press, 1987.

Biggers, Don H. *German Pioneers in Texas: A Brief History of Their Hardships, Struggles and Achievements*. 1925; reprint, Austin: Eakin Press, 1983.

Brooks, James F. *Captives and Cousins: Slavery, Kinship, and Community in the Southwest Borderlands*. Chapel Hill: The University of North Carolina Press, 2002.

Carlson, Paul H. *The Buffalo Soldier Tragedy of 1877*. College Station: Texas A&M University Press, 2003.

Carter, Robert G. *The Old Sergeant's Story: Winning the West from the Indians and Bad Men in 1870 to 1876*. New York: Frederick H. Hitchcock, 1926.

———. *On the Border with Mackenzie, or Winning West Texas from the Comanches*. Mattituck, N.Y.: J. M. Carroll & Co., 1935.

Cates, Cliff D. *Pioneer History of Wise County*. Decatur, Tex.: [n.p.], 1907.

Comanche Language and Cultural Preservation Committee. *Taa Nꞟmꞟ Tekwapꞟ?ha Tꞟboopꞟ (Our Comanche Dictionary)*. Lawton: Comanche Language and Cultural Preservation Committee, 2003.

Cook, John R. *The Border and the Buffalo: An Untold Story of the Southwest Plains*. 1907; reprint, Austin: State House Press, 1989.

Corwin, Hugh D. *Comanche and Kiowa Captives in Oklahoma and Texas.* Guthrie, Okla.: Cooperative Publishing Co., 1959.

De Shields, James T. *Border Wars of Texas.* Tioga, Tex.: The Herald Co., 1912.

Drimmer, Frederick, ed. *Captured by the Indians: 15 Firsthand Accounts, 1750–1870.* 1961; republication, New York: Dover Publications, Inc., 1985.

Ebersole, Gary L. *Captured by Texts: Puritan to Postmodern Images of Indian Captivity.* Charlottesville: University Press of Virginia, 1995.

Exley, Jo Ella Powell. *Frontier Blood: The Saga of the Parker Family.* College Station: Texas A&M University Press, 2001.

Families of Kimble County. Vol. I. Junction, Tex.: Kimble County Historical Commission, 1985.

Fehrenbach, T. R. *Comanches: The Destruction of a People.* 1974; reprint, [Cambridge, Mass.]: Da Capo Press, 1994.

———. *Lone Star: A History of Texas and the Texans.* 1968; rev. ed., [Cambridge, Mass.]: Da Capo Press, 2000.

Fisher, O. C. *It Occurred in Kimble.* 1937; reprint, San Angelo: The Talley Press, 1984.

Freeman, Martha Doty. "Historic Properties Associated with the Henry M. Smith Family." In Gregg C. Cestaro, Martha Doty Freeman, Marie E. Blake, and Ann M. Scott, *Cultural Resources Survey of Selected Maneuver Areas at Camp Bullis, Bexar and Comal Counties, Texas: The Archeology and History of 3,255 Acres Along Cibolo Creek.* Fort Worth: U.S. Army Corps of Engineers, 2001, 119–27.

Gamel, Thomas W. *The Life of Thomas W. Gamel.* Dave Johnson, ed. Mason, Tex.: Mason County Historical Society, 1994.

Gard, Wayne. *The Great Buffalo Hunt.* 1959; reprint, Lincoln: University of Nebraska Press, 1968.

Gillett, James B. *Six Years with the Texas Rangers, 1875 to 1881.* 1921; reprint, Lincoln: University of Nebraska Press, 1976.

Greene, A. C. *The Last Captive.* Austin: The Encino Press, 1972.

Hagan, William T. *Quanah Parker, Comanche Chief.* Norman: University of Oklahoma Press, 1993.

———. "Squaw Men on the Kiowa, Comanche, and Apache Reservation: Advance Agents of Civilization or Disturbers of the Peace?" In *The Frontier Challenge: Responses to the Trans-Mississippi West.* John G. Clark, ed. Lawrence: The University Press of Kansas, 1971, 171–202.

———. *United States—Comanche Relations: The Reservation Years.* 1976; reprint, Norman: University of Oklahoma Press, 1990.

Haley, James L. *Apaches: A History and Culture Portrait.* 1981; reprint, Norman: University of Oklahoma Press, 1997.

―――. *The Buffalo War: The History of the Red River Indian Uprising of 1874.* Garden City, N.Y.: Doubleday and Co., 1976.

Haley, J. Evetts. *Fort Concho and the Texas Frontier.* San Angelo: San Angelo Standard-Times, 1952.

Harston, J. Emmor. *Comanche Land.* San Antonio: The Naylor Co., 1963.

Heard, J. Norman. *White into Red: A Study of the Assimilation of White Persons Captured by Indians.* Metuchen, N.J.: Scarecrow Press, 1973.

Hill, Edward E. *The Office of Indian Affairs, 1824–1880: Historical Sketches.* New York: Clearwater Publishing Co., Inc., 1974.

Hixson, Robert. *Lawrie Tatum, Indian Agent: Quaker Values and Hard Choices.* Wallingford, Penn.: Pendle Hill Publications, 1981.

Hodge, Frederick Webb, ed. *Handbook of American Indians North of Mexico.* 2 Vols. New York: Pageant Books, Inc., 1959.

Hunter, J. Marvin. *Horrors of Indian Captivity.* Bandera, Tex.: Frontier Times, 1937.

Johnson, Adam R. *The Partisan Rangers of the Confederate States Army.* William J. Davis, ed. Louisville, Ky.: George G. Fetter Co., 1904.

Jones, Douglas C. *The Treaty of Medicine Lodge: The Story of the Great Treaty Council as Told by Eyewitnesses.* Norman: University of Oklahoma Press, 1966.

Jones, Jonathan H. *A Condensed History of the Apache and Comanche Indian Tribes* [*Indianology*]. 1899; reprint, New York: Garland Publishing, Inc., 1976.

Jordan, Gilbert J. *Yesterday in the Texas Hill Country.* College Station: Texas A&M University Press, 1979.

Jordan, Terry G. *German Seed in Texas Soil: Immigrant Farmers in Nineteenth-Century Texas.* Austin: University of Texas Press, 1966.

Katz, William Loren. *The Black West.* 1971; 3d ed., Seattle: Open Hand Publishing Inc., 1987.

Kavanagh, Thomas W. *The Comanches: A History, 1706–1875.* Lincoln: University of Nebraska Press, 1996.

Kendall County Historical Commission. *A History of Kendall County, Texas.* Dallas: Taylor Publishing Co., 1984.

Kvasnicka, Robert M., and Herman J. Viola, eds. *The Commissioners of Indian Affairs, 1824–1977.* Lincoln: University of Nebraska Press, 1979.

Lehmann, Herman. *Nine Years Among the Indians, 1870–1879.* J. Marvin Hunter, ed. 1927; reprint, Albuquerque: University of New Mexico Press, 1993.

Llano County Family Album: A History. Llano, Tex.: Llano County Historical Society, Inc., 1989.

Lockwood, Frank C. *The Apache Indians.* 1938; reprint, Lincoln: University of Nebraska Press, 1987.

Mason County Historical Book. Mason, Tex.: Mason County Historical Commission and Mason County Historical Society, 1976.

McConnell, Joseph Carroll. *The West Texas Frontier, or a Descriptive History of Early Times in Western Texas.* 2 Vols. Palo Pinto, Tex.: Texas Legal Bank and Book Co., 1939.

Morgan, Jonnie R. *The History of Wichita Falls.* 1931; republication, Wichita Falls, Tex.: Nortex Offset Publications, Inc., 1971.

Mortimer, Barbara. *Hollywood's Frontier Captives: Cultural Anxiety and the Captivity Plot in American Film.* New York: Garland Publishing, Inc., 2000.

Moulton, Candy. *The Writer's Guide to Everyday Life in the Wild West.* Cincinnati: Writer's Digest Books, 1999.

Namias, June. *White Captives: Gender and Ethnicity on the American Frontier.* Chapel Hill: The University of North Carolina Press, 1993.

Neal, Charles M. Jr. *Valor Across the Lone Star: The Congressional Medal of Honor in Frontier Texas.* Austin: Texas State Historical Association, 2002.

Neeley, Bill. *The Last Comanche Chief: The Life and Times of Quanah Parker.* New York: John Wiley and Sons, Inc., 1995.

Newcomb, W. W. Jr. *The Indians of Texas: From Prehistoric to Modern Times.* Austin: The University of Texas Press, 1961.

Noyes, Stanley, with Daniel J. Gelo. *Comanches in the New West, 1895–1908.* Austin: University of Texas Press, 1999.

Nye, Wilbur Sturtevant. *Carbine and Lance: The Story of Old Fort Sill.* 1937; 3d ed., Norman: University of Oklahoma Press, 1969.

———. *Plains Indian Raiders: The Final Phases of Warfare from the Arkansas to the Red River.* Norman: University of Oklahoma Press, 1968.

Nystel, Ole T. *Lost and Found; or Three Months with the Wild Indians.* 1888; reprint, Clifton, Tex.: Bosque Memorial Museum, 1967.

Oatman, Wilburn. *Llano: Gem of the Hill Country.* Hereford, Tex.: Pioneer Book Publishers, Inc., 1970.

Peavy, Linda, and Ursula Smith. *Frontier Children.* Norman: University of Oklahoma Press, 1999.

Penniger, Robert. *Fredericksburg, Texas: The First Fifty Years.* Charles L. Wisseman Sr., trans. 1896; English ed., Fredericksburg: Fredericksburg Publishing Co., Inc., 1971.

Pierce, Michael D. *The Most Promising Young Officer: A Life of Ranald Slidell Mackenzie.* Norman: University of Oklahoma Press, 1993.

Polk, Stella Gipson. *Mason and Mason County: A History.* Austin: The Pemberton Press, 1966.

Ponder, Jerry. *Fort Mason, Texas: Training Ground for Generals.* Mason, Tex.: Ponder Books, 1997.

Richardson, Rupert Norval. *The Comanche Barrier to South Plains Settlement.* Kenneth R. Jacobs, ed. 1933; rev. ed., Austin: Eakin Press, 1996.

Rister, Carl Coke. *Border Captives: The Traffic in Prisoners by Southern Plains Indians, 1835–1875.* Norman: University of Oklahoma Press, 1940.

———. *Fort Griffin on the Texas Frontier.* Norman: University of Oklahoma Press, 1956.

Roberts, Dan W. *Rangers and Sovereignty.* 1914; reprint, Austin: State House Press, 1987.

Robinson, Charles M. III. *Bad Hand: A Biography of General Ranald S. Mackenzie.* Austin: State House Press, 1993.

Rochlin, Harriet and Fred. *Pioneer Jews: A New Life in the Far West.* Boston: Houghton Mifflin Co., 1984.

Rocksprings Woman's Club Historical Committee. *A History of Edwards County.* San Angelo: Anchor Publishing Co., 1984.

Roemer, Ferdinand. *Texas, with Particular Reference to German Immigration and the Physical Appearance of the Country.* Oswald Mueller, trans. 1849; English ed., 1935; reprint, Austin: Eakin Press, 1983.

Schaefer, Harvey. *Dripping Springs, Comal County, Texas: A Supplement to "The Boy Captives."* San Antonio: Omni Publishers, Inc., 2000.

Schilz, Thomas F. *Lipan Apaches in Texas.* El Paso: Texas Western Press, 1987.

Schubert, Frank N. *Black Valor: Buffalo Soldiers and the Medal of Honor, 1870–1898.* Wilmington, Del.: Scholarly Resources Inc., 1997.

———. *Voices of the Buffalo Soldier: Records, Reports, and Recollections of Military Life and Service in the West.* Albuquerque: University of New Mexico Press, 2003.

Skogen, Larry C. *Indian Depredation Claims, 1796–1920.* Norman: University of Oklahoma Press, 1996.

Slotkin, Richard. *Regeneration through Violence: The Mythology of the American Frontier, 1600–1860.* Middletown, Conn.: Wesleyan University Press, 1973.

Smith, Clinton L., and Jefferson D. Smith with J. Marvin Hunter. *The Boy Captives.* Bandera, Tex.: Frontier Times, 1927.

Sörgel, Alwin H. *A Sojourn in Texas, 1846–47: Alwin H. Sörgel's Texas Writings.* W. M. Von-Maszewski, trans. and ed. San Marcos, Tex.: German-Texan Heritage Society, 1992.

Strong, Henry W. *My Frontier Days and Indian Fights on the Plains of Texas.* [Waco, Tex.: n.p., 1926].

Tate, Michael L. *The Indians of Texas: An Annotated Research Bibliography.* Metuchen, N.J.: The Scarecrow Press, Inc., 1986.

Tatum, Lawrie. *Our Red Brothers and the Peace Policy of President Ulysses S. Grant.* 1899; reprint, Lincoln: University of Nebraska Press, 1970.

Tiling, Moritz. *History of the German Element in Texas from 1820–1850.* Houston: Moritz Tiling, 1913.

Tyler, Ron C., Douglas E. Barnett, Roy R. Barkley, Penelope C. Anderson, and Mark F. Odintz, eds. *The New Handbook of Texas.* 6 Vols. Austin: Texas State Historical Association, 1996.

Viola, Herman J. *Diplomats in Buckskins: A History of Indian Delegations in Washington City.* Washington, D.C.: Smithsonian Institution Press, 1981.

Wallace, Ernest. *Ranald S. Mackenzie on the Texas Frontier.* College Station: Texas A&M University Press, 1993.

———, ed. *Ranald S. Mackenzie's Official Correspondence Relating to Texas, 1871–1873.* Lubbock: West Texas Museum Association, 1967.

———, and E. Adamson Hoebel. *The Comanches: Lords of the South Plains.* Norman: University of Oklahoma Press, 1952.

Wilbarger, J. W. *Indian Depredations in Texas.* 1889; reprint, Austin: Eakin Press, 1985.

Wilbert, Hulda C. *Kernels of Korn: The Historical Events of a Pioneer Family.* Burnet, Tex.: Nortex Press, 1982.

Winfrey, Dorman H., and James M. Day, eds. *The Indian Papers of Texas and the Southwest, 1825–1916.* 5 Vols. Austin: The Pemberton Press, 1966.

Acknowledgments

For information on the white Indians that could not be obtained from public archives, I relied heavily on the kindness of strangers, many of whom became my friends and regular correspondents. I am deeply indebted to these genealogists, fellow researchers, and descendants of the individual captives whose lives I followed:

Dot and Banc Babb: Eugene T. Babb, Leslie Hargus, Anna Crooks, Daniel Crooks, Claudia Crooks, Roy Slonaker, Bette S. Anderson, Roslyn Shelton, Bill Lynch, Debby McClintock, Carol Schmitt, Marca Kent, Lydia Tilbury Hair, Marcy George, Claud Elsom Jr., and Molly Culver.

Minnie Caudle: Damon W. Benson, Neoma Benson Cain, Frank Modgling, Johnie Lee Reeves, Wayne Benson, Dave Johnson, Debbie Modgling Rieger, Janine Modgling, Kathleen Burns, Jodie H. Benson, Audrey Vodehnal, Christopher H. Wynkoop, and Cindy Gettelfinger.

Rudolph Fischer: Josephine and Edward Wapp, Teresa Parker, Lorene Kerchee Pewewardy, Betty Crocker, Kenn Knopp, and Sallie Tonips.

Temple Friend: William A. Hadwiger, Tom W. Locke, and Tom Kingery.

Adolph Korn: Lela Korn Hennigh, Jerry Korn, Gene Zesch, Lora Hey, Susie Ellison, Peggy Laverty, Patty Moss, Max Hey, Ron Sheets, Patricia McCrory, Johnita Bohmfalk, Al Dreyer, Neil Fisher, Gerald Geistweidt, Delvin Bauer, and Gerry Gamel.

Herman Lehmann: Gerda Lehmann Kothmann, Esther Lehmann, Vanessa Burzynski, Buzzy Parker, Carlos Parker, and Don Dye.

Clinton and Jeff Smith: Edda Raye Smith Moody, Carlene and Tom Smith, Beth and Allen Smith Jr., Clint and Nettie Smith, Kay Dean, Emmett "Buddy" Smith, C. L. Smith, Joe and Molly Butcher, Jerome Janca, and many other family members who welcomed me at the Smith reunion.

For information on other individual characters in the story: Sarah Franklin, Elizabeth Mahill, Billy Markland, Sam Oatman, Kay Reichenau Ponder, Anita Sanders, and Bobby Wadsworth.

The following staff members and volunteers at research centers patiently and cheerfully responded to my requests for information, often steering me toward sources I otherwise would not have found:

Towana Spivey, Ramona East, and Jo Ruffin, Fort Sill Museum Archives, Fort Sill, Oklahoma;

Deborah A. Baroff, Museum of the Great Plains, Lawton, Oklahoma;

Kristina Southwell, Josh Clough, and John R. Lovett, Western History Collections, The University of Oklahoma Libraries, Norman, Oklahoma;

William D. Welge, Chester Cowen, Bill Moore, Oleta Kite, Tressie Nealy, Lillie Kerr, and Phyllis Adams, Oklahoma Historical Society, Oklahoma City, Oklahoma;

Jill Abraham, George Briscoe, Richard Fusick, and Mary Frances Morrow, National Archives and Records Administration, Washington, D.C.;

Rodney Krajca, National Archives and Records Administration, Southwest Region, Fort Worth, Texas;

Dulcinea R. Almager and Betty L. Bustos, Panhandle-Plains Historical Museum, Canyon, Texas;

Jim Bradshaw, Norma Thurman, and Nancy Jordan, Nita Stewart Haley Memorial Library, Midland, Texas;

George Elmore, Gia Lane, and George Butler, Fort Larned National Historic Site, Larned, Kansas;

Mark Vargas, Mitzi Kay Cook, and Dianne Carroll, University of Science and Arts of Oklahoma, Chickasha, Oklahoma;

Robert S. Cox and Valerie-Anne Lutz, American Philosophical Society, Philadelphia, Pennsylvania;

Susan McElrath, Smithsonian Institution National Anthropological Archives, Suitland, Maryland;

Jane Hoerster, Julius DeVos, Wanda Hitzfelder, Robert and Linda Laury, and Jerry Ponder, Mason County Historical Commission, Mason, Texas;

Mary Jo Cockrell, Heartsill Young, Theresia Schrampfer, and Janice Walters, M. Beven Eckert Memorial Library, Mason, Texas;

Beatrice Langehennig, Mason County and District Clerk, Mason, Texas;

Frederica Burt Wyatt, Kimble County Historical Commission, Junction, Texas;

Becky Matticks, Edith Williams, and Anna Louise Borger, Butler County Historical Society, El Dorado, Kansas;

Rosalie Gregg, Carla Womack, and Shirley Zedaker, Wise County Heritage Museum, Decatur, Texas;

Paul Follett and Mary Lou Gorthy, Lawton Public Library, Lawton, Oklahoma;

Rob Groman and Gayle Brown, Amarillo Public Library, Amarillo, Texas;

Sue Steiner, Reedsburg Public Library, Reedsburg, Wisconsin;

Peter Shrake and Mary Farrell-Stieve, Sauk County Historical Society, Baraboo, Wisconsin;

Alice Laforet, Fredericksburg Genealogical Society, Fredericksburg, Texas;

Richard Himmel, Morris Martin, Mary Durio, and Cynthia Beard, Willis Library, University of North Texas, Denton, Texas;

Andrew Jelen, Wichita Falls Public Library, Wichita Falls, Texas;

John M. Cahoon, Seaver Center for Western History Research at the Natural History Museum of Los Angeles County, Los Angeles, California;

Martha Utterback, Daughters of the Republic of Texas Library, San Antonio, Texas;

Paul Camfield, Gillespie County Historical Society, Fredericksburg, Texas;

And the many knowledgeable librarians and archivists who assisted me at the Center for American History at the University of Texas at Austin; San Antonio Public Library; Texas State Archives; New York Public Library; the Library of Congress; Kansas State Historical Society; Fort Concho Museum Library; Southwest Collection at Texas Tech University; University Library at the University of Texas at El Paso; National Archives and Records Administration at College Park, Maryland; Dallas Public Library; Houston Public Library; Charles E. Young Research Library at the University of California at Los Angeles; Llano Public Library in Llano, Texas; Pioneer Memorial Library in Fredericksburg, Texas; and Chico Public Library in Chico, Texas.

For insight into the Comanche way of life, I extend my warmest thanks to Barbara and Ken Goodin, Dan Gelo, Tom Kavanagh, Vernon Cable, Larry Liles, Billie Cable Kreger, Ron Red Elk, the elders of the Comanche Language and Cultural Preservation Committee, and the members of the Petarsy Indian Methodist Church.

For access to several privately owned sites described in the story, I am grateful to John and Joyce Haynes, Mike Haynes, Estella Hoerster, Dorothy and John Harold Schuessler, Anthony and Gloria Nebgen, Edgar James Moss, and Bill Knox.

My good friends Steve Adams and Mary Cook invested a great deal of time meticulously reading my first draft, and the finished product is much better as a result of their wise observations and suggestions.

A host of supportive relatives, friends, and fellow historians and writers provided me with overnight accommodations, work space, meals, leads, opinions, keen readers' eyes, and good company while I was working on this book, among them Jerialice Arsenault, Darlene Bryand, Marc Castle, Chan Chandler, Anne Dempsey, Jane Dentinger, David and Mary Dreyfus, Karl Field and Mary Jordan, Glenn Hadeler, Matt Hey, Alan C. Huffines, Jo Ann Hughen, Sam and Jun Hurt, Jamie Smith Jackson, Tom and Janet Jones, Misha Jordan, Quentin Jordan, Terry Jordan, Katye Kowierschke, Louise Larson, Peggy and Bill Laverty, Laura Lewis, Matt Loynachan, Bill and Modena Marschall, John McEwan, Fran and Skeeter Merritt, Greg Michno, Karen and Greg Mitchell, David Murray, Steve Mustoe and Rhonda Stoltz, Dean, Kim, and Austin Nolan, George Ward, Susan and Tanner Weil, Norman Weiss, Jackie Wertheimer, Casey and Lucinda Zesch, and Gene and Patsy Zesch.

The Captured was transformed from manuscript to book through the diligent efforts and creativity of Meryl Gross (production editor), Michelle McMillian and Deborah Kerner (designers), Cathy Turiano (production manager) David Cain (cartographer), Deborah Miller (copy editor), and Liz Catalano (proofreader).

My agent, Jim Hornfischer, shepherded this project from concept to completion with unfailing enthusiasm, care, and acumen. My initial editor, Julia Pastore, gave generously of her attention and encouragement, and I was most appreciative of her sound counsel and her belief in this venture. Editor Joe Cleeman steered the book through the latter phases of the publication process with exemplary finesse and dedication. It has been my greatest pleasure to work with all three of them.

Index

Ackerknecht, Erwin H., 112
Adobe Walls, battle of (1874), 206–7
African-Americans, xviii, 49, 57, 89,
    316n11
    as Cavalry soldiers, 95, 134, 218
    killed by Indian raiders, 67
alcohol, effects of, 130–31
Anderegg, Johann and Margretha, 94
Anderson, Bette S., 284
anthropologists, xviii, 23, 111, 112,
    126–27
Apaches, xvi, xix, 14, 36, 89
    abduction of Adolph Korn and, 4,
        18–19, 299–300, 306–7n11
    abduction of Lehmann brothers,
        95–101
    abduction of Smith brothers, 104
    in battle with Texas Rangers,
        208–13, 315n9
    federal Indian agents and, 151–52
    Jerome Commission and, 253
    massacred by U.S. Army, 136
    in Mexico, 194
    psychology of captives of, 112
    relations with Comanches, 121
    on reservation at Fort Sill, 146, 193,
        261
    war councils, 134–35
    ways of life, 109–10, 130–33
    . *See also* Lipan Apaches
Arapahoes, 65
Arizona, 18
Asbury, Capt. Henry, 82–83
Asewaynah (Gray Blanket). *See* Fischer,
    Rudolph
Asian-Americans, 89
Aue, Max, 105

Augur, Brig. Gen. Christopher C., 179,
    186
Austin, 84
Axtell, James, 64, 115

Babb, Banc, xix, 41–49, 102, 115, 181,
    301
    adjustment to Comanche way of life,
        50–52
    bid for adoption by Comanches,
        253–55, 256, 257
    captive psychology and, 111
    Comanche name of, 45, 127
    death of, 284
    efforts to secure release of, 59–62
    final years, 283–84
    Indianization of, 112–13, 247
    as last white Indian, 284
    return to white society, 62–64,
        229
Babb, Court, 43, 56
Babb, Dot, xix, 41–49, 85, 115, 132
    adjustment to Comanche way of life,
        53–56
    Comanche name of, 127
    continuing appeal of Indian life to,
        248–50
    death of, 63, 281
    defense of Indian captors, 86–87
    efforts to secure release of, 57, 59,
        60 62
    final years, 280–81
    Hollywood and, 263–64
    Indianization of, 112, 245
    on Indians' treatment of captives,
        102
    as killer, 137

Babb, Dot *(continued)*
  memoir of, 263, 264, 270
  personal injury claims of, 252, 255
  post-return career, 239
  religious views, 113
  return to white society, 62–64, 229
Babb, Isabel, 42–44, 45, 56
Babb, John, 43, 44, 56, 60, 62
Babb, Margie, 43, 45, 56
Backecacho (End of a Rope). *See*
  Smith, Clinton
Bald Head. *See* Tatum, Lawrie
Ball, Thomas, 290
Bank Robbery, The (film), 263
Bartruff, Johanna. *See* Korn, Johanna
  Bartruff
Batsena, 136
Bauer, Frank, 288–89
Bauer, Jacob, 288
Bell, Banc Babb. *See* Babb, Banc
Bell, Jefferson Davis, 240
Benson, Damon, 79, 85, 137, 279
Benson, James M., 244
Benson, Mose, 280
Bent, William, 206
Bettina (German settlement), 34
Black Crow, 235, 309n17
Black Horse, 235
Boy Captives, The (Smith brothers),
  272–73, 316n15, 330n9
Bradford, Jack, 74, 76, 85
Bradford, Samantha, 69, 73, 74, 85
Brady, Matthew, 170
Brazos River, 24
Briscoe, Eliza and Isaac, 82
Brite, John, 94
Buchmeier, Auguste, 91, 93–94, 97
  Colonel Mackenzie and, 227–28
  defense against Indian raid,
    99–101
  General Sherman and, 140–41
  search for son, 142, 193
  son's return and, 231
Buchmeier, Mina, 91, 99
Buchmeier, Phillip, 91, 94, 97, 99,
  193, 227
Buckelew, Frank, 112, 113, 265

buffalo, 47, 66, 67, 107, 158
  commercial hunting of, 202–4,
    215–16
  scarcity of, 82
buffalo hunters, 203–4, 215–18, 251,
  259–61, 295
Burks, N. E., 242
Burr, J. G., 271
Butler, Josiah, 182, 183
Butler, Lizzie, 182

Cable, Vernon, 49–50
Caboon, George, 154–55, 157, 179
Cachoco. *See* Korn, Adolph
Caddoes, 54–55, 59, 204
Cain, Neoma Benson, 81, 85, 240,
  244–45
Canadian River, 47, 50
captives
  acculturation of, 62, 63
  assimilation of, 64, 85, 112, 113,
    261
  defense of Indian captors, 85–87
  descendants of, xix–xx
  equal treatment by Indians, 124
  ethnic diversity of, xviii
  former captives' drift back to
    Indians, 248–51
  journalists and, 226
  as killers, 137–38
  Mexican, 27, 28, 32, 55, 255
  negotiations for release of, 81–84
  parents of, 141–43
  post-return careers of, 239–41
  psychological situation of, 111–15
  ransomed, 157
  readjustment to white society,
    199–201
  reasons for taking, 49–50
  searches for, 56–59, 75–79,
    141–43
  slain, 75, 76–78, 85
  timetable of events concerning, 301
  traded between tribes, 155–56
  treatment by Indian captors, 102–3
  white society despised by, 133–39
  . *See also* white Indians

Menardville (town), 68
Methodist church, 4, 6, 113, 146, 242
Meusebach, John O., 27–31, 29,
    30–32, 33, 34, 35
Mexican-Americans, xviii, 67, 89
Mexicans, xviii, 25, 27
  as captives, 32, 49, 55, 60, 255
  former captive as searcher, 154
  in San Antonio, 190
Mexico, 55, 63, 194–95
Mihecoby, 255
Modgling, Frank, 81, 246
Modgling, Henry, 279
Modgling, William F., 244
Monewostuki, 109, 125, 162, 163,
    168
Moniwoftuckwy, 129, 318n5
Montechema. *See* Lehmann, Herman
Moody, Edda Raye, 239, 240, 243,
    248, 278
  memorial of Clinton Smith, 279
  on western shows and reunions, 267
Moore, Daniel, 16
Moore, Rance, 16
Mopechucope (Old Owl), 24, 29, 31,
    34, 35, 36
Morris, Charles, 251
mountain lions, 96, 97
Mowway (Shaking Hand), 107–8, 124,
    154, 173, 311n10
  Comanche prisoners and, 180–81
  Indian agent Tatum and, 155–57
  Red River War and, 208
  trip to Washington, D.C., 159, 160,
    169–71, 175
  village on Red River, 158–60,
    161–66
Murphy, Thomas, 84

Nadernumipe (Tired and Give Out).
    See Babb, Dot
Native Americans, xvi, xx, 25, 151
  commercial buffalo hunting and,
    202–4
  cultural differences with other
    Americans, 241–42
  disease epidemics and, 149

film industry and, 263–64
kidnapped by other Native
    Americans, xviii
raids against white settlers, 10–13
reasons for taking captives, 49–50
spiritual practices, 113
treaties with United States, 65–66
twentieth-century reunions with
    settler adversaries, 265–69
. *See also* Southern Plains Indians;
    specific tribes and divisions
New Braunfels (town), 5
New Mexico, 18, 20, 60, 83, 98, 122
  captives in, 147–49
  U.S. Army campaigns in, 161
Newcomb, James P., 144
Nicholson, William, 222–23
*Nine Years Among the Indians
    1870–1879* (Lehmann), 271–72,
    314n6
Nokonis (Comanche division), 42, 56,
    60, 61, 174
Nooki, 136
Nusticeno, 210–13, 266
Nystel, Ole, 112, 113

Oatman, Hardin, 76, 77
Oatman, John, 76–77
Oklahoma, xx, 47, 49, 59, 262
Oklahoma Motion Picture Company,
    263
Old Texas (film), 264
Old Trail Drivers Association, 265,
    269, 272, 279
Omercawbey (Walking Face), 44
Our Red Brothers (Tatum), 150

Pacer, 151–52
Palo Duro Canyon, 79
Panhandle-Plains Historical Society,
    281
Parker, Rev. White, 283
Parker, Carlos, 267–68
Parker, Cynthia Ann, 124, 205, 229
Parker, Ely S., 144
Parker, Harold, 259
Parker, Len, 251

INDEX

Topay, 133
"Toppish," 176, 178, 180, 189,
    277–78
. See also Maxey, John Valentine
Tosacowadi (Leopard Cat), 108–9,
    125, 129, 131, 319n12
    death of, 168, 199, 321–22n5
    idolized by Clinton Smith, 135
    U.S. Army attack and, 162
Tosawa (Silver Brooch), 156
Townsend, Amanda, 70, 75, 78
Townsend, Nancy, 70
Townsend, Spence, 76, 78
traders, 146–48
Turpe, Albert, 194
Twovanta, 126

U.S. Army, 5, 8, 19, 66
    buffalo hunters and, 203
    Comanche prisoners of, 179
    defeat of Indians, 287
    destruction of Mowway's village,
        159–66
    forts established by, 35
    massacres of Indians by, 136, 163,
        166, 218
    Sherman in command of, 63, 140

Verein zum Schutze deutscher
    Einwanderer in Texas (Society for
    the Protection of German
    Immigrants in Texas), 25, 26
Victorio, 134

Waco tribe, 33, 59
Walker, Francis J., 170–71, 186
Walker, Lt. Mark, 60, 61, 62
Wapp, Josephine, 41, 241, 276
Washington, D.C., 24, 58, 84, 94, 95
    Comanche chief in, 159, 160
    Korn family's appeal to, 144
Washita River, 62
Watchoedadda (Lost Sitting Down), 53
westerns (movies and novels), xvii, xx,
    7, 11, 263–64
White, Eugene E., 249

white Indians, xviii, xix, 29, 41, 90
    cruelty of, 120, 123
    legends about, 276
    participation in raids by, 119–21
    psychology of, 112
    published memoirs of, 263, 264
    at twentieth-century reunions,
        266–69
. See also captives
white settlers, 24, 303
    changing patterns of settlement, 36
    killed by Indians, 10–12, 15–16, 37,
        40, 68, 69
    pressure on Indian hunting grounds,
        66
    twentieth-century reunions with
        Native adversaries, 265–69
    ways of life, 114
. See also European-Americans;
    German immigrants
Whitworth, Sidney M., 246–47, 267
Wichita Mountains, 183, 221
Wichitas, 204
Wild West shows, 268, 273–75
Williams, Capt. John, 11
Williams, Thomas G., 194
Winnebagos, 43
Wisconsin Territory, 43
Wise County, 42, 53, 56
wolves, 96, 97, 213
women
    Apache, 109–10
    Comanche, 33, 34, 81, 168
    German, 32
    white captives, 14, 49
Wounded Knee massacre, 235
"Wrinkled Hand Chase," 208
Wynkoop, Col. Edward W., 82, 83
Wynkoop, Louise, 83

Yamparikas (Comanche division), 170,
    181
Yellow House Canyon, battle at,
    217–18

Zesch, Gene, 293